Past Due

Past Due

The End of Easy Money
and the Renewal
of the American Economy

Peter S. Goodman

Times Books
Henry Holt and Company
New York

Times Books
Henry Holt and Company, LLC
Publishers since 1866
175 Fifth Avenue
New York, New York 10010
www.henryholt.com

Henry Holt® is a registered trademark of Henry Holt and Company, LLC.

Library of Congress Cataloging-in-Publication Data

Goodman, Peter S.
    Past due : the end of easy money and the renewal of the American economy / Peter
S. Goodman.—1st ed.
        p. cm.
    Includes bibliographical references and index.
    ISBN: 978-0-8050-8980-6
    1. United States—Economic conditions—2001—   2. Credit—United States.
3. Financial crises—United States.   4. Unemployed—United States.   I. Title.
    HC106.83.G66 2009
    330.973—dc22   2009012848

Henry Holt books are available for special promotions and premiums.
For details contact: Director, Special Markets.

First Edition 2009

Designed by Meryl Sussman Levavi

Printed in the United States of America
10   9   8   7   6   5   4   3   2   1

For Deanna Fei

My fortunes soared the minute I laid eyes on you.

Contents

Past Due

Dust Ourselves Off

In early 2008, the bill finally came due for Dorothy Thomas. The accumulated costs of years of living in excess of her income washed over her with a vengeance. First, she lost her car, and then she couldn't get to work, so she lost her job. With no wages, she couldn't pay her rent, so she lost her home. Within a matter of months, she had slipped from waking up in a desirable community in northern California to squatting in a drug-infested neighborhood. By year's end, she was occupying a bunk at a homeless shelter. And then her lousy credit prevented her from getting another job, making it nearly impossible to dig out from the commonplace financial disaster that had upended her life.

For two decades, Thomas had lived strategically beyond her means. She had rented houses in better neighborhoods than she could really afford, the monthly payments straining the paychecks she earned selling makeup at department stores or scheduling medical appointments at doctors' offices. Like millions of other Americans, she had tapped too many credit cards and paid too few bills while focusing on the immediate concerns of keeping food on her table, gas in her car, and ample clothing in the wardrobes of her two girls.

Across the United States—a country grappling with its worst economic downturn since the Great Depression—a sense has taken hold that this new age of reckoning is predominantly the result of national profligacy. Extravagance is clearly part of our national crisis, and yet it is only part of the explanation. Millions of people have been living beyond their incomes for the simple reason that those incomes have been outstripped by the cost of middle-class American life. Thomas exceeded her finance not out of craving for a prestigious address, but in order to put her two daughters in better school districts, while exposing them to the loftier aspirations of wealthier children. She wanted both girls to complete college, something she had sought for herself but failed to grasp.

Born in 1958, Thomas had grown up poor in Muskogee, Oklahoma, raised by her grandparents because her mother struggled with drinking and addiction. In the second grade she was sent to a forcibly integrated elementary school, one of a handful of black children delivered into a largely hostile white community. From the first day of school, Thomas, then seven, felt a deep sense of terror—as her grandmother held her hand and put her on the bus, crying; as the bus pulled up to school and she stepped into a crowd of enraged white parents waving protest signs; as a hall monitor with piercing blue eyes stared at her with naked hostility. "To this day, I don't like blue," she said. "She always made me feel unclean or dirty. I don't think I learned anything that first year. I just remember being scared all the time."

After graduating from high school in 1976, Thomas enrolled at the University of Oklahoma to study nursing. But soon she got pregnant with her first daughter, Shawn. The girl's father—her high school boyfriend—paid no child support. She felt pressured by her grandparents to start making money, so she shelved her thoughts of upward mobility through education, dropped out of college, and started looking for a job. "My grandparents just damn near came from the slave fields," Thomas said. "They were very frank. 'We ain't got no money. Go to college? You might just forget about that. You want to be somebody, you better be somebody with a job.' Every dream you had got squashed."

She moved to northern California, invited by her sister, who was already living there. At first she rented a cheap apartment in a largely African American neighborhood in Sacramento. In her twenties, Thomas had a glamorous quality about her, a smooth voice, and fine features. She was making her living selling makeup at a department store, and she decided to move to the more exclusive community of Southland Park. The extra

$200 a month in rent she paid for the town house was hard to come by. Yet, far from a profligate act, moving there seemed like a wise investment in her daughter's future. The new community was more diverse, with white and Asian families, and its schools had good reputations. Thomas assumed that being around higher-income people and better schools would make Shawn accustomed to that life, conditioned to strive for it.

"I truly bought into the idea that education is the way out of poverty," Thomas said. "It just seemed like basic common sense that the nicer areas would have better schools. It doesn't take a rocket scientist to figure out that if your kids are going to school with kids who are preprogrammed to go to college, then that's what they will expect."

She took Shawn by the hand to the local elementary school, uncertain what sort of reception to expect, and determined to secure her a spot. "I just applied," Thomas recalled. "I said, 'If they aren't going to take me, I'm going to raise a ruckus.'" None was required.

Thomas's second daughter, Amber, was born in 1986. Her relationship with Amber's father soon fell apart as he began using drugs in the house they shared. Seeking a clean break, Thomas took the girls south to San Jose, joining her sister. Again, she selected a middle-class neighborhood, the Berryessa district in the heart of booming Silicon Valley, which strained her finances but ensured her girls would attend good schools. She rented a house for $1,400 a month from a Filipino family that gave her a bit of a break on the rent, and she treated the place as if it were her own, adding magnolia trees to the backyard and flowers to the front. "I came to think of that house as my home," she said. She remained there for sixteen years.

Thomas made as much as $22 an hour in those years, mostly as a receptionist at medical offices. It was enough to pay the rent and keep her kids in books, clothing, and food. She worked as a cocktail waitress at private events on weekends so she could come up with funds to send the girls to science camp in the summer; to buy Amber an expensive cheerleader outfit; to make sure her daughters didn't feel inferior to their peers.

In addition to accruing credit card debts, she sometimes opted not to pay the gas bill so she could pay the rent. She tossed the cable bill so she could buy school supplies for the girls, or a pair of shoes for work. Partially, this was because most of the spending seemed crucial. Partially, it was because no one had ever taught her how to budget. "We were never taught to manage money, because we never had money," Thomas said. "Being poor, you think about rent, lights, gas, and food, and nowadays cable and car insurance. Those are the bills you focus on. You're always robbing Peter to pay Paul. You're forced to make choices of survival."

Both of her girls graduated from high school and went off to college. Shawn attended Cal State–Long Beach, and then the University of Hawaii for a master's in education. She has remained in Hawaii, working as a public school teacher. Amber enrolled at Chico State. Thomas justifiably takes pride in having raised her girls to success, attaining levels of achievement that towered over the world into which she was born and raised. And yet the bills were still coming due, years after her daughters established their own lives.

In 2006, with long-standing credit card balances absorbing her income, Thomas had failed to pay a $10 fee for the registration sticker on her car, a 1996 Toyota Corolla. Then she failed to pay a ticket for having an expired registration. And then, one afternoon in November, a cop pulled her over in San Jose and wrote her another ticket. He checked the records, discovered it was her second offense, and had her vehicle towed away.

"I got down on my knees and begged that officer," Thomas recalled. It was no use.

With little cash, Thomas could not afford to pay the fees required to extract her vehicle from the lot. As it sat unclaimed, those fees swelled beyond $1,600. Without a car, she could no longer get to work, so she lost her job as an administrator at a hospital. Without a job, she could no longer pay rent, and with neither savings nor decent credit she was in no position to rent even a smaller, cheaper place while she tried to start over. So she moved to Oakland, the blue-collar cousin to aristocratic San Francisco across the bay, where her friend, Yvonne, had rented a ramshackle place on Adeline Street, a rough part of town, agreeing to put her up while she looked for work.

This was how Thomas—a product of poverty who had managed to raise two college students—found herself living on what she came to call Crack Avenue.

Yvonne's rental was a beat-up white Victorian in the flatlands of West Oakland, on a block where all the houses sat in various states of disrepair, with sagging roofs, loose tiles, and front windows covered by taped newspapers or boards. Emaciated people loitered on the corners and congregated in front of the check-cashing place across the street, in front of the bodega, and at the liquor store where the merchant stood behind bars. Inside the house, purple mold spores dominated one wall. Drunks and addicts often turned up to sleep on the back porch. Thomas and her friend called it "the monster house."

"We had to laugh about it," Thomas said. "That was the only way to get through it."

One day, Thomas opened some mail that had come for the landlord. It was from a bank. The owner was behind on the mortgage payments. Foreclosure loomed. Their rent was supposed to include utilities. But soon the gas and water were cut. They went across the street to Yvonne's boyfriend's house to use the shower. They carried buckets of water back with them to flush the toilet.

She took the bus to a job center downtown and looked for work, growing despondent as rejections mounted. Each month, the unemployment rate climbed, adding hundreds of thousands of more jobless Americans to the hunt for diminishing opportunities.

Thomas had clearly lived beyond her means. She had tapped credit she was in no position to pay back, putting herself in danger. Her troubles were of her own making. Yet it was hardly decadence that had put her where she was. She had reached for something that society was telling her she had to provide for her children at any cost—a decent education.

"I didn't get myself out of poverty," she said. "But I got my daughters out. I was the bridge."

☙

In November 2007, when I began writing about the national economy for the *New York Times*, some economists were beginning to worry about the possibility of a recession. But hardly anyone—save for a few then written off as veritable kooks—grasped that economic crisis was about to become the dominant issue of our day, or that daily conversation would soon revolve around comparisons with the Great Depression. "This economy is flexible," President George W. Bush had said as he addressed business and civic leaders that month in Indiana, dismissing the emerging signs of trouble. "It is dynamic and it is competitive enough to overcome any challenge we face."

Yet as soon as I began to leave my cubicle in New York to get a sense of what was happening in different parts of the country, I became convinced that the economy was spiraling down. In Reno, Nevada, a once hot housing market that had gone bust, I fell in with a bunch of guys in their thirties who had been speculating heavily on real estate in recent years. As housing prices rose, they amassed new cars and clothes, enjoyed expensive dinners, and spent as if their paper gains were real. Now, their paper gains were a memory, and most were hunkering down. Shops and restaurants throughout the area were suffering an evident pullback. In Cape Coral, Florida, an entire metropolitan area was reeling from the strain, as enormous quantities of wealth were swiftly eliminated, and housing prices plunged—an early indication of what lay ahead for other formerly booming real estate markets as joblessness spread and government revenues plunged. In January 2008, as I reported a story on the implications of Americans losing access to credit, I spoke with Fran Barbaro, a highly educated, highly paid technology entrepreneur in Boston who had gotten herself in such trouble—borrowing energetically against the value of her home—that she was facing the threat of foreclosure. In Oakland, California, a city that had yet to gain back the jobs it had lost in the last recession and was already losing more, I spent the afternoon with Greg Bailey, an able-bodied, intelligent man of forty who had spent much of the last year futilely applying for the sorts of low-wage warehouse jobs he had turned down years earlier. In Miami in the summer of 2008, I met Willie Gonzalez, a liquor distributor whose commissions were drying up along with Florida's spending power. By the end of the year, he would surrender his house to foreclosure. I met Dorothy Thomas, who broke down in tears as she described how she had damaged her credit by living in better neighborhoods than she had been able to afford so she could send her daughters to better schools.

There were plausible reasons why each of these people might individually have landed in danger, reasons that could perhaps be distinguished from the troubles afflicting the broader economy. Bailey was an African American man in a city with high black unemployment. Thomas was a single mother who had run up bills she could not pay. The people I met in Reno had lived far beyond their incomes, assuming that something akin to a cash advance on future earnings would be easy to repay.

Cape Coral had been a den of reckless speculators who had driven up real estate prices beyond any rational connection to affordability.

But, taken as a whole, it was hard to dismiss these struggles as the ordinary distress found within any economy. That sense only deepened as a range of government data confirmed the weakening of the job market and the broad economy over the next several months, shrinking job opportunities for nearly everyone, from lower-skilled blue-collar workers to those with advanced degrees.

࿔

There has always been poverty in the United States. There has always been unemployment and foreclosure and bankruptcy. Even in good times, many people fail. Such is the reality of capitalism, the downside of the growth and innovation contained within a system in which people are free to take great risks and pursue great rewards. Yet the more I encountered these commonplace troubles, the harder it became to accept that this was just the usual, temporary downturn for the American economy.

Midway through 2008, the economy was losing hundreds of thousands of jobs a month and would continue to do so for months afterward. Most economists had concluded that a recession was well under way, though President Bush ridiculed such talk. "You can listen to these economists," Bush said in West Virginia. "On the one hand, they'll say, and then on the other hand. If they had three hands, it would be on the one hand, the second hand and the third hand."

For most, however, the debate was purely academic.

"All my cousins already know it's a recession," said Robert Barbera, chief economist at the research and trading firm ITG, speaking that July. "They have the luxury of not having PhDs. The auto companies are in dire straits. The airlines have been shutting down flights and firing pilots. The truckers are in near hysteria because of the price of diesel. If you round up the usual suspects, this is a bad circumstance. And the word we usually use for a bad circumstance is a recession."

Not until late 2008 did the official validation come from the National Bureau of Economic Research, the private organization that ultimately decides whether and how to label bad circumstances. Back in

December 2007, the American economy had indeed slipped into a recession, the panel concluded.

The use of the recession label removed any remaining doubt that the suffering of so many Americans was part of a broad trend. Yet it also implied that all would soon be right again. Economists tend to think in cyclical terms. In good times, businesses invest in new factories and machinery and hire more workers, and the economy expands. Workers spend their wages, distributing their dollars throughout the economy—to butchers, hardware stores, movie theaters, dry cleaners—and the economy expands some more. That creates additional jobs at businesses that capture the extra dollars. More wages supply more people the wherewithal to buy, and the economy expands still more. But eventually expansion ends, as all things must. Maybe an external shock such as an oil crisis causes the downturn, inflating fuel costs and making people unable to spend as much on other goods (as seemed to be the case in the summer of 2008). Maybe factories and merchants invest too aggressively in good times and generate more products and services than the economy needs, leaving too much stuff lying around unsold. They cut back on production and stop buying parts and raw materials from their suppliers. That prompts those suppliers to lay off workers. The newly unemployed cut their spending, depriving other businesses of sales. In this fashion, the forces of retrenchment ripple through the economy until economic activity actually shrinks, the very definition of a recession. But after a pause of a few months or perhaps a year, order is restored and the economy starts growing again. Because growth is the natural course of events, as economists see things. People want more. Businesses want to expand.

In the thinking of economists, the business cycle is an inextricable part of economic reality, as elemental as the changing seasons. So when the recession began in late 2007, one could reasonably draw on that established pattern to take comfort that better days were surely on the way, just as certainly as spring follows winter.

But that was wrong. This downturn was unusual. It was the result of two decades' worth of excessive debt building up within the American economy. The recession was caused not just by too much investment—though the trigger was plunging real estate prices resulting from exuberant construction—but also by broad dysfunction in the financial system. Banks had indiscriminately lent stupendous amounts of money to home owners, and much of that money was gone forever. As banks recoiled in horror at the sudden worthlessness of trillions of dollars' worth of investments linked to mortgages—investments that had only recently seemed rock solid—they discovered that they had participated in the enticing make-believe that housing prices could never fall. The banks had lost the courage to lend to almost anyone.

This was catastrophic. Banks function as the arterial system of the economy. They deliver capital to businesses and households that need it. When the system struggles, as it did in the summer of 2007 before worsening in the months after, companies and households could not get their hands on money. People who wanted to buy cars could not arrange financing, so the companies that manufactured and sold cars, from the Big Three automakers in Detroit to the sales lots in every community, suffered withering shortfalls and potential bankruptcy. Stevedores at ports from Portland, Oregon, to Baltimore lost working hours as fewer cars arrived on American shores from Asia and Europe. Companies that contemplated adding equipment or expanding their workforce were unable to borrow capital, so they deferred expansions, depriving suppliers of fresh orders and would-be workers of jobs. Potential homebuyers could no longer secure mortgages, so they stopped buying homes, and housing prices fell more, decreasing business for real estate agents, title companies, appraisers, and construction workers. Anyone who had gotten accustomed to financing purchases—or paying their bills—on credit faced a grave situation, because they could no longer roll their debts over to new loans as their old loans came due. They had to pay back what they owed. And in late 2007, as the financial system became consumed by a paralyzing fear, an awful lot of Americans owed an awful lot of money.

૭

For years, the economy had been juiced by the coursing stream of borrowed finance. By 2008, consumer credit exceeded $2.6 trillion, up from $300 billion three decades earlier.

The run-up in debt was itself reflective of another reason why the recession was far more severe than a typical dip in the cycle: Americans had been borrowing exuberantly not simply because Americans are extravagant spenders—though that is certainly part of the explanation—but because the economy has for many years failed to create adequate numbers of high-quality jobs, the sorts of jobs that pay enough to finance a middle-class life. The recession that began in December 2007 landed atop a lengthy period of extraordinarily lean economic gains among American workers.

Between the end of World War II and the 1970s, the economy lifted nearly all Americans. Women and minorities entered the workforce in greater percentages than ever. Economic inequality was accelerating, but so was wage growth for nearly everyone. If people in penthouses saw their incomes increase faster than everyone else, at least the people who vacuumed their floors, catered their weddings, and sold them insurance were also making progress. In 1964, the average rank-and-file American worker—about 80 percent of the American workforce—brought home about $300 a week, in inflation-adjusted dollars. By 1973, those same weekly earnings had swelled above $330, a jump of about 10 percent in a little less than a decade.

But even as the economy mostly grew in the years that followed, average weekly earnings dipped below $260 by 1996, a slide of more than one-fifth over twenty-three years. By October 2008, those same weekly earnings had only inched up to $279, roughly the same level as in 1983. In short, a quarter-century had come and gone with the average American stuck in place.

To be sure, some of the drop can be explained by the changing composition of the American workforce. As more women and immigrants have entered the workforce, this has pushed wages down overall. Still, many economists see in this data the broad outlines of distress. "For middle- and low-wage workers, the median wage basically went nowhere over these years," said economist Jared Bernstein. "These were tough years for working people."

Economists are inclined to measure progress in terms of productivity—that is, how much stuff can be made with a given amount of labor. From 1947 through about 1978, wages and benefits for rank-and-file workers grew roughly in tandem with the overall productivity of the U.S. economy: both more than doubled over that period. American businesses became increasingly efficient, churning out twice as many goods and services for the same hour of labor. Workers reaped benefits, seeing their compensation increase by roughly the same magnitude.

Between 1979 and 2007, productivity shot up by another 70 percent. But compensation for the American rank and file hardly moved, inching up only 5 percent, after factoring in inflation. In recent decades, only the elite—those in the top tenth of income distribution—saw their real earnings keep pace with gains in productivity.

How and why most workers extracted so little from those years of mostly robust expansion is the subject of a debate that could fill its own book. The highlights include the declining power of unions in organizing contracts, the rise of off-shoring—which has allowed companies to shift production to regions where labor is cheap, such as Latin America and Asia—and the steady march of economic inequality, with the bulk of the economic rewards flowing mostly to those with college educations. But the bottom line is clear: while the economy has grown and the rich have prospered, most Americans have seen meager improvement in their material well-being over the last quarter-century.

Even as the value of many wages slid, the cost of living dropped. Many products became very cheap—particularly clothing, cars, and furniture—as globalization accelerated. Before speculation overtook the real estate market, home ownership was expanding, as low interest rates made mortgage payments manageable for many who had previously been shut out. Yet what the earnings numbers bring home is something that many people already know intuitively, without consulting a government database: something has gone wrong with the economy, something subtle and pernicious. The economy has been suffering from a chronic shortage of work and income. Easy money filled the gap.

Americans have long compensated for the reality of declining wages and growing insecurity by tapping an assortment of credit options served up by Wall Street, from second mortgages on houses to high interest "payday loans." "The middle-class way of life can be maintained for quite a while with smoke and mirrors—and many credit cards," declared Teresa A. Sullivan, Elizabeth Warren, and Jay Lawrence Westbrook in their 2000 book, *The Fragile Middle Class*. Growing debt translated into growing vulnerability to changing economic conditions. The researchers found a fourfold increase in personal bankruptcy filings between 1979 and 1997, a period of relatively robust growth. When they surveyed those who landed in bankruptcy, they were surprised to discover that these people were much like other middle-class Americans, except for some recent misfortune that has pushed them over the edge—a lost job, an illness, a divorce.

Even households that have gotten ahead have found progress tenuous and subject to unexpected reversals, as the investment binges and busts of recent times have made incomes more volatile, according to some data. Between the early 1970s and the early 2000s, the percentage of working-age people who saw their family income drop by half or more climbed from 4 percent to almost 10 percent, according to one study. This trend was worst for those at the lower end of the economic spectrum, but the rising instability afflicted nearly every demographic group. The growing prevalence of two-income households has cushioned that instability but can also exacerbate trouble: two earners means two shots at a layoff or reduced working hours. Most families tie their purchases of major items such as houses and cars to their combined household income, leaving them vulnerable to default when one spouse loses a job. Two incomes often requires costly child care, take-out food to make up for lost hours of parenting and cooking, and the expenses of owning and operating two cars. But a second income typically does not get a family ahead; it merely holds them in place while increasing the stresses and logistical difficulties of everyday life—a phenomenon Harvard Law School professor Elizabeth Warren calls "the two income trap."

Government policies that entrusted more of American economic security to the markets ratcheted up volatility. President Bush liked to talk about what he called the "Ownership Society," a new era in which Americans would enjoy direct control of their financial fate, as opposed to relying on government. This was the spirit in which he pushed unsuccessfully to privatize Social Security. This was the thinking behind his campaign to expand home ownership.

Such policies seemed attractive when housing prices and stock markets were rising, but they rendered formerly stable areas of middle-class life significantly riskier. A modest retirement was once guaranteed for many American workers, particularly those in unions, whose contracts offered traditional pensions that paid out a monthly lump sum until the end of life. How the company came up with the money for that monthly check was its problem. But in the 1980s, as union power eroded, many employers quit offering pensions and shifted to the then new 401(k) retirement savings plans, to which they made only limited contributions. Employees themselves contributed the bulk of the money, choosing from a basket of mutual funds and stocks in which to invest, much to the delight of Wall Street banks that earned profits by managing the money. In 1983, less than 7 percent of all private retirement savings was parked in such accounts; by 1998, they held more than half of private retirement savings. For households headed by workers in their mid-forties and younger, nearly two-thirds of retirement savings were in 401(k) accounts, placing a majority of Americans' retirement prospects in stock investments. The value of these accounts tended to be smaller than a pension. Cutbacks to Social Security brought total retirement benefits down further, while encouraging people to entrust their retirement savings to riskier investments, favoring stocks over bonds. Between 1983 and 1998—a period synonymous with breathtaking gains in stocks—the typical family approaching retirement wound up with 11 percent less stashed away than the same sort of family had at the beginning of those years.

As a result, Americans became obsessed with the short-term gains of their stock portfolios and home prices, much to their detriment, argues the Yale economist Robert Shiller. "There is indeed much to be said for the ownership society in terms of its ability to promote economic growth," Shiller writes in *Irrational Exuberance*, the classic account of the tech and housing bubble years. "But by its very nature it also invites speculation, and, filtered through the vagaries of human psychology, it creates a horde of risks. . . . People still place too much confidence in the markets and have too strong a belief that paying attention to the gyrations in their investments will someday make them rich, and so they do not make conservative preparations for possible bad outcomes."

For people with the means to buy stocks and real estate, the technology boom of the 1990s and the housing bubble of the 2000s served up the ultimate opportunity to spend in brazen disregard of incomes and debt levels. By Shiller's calculation, between 1996 and 1999 the increase to average American household wealth that could be attributed to the appreciation of stock holdings was more than twelve times that of personal savings. Between 2001 and 2003, increases in house prices dwarfed savings tenfold as a source of increased wealth. "Saving for the future seemed almost irrelevant in view of the increase in asset values that came from doing nothing more than just buying and holding," Shiller writes. No one feels the need to save when money is just lying there for the taking. For several years before the recession began in late 2007, the national savings rate had been negative: households were spending more than they were earning. Americans had no cushion to turn to in tough times.

And this was no ordinary pullback. The recession unfolded with punishing consequences. As the mortgage crisis burst into a broader financial crisis, the U.S. economy became locked in a downward spiral. As housing prices fell, so did household spending, prompting businesses to lay off millions of workers. Jobless people cut their spending, intensifying the downturn, and many fell behind on their mortgage and credit card payments. As banks saw greater losses, they cut back on lending, squeezing the clamps tighter on the economy and prompting more layoffs still.

∽

In late 2008, as it emerged that the United States was experiencing the worst downturn since the Great Depression, a public bewildered and beleaguered became obsessed with a stunning financial scandal. The money manager Bernard Madoff, widely celebrated for his supposedly steady hand and his generous philanthropy, confessed to running a criminal ruse over many decades. Madoff had been attracting investment by lying about past profits and then handing out these new funds to existing shareholders to perpetuate the illusion of profits. Prosecutors described it as the largest Ponzi scheme in history, one whose losses reached $65 billion. In the midst of a terrible financial crisis, one that entailed no end of impenetrable financial jargon, the abstract complexities of economics, and a great deal of distress, Madoff's misdeeds seemed to offer an enticingly simple explanation for all that had gone wrong.

In the course of the year, the stock market had wiped out $7 trillion worth of wealth. Some 50 million Americans whose retirement savings were entrusted to the markets saw $1 trillion in value annihilated in little more than a year. The downturn destroyed 2.6 million jobs during 2008 — the largest one-year drop since 1945. Real estate prices had plummeted and millions of ordinary people were surrendering their homes to foreclosure. Seemingly indomitable Wall Street investment banks had collapsed and disappeared — Merrill Lynch, Lehman Brothers, Bear Stearns, all gone. There was talk of Fannie Mae and Freddie Mac, which, despite their country cousin names, were mortgage companies whose near collapse threatened to take down much of the global economy. Collateralized debt obligations and derivatives, whatever the hell they were, seemed to be implicated. President Bush, an eternal optimist, had put aside a quarter-century of dogmatic devotion to free markets and begged Congress to deliver a $700 billion taxpayer-funded Wall Street bailout, warning that the alternative was something akin to financial Armageddon. "Our entire economy is in danger," he intoned during a nationally televised speech that September. For the first time since the early 1990s, the indomitable American consumer had started conserving. Some economists openly worried that the country was in danger of sinking to the depths once explored by Japan, where the end of a speculative real estate bubble in the 1980s ushered in a so-called Lost Decade of joblessness and despair. "The open question is whether we're in for a bad couple of years, or a bad decade," declared Kenneth S. Rogoff, a former chief economist at the International Monetary Fund.

Then along came Bernie Madoff. Even though his victims were generally well-heeled investors, here was a face to blame. Indeed, by February 2009 an opportunistic toy company had released the "Smash-Me Bernie Doll," a diminutive version of Madoff dressed as a red devil with a pitchfork and packaged with a hammer. For a mere $99.95, buyers could take out their frustrations on Madoff in effigy.

And yet how was Madoff's scam fundamentally different from the one that Americans had used to power the economy for many years? Americans had become addicted to dreaming up stories that prompted money to change hands, and calling that economic progress. A nation skilled in engineering, innovation, and craftsmanship had relinquished its traditional focus on producing goods and services of intrinsic value in favor of financial make-believe. From the technology boom of the 1990s through the housing boom of the 2000s, Americans had participated in a lucrative exercise in collective delusion, subscribing first to the idea that the Internet justified a near-limitless appreciation of stock prices, and then to the notion that housing prices could only rise. On the backs of these two fantasies, the financial system had lent out ridiculous quantities of money to businesses and home owners, as if the old laws of supply and demand had been repealed. This generated economic growth and scattered riches. It also inflicted the economy with a debilitating case of disillusionment. The markets lost faith in the make-believe that had long propelled investment, starving the economy of capital. And even Americans like Dorothy Thomas who barely benefited from the make-believe were widely suffering the consequences.

For many years, the economy has existed in a state of Neverland akin to that depicted in J. M. Barrie's classic tale *Peter Pan*; Americans have operated as if we can fly, borrowing increasingly enormous sums of money while making believe it need never be paid back, while Wall Street has cavorted across an island of unlimited adventure with no adult supervision.

Peter Pan taught the Darling children of London that they could fly simply by believing in "lovely wonderful thoughts." Fantastical thinking about financial engineering and free markets helped propel the American economy through two decades of extraordinary reliance on borrowed money and unregulated commerce. We have availed ourselves of too much fairy dust, the easy money offered up by the financial system in the form of home equity loans and low-interest credit cards. All the while, the legendary chairman of the Federal Reserve Alan Greenspan, repeatedly assured us that financial innovation and the magic of market forces obviated the need for government regulation. Whenever anyone warned that deregulation and too much easy money were setting up a crash, Greenspan shushed them with assurances that the markets were hedging all risks, a dose of make-believe.

Neverland has its vulnerabilities. Fairies can only survive for as long as children believe in them. Once their belief dies, fairies die, too, along with their magic dust.

When the markets lost belief in the "lovely wonderful thoughts" that propelled virtually unlimited investment in housing and technology companies, the consequences were lethal. Real estate prices and tech stocks came crashing back to earth, millions of people lost jobs, trillions of dollars of paper wealth were destroyed, and the economy stopped functioning.

In *Peter Pan*, the pedestrian skills of reading, writing, and arithmetic seem not worth cultivating. "I don't want to go to school and learn solemn things," Peter Pan tells Wendy Darling as she tries to persuade him to forsake the fantastical Neverland and join her family in the brick solidity of London. Millions of Americans likewise disdained sober financial planning and accounting, and did not bother scrutinizing the fine print of their mortgage documents. Banks and their regulators did not bother contemplating the broader implications of the complex investments known as credit derivatives that summoned trillions of dollars in investment capital from thin air while dramatically increasing the risks weighing on the financial system. Budgeting seemed anachronistic as skyrocketing technology stocks seemed to render retirement savings superfluous, and as rising home prices allowed households to spend as if bills were meaningless.

Ultimately, fantasy cannot sustain flesh and blood. In *Peter Pan*, the Lost Boys tire of having to "make-believe that they had had their dinners." The Darling children opt to go home to their warm beds and their parents. During the technology boom, investors eventually grew disenchanted with make-believe earnings—the voluminous profits that were always just over the horizon. And when they stopped believing, they yanked their money from the markets, depriving even legitimate tech companies of capital. This happened again in the summer of 2007 as investors finally figured out that the values of mortgages depended upon willful disregard of the reality that a lot of borrowers would never be able to pay back their loans. So the investors spurned mortgage-linked investments, and the financial system shut down. In the end, even Alan Greenspan admitted that his faith had been excessive.

෯

On January 20, 2009, Barack Obama stood on the grand staircase of the Capitol in Washington, D.C., and looked out at the crowd of more than a million thronging the Mall to deliver his inaugural address. Obama declared, "Starting today, we must pick ourselves up, dust ourselves off, and begin again the work of remaking America." The new president might well have been referencing the fairy dust of *Peter Pan*. It was time to stop pretending we could fly. It was time to build a real new economy powered by solid investment, sober-minded thinking, and honest work—not make-believe.

The economy was in such crisis that an extraordinary political consensus had emerged. The new president and both political parties were in agreement that an enormous sum of public money had to be swiftly unleashed to give the economy a jolt. Even before he assumed office,

Obama crafted plans to spend $800 billion in taxpayer money over the first two years of his term. He aimed to expand unemployment benefits, distribute additional food stamps, and create as many as 4 million jobs through large-scale construction projects. In ordinary times, such a budget request would have been a nonstarter, or at least required several months of hearings and horse-trading before the required votes could be amassed. But these were not normal times. Each week seemed to bring a fresh indication that the economy might be sliding toward the abyss. Although there was griping, Republican dissent, and compromise, Congress approved Obama's stimulus spending bill within his first month in office.

The stimulus bill took the edge off the worst economic fears and raised hopes that the suffering would diminish. It would generate needed paychecks. It would provide relief to those laid off. It would spare jobs that would otherwise have been lost by sending aid to strapped states, enabling them to proceed with construction projects.

But it would not get at the roots of the crisis. It would not restore order to so many facets of the economy that had been warped by years of recklessly destructive financial management, and by failed government experiments in letting markets run free of regulation.

The economy was not merely ailing. Its basic mechanisms had broken down. A country that had in recent years gorged itself on consumer goods without limit, courtesy of rising home prices and seemingly bottomless credit, was choking on the aftermath of a real estate bust and the ensuing financial crisis. Easy money and a devil-may-care attitude toward debt had been replaced by shrinking incomes, revoked credit, forced austerity, and downward mobility.

Americans were buffeted by a swirl of mixed messages. On the one hand, a new catch phrase insinuated itself into the conversation: Americans had to *live within our means*. Pundits seized on this phrase like a badge of wisdom, asserting that consumer profligacy had brought the nation to its knees. At the same time, in the summer of 2008, the government had mailed out $100 billion worth of tax refund checks and urged people to head to the shopping mall.

"What do they want from us, anyway?" asked an exasperated Michael Kinsley in an op-ed piece in the *New York Times*. "Without consumers to lead the charge, an economic recovery will be hard to achieve. And yet everyone agrees that we need to start saving more. So should I buy that coffee maker to stimulate the economy? Or should I save the money in order to 'grow' the economy and provide for my own old age? I can't do both."

⌘

How did we get so addicted to make-believe that we turned our economy into a hoax? How did we manage to take an economic system that had lifted most Americans for many generations and transform it into a dysfunctional heap? How can we repair it so that it works again, generating jobs that finance traditional middle-class lives? This book looks back at our recent history in the service of moving forward, using an exploration of the past as a springboard toward building a better future, one centered on enduring areas of our strength.

From the ashes of the failed era of easy money, Americans must get back to honest work. We must generate the sorts of jobs that can support middle-class American life. We must invest in inherently productive enterprises, such as renewable energy and biotechnology and other areas yet to be forged. Above all, we must ground our plans not in financial make-believe but in the world we inhabit today—a world with plenty of adventures and risks still worth taking.

This book will unfold as a wide-ranging tour of the American landscape and beyond, from Silicon Valley in the 1990s, to China in the first decade of the new millennium, to Florida, California, and Nevada in the midst of the real estate bubble, and on to North Carolina, Iowa, Ohio and elsewhere in exploration of the potential underpinnings for a healthier economy. It will take readers behind the headlines, consulting a range of experts and analysts, but more important, it will probe the lives of real people whose experiences shed light on how we got to this troubled moment and how we might move forward.

The fundamental challenge now confronting American society is how to transition from an era in which we spent and consumed in brazen disregard of traditional limits to a new period in which we live on what we earn. Americans are beginning to save again. Cut off from myriad forms of credit and forced to contemplate a future in which free money cannot be pulled from their houses, Americans have returned to the necessary discipline of financial planning. These are healthy developments, and yet austerity and budgeting will not be enough to right the economy, not after years in which earnings have been steadily deteriorating and jobs have been disappearing. Work must once again become a more rewarding pursuit. The government must once again regulate the financial system to protect the economy from investment binges.

This is the story of how things got so out of hand, and how we might move on to something better.

PART I

∽

The Age of Easy Money

1

The Credit Diet

"The money was always there."

In late 2007, Fran Barbaro, a white, fifty-year-old mother of two boys, with an MBA and a résumé full of six-figure-salary computer industry jobs, found herself confronting a previously unimaginable situation: she could no longer keep up with the mortgage payments on her three-bedroom house outside Boston. The bank was threatening to foreclose.

Barbaro had enjoyed years of enviable incomes. During the technology boom of the 1990s, the value of her stock portfolio had swelled beyond $1 million, giving her the financial freedom to purchase symphony tickets, original art, and tropical vacations. During the subsequent real estate boom, the value of her home in an exclusive suburb swelled to nearly $1 million, allowing her to borrow against this increase to continue her lifestyle of plenty. All of that money was now gone, her stock portfolio exhausted, and her home worth less than she owed the bank. Barbaro had moved into an apartment in the basement of a house owned by her parents in an effort to economize and avoid bankruptcy. Her two boys occupied the lone bedroom. She spent her nights on a pull-out sofa in the living room.

Like millions of other Americans, Barbaro had run through her money. She had shelled out again and again for what she considered the staples of upper-middle-class American life: special after-school programs for her boys, who suffered learning disabilities, which ran $25,000 a year; summer camp; a new kitchen. Not to mention the run-of-the-mill costs of keeping gas in the car, food on the table, and the lights on. "These were simple day-to-day expenses," Barbaro explained. "I always made a lot of money. The money was always there."

More than two centuries earlier, Benjamin Franklin had counseled those fortunate enough to enjoy credit to take care to distinguish between borrowed funds and income. "Beware of thinking all your own that you possess, and of living accordingly," he wrote. "It is a mistake that many people who have credit fall into. To prevent this, keep an exact account for some time, both of your expenses and your income."

Franklin had of course never confronted Internet stocks whose value doubled inside of a week. He had never encountered a variable rate mortgage, a home equity line of credit, or a zero-interest credit card— financial innovations with exotically lenient terms that made almost any purchase eminently doable for people of Barbaro's means. She never felt any compulsion to square her outlays against her income. In place of that seemingly antiquated accounting exercise, she had her stock portfolio, most of which was invested in technology companies. She could dip into her stock winnings at will, and that gave her a sense of security. It made every expenditure seem reassuringly manageable, even responsible. What parent would turn down a special program for a child struggling to read when the money was just sitting there? Why skimp on summer camp?

After the markets collapsed in the middle of 2000 and the Nasdaq ceased to function as a dollar printing machine, Barbaro's house assumed that role. The real estate speculation that unfolded over the subsequent years lifted the value of her home to heights that would have seemed absurd, except that the same story was playing out throughout Boston and in much of the country, from suburban Atlanta to the deserts encircling Phoenix. When her continued spending swelled her credit card balances to levels requiring monthly payments she could no longer manage, Barbaro was able to pick from a crowded buffet of mortgage companies and banks eager to turn her increased paper wealth into cash in hand.

In 2004, she arranged a new mortgage on her house to take advantage of low rates, and she tacked on a $44,000 home equity line of credit to pay off the credit cards. Still the banks kept stuffing her mailbox with offers for more money, right now, no documentation required, most of the come-ons wrapped in a reassuring veneer of responsible financial planner speak: "Consolidate your debts." "Put your money to work for you." Barbaro accepted their offers, taking on more debt in the belief that there was plenty of credit left.

Until there wasn't any more. By the end of 2007, her stock portfolio was exhausted, the proceeds shrunken by the collapse of the market in 2000 and the remainder spent on everyday living expenses while she recovered from surgery and a memorable trip to Belize with her boys. After she separated from her ex-husband in 1999, becoming the sole breadwinner, she pulled money from her 401(k) retirement account through a so-called hardship withdrawal, and she was on the hook for the resulting taxes. She had borrowed against the value of her home so aggressively that she could borrow no more. She owed more than $800,000 on her mortgage and home equity lines of credit, yet her house was worth less than $700,000. In the parlance of the time, she was "upside-down." The same banks that for years had been begging her to borrow were suddenly shunning her as an unsavory risk.

Barbaro's latest mortgage had begun with a promotional rate that made the monthly payment a manageable $2,600 a month. For reasons she could not understand—reasons buried in the fine print of loan documents she had not read closely—the payments were spiking to $3,300 a month. She worried that the next stop on her journey would be foreclosure.

Barbaro spoke in the demanding voice of someone accustomed to getting her way. She could be loud and confrontational, her words tinged with the nasal inflection of New England. She was no candidate for food stamps or a winter coat donated by a church. She still had a job that the majority of Americans would envy, bringing home $5,200 a month from a local software developer. But her monthly debt payments alone were absorbing more than $4,000. Like so many, she had become a reluctant participant in a lifestyle that recent times had rendered strangely quaint: she would have to live within the confines of her income.

She quit shopping at Whole Foods, with its high-end organic produce and European cheeses, and started buying groceries at discount
supermarkets. She relinquished thoughts of another vacation. She
rented out her house, moved into the basement apartment at her parents'
place, and began to negotiate with the bank to try to lower her mortgage
payments.

"You're sacrificing certain things," she said. "How do you salvage
what you had and hopefully go back?"

That question was reverberating across the country. Ben Franklin's
admonition was suddenly relevant again. The old days of being bom-
barded with alternative sources of cash were gone.

✍

On the other side of the country, in Oakland, California, Greg Bailey
had missed out on the spoils of the age of easy money. He had never owned
a home or a stock portfolio, living paycheck to paycheck while people
like Barbaro feasted on credit and technology stock proceeds. Yet, as the
economy sank into a deep recession in 2007 and 2008, he was drawing
an outsize share of the hurt.

Tall and athletic, with a neatly shaved head and a closely cropped
beard, Bailey sat in front of a computer terminal at a downtown jobs
center. He rearranged his body to take the pain off his back—the result
of years of lifting and bending and straining—as he squinted at the
screen in search of his next job. Then forty, Bailey had a cool air about
him, the gentle sort of friendliness that often characterizes people accustomed to being physically larger than those around them. He exuded an
inner confidence that testified to the high school basketball star he had
been, and the ladies' man he clearly still could be, even as he rolled his
eyes in beleaguered fashion when the subject of women came up. His
broad shoulders more than amply filled out his lone sport jacket, which
he wore on days he went to look for work.

For the last two decades, Bailey had worked with his hands, a life that
seemed to him accidental, the result of his plans for college undone by a
family crisis. When I first met him in February 2008, he had been almost
continuously without work for the past eight months, arriving at the job
center day after day, sitting in front of a computer, looking through listings and sending out fresh applications.

"There's no jobs out there," he said. "It's depressing."

Bailey had grown up in Oakland, a city whose very name—fairly or otherwise—carried the whiff of plans gone awry, hopes deferred, urban decay, and stubborn poverty, particularly among African Americans, who make up more than one-third of the city's roughly 400,000 people. As a child, Bailey had grown up comfortably. His mother earned $70,000 a year as a customer service representative for the local telephone company into the mid-1980s. She bought a house in East Oakland, a cozy orange stucco place on a dead-end street, allowing Bailey and his little brother to ride their bikes on the pavement and play basketball at hoops set up in surrounding driveways. Her wages were enough to bring home clothes, groceries, and plenty of toys at Christmas; enough to pick up the tab at seafood restaurants by the bay. His grandparents owned a home in North Oakland, in a solidly middle-class African American neighborhood. He never knew his father, who was somewhere off in Michigan, but he spent a lot of time with his grandmother—"She was beautiful," Bailey said. "Like Lena Horne"—and he felt no absence. "We got almost everything we wanted," he said. "I was a happy kid."

Bailey attended Bishop O'Dowd High School, a private Catholic institution on a well-groomed campus on a bluff overlooking the San Francisco Bay. Bishop O'Dowd was a perennial basketball powerhouse, and Bailey made the varsity squad, blossoming into a formidable player. His junior year, he came off the bench on a team that included the future NBA player Brian Shaw. They made it to the northern California finals, playing in front of some ten thousand people at the Oakland Coliseum. By his senior year in 1984, he was the starting shooting guard on a team that included two seven-footers. "I was a basketball star," he said, disclosing this status matter-of-factly, without bravado, but with pride, now tinged with pain about how it worked out. His senior year, the college recruiters began calling. At a Christmas tournament in Las Vegas, he played in front of three hundred of them, drawing attention for his scoring knack. They dangled scholarships to campuses near and far—San Jose State, the University of Alaska. Basketball was a means, Bailey understood, not the end. It was a ticket to college and the opportunities it would unlock for him. A college degree would give him access to the white-collar world to which his mother was already accustomed, and with far greater possibilities.

But that same year, Bailey's mother succumbed to addiction to crack cocaine, the pernicious drug then sweeping Oakland and much of inner-city America with the force of an epidemic. She lost her job. Then she stopped bringing home food. And then she stopped coming home at all, leaving Bailey and his brother to look after themselves. "I had two pairs of pants to start my senior year," Bailey said. "We'd wait for groceries and she'd never come. She was so far gone."

His mother settled in with his grandmother, who was then so frail she was unaware of the rampant drug use in her home. Bailey's brother, three years younger, soon moved out to live with his father. Bailey stayed in the house alone. As his senior year progressed, he turned down scholarship offers that would have taken him away from Oakland, so he could keep an eye on his mother. To support himself, he got a job as a gopher at a law firm, earning $8 an hour for three or fours a day after class. After graduation, he enrolled in part-time classes at a local community college. But the demands of work and school proved too much. He dropped out and got a full-time job driving a truck for a tile shop in Berkeley, the bohemian university town to the north, with its cappuccino bars and used bookstores. As the fall semester unfolded around him, with students bicycling to campus and attending parties in the scruffy bungalows off Telegraph Avenue, Bailey spent his days loading boxes of tile into the back of a truck at the warehouse, and then delivering them to construction sites, earning $7.25 an hour. Nights he spent back at his mother's house, alone, reading books by candlelight: the electricity had been cut off for lack of payment. Soon, the water and gas were gone, too. Bailey would wake up and drive to a nearby gas station to wash up in the men's room, before going to work at the tile shop. After about a month, he borrowed money from his boss and rented a small studio apartment in Oakland for $450 a month. His mother's house was relinquished to foreclosure.

He was nineteen years old, living on his own, and working a blue-collar job. In the story he told himself, this was a brief and unexpected detour before his mother regained her footing and his real life resumed on some college campus.

"I was happy to be making some money anyhow," he said.

But months passed, and then years. What had seemed like a temporary stint became Bailey's life.

In 1987, he tried to go back to school, enrolling at nearby Merritt College. He joined the basketball team, scoring twenty points in his first game. But his mother had listed him as a dependent on her taxes, so he could not qualify for financial aid. What savings she had were being drained by her deepening addiction. Between the costs of tuition and the tug of concern for his mother, school did not fit into the picture. So Bailey put his studies aside for a second time and concentrated on paying the family bills.

It was all sideways from there, a series of jobs delivering home furnishings, seafood, and plumbing supplies. He apprenticed to become an electrician—his grandfather's job as a young man—but quit in disgust when the white journeyman he shadowed ceaselessly cracked racist jokes. He worked as an appliance installer, delivering washers and dryers to homes throughout northern California.

His own home was a malleable concept, one that fluctuated with his relationship status and his tolerance for being around his mother, who was ensconced in his grandmother's house with a loose collection of fellow addicts. For a few years, he had lived in his own apartment in Oakland. Then he lived with a girlfriend in San Francisco, who didn't want him to work, suffocating him. In recent years, he had been shuttling between his grandmother's house and the apartment where he sometimes lived with his longtime girlfriend and their nine-year-old son, while trying to cadge together the security deposit required for a place of his own.

Yet, through the years Bailey had never lost the drive to make a better life. In 2007, he invested his time and hopes in a government-funded training program that was supposed to land him a job in biotechnology, a career with a future. He sent dozens of applications to the biotech firms clustered in Emeryville, next to Oakland, but one rejection yielded to still another. Not one to dwell on disappointment, he pragmatically adjusted his aspirations down. He would take any decent-paying job—even the sort of job from which he had hoped to escape for the sake of his back and the high blood pressure that the doctor said was the result of too much stress, too many hours driving a truck, hauling refrigerators up stairs; too many "energy drinks," the highly caffeinated concoctions he pounded down to keep working. He would willingly take another job that hurt his body and paid less than he made before, if that was all that was available.

He was trying to carve out a modest perch in a city where wealthy families mostly lived up in the hills, on landscaped spreads laced by flowering vines, their bay windows looking out toward the water—the postcard view he had enjoyed from his high school. Those lives were now as far from Bailey's everyday existence as the moon. The trickle of prosperity long promised amid successive tax cuts had never made it down to the flatlands of Oakland. But as the recession intensified, pain was pouring down with a vengeance. Even people with six-figure salaries were cutting back on their spending, and as banks stopped lending, the strains of the formerly comfortable were rolling downhill, assailing Bailey and the other unemployed people at the job center. The American economy was spooked. Businesses alarmed by the prospect of households tightening up were reluctant to expand or hire. Joblessness was growing—especially among African Americans like Bailey, and especially in cities like Oakland, where manufacturing had long sustained less educated people and was now mostly a memory.

The warehouses that had ringed downtown when he was growing up—low, brick buildings clustered near the port of Oakland and the rail lines reaching into the prodigious farmland of the Central Valley—had been mostly given over to residential loft spaces. The same structures in which men had hoisted crates of tomatoes had been transformed into homes for commuters with stock-option jobs in the Valley, the brick walls and exposed plumbing retained as stylish design counterpoints. There was still warehouse work to be had to the south, off the snake's nest of freeways in Fremont and Hayward. But you needed a car to get to those places, and Bailey couldn't afford one. After years of living week to week, he had failed to build up his credit, a classic Catch-22 that confined many low-income people in a nation of sprawling cities and scant public transportation: without a steady job, he could not buy a car. Without a car, it was nearly impossible to get a job.

In December 2007, Bailey applied for a night stocking position at a Walmart in a part of Oakland marked by street gangs, broken glass, and discarded syringes. After several interviews, the woman doing the hiring stopped returning his calls. She had been fired, it turned out, and nobody seemed to know or care what had happened to his file. If he wanted a career at the world's largest retailer, he would have to start over—all this, for a minimum-wage job that was purely a means to earn a few dollars so he could buy Christmas presents for his son. No presents this year. Bailey took his job search elsewhere. He got a job that paid $11 an hour at a computer chip company, where he worked in the warehouse, pulling orders off the shelves. Getting there involved taking the BART—the Bay Area Rapid Transit, the metropolitan commuter train service—down to South Hayward, and then walking two miles along a desolate industrial strip, past lots ringed by barbed wire, because no buses traveled the area. His shift ran from two in the afternoon until eleven at night. He had to hustle to make the last train back to Oakland before the BART shut down at midnight. He got home after 12:30 A.M. By the time he decompressed, it was two or three in the morning. And by the time he woke up, it was practically time to go back to work again, giving him no chance to search for a job in one of the biotech companies for which he had trained. His bosses told him there was no raise in his future. So, after two weeks, Bailey quit the warehouse to look for something better. "I was afraid I'd get stuck," he said.

Several weeks later, he had nothing.

"I'll just look for anything now," Bailey said with a shrug. "It doesn't matter."

As he reconciled himself to his prospects in early 2008, employment options were shrinking dramatically. The economy was shedding hundreds of thousands of jobs a month. By the end of 2008, the unemployment rate among black Americans would reach 11.9 percent, its highest level in fifteen years.

On a February afternoon, Bailey resolved that he would take a job as a forklift driver at a warehouse for $9 an hour—barely two-thirds of what he had been earning three years earlier. "It's just picking up boxes," he said. "That's all right. I've got to do something."

Even then, he had no luck. The boss never called back to finalize the deal, concerned that Bailey was overqualified. "I think he knew that I wasn't going to stick with it," Bailey said. "I was like begging him, but he just wouldn't give it to me."

He was at a place in his life where you could at once see the teenager he had been, the enthusiastic basketball player with the scoring touch, a ready grin, and a mischievous streak—"a really nice kid," his assistant coach called him—as well as the frustrated man he was becoming, with worry lines carved into his forehead and dark circles under his eyes. And those back pains. The tightness made him stiffen just a bit as he got up out of a chair. You could hear the weariness in his voice from not having a home, the embarrassment from not having a car—in California, of all places. You could see him wrestling with bitterness and resignation as most of the job applications he sent out vanished without a response. Day by day, he was succumbing to the realization that things were not working out. He was sinking into a state of quiet desperation.

According to the guiding narrative of the American economy, Bailey was precisely the sort of person who was supposed to be able to count on upward mobility. He had demonstrated a willingness to adapt and acquire marketable skills. He was reliable and clearly eager for work. But here he was, just beginning his forties—prime earning years. He was strong-bodied, well-spoken, computer-literate, and charming. He was handsome and self-possessed. He had grown up in the middle class and was accustomed to thinking of this as his station. He was a black man in a society in which some employers still carried negative preconceptions, but he had the sort of dependable demeanor that companies were always saying they needed. Addiction had swirled around him for most of his adult life, and he had not succumbed. Bailey did not blame his problems on society, merely expressing bewilderment and fatigue. He had earned a living through physically arduous work for more than two decades, and he was willing to sign up for more. He had pursued a state-supported plan to get ahead, to get educated, and to make use of his brain in addition to his body. Bailey did not want a handout. He wanted a job. Yet he kept sliding backward.

‿

Threaded into the conversation about the American reckoning with excessive debt and consumption was a smug satisfaction that people like Thomas and Fran Barbaro were getting their comeuppance, while the nation as a whole was forced to return to a more wholesome mode of living. Americans had indulged their habit for easy money for too long, pundits intoned. Voluntarily or not, many were now forced to kick their addiction to credit, live within their incomes, and perhaps even save. It sounded so healthy, like a diabetic forgoing another trip to a fast-food joint in favor of a farmer's market or a backyard garden. It was the end of "financial decadence," as David Brooks put it in a column in the

New York Times, "the trampling of decent norms about how to use and harness money."

Others suggested that the downturn offered an opportunity to forge a more sustainable lifestyle. As food prices soared in the spring of 2008, intensifying the squeeze on household finances, some advocates for the environment and healthier eating celebrated the prospect that fast food would become more expensive, perhaps encouraging more people to embrace locally grown, organic produce. "We're talking about health, we're talking about the planet," said Alice Waters, the legendary California restaurateur. "Make a sacrifice on the cell phone or the third pair of Nike shoes." But a lot of Americans were eating Big Macs and Chicken Nuggets instead of goat cheese and endive salad not because they had blown their money on sneakers, but because they had small incomes. They had gotten into debt not so much out of decadence, but because they had no other way to finance everyday expenses such as education and health care.

For generations, Americans have been schooled on the comforting notion that a basic compact guarantees ample rewards for those who make a sufficient effort at advancement. A positive attitude, hard work, punctuality, and moral rectitude bring the appurtenances of middle-class life. This neat formulation speaks to the frontier identity embedded in the national DNA, the idea that the United States holds limitless opportunities, with treasure available for anyone willing to labor. It is a notion that affords wealthy people the satisfaction that they have earned their lot, rather than inheriting the good fortune to be sent to better schools, nurtured by parents with ample leisure time, and aided by social peers as they forge careers. It is a conception that works in the service of a peculiarly American insistence that ours is a classless society, even as the gap between rich and poor widens. And it gives working people a daily incentive, offering assurance that their aspirations are attainable, not a gamble against the odds.

This idea of just rewards for the virtuous is of a piece with the religious cosmology that has been the bedrock of American thinking since the nation's inception. The German sociologist Max Weber called it the Protestant work ethic, finding in the prosperous, Calvinist-influenced societies of early-twentieth-century America and northern Europe a shared understanding that people toiled according to their calling and a divine plan. Making profits was an exercise blessed by the heavens; work and the pursuit of profit amounted to a moral code. "The middle-class employer became conscious of himself as standing in the full grace of God and as visibly blessed by Him," Weber wrote in *The Protestant Ethic and the Spirit of Capitalism*. "If he stayed within the bounds of formal correctness, if his moral conduct remained blameless, and if the use he made of his wealth was not offensive, this person was now allowed to follow his interest in economic gain, and indeed *should* do so." As for employees, "work constitutes a particular defense mechanism against all those temptations summarized by the Puritan notion of the 'unclean life.'"

In the nineteenth century, Horatio Alger penned dozens of novels depicting enterprising young Americans of humble background relying on their innate likeability and hard work to forge success. *Ragged Dick*, published in 1868, depicts the triumph of a fourteen-year-old homeless shoeshine boy who works the gritty streets of New York. Soon befriended by a customer who admires his industriousness and good looks, Dick is introduced to the man's nephew, who buys him a new suit to replace his dirty rags, giving him a taste of a better life. Dick later rescues a drowning man, selflessly jumping off a ferry to save him. The grateful recipient of this heroism is a wealthy industrialist, who promptly rewards Dick with a high-paying job as an office clerk. *Ragged Dick* typifies Alger's world, one in which virtue and effort are reliably rewarded with advancement and material comfort. More than one hundred titles later, the Horatio Alger story became cemented as a core piece of the American identity, attesting to the notion that anyone can make it in the United States, while indirectly supporting views that those who fail have simply not tried hard enough.

In more recent times, the Horatio Alger mythology has been transformed into a singular devotion to the workings of the unfettered market. If opportunities are abundant and accessible to all, if anyone can make it, then it follows that the results of American-style capitalism are fundamentally fair. Charity and philanthropy still have their place, but the unfortunate are isolated cases, people deserving of pity and support, but certainly not cause to doubt the soundness of the broader economic system. In this way of thinking, the market is an organic entity whose judgments carry the force of natural law and an enlightened government is one that simply gets out of the way and lets the market work its magic, separating winners from losers and maximizing prosperity for all.

For much of the first half of the twentieth century, such ideas were confined to the minority of American thinking. Government was generally cast as a crucial player in a healthy economy, a guarantor of jobs and material security in a world in which the swings of the market could be punishingly unpredictable. In the years after the Great Depression, the leading economic thinker, John Maynard Keynes, argued that government needed to spend money when times were hard in order to stimulate the economy and ensure that people were working—the calculus behind Roosevelt's New Deal. That stance brought the wrath of laissez-faire economists, who saw Keynes's prescriptions as heretical: in the long run, the market was always right. But as Keynes famously declared, "In the long run, we are all dead." It was government's job to watch over the here and now; to confront momentary excesses and failures in the market—not least, weak demand for labor—and then step in and stimulate growth.

This tension between competing notions of market forces and the role of government runs through U.S. history. But in the decades leading up to the current financial crisis, the champions of the omniscient market enjoyed near-total control of the policy levers, rolling back the regulatory encroachment of government in many commercial realms. The chief apostle in this mission was the economist Milton Friedman, whose corpus of libertarian ideals was elevated to dogma when Reagan claimed the White House in 1980. Friedman and his acolytes—not least, Alan Greenspan, who would later run the Federal Reserve—portrayed government as an elite club of ham-handed bureaucrats whose good intentions consistently led the economy astray. Friedman pinned the blame for the Great Depression on "government mismanagement." So deep was his disdain for bureaucratic intervention that he once said: "Thank God for government waste. If government is doing bad things, it's only the waste that prevents the harm from being greater."

At Friedman's urging, the Reagan administration removed regulatory strictures from a host of industries, systematically attacked the power of labor unions, and rolled back taxes. It allowed the market free run as a new crop of swashbuckling gamblers pioneered the use of so-called junk bonds—loans backed by risky collateral, enticing investors with potentially high returns—to go on a corporate merger spree. The result was fat profits for those at the table, economic growth overall, but growing instability for millions of workers as huge companies swiftly changed hands like poker chips at a card table, laying off workers to cut costs and please Wall Street.

Not that this instability shook belief in the guiding theory, or occasioned concern for the volatility it sowed. Radical faith in the judgment of the market effectively institutionalized a callous disregard for the declining fortunes of many. If the market is an almost mystical source of wealth, and if opportunities are available for anyone willing to work, then it follows that those not prospering have only themselves to blame. They have failed to exploit the abundance around them. The market fundamentalism of the last three decades has provided the materials to spin a lack of concern about economic struggles into a moral virtue. If the solution to life's problems was to unleash the market, then it was morally courageous to oppose anything that interposed itself between the market and the citizenry. So labor unions were effectively hurting people they aimed to help by interfering with the market. Using public funds to address the crisis of joblessness among black men by offering job training amounted to impeding the fix that free enterprise would otherwise provide. Any barriers preventing minorities from claiming success would be swept away by the power of the market. In the course of what became known as the Reagan Revolution, these sorts of ideas rose to the fore. The Horatio Alger story was upgraded from a source of heartwarming inspiration into the guiding narrative of economic policy. Anyone could make it in this land of opportunity—black and white; graduates of prep schools with $50,000-a-year tuitions and graduates of inner-city schools with leaky ceilings. Americans were not gutless Europeans who needed the nanny state to protect them from the vagaries of the market. They were rugged individualists whose resilience had been forged in the New World, in immigrant homes from which parents and grandparents had managed to find their way to better lives. If they did it, then so could you. And if you failed, you had only yourself to blame. In post-1980s America, failure was a uniquely personal outcome, something to be explained away by laziness or stupidity or moral weakness, and never ascribed to systemic trouble. Regulations were dangerous impediments to the wisdom of the market.

∽

Amid the wild, antiregulatory climate of the Reagan years, Wall Street unleashed its creative powers toward crafting new ways to extract profits through increasingly aggressive borrowing and lending. It was not merely individuals such as Fran Barbaro and Dorothy Thomas who came to rely upon growing volumes of credit: the financial system as a whole became governed by a reckless denial of the mounting dangers of excessive borrowing. Investors and regulators, who should have been paying attention, soothed themselves with the belief that financial innovation would prevent any crisis.

On Wall Street beginning in the 1990s major financial institutions bet trillions of dollars in a shadow financial system that operated beyond the purview of standard bookkeeping. These transactions involved enormous amounts of borrowed money, and yet the government officials tasked with protecting the system left it to unsupervised markets to manage whatever dangers might lurk. The key proponent of this philosophy was Alan Greenspan, who chaired the Federal Reserve from 1986 to 2006, and who carried an outsize reputation as a wise man. As leverage built up within the financial system during his tenure, Greenspan repeatedly counseled Congress to allow Wall Street to carry on with the dangerous games of financial make-believe that ultimately brought the system down.

A self-identified libertarian, Greenspan counted among his formative influences the novelist Ayn Rand, who portrayed collective power as an evil force set against the enlightened self-interest of individuals. Each time a crisis presented itself and was successfully managed, Greenspan pointed to the fact that a meltdown had been averted as vindication for his laissez-faire philosophy, evidence that the system could indeed be trusted to regulate itself.

The credit bubble that eventually metastasized into the contemporary financial crisis had its roots in Reagan free-market ideology, when the government also lifted long-standing rules regulating savings and loan institutions, regional banks that lent money to home owners with public backing. The S&Ls had been restricted to doing business within fifty miles of their headquarters. The interest rates they could pay depositors were capped, but those deposits were insured by the government. In the late 1970s, the S&Ls found themselves under assault from a nasty combination of high interest rates and accelerating inflation. Depositors withdrew funds to take advantage of higher interest rates available elsewhere. Inflation cut the value of the payments S&Ls received on long-term mortgages. In response, Reagan looked to market forces to straighten out the mess. He removed the old strictures and allowed the S&Ls to invest in whatever they chose, while leaving in place the government guarantee on deposits.

For the people running these institutions, here was an intoxicating opportunity. They were free to gamble as much as they liked, while secure that Uncle Sam was on the hook for any resulting losses. They did not fail to exploit what seemed a once-in-a-lifetime opportunity. Through the first half of the 1980s, the S&Ls bought their infamous junk bonds, issued high-interest credit cards, and sank billions into skyscrapers and condominiums. Hucksters, mobsters, looters, dreamers, and incompetents plowed into real estate, chasing a piece of the action. The S&Ls racked up enormous losses. Some of their funds were pilfered through various flavors of fraud. Some were sunk into erecting a glut of vacant real estate, predominantly in the Sun Belt. As properties stayed empty and real estate prices fell, the S&Ls took bigger losses than ever. As the losses spiraled out of control, the government stepped in and shut down failed lenders, taking over properties pledged as collateral and selling what it could. Before the books were closed, the debacle cost taxpayers $124 billion.

But that episode—taxpayer bailout and all—did not tame the gambling culture that ruled American finance. Out of the wreckage of the old mortgage finance system, the aggressive bond traders at Salomon Brothers, the Wall Street giant, sniffed out a lucrative opportunity that exponentially increased the overall risks in the financial system. As Niall Ferguson recounts in his financial history, *The Ascent of Money*, when the S&Ls teetered toward collapse in 1983, they unloaded many of their holdings to raise cash. Salomon began buying their mortgages en masse at fire-sale prices, then pooling them together and reselling them as bonds. The buyers of these bonds collected the payments that home owners made on their mortgages. This process, known as securitization, was widely hailed as a great financial innovation. As banks off-loaded their mortgages, they collected capital they could plow into writing more loans, making it easier for Americans to buy houses. Investors found the bonds attractive because large-scale defaults on mortgages seemed unlikely amid the widespread notion that housing prices could not simultaneously fall across the entire country. Even if housing prices did fall and losses resulted, that risk was covered by somebody else. Most of the mortgages that Salomon was pooling and selling were guaranteed by Fannie Mae, Freddie Mac, or Ginnie Mae, three private but government-sponsored institutions that bought home loans. If home owners stiffed the banks on their mortgage payments, these institutions—not investors—would be stuck with the losses.

Salomon, soon joined by a crowded field of competitors, unloaded swelling volumes of so-called mortgage-backed securities, portraying them as little riskier than Treasury bonds. Between 1980 and 2007, the value of mortgage-backed securities guaranteed by a government-sponsored entity swelled from $200 million to $4 trillion. Without that enormous reservoir of cash, real estate speculation and housing prices could not have built up to such astronomical levels.

Other forms of investment built upon borrowed money sprouted from the market's risk-embracing culture. The hedge fund Long-Term Capital Management—overseen by a pair of certifiable geniuses, the Nobel Prize–winning economists Myron Scholes and Robert Merton— had developed a trading system that supposedly promised protection from the wild swings of the market. The fund traded aggressively in derivatives, the exotic investments whose value was linked to movements in the price of something else, in a murky and largely unregulated process. Long-Term Capital borrowed hellacious amounts of money, spreading it around the world on bets placed on minute movements in other investments. In the fall of 1997, the fund had net assets of $6.7 billion on its balance sheets, but another $126 billion in assets financed by debt. In other words, it was leveraged up to its eyeballs. It had nowhere near enough cash on hand to cover its loans if anything went wrong. Its partners assumed that while one or two of its trading strategies might cause losses at any moment in time, it employed so many that they could not all fail at once. Suddenly, in 1998, an awful lot was going wrong, and all at once.

Through much of the 1990s, money had been rushing into the fast developing "tiger" economies of Thailand, South Korea, Indonesia, and Malaysia, financing real estate ventures and factories. A middle class was taking root and prospering in these once poor countries, filling suburban-style villas on the edges of Jakarta and high-rise apartment complexes crowning Bangkok, Kuala Lumpur, and Seoul. People hungered for the accoutrements of modern living, from air conditioners and refrigerators to cars and hair dryers. In 1997, as it became clear that global investment had generated too much real estate in these countries, money rushed out. Banks from Frankfurt to Tokyo that had lent money to Asian ventures suddenly demanded repayment of their loans, making capital tight.

By the summer of 1998, the so-called Asian contagion had spread to Russia, where foreign banks had similarly loaned money for overexuberant development projects. Investments there were souring, too. Russia defaulted on its dollar debts, racking up investor losses and prompting financial institutions to further tighten their lending. As borrowing became more expensive, this put pressure on so-called hedge funds like Long-Term Capital.

Between the Asian crisis and the Russian crisis, Long-Term Capital was suffering huge losses. On a single day, Friday, August 21, 1998, the fund—its name suddenly turned ironic—lost $550 million. Collapse appeared imminent. The fund was dumping investments onto plummeting markets to raise cash, sending values of many assets down around the globe. Given the size of the company's debts to other institutions, failure was certain to be a collective experience. Faced with this deeply unpalatable scenario, the Federal Reserve Bank of New York convened a room full of private bankers and demanded that they quickly do something to prevent the fund's collapse. The banks together came up with $3.6 billion to bail out Long-Term Capital. Order was restored.

One might reasonably have concluded from this experience that leverage had gotten out of hand on Wall Street. Regulators might have opted to step in to ensure that, in the future, institutions set aside sufficient funds against the possibility of their investments going bad. Long-Term Capital's near-death experience reinforced calls on Capitol Hill for rules on derivatives investing. The hedge fund manager George Soros warned that putting off substantial regulatory reform "will surely lead to the breakdown of the gigantic circulatory system which goes under the name of global capitalism."

But faith-based regulation carried the day. The key to keeping it going was Greenspan, who was resolute that the people participating in the market would behave responsibly if left to their own devices. As leverage grew within the American financial system, Greenspan—not for nothing known as "the maestro"—successfully killed proposed rules that would have forced financial institutions to set aside more funds as a reserve against bad investments. "Risks in financial markets, including derivatives markets, are being regulated by private parties," Greenspan said during a 1994 appearance on Capitol Hill. "There is nothing involved in federal regulation per se which makes it superior to market regulation." For Greenspan, the near collapse of Long-Term Capital did not register as a sign of the dangers building up in the unregulated financial system, but rather as an affirmation of his belief that the good people of Wall Street could be counted on to do the right thing; that, despite the occasional bumps in the road, the market knew where it was going. "By facing the harsh reality and acting in their self-interest, [the banks] saved themselves and, I suspect, millions of their fellow citizens on both Main Street and Wall Street a lot of money," Greenspan later wrote in his memoir, *The Age of Turbulence.*

In the wake of the Asian, Russian, and Long-Term Capital crises, the credit markets became unwilling to lend freely, choking off economic activity. At the Federal Reserve, Greenspan employed the tool that would define his tenure: he dropped interest rates three times in the fall of 1998 in a bid to spur the economy. Money fleeing Russia and lending going stagnant worldwide represented "not judgment but panic," Greenspan wrote. "Panic in a market is like liquid nitrogen. It can quickly cause a devastating freeze."

If banks, along with stock and bond markets, are the arterial system of the economy, distributing capital to businesses and consumers, the Fed can be considered the heart of the beast. The Fed, through its lending to financial institutions, guides the interest rates at which banks exchange money with one another to settle up their balance sheets overnight. That target rate forms the key reference point within the American financial system, indirectly determining what lenders charge for mortgages and business loans and what credit card companies charge for cash advances. When the Fed drops interest rates, it essentially prods companies and ordinary people to make use of money, to spend it, and bet it on new ventures, rather than keep it in savings accounts and government bonds. Lowered interest rates take some of the risk out of business, which also stimulates investment. When money can be borrowed more cheaply, it hurts less to lose it, and companies and investors become more likely to take risks in pursuit of profit.

So, as the Fed dropped rates in 1998, banks and investment funds got more aggressive. They started plowing larger and larger amounts of money—mostly borrowed money—into an area of the economy that had already blossomed into a modern-day gold rush. They invested in technology, and particularly into a fresh crop of businesses focused on extracting riches from a new thing called the Internet.

2

Profits of Neverland

"The biggest smoke and mirrors deal of them all."

During the late 1990s, Americans became enthralled by the transcendent powers of technology. Amid an investment mania, many built up unrealistic cravings for immediate wealth. A few actually realized their dreams: in the space of a few years, Eric Bochner went from borrowing money from his parents so he could buy a modest condo to living with his girlfriend in a $2.6 million 5,000-square-foot estate carved into the side of a hill south of San Francisco, with his and hers Ferraris in the garage.

Born and raised in Chicago, Bochner had attended both college and law school at the University of Michigan in Ann Arbor before he landed in Silicon Valley in 1992, attracted by the promise of technology. At first, he worked in a law firm in Palo Alto, the swath of suburbia that is home to Stanford University, where he represented tech companies. Then he began working directly for the companies, which was both more exciting and more lucrative. He shepherded investments into new, high-flying businesses that specialized in selling themselves as the beneficiaries of unprecedented technological change. In October 1999, Bochner joined a start-up called Ariba. Launched three years earlier on the strength of a business plan that had supposedly been sketched in crayon on a paper tablecloth in a San Francisco restaurant, the company was in the process of raising billions of dollars with the story of how it was poised to become a veritable linchpin of global capitalism.

Ariba created business software that simplified and sped up procurement within companies. It linked everyone inside a client company through a single, shared computer program. A company using its program could tap into an online database of suppliers. When an employee needed to purchase something—copy paper, cement, an office chair— he or she could buy it immediately, using a centralized list of agreed-upon vendors, rather than filling out a requisition form, sending it to the appropriate office, and awaiting authorization. Every employee inside the company could see and track what was happening from his or her own screen, in real time. That gave the company greater control over its inventory and ensured that it was getting the lowest price. For Ariba, the goal was to capture a piece of transactions between businesses. When a hotel chain used its software to purchase staplers from an office supply wholesaler, Ariba would get a little slice of the deal. When a food processing company ordered salt in bulk, Ariba would net a cut.

Ariba had yet to count a dollar in profit, but that was beside the point: the power of its narrative alone, the image of the company strategically placing itself at the center of so much commerce, attracted staggering quantities of capital. Four months earlier, in July 1999, it had sold its stock in an initial public offering, pricing the shares at $23 each. By day's end, they had nearly quadrupled in value, closing at $90, and making the company worth a cool $3.7 billion. By year's end, Ariba's shares would be worth more than $500 each.

Lean and athletic, Bochner, then only thirty-three, was already considered a veteran of Silicon Valley, land of the twenty-four-year-old stock option millionaire. He was accustomed to the fashion of making money not by selling products but by selling investors on a narrative describing an incalculable volume of future revenues. That was how the Valley worked. Yet this new job was unlike anything he had seen before. Ariba took make-believe to a whole new level. "That was the biggest smoke and mirrors deal of them all," Bochner said. "It still boggles my mind."

Unlike many start-ups, which were still developing their products, Ariba already had one for sale. But there were obvious limitations to how much money Ariba could make selling its software. It was aiming its product at the big Fortune 500 companies. What happened when Ariba ran out of customers? So Ariba did what many tech companies were already doing: it shifted its focus from selling its product to selling its stock. It announced that it was building a "network," employing one of the easy money words of the era. The network jargon was supposed to indicate the limitless power of the Internet, whereby every company on the planet could buy and sell from one another. In place of the slow-moving business of selling product to one company at a time, Ariba would convene a series of cyberspace marketplaces that could attract hundreds of companies at once, capturing a little piece of every transaction.

Even by the audacious standards of the time, this was a particularly compelling story. Investors had grown jaded about the parade of dot-com companies that had come into being and were now swiftly disappearing, having exhausted their venture capital while offering up services of dubious logistical possibility. Back in 1999, the world was not yet ready to buy living room furniture or pet food over the Internet, as two high-profile flame-outs, Furniture.com and Pets.com, discovered. Profit could not be extracted by unleashing a fleet of scooters to deliver single bags of potato chips across lower Manhattan. Ariba seemed refreshingly solid. It was aiming at a part of the commercial world that was well-established and inarguably enormous: plain vanilla transactions between businesses. It was part of a new industry defined by its own lucrative jargon—b2b, for business-to-business, which distinguished it from those failed dot-coms aimed at consumers. A flood of money would surely land at the company's door, if only it could secure just a fraction of a percent of the dollars spent on paper clips or widgets or whatever else.

"The era of green-field opportunities in business-to-consumer E-commerce is over, but business-to-business is the next wave," proclaimed the Merrill Lynch analyst Henry Blodget, the archetypal hype artist of the era, on the day that Ariba first sold shares to the public. "Ariba isn't profitable yet, but it's in a great position to capitalize on that wave." "By anyone's measuring stick, the growth in b2b commerce over the next several years will be nothing short of spectacular," gushed the trade periodical *Interactive Week*, citing a forecast that b2b transactions would exceed $1.3 trillion by 2003. Not to be outdone, an analyst at

Banc of America Securities declared the total annual value of all *potential* business-to-businesses transactions was already $50 trillion a year, a figure then larger than the global economy. "Something really big is going on," the analyst declared. "It is the new e-conomy."

Ariba could not merely say it was doing what it claimed to be doing. The company had to seem like it was really constructing a global marketplace. Bochner, freshly arrived with the title of vice president of commerce services, was employed as the lead man in creating this impression. "My job was to build network revenue," he said. "We were telling Wall Street we were building a network, and it was clear that we needed the story to be sold sooner rather than later. We're all like, 'Well, what can we do today?'"

From the beginning, Bochner saw this as a rather impossible task. It involved getting companies that manufactured metal tables to utilize the same vendor markets as those that manufactured coils of steel. It meant grouping together cork board–makers with wine bottlers. Every industry that overlapped with another in its demand for a given commodity had to use Ariba's software and use the same virtual marketplaces for them to function at sufficient scale. "It basically requires the world to reorganize," Bochner said. "It might happen eventually, but it would take thirty years for that to happen."

The stock was priced for it to happen now. And the stock was the only thing that mattered. A valuable stock gave Ariba currency it could use to buy other companies, which gave its public relations staff reason to put out fresh press releases asserting its mission in the market-pleasing language of the era: "Through the Ariba B2B Commerce platform—an open, end-to-end infrastructure of interoperable software solutions and hosted Web-based commerce services—the company enables efficient on-line trade, integration and collaboration between B2B marketplaces, buyers, suppliers and commerce service providers." Impenetrably dense, jargon-laden descriptions such as this gave analysts like Blodget—most of them working for the investment banks then brokering the deals—another opportunity to describe a future colored in gold, broadcasting Ariba's promise through cable television appearances, in print, and via online news. And that made the stock continue its swift ascent into the stratosphere.

In the idealized version of American business, companies are supposed to concentrate on developing and selling their products. If they succeed and their businesses grow, their stock prices rise accordingly. But during the technology boom, maintaining the stock at a high level *was* the business. Everything else was subsidiary. This perversion of the norms of commerce was the defining factor of the era, and it lived on long after technology companies like Ariba lost their luster with the investing public. Believers trumpeted the arrival of a New Economy that superseded the traditional assumptions of economics. In the logic of this new economy, when profits and revenues couldn't be measured, that meant they were limitless.

～

Back when Bochner was a kid in Chicago, his father, who worked as an accountant at a commodities trading firm, told him how markets worked. A big trader would call in a big order—say, one thousand pork bellies. The trader on the floor who took the call was invited to buy fifty for himself before he placed the client's order, and then sell right after. Just a little for himself, not enough to bump up the market—which would have forced the client to pay more for his own order—but enough to benefit from the rise in prices that was sure to follow. The trader on the floor had no idea if pork bellies or live cattle rationally *should* be priced higher based on the fundamentals that affect the value of pork or beef—the price of grain, the prevalence of disease afflicting livestock, the demand for meat. All the trader knew was that money was about to surge into his part of the market, sending prices up and creating a momentary profit opportunity.

Bochner often thought of this story as he launched into the shadow play of building Ariba. It was never about creating a real business, he said. "The whole idea was attract investment, sell your story to the Street and then get yours out."

At first, Bochner says, Ariba resorted to aggressive bookkeeping—par for the course in that day. It labeled as "network revenues" the money it earned from maintaining its software. It put together a PowerPoint presentation that laid out its story and showed it to fund managers, who bought the stock. Then Bochner started pursuing mergers, buying other companies that appeared to be doing what Ariba was supposed to be doing. "It ended up being a disaster," Bochner said. Nobody at Ariba knew how to run any of these businesses, and there was dissension between the people already at the company and the new people who joined the company through the mergers. But before Ariba's reality eclipsed the lovely wonderful thinking behind its stock price, bringing it down to earth—before the whole tech bubble burst—the strategy worked brilliantly.

Bochner earned a base salary of about $150,000 a year, while pulling in bonuses of $20,000 a quarter. In late 1999, he moved into his new estate in Hillsborough, between San Francisco and Silicon Valley. Like virtually everyone at the company, from the chief executive to the entry-level secretaries, he was drawing stock options that were soaring in value as the company's stock price exploded, reaching nearly $1,000 a share by late February 2000. The market handed money to Ariba as if it actually had a network in place and was booking a little piece of countless transactions between the world's businesses. At this height, the company was worth more than $40 billion on paper, and Bochner had a seven-figure bank account. His then girlfriend, who worked in Ariba's human resources office, had sold some of her options to raise the money needed to buy the house in cash. They bought the two Ferraris.

Bochner started taking flying lessons from a guy who had quit his job as an engineer at a hardware company, having bought Cisco Systems stock early on and then holding it while it swelled exponentially. After he got his pilot's license, Bochner bought a single-engine plane, paying about $500,000. "I didn't think it was that big of a deal at the time," he said. One of Ariba's founders had three aircraft. "I thought, well, I'll just buy a plane."

But then the tech bubble burst as the market lost patience with storytelling and demanded profits for its shares. Trillions of dollars in paper wealth were annihilated. Ariba's reckoning came quickly. By mid-December 2000, its stock was down to one-third of its peak value. Bochner lost his job in a wave of recriminations. "People were pissed off about the valuation and they were looking for people to shoot," he said. "I got shot."

He went back to school for a while, pursuing a PhD in physics at the University of California at Berkeley, but he got restless and quit. He visited his parents in Chicago and decided to stay while he figured out what to do with the rest of his life. He liked the thought of doing something with his hands, producing something of tangible value, in contrast to his days in Silicon Valley. And he liked to cook. So he enrolled in pastry school, graduating in December 2002. He moved to Iowa City to be with his new girlfriend, who was a doctor there. A few months later, they were married. Bochner launched a chocolate factory, bringing in specialty machinery from Europe and Japan. He imported Swiss chocolate, aiming to produce confections of distinctively high quality. By 2007, he had gained a major retail chain as a customer, racking up sales of $3.5 million.

When I met him in Iowa City in August 2008, Bochner gave me a tour of the factory—a broad, low building on the edge of town that had been a hardware store in its previous incarnation. He wore blue jeans and a T-shirt emblazoned with the logo of the Southern rock band Lynyrd Skynyrd. We walked past the employee entrance, where a time card system was mounted to the wall, down a fluorescent-lit corridor, and then out onto the factory floor. He showed me the stainless steel contraptions that melted and mixed chocolate; the machines that squirted it into molds. His employees wore white gowns and hairnets as they plucked finished chocolates from a conveyor belt and deposited them into boxes.

We had lunch at a local barbecue joint a short drive away, where we carried our food over to our table on a plastic tray, stopping to pick up straws and condiments. It felt an awfully long way from Silicon Valley.

"There it was about creating something intangible," Bochner said. "This is real. I have to actually work for my money." He cracked a grin.

He had a firm grasp of his costs and his profits from month to month. He oversaw a stockroom full of real materials, a logbook, and contracts that required that he deliver real product. He paid his employees in dollars, not stock options.

Looking back on those years in the Valley, Bochner could see how the atmosphere had perverted the process of valuation. It sapped any incentive to plan for the future or distinguish make-believe from reality. "It warped everything about everything," he said. "You lose total perspective. The money I had then, I wish I had now."

Hadn't he been saving a lot of it? Bochner's eyes widened. "*Saving?*" he said. "I had put away $100,000 in case the whole world blew up. But it just didn't make sense to really save anything, because everything was going up. My salary was ridiculous. Why save? Who gives a shit? I'm going to make more money tomorrow. If you needed to, you could dump just your stock options and make hundreds of thousands of dollars anytime you wanted to. There was no point to it. What were you saving? You spend on everything you want, because you can.

"It's outer-worldly," he said. "You felt like you were anointed. I'm in the right place at the right time and I'm a super-genius."

Still, Bochner chafed at the idea that the chocolate factory represented something real and solid, a healthy return from his days at Ariba. "I remember those times," he said. "We were flying around the world in business class, drinking champagne, eating Kobe beef, and meeting lots of interesting people. You felt powerful. You knew that whole world-changing thing was as much for internal consumption as it was for Wall Street. You felt like you were doing something important. It's not as glamorous now. We're not changing the world. We're just making frickin' chocolate."

⸎

The ethereal nature of the boom that fueled the economy through most of the 1990s was in part the result of genuine technological breakthroughs. The investment euphoria inflated a stock market bubble, but it also produced a new telecommunications infrastructure that continues to generate returns for merchants selling products and creative minds dreaming up ways to beam valuable information to people on the go. While Pets .com and Furniture.com still rank among the more spectacular failures of the era, a decade later people do buy dog food and living room sets online. Millions of former commuters work from home, eschewing clogged and polluted freeways, linking to their offices via the Internet. Yet so much of the Internet boom was simply pumped up by Wall Street's financial engineering, Madison Avenue's branding power, and the media's willing naïveté.

Investment banks skillfully exploited growing public fascination with the Internet to sell shares of new companies that built and programmed the global computer network, designed hardware that used it, and constructed new businesses that rode its connections to reach customers. For Wall Street, tech stocks were the answer to the breakdown of its previous business model. In decades past, large investment banks enjoyed an effective monopoly over stock trading, owing largely to their substantial research operations. Through the 1970s and '80s, information about individual companies and stocks was scarce and expensive. Only the largest brokerage houses could afford top-shelf research offices, where analysts combed through microfilm versions of corporate financial statements and government data in search of industry trends. These analysts alerted traders to news about companies and the economy over in-house public address systems known as squawk boxes. If an ordinary investor wanted access to that intelligence, they had to have an account with one of the big Wall Street brokers, paying steep commissions.

By the mid-1990s, all that had changed. The Internet delivered as much data as any amateur investor could desire—the same government reports and corporate financial statements once accessible only to the professionals—and most of it was free. *Squawk Box* became the name of a popular show on CNBC, a financial news channel available to anyone with cable television. The same Wall Street analysts whose thoughts had once been available only to bank clients frequently appeared on the show, offering their stock picks to the world. A new crop of discount brokerages emerged and prospered, allowing investors to buy and sell shares for commissions of less than $10 a trade. Anyone with a modem could buy stock with the mere click of a mouse.

Shorn of their ability to attract customers with their exclusive hold on information, the old Wall Street investment banks had to cook up new means of generating business. They had to find a new mission for their armies of analysts. They settled on technology stocks, unleashing their research prowess toward locating promising companies that had not yet sold shares to the public. "Their old business model went away and they had to figure out something new to do," said Mark Sunshine, president of the commercial bank First Capital. "So they found these hot companies that would show astronomical growth, and you can only get them from us. They had to make the research special."

The new profit stream for the investment banks was centered on the initial public offering, the first sale of shares. The banks deployed their analysts as salespeople, fanning up feverish excitement for the companies' new stocks. They priced the first shares low, counting on the media buzz that would accrue when the price multiplied on the first day of trading. The key to the deal: only clients of the Wall Street banks that led the stock offerings were allowed to buy the first shares. That gave customers good reason to continue to pay the $50 and $100 commissions still being charged for trades by JPMorgan Chase, First Boston, Merrill Lynch, and other stalwarts, even as discount brokerages multiplied.

The strategy proved to be a stupendous success. Netscape, the company that developed an early Web browser, had been in existence for little more than a year and had yet to count any profits when it sold its first shares to the public in August 1995. At the opening, the shares were priced at $28 each. By lunchtime, they had nearly tripled in value, before settling at more than $58 each. At the end of the day, the company's twenty-four-year-old vice president of technology, Marc Andreessen, owned a stake worth more than $58 million.

Far from an aberration, Netscape's experience became the template. For several years, it seemed that any idea ending with the magic words *dot-com* was deserving of rock star treatment. It began with the stories in the business press, profiles of irreverent young chieftains with little or no business experience that indulged words like *wunderkind* and *prodigy*. "Tech stardom started, as usual, amid pizza boxes," began a typically breathless 1998 *Fortune* magazine paean to the two boy wonders behind the search engine Yahoo. "For two Stanford engineering students, Jerry Yang and David Filo, the launching pad was an oxygen-depleted double-wide trailer, stocked by the university with computer workstations and by the students with life's necessities—golf clubs, sleeping bags, and enough half-empty food containers to prompt a friend to call the scene a 'cockroach's picture of Christmas.' It was the first headquarters of Yahoo!, now the most successful company ever spawned by the World Wide Web." Then, the road shows, at which these youthful geniuses dazzled pin-striped bankers, persuading them to hand over the keys to the vault. Finally, payday: the IPOs, with the trading floors of Wall Street investment houses suddenly seeming as glamorous as a ringside seat at a prizefight.

On the strength of this celebration of technology, the Nasdaq composite stock index, loaded with tech companies, doubled in value between the summer of 1995 and the end of 1998. By early 2000, it had doubled again, peaking above 5,000 in March of that year. By then, stocks trading on the Nasdaq were collectively worth $6.2 trillion—an increase of more than $5 trillion from the day Netscape sold its first shares.

Back in the 1960s, John Maynard Keynes had criticized fervent belief in the efficient markets theory, which holds that the price of anything in a market system—a share of stock, a house—rationally reflects myriad factors shaping its value. Far from a dispassionate judge of value, the market functioned more like a beauty contest, he argued, one that did not even bother to figure out who was most beautiful, but merely who was most likely to be deemed most beautiful by others. "A conventional valuation which is established as the outcome of the mass psychology of a large number of ignorant individuals is liable to change violently as the result of a sudden fluctuation of opinion," Keynes warned. "The market will be subject to waves of optimistic and pessimistic sentiment, which are unreasoning."

As the great bull market took shape in the 1990s, the Yale economist Robert Shiller updated that warning. "Prices change in substantial measure because the investing public en masse capriciously changes its mind," he wrote. By the middle of the decade, more than a few analysts were sounding the alarm that stock prices had reached heights unsupported by any logic. "It's insanity," scoffed Michael Metz, chief investment strategist at Oppenheimer & Company, in a 1996 *Barron's* article headlined "Market Mania." "There's no rational way to value some of these companies." Even Fed chairman Alan Greenspan momentarily doubted the market's wisdom. During a dinner appearance in Washington, D.C., in December 1996, he raised the possibility that markets were under the thrall of "irrational exuberance"—the phrase Shiller took as the title of his book, in which he argued that stocks were wildly overvalued.

But such warnings were faint amid a shouted chorus of buying. Momentum was propelled as analysts crafted an overarching justification for the bubble, hanging its legitimacy on the utopian vision they christened the New Economy. Technology had effectively transcended gravity, justifying fabulous increases in stock prices. The old ups and downs of commercial life had been tamed. In 1997, political scientist Steven Weber pronounced last rites on the business cycle in the august pages of *Foreign Affairs*, concluding that effective government policy and technological innovation had flattened out the old rises and falls that had characterized economic reality for generations. "The waves of the business cycle are becoming ripples," he wrote.

The boldest, most ridiculous assertion of the era came in the fall of

1999, with the publication of *Dow 36,000: The New Strategy for Profiting from the Coming Rise in the Stock Market*, written jointly by newspaper columnist James K. Glassman and economist Kevin A. Hassett. As their book appeared on shelves, the Dow was above 10,000, having more than doubled inside of four years. "Stock prices could double, triple, or even quadruple tomorrow and still not be too expensive," Hassett and Glassman proclaimed, arguing that the old models of valuing stock reflected too much worrying and not enough recognition that risks had been greatly diminished by innovation. "No area of inquiry is more ripe for a paradigm shift than modern finance," they concluded. The book immediately hit the best-seller list, and Glassman—already a syndicated columnist for the *Washington Post* as well as a contributor to the *Wall Street Journal*—became a fixture on the talk show and speech circuit. Even as the market failed to comply with his prognostications, Glassman endorsed the New Economy without qualification. "The message I have is reassuring," he told a room full of investors in New York in October 2000, with the Dow down about 1,000 points since the release of his book. "We are on the verge of a tremendous wealth explosion, the likes of which has never been seen."

Such messages transmuted a viruslike strain of gold rush fever to ordinary Americans who now increasingly relied on investments, rather than pensions, for their retirement nest eggs. Talk of stocks became an acceptable form of dinner party conversation. Some people quit their jobs and became day traders, buying and unloading thousands of shares per hour. Had these same people stayed home to play the horses or online poker, they would have been subject to criticism as derelict gambling addicts. But because the objects of their speculation had names like Internet Capital Group, these traders were popularly celebrated as gutsy—if envelope-pushing—investors, making their own Horatio Alger stories.

A nation that had long prided itself on its Protestant work ethic and levelheadedness now rejected these virtues as impediments to attaining "self-made" wealth. In place of the traditional view that you work a decent job for a lifetime, sock away savings, and collect a pension—that, in essence, you construct a comfortable future through hard work, patience, and planning—came the invitation of comfort and gratification, at Internet speed, for anyone with a brokerage account and a dream.

The tech start-ups and their Wall Street handlers implicitly ridiculed the work ethic as an antiquated notion while speaking to a different lobe of the American brain—the part ruled by the frontier dream of finding a mountain of gold and never working again.

Television ads for the discount brokerage Ameritrade perfectly encapsulated the cultural moment, employing a pitchman named Stewart who would become an icon. With spiked hair, long bushy sideburns, and twenty-something energy, Stewart embodied the idea that online trading was a populist insurrection. In one memorable spot, he is working at a sterile office, bored to the point of photocopying his face, when his boss—a round, middle-aged man in a drab suit—catches him in the act. The boss summons Stewart to his office and shuts the door. Stewart thinks he's in trouble. But, no, a revolution is under way, and the boss wants in. He has just opened an Ameritrade account. He needs Stewart's help to buy his first shares of stock online. Stewart nods conspiratorially, then barks, "Let's light this candle. . . . Let's buy!" His boss is inclined to purchase a mere one hundred shares. "How about five hundred?" Stewart prods. When the older man hesitates, Stewart flaps his arms and squawks like a chicken. "Ride the wave of the future, my man!" Stewart crows as the transaction goes through. "Rock on." Traditionally, ads for financial services had emphasized the conservative, time-honored predictability of bankers overseeing a lifetime's savings. Ameritrade took direct aim at that image, casting itself as a progressive force that would cut out the overpaid hacks on Wall Street. The fictional boss's trade cost just $8, compared to the $200 charged by his broker. But the ad also played to the get-rich-quick impulses of the era. Investing was simply about having the courage to click "buy." Reasoned analysis and professional assessment were time-wasting obstacles to making money right now.

In another ad in the same campaign, Stewart visits a girlfriend at her parents' suburban home, with a manicured garden and swimming pool. Her parents are dressed for tennis. As Stewart emerges from the pool, revealing an American flag tattooed across his chest, his girlfriend announces that he likes to trade online, drawing a condescending smile from her father. "I'm a stockbroker, son," he says, laying a hand on Stewart's shoulder. But Stewart's iconoclasm again carries the day. He ridicules the dad—the very archetype of a square—for settling for merely market-beating returns. "I don't want to beat the market," Stewart says. "I want to grab it, sock it in the gut a couple of times, turn it upside down, shake it by the pants." The soliloquy waved the banner of financial democratization: it invited the rabble—the rank and file—to break into the elite country club of Wall Street and seize the American dream for themselves. And a mere piece of the dream would not do. Ameritrade's campaign urged Americans to be greedy, to adopt a new model of financial planning that celebrated greed as an unabashedly American impulse: you had to be in it to win it, and the winnings were just sitting there waiting.

The technology boom did not destroy financial planning so much as insinuate its exaggerated expectations into Americans' thinking, making trading in risky and dubiously valued assets seem sensible and commonplace. Indeed, those who eschewed such stocks were barraged with the message that they were fools. "If you're out of this sector, you're going to underperform," declared the money manager Alberto Vilar, as his Amerindo Technology Fund more than doubled in value in 1999. "You're in a horse and buggy and I'm in a Porsche. You don't like tenfold growth opportunities? Then go with someone else."

৩

Fran Barbaro did not relate to such gambling or day trading. She neither felt impulsive nor intoxicated by easy money as she bought and sold stocks in what was to her a deliberative fashion. Through the 1990s, she read the *Wall Street Journal* and the *Financial Times*, keeping abreast of the latest happenings in technology. She applied what she learned toward buying shares of the companies she most admired. She placed her orders through Charles Schwab, the discount broker, which charged her such tiny commissions that she could afford to trade whenever she spotted an opportunity.

The bulk of Barbaro's portfolio was tied up in what seemed like sensible investments. She saw right through the dot-coms and did not bother with them. "They always seemed like fluff to me," she said. "They had no underlying technology." Instead, she invested in large, well-managed businesses with established histories of making real money—IBM, Intel, and Cisco Systems, companies that were designing and constructing the long-term infrastructure of the Internet. Whenever she needed extra cash, she could just sell a small portion of her holdings.

Barbaro had been diagnosed with a debilitating illness, chronic pancreatitis, which entailed having painful stones lodged in her ducts. She required eighteen surgeries over more than a decade, each one requiring her to miss work for as long as two months as she recuperated. Though her insurance paid for the operations and the hospital stays, nothing compensated for the lost wages. Her stock-picking bridged the gap.

In the spring of 1995, Barbaro and her then husband went out looking at houses. The place they lived in at the time was on Route 60, a busy highway. The sounds of truck engines and car horns penetrated directly into their rooms, making them eager to move. With a new baby on the way—Gabriel, joining his five-year-old brother, Michael—they needed some extra room. They found a modest place in a quiet suburb, 2,272 square feet, set back from the street behind flowering shrubbery. "A little house, three bedrooms, nothing to it," Barbaro thought, as the agent pulled past the oak trees lining Juniper Road and into the driveway. "Just a modern old '50s ranch house."

The house was in dreadful shape, which explained why it had been sitting on the market unsold for two years. The septic system had failed. The roof leaked. The kitchen had never been upgraded from the day the house was completed. The linoleum floors were stained with grease, mud, and animal waste. And the asking price seemed ridiculous—$562,000, a price entirely out of proportion with the work needed to make it even modestly inhabitable.

Still, in key respects it was perfect. It was in Belmont Hill, a suburb of Boston, on a semirural street to the north of the town. An exclusive neighborhood, the real estate agent said. It sat about halfway between the Belmont Country Club, with its golf course, and Belmont High School, a reliable portal to college. "The community is well-established, suburban, residential; above average income," the school Web site declared. "Many community residents are prominent leaders in professional fields."

Though the house was a humble affair, it sat on the same shaded street as Tudor estates and old Victorians with elaborate fretwork and stained glass windows. Living there, Barbaro's boys could attend the same schools as the wealthier kids in Belmont, with its median household income reaching nearly six figures. They could get a head start in a nation in which preschools marketed themselves as the first step toward Harvard.

Barbaro had been working for several years at Adobe Systems, a successful software company, where she negotiated business deals. The frequency of her bouts with illness made her loath to buy an expensive home that would surely require a six-figure sum to renovate. But they had the money. She earned $150,000 a year. Her husband was bringing home a six-figure salary from his own technology job. Her stock portfolio seemed a veritable fountain of cash. So they negotiated a deal—$387,500. Barbaro sold some of her Adobe stock to raise the down payment. Then they found a contractor, sinking another $150,000 into fixing the place up. They put up a new roof. They tore out the old kitchen and replaced it. Juniper Road became their home.

The following year, Barbaro took a job at a software start-up that quickly ran through $13 million in venture capital and shut down without ever shipping a product. Despite her resulting unemployment, she felt no need to conserve. Her stock portfolio was still worth about $500,000—more than enough to pay the mortgage and the other bills while she set up a consulting business and still feel that she had ample savings salted away.

Far from an anomaly, Barbaro was representative of a new class of American investors for whom saving and speculating had become indistinguishable, embracing technology stocks as a means of bypassing the traditional limits of household finance.

In *Irrational Exuberance*, Shiller delineated the key factors that made investors so hungry for tech stocks, bidding up prices more sharply than any time in recorded history. An increase in the frequency of layoffs sowed insecurity, instilling ordinary Americans with the feeling that their financial needs rested on their ability to find money independent of their jobs. As pensions continued to give way to 401(k) plans, more and more people turned to stocks and mutual funds, exposing them to the market's hype. The spread of technology, with computers and the Web entering most homes for the first time, supported the impression that the world really was being upended and that the technology companies were justified in their promises of extraordinary profits. By keeping interest rates low, Alan Greenspan made sure finance was abundant, even after he publicly worried about the effects of irrational exuberance. Even the spread of legalized gambling—both online and in Indian casinos across the country—made investing in technology companies with no earnings seem comparatively conservative.

Wall Street and Madison Avenue skillfully played to these new realities. Throughout the history of business, marketers had sold products by making them seem like bearers of much bigger things. Americans who might never leave the cornfields of Illinois were invited to drink Coors beer as a virtual pilgrimage to the Rocky Mountains. Razor blades were sold not as mere devices to remove whiskers, but as conveyors of manhood.

During the technology bubble, the product was tech stocks, with shares sold as avatars of an almost mystically lucrative future. Companies pumped up their aura of limitless potential by casting themselves as far more than providers of goods and services. They were liberators intent on breaking through barriers to human potential. Steve Case, the salesman extraordinaire who pioneered America Online and brought millions of people to the Internet for the first time, talked ceaselessly about how his company existed to make the world better. Qualcomm, which developed computer chips to power cell phones, sold itself as a means of freeing humanity from its tether to wires, offices, and social convention. John Chambers, the chief executive of Cisco Systems, was not content that his company be seen as good at making telephone and Internet equipment. "We can be the one company that can change the world," he said repeatedly. "It's maybe the first time there's ever been such a company."

Tech companies amplified this sense that they were far more than mere businesses by appropriating the language of liberation and the trappings of bohemian irreverence—rock music, disdain for business attire, and relentless talk of revolution. In *One Market Under God*, published in 2000, the journalist Thomas Frank explored how this worked in the service of market fundamentalism: it cast big business as a populist force working to elevate the people, and rendered anyone standing in its way as a retrograde enemy of the public good. As they rolled out their "solutions" and sold their stock, the technology chiefs railed against regulators who might interfere with their gargantuan mergers or impede the exotic forms of finance enabling them. Their revolutionary shtick connoted the message that they were the vanguard of innovation. They were fighting on the side of freedom, striving to give the world what it craved, if the regulators would only get out of their way. "As business leaders melded themselves theoretically with the people, they found powerful new weapons with which to win their 'grand argument' with those who sought to regulate or control any aspect of private enterprise," Frank wrote. "Since markets express the will of the people, virtually any criticism of business could be described as an act of despicable contempt for the common man."

In this spirit, tech companies and their public relations apparatus took great pains to make their doings seem youthful and spontaneous. The reliable prop in this mission was the foosball table, whose presence seemed to require mention in every feature story about the newest Silicon Valley start-up, typically opposite a photo of twentysomething computer programmers dancing atop their desks. It was all served up with a purpose, aiming to preempt the critical questions that stock analysts and journalists should have been asking about balance sheets and debt levels and business models.

The stock analysts had a reasonable excuse for swooning for the tech companies, falling in line as apparatchiks in their mission to sell shares to the public: they worked for the investment banks that were making fortunes brokering the deals. We journalists, on the other hand, had only our inexperience and our vanity to blame. Nobody bought us off for our participation in the great con. The public relations outfits were skilled at feeding journalists grandiose angles about technology changing everything, and too many in the trade proved susceptible. Journalists liked the idea of writing about things that had never happened before, things that were worthy of historical treatment. Taking aim at the spectacle would have diminished its importance, and thus our own place in the proceedings. Moreover, many of the people running the companies were indeed compelling figures and some of their ideas were brilliant.

But the ultimate reason the press coverage enabled the boom more than checked its excesses was because many journalists lacked the analytical tools and the memory of past investment binges that would have aided more critical reporting. I had been a career political and environmental reporter when I began covering telecommunications for the *Washington Post* in 1999, at the age of thirty-three. I was more than willing to seek out analysts and solicit their aid in making sense of the technology being unleashed. But many of those analysts, employed by the investment banks, were less than impartial observers. I had no problem reading reports and calling consultants who could explain the strategic imperatives of whatever new mega-merger was on tap. Cultivating sources and enlisting their help in making sense of news had been my life for a decade. But the balance sheets and corporate filings with the Securities and Exchange Commission were a foreign experience, not just because I was new to the beat but because new methods of accounting were being invented to deliver future profits today. The shamelessness of the PR people who called dozens of times a week with transparently absurd pitches added to my gut feeling that much of what was happening in technology amounted to a ruse. Limo rides were proffered by tech companies to ferry the media from trade shows to their private parties in San Francisco and Las Vegas, where reporters drank martinis and were rewarded with off-the-record conversations with strategic gurus. Yet even with that skepticism fully intact, the relentless waterfall of huge deals, product announcements, and regulatory changes absorbed most of the hours of any news day. Faced with another huge corporate merger—America Online buys the cable and media giant Time Warner!—my colleagues and I tended to explore whether the deal would really bring the advertised "synergies" and whether it would pass regulatory muster. We could try to figure out what to make of the accounting in the latest deal, the corporate compensation structure, but that was a swim upstream against the companies and their public relations juggernaut.

There was plenty of illuminating reporting, to be sure. Enron's elaborate con was ultimately exposed after *Fortune* writer Bethany McLean properly scrutinized its balance sheet. Every major newspaper featured sensible analysis by writers who doubted whether the boom could go on. But such words tended to be drowned out by the latest profile of the latest darling company that had doubled in price. Not until after the markets collapsed and the Nasdaq lost about $5 trillion in paper value in 2000 did journalists probe en masse, arriving like investigators at the scene of a plane crash, suddenly curious why the airline had been serving champagne in the cockpit.

The image-maintenance machine of the technology companies

shaped their chieftains into courageous visionaries bent on elevating human existence. In rare moments, some would offer a wink and a nod in recognition of what was really going on. In an exchange with my *Post* colleague Mark Leibovich, Larry Ellison, the chief executive of the software giant Oracle, stuck two fingers in his mouth and gagged as he disdained the world-saving spiel favored by his technology brethren. "Oh, well, the reason we're doing software here at Oracle is because someday children will use this software, and we wouldn't want to leave a single child behind," Ellison said, in mock sincerity. "If I could just make the world a better place, what I really care about is making the world a better place, and that's why I'm doing this. And all my money's going to medical research so we can help people who are sick." Then Ellison gagged again. "People say this and get away with it," he pronounced. "I can't deal with the fog of deceit."

The central impetus for the spin campaign was not to make companies seem benevolent as much as to render their doings historically unprecedented—an image that worked to justify the otherwise impossible valuations assigned by the markets. If the tech companies were transcending the limits of old-fashioned business models, then the means of measuring them had to be scrapped in favor of new measurements of valuation. Then and only then could Webvan—an early online grocery store that soon went bankrupt—be worth considerably more in 2000 than Winn-Dixie Stores, a profitable supermarket chain that counted annual revenues of $14 billion.

Dot-com stocks were valued by the number of "eyeballs" they could capture, the number of visitors they attracted to their Web sites, the mouse clicks those visitors made, or some other metric designed to generate the impression of explosive growth. Companies selling equipment to the dot-coms were to be valued with something called EBITDA—earnings before interest, taxes, depreciation, and amortization—as if it would be unfair to hold frontier businesses to the stodgy standard of needing to actually take in more dollars than they paid out. These measures of valuation—touted by the investment banks doing the deals—were duly affirmed when the anointed stocks rose.

American markets were governed by a feedback loop of validation. Those brash young entrepreneurs were securing seven- and eight-figure checks from venture capitalists. The parking lots of Silicon Valley were shimmering with new BMWs. So surely these strange new ways of measuring companies had to make sense, just as otherwise unfathomable housing prices would make sense a few years later, based on how much the neighbors just got for theirs. Even if the prices didn't make sense to *you*, they made sense to the *market*, and that was the only vote that counted.

3

The Debts of the New Economy

"I bought into the same elixir that everyone else did."

Investment manias create their own reality. When enough money buys into the tenets of a lucrative fantasy, the broader economy is affected as if the fantasy is solid truth. Even sober-minded people—those not willfully participating in the make-believe—are sucked in nonetheless, making decisions that prove catastrophic once reality inevitably intrudes.

When demand is growing feverishly for almost anything of value, the market is prone to produce it as if demand were unlimited. Companies whose fortunes are tied to stock market performance have an interest in perpetuating a sense of insatiable consumer demand. Their apparent success creates business opportunities for other companies, which sell the goods and services needed to run a business. That keeps money flowing, making it seem as though economic growth is dependable.

I learned this lesson up close through the adventures of a company that became synonymous with the tech bubble: WorldCom. In the fall of 1999, I was attending an Internet conference in the ballroom of a hotel not far from the White House. It was a typical gathering for its time. Several hundred people—some in conservative suits and ties, with the more powerful favoring jeans and turtlenecks—sat in velvet-backed stackable chairs listening to the bravado of the leaders of major Internet companies. Among the speakers was John W. Sidgmore, then World-Com's chief operating officer.

Sidgmore was one of a community of wealthy technology chieftains clustered in the office parks of northern Virginia. Short, bearded, and pugnacious, he walked across the stage to the podium with a swagger. He had launched a business in the early 1990s called UUNET, the first commercial Internet service provider. It became the largest Internet "back-bone" in the world, a global highway of fiber optics cables that carried digital bits, credit card transactions, video feeds, and telephone calls. He had sold that company to another firm, which in turn was swallowed up by WorldCom, an enterprise built on one merger after another.

WorldCom occupied the very peak of the telecommunications world. In the configuration of the day, telecom was neatly divided into the monopolists and the upstarts. The monopolists were the Bell companies with their near-total grip on local telephone markets. The upstarts derided the Bells as dinosaurs forged in a culture of guaranteed, state-regulated profits, unfit for the new battle at hand, which would be decided on grounds of innovation. These new companies used a host of creative technologies to carve out their own markets—wireless telephone connections, satellite links. A landmark law, the Telecommunications Act of 1996, had granted them the rights to lease key pieces of the Bell networks, a major driver in the technology boom. The law generated the impression—actively encouraged by the Clinton administration—that competition would rule telecom, making it fertile frontier for investors. Hundreds of billions of dollars of investment poured into the industry in pursuit of the spoils.

But the new crop of eager competitors had fundamental troubles. For one, they were mostly small and untested, and they needed vast amounts of capital to build out their businesses. Despite the Telecom Act, the Bells had a multitude of ways to deny access to their wires, and they used them all, effectively monkey-wrenching the upstarts. World-Com cast itself as the white knight in this story. It was neither small nor untested, and its very roots went back to the long-running battle with Ma Bell. WorldCom's founder and chief executive, Bernie Ebbers, was a towering bear of a man, a plain-spoken former basketball player who kept the company headquarters in Mississippi long after it became an international brand, and who famously favored cowboy boots. Decades earlier, Ebbers had sketched out a way to buy cheap wholesale long-distance telephone service from AT&T and sell it retail. He had convinced Wall Street that WorldCom was singularly poised to triumph in the modern telecom battle.

On that day in 1999, Sidgmore flashed a PowerPoint slide on the screen behind him. It showed a graph of the growth in Internet traffic — the volume of telephone calls and digital blips coursing through the company's network of cables. Demand was exploding off the chart, seemingly unlimited. The inference was obvious: WorldCom's upside was without limit. The company's stock price rose higher, month after month.

Sidgmore was accustomed to showing this chart and hearing audible gasps. On this day, a skeptical hand went up in the ballroom. The questioner asked how all that Internet usage would spell profit. So many networks were being built to carry Internet traffic. Wasn't a glut taking shape? If that was true, the basic law of supply and demand suggested that the prices commanded by WorldCom and its competitors would soon plummet. Sidgmore scoffed at this idea. A *glut*? He pointed again to the chart. Demand was growing, and that was the only truth that mattered.

Among technology analysts at that time, it was widely accepted that WorldCom was a real business making serious money and positioned to dominate. Companies like Ariba needed stories to win the markets. WorldCom was erecting something you could see with your eyes, as construction crews ripped open the streets to lay down another length of fiber optics cable. Whether Webvan or Furniture.com or Ariba proved viable did not matter to WorldCom. WorldCom *was* the Internet. But a glut was indeed taking shape. It was not the first time an explosion in demand prompted speculators to build too much of something, nor would it be the last. There really had been plenty of desire for modern housing in Bangkok in the mid-1990s — just not enough to fill the apartment towers that packed the skyline of Thailand's capital before the money flooded out of Southeast Asia. There really was strong demand for houses during the real estate boom of the mid-2000s, just not enough to fill the subdivisions that got built by a construction industry operating with essentially free finance.

Between 1997 and 2001, local and long-distance telephone companies spent more than $300 billion erecting their networks, distributing their dollars across the technology spectrum to consultants and engineers, to software companies, and to electronics vendors such as Cisco Systems. But all that spending generated so much supply that prices to use the networks were falling through the floor. Between October 1998 and February 2002, the transmission capacity for moving Internet data beneath the Atlantic Ocean, between North America and Europe, expanded almost twentyfold. During the same period, the price of leasing a transmission line dropped from $125,000 a year to $10,000. The companies that had laid down the cables were swimming in debt. By the end of 2001, the eight largest telecom companies owed $191 billion, by one estimate. That meant they needed cash immediately, just to keep up with their debt payments. And that gave them greater incentive to charge low prices to ensure they got business, and lower prices tightened the noose around all of them.

"Demand was poised to go up 30, 40, 50 percent per year and prices were going down and you were going to make up in volume what you lost on price," said Leo Hindery, a longtime cable television executive who briefly headed a WorldCom rival, Global Crossing. "If there was just a hiccup in that, you were going to get crushed."

For WorldCom, the hiccup came courtesy of antitrust authorities. Ebbers had built his company on the relentless pursuit of scale. For two decades, he had been using his escalating stock as currency to buy the next company in a string of more than sixty mergers. Each deal allowed for creative accounting—the use of special, merger-related charges—to blur the details of his overall balance sheet. The public kept buying in, bidding up the stock, and handing WorldCom the currency to do the next deal. But in the spring of 2000, the Justice Department and the European Union both filed lawsuits to block WorldCom's $129 billion purchase of another Internet and telecom giant, Sprint, concluding that the merger would hurt competition. Suddenly, Ebbers had to run what he had amassed, rather than simply plot the next merger. He had to generate profit by operating his company.

As prices fell and more competitors completed their networks, that became impossible. At a board meeting in April 2001, WorldCom's senior leadership gathered at the corporate headquarters to ostensibly hear their chief executive outline his vision for righting the company. Instead, Ebbers reprimanded them for using too much coffee in the employee break room, underscoring just how desperate the situation had become. The company ultimately resorted to illegality to avoid coming clean with the markets: it booked its maintenance expenses and fees paid to other telephone companies as one-time-only investments in the future, turning huge losses into apparent gains. Ebbers would eventually go to prison for doctoring the books.

The demise of WorldCom and other large Internet companies reverberated through the technology world in a way that foreshadowed what would happen to the financial system when the giant investment bank Bear Stearns collapsed in the spring of 2008, a victim of its speculative excesses in the mortgage market: it forced a reevaluation of all of the operative assumptions driving the markets, and it triggered a daisy chain of reckoning. Businesses that had been selling products and services to WorldCom—companies that made fiber optics cables such as Corning and the electronics makers such as Cisco and Nortel—saw their sales plunge.

WorldCom's ascent and disintegration illustrated another dynamic that came to define the economy of the 2000s: when one large player wins the market's favor through reckless behavior, competitors feel enormous pressure to do likewise or get left behind. As WorldCom delighted investors with unexpectedly huge revenue gains through much of the 1990s, executives at AT&T, the nation's largest long-distance telephone company, scratched their heads in amazement and tried to figure out how to keep up. AT&T was in the same business, chasing the same customers, buying the same technology, and hiring the same consultants and market researchers. Yet its growth rate was always eclipsed by World-Com's. AT&T grasped to develop its own visionary plan to wow the market, in part leading it to sink more than $100 billion into acquiring cable television companies and outfitting them to become telephone and Internet services. AT&T eventually aborted this strategy, selling off its cable holdings for far less than it paid for them, and then selling itself to a local telephone company, SBC Communications. In the end, AT&T's cable strategy proved one of the grandest, most disastrous bets in the history of capitalism. And one of the reasons it came about was because AT&T's primary competitor, WorldCom, was playing with fairy dust, using an inflated stock to buy companies that produced the illusion of growth. That changed the market for everyone else.

This sort of madness becomes not only infectious but imperative. Risk taking and indulgence in one headquarters forces others to follow suit, lest they miss out on the spoils. This dynamic spread through American financial life. In recent years, faced with this conundrum, the people running major banks, including Bear Stearns, Lehman Brothers, and Citibank, kept trading in risky mortgage-linked investments because everyone else was doing it, too. Pulling back to avoid future losses meant missing out on the near-term profits being harvested by competitors, and the markets would surely take note, sending their stock prices down, perhaps costing them their jobs. As Citgroup's then chief executive Charles Prince famously put it in July 2007: "As long as the music is playing, you've got to get up and dance." Of course, after the music stopped in 2008, Citigroup nearly collapsed, requiring a $45 billion taxpayer-financed bailout. But during the credit bubbles, sensible risk management was an impediment to keeping pace with the competitors.

In April 2002, WorldCom's board forced Ebbers to resign, blaming him for the company's plunging stock price amid an investigation from the Securities and Exchange Commission into how the company had been accounting for its many mergers. By the time the WorldCom accounting scandal emerged in June 2002, Sidgmore was running the company. I called him in his office for a retrospective article on how WorldCom had brought itself to ruin, and I reminded him of the speech he had made nearly three years earlier, and how he had sneered at the questioner who had asked about a glut. Sidgmore became irate, accusing me of unfairly singling him out for blame when he had simply done what his contemporaries had all been doing. "I bought into the same elixir that everyone else did," Sidgmore said. "There is no way that anyone predicted all this.

"You look at Andy Grove's speeches," he said, referring to the founder of Intel, "John Chambers's speeches," referring to the chief executive of Cisco. "They're all bullshit. Same as mine."

∾

In one central regard, the technology boom was a mirage, an elegantly simple process of constructing an abundant present at the cost of the future, generating a sustained hangover that still grips the American economy. The financial system took on debt—enormous quantities of it—and unleashed these borrowed funds across the virtual landscape in pursuit of riches. Between 1989 and 1999, the total outstanding debt in the financial system increased by an amount that exceeded Japan's annual economic output, swelling from $2.4 trillion to $7.6 trillion. Investment bankers and venture capitalists sprinkled those funds on the upstart companies, and those companies used their money to buy things from other companies, and so on and so forth until the economy was running at a fevered pitch. The future was aggressively mortgaged to pay for the present, but it wasn't supposed to be a problem because the future was inestimably enormous. It was as if you and everyone you knew drew the maximum cash advance on your credit cards, pulled second mortgages on your homes, and threw a party worthy of Jay Gatsby. At the height of it—with bands playing on the lawn, canapés and champagne in hand, people coiffed to the nines—you might reasonably conclude that some new fountain of wealth had been discovered. Until the bills began piling up in the mailbox, past due.

The problem for the American economy was that businesses and ordinary people made important decisions about savings and social policy based on the assumption that the bubble *was* real; that companies propped up by easy money and inflated demand would continue to receive orders; that jobs would continue to be plentiful. It was as if the local catering and tuxedo rental companies took your credit-financed party as a reliable indication of the future and planned accordingly, erecting new stores and hiring more employees to service your anticipated demand.

Between 1992 and 2001, telecommunications roughly doubled as a source of activity in the American economy, delivering two-thirds of the new jobs created and one-third of the new investment. The new companies leased office space and bought telephones and computers. They bought insurance policies and legal and accounting services. They shelled out for vehicles and airplane tickets and hotel rooms, and they rented hotel ballrooms for meetings and trade shows, generating sales for myriad other businesses. The benefits of the boom spilled out broadly, amplifying demand for goods and services across the nation. Money washed through the insurance firms of Hartford, Connecticut; the commercial banks of Charlotte, North Carolina; the interior design outfits in Los Angeles; the food processors outside Chicago; and the warehouses of Memphis. Business swelled at truck stops, restaurants, plumbing dealerships, maid services, temp agencies, and dry cleaners. Landscape gardeners in California found themselves paid as well as top-drawer accountants, as they tended to the flowering shrubbery of stock option millionaires, and they distributed their winnings to wine merchants, car dealers, and home furnishings suppliers. Money was landing in seemingly every crook and crevice of the American economy.

It was what economists call a virtuous cycle. The dollars sluiced through the economy, each advance generating fresh business for someone new, extending prosperity. People who previously had not been able to find jobs were in demand. By the end of the 1990s, the national unemployment rate was down to 4 percent, its lowest level in thirty years. A lot of people were lifted up by the boom. And a lot of people were set up for a crash when the make-believe gave way to reality.

Willie Gonzalez's experience exemplified both the promises and the pitfalls of the tech bubble for working people, whose real lives had nothing to do with trading stock. He had grown up simply but comfortably in Oakland and Miami, the seventh of seven children in a Cuban American family. He had run his own construction company in Miami for much of the 1980s, but business deteriorated as housing prices fell near the end of the decade. Then, in 1992, Hurricane Andrew devastated his neighborhood. Wanting to get away from the destruction, Gonzalez, his wife, Ibis, and their three children moved across the country to Modesto, California, where a cousin promised to put them up and help him get a job.

Gonzalez's cousin worked at a cardboard packaging factory in Livermore, a sixty-mile commute away on the eastern edge of the San Francisco Bay Area. He helped Gonzalez get hired as a night forklift driver for $6 an hour. "I said, 'I have to start somewhere,'" Gonzalez said. "We arrived out there with nothing. I needed to start getting my family on their feet, so I took the first thing I found."

The plant made packaging for a host of manufacturers in the area, among them a pair of major technology companies—Hewlett-Packard, the computer manufacturer, and Cisco Systems. For Gonzalez, the wages were lean, but life was cheaper in Modesto than in Miami, and the company was expanding to meet the demands of the tech boom. Within a few months, he worked himself up to the dayshift, which brought a modest raise. By 1994 he had saved enough to buy a four-bedroom house with separate living and dining rooms, and a large yard—all for $130,000. His kids were studying karate. Modesto was peaceful and predictable, its flat streets running straight and undistracted past ball fields and houses with porches, beneath shady trees that warded off the Central Valley sun.

By the end of 1995, demand for the packaging being churned out by the Livermore plant was exceeding the supply of people capable of delivering it. The factory managers asked Gonzalez if he was interested in training to drive an eighteen-wheeler tractor-trailer truck. He agreed on the spot. Soon, he had a license. As a driver, Gonzalez's salary began at $12 an hour, double his beginning wages, but he had designs on better. Less than a year later, in the spring of 1996, he drove by a Freightliner dealer in Stockton, California, where he spotted a repossessed Mercedes-Benz truck. He bought it for $50,000—all on credit—and immediately quit his job, sure that he could make far more money working for himself. He was on the hook for a monthly truck payment of $1,884, a daunting sum. But a truck driver with his own rig in northern California was greatly in demand. The boom was in full swing, and the products it generated and consumed were jamming the highways.

Gonzalez picked up a contract with a company called Eagle Global Logistics, which hauled cargo for Hewlett-Packard. Most days, he pulled out of his home in his trailer around noon outfitted in blue jeans and a company T-shirt, drove west to Livermore to pick up pallets of computer gear produced overnight by the factories there, then drove further west to Hayward to pick up more. He then crossed the bay to San Francisco, to Eagle's cargo hub. There, he dropped the trailer he had been carrying and picked up another one, an airfreight trailer, loaded with electronics. He ran it down to the San Jose airport, where a crew loaded it into the belly of a cargo plane.

He frequently did not get home to Modesto until one or two in the morning. Sometimes, he ran so many legs in one day, so many miles and hours gone, that he succumbed to exhaustion on the roadside, parked near the warehouse, and slept in his truck. But the hours and stress were eased by the money he was bringing home, as much as $5,000 a week. As he recalled those days more than a decade later, his eyes took on a pronounced glow. "I always loved trucks," he said. "Some kids want to be firefighters, because they like fire trucks. My dream was my own eighteen-wheeler. My passion was to drive a nice, clean truck, with state-of-the-art equipment. It was a real good life."

Between 1996 and the end of the decade, Gonzalez brought home more than $150,000 a year. The same market magic that put a pair of Ferraris in Eric Bochner's garage and art on Fran Barbaro's walls changed life at the Gonzalez residence, too. He sent his wife home to visit her family in Puerto Rico and surprised her with a Jacuzzi on her return. He put a swimming pool in the backyard and took the family out to local steakhouses. Some weekends, they drove down to Santa Cruz, a town set in the redwoods along the Pacific, where they strolled the boardwalk, rode the roller coaster, and dipped their toes in the foam.

Gonzalez brought home between $10,000 and $20,000 a month. About $7,000 went to pay the mortgage, the truck payment, his insurance, and his gas, a bill that increased when he traded in his aging rig for a new Peterbilt truck that cost $120,000. He spent about $3,000 a month on groceries, clothing, and fun, he said. Whatever was left—sometimes as much as $10,000, sometimes nothing—he put in the bank. He did not live within a proscribed budget. He had no financial plan, leaving him vulnerable to an abrupt change in fortunes. He spent money as if it was abundant and would continue to be so, the same bad bet made by so many others. But the way Gonzalez saw it, he was not living extravagantly. He worked hard and paid his bills. By the middle of 2000, he had saved about $50,000.

By then, the New Economy companies were cutting back production in the face of falling sales. Hewlett-Packard shifted production to Mexico, and that reduced the volume of goods on the California freeways. Gonzalez's monthly take slipped from $5,000 to $1,700. "Everything just slowed down for everybody," he said.

He quit driving for Eagle Global and began hauling produce for Trader Joe's, the specialty grocery chain. By the summer of 2002, the economics of driving a truck had deteriorated to the point where it wasn't even worth turning the ignition. A Trader Joe's dispatcher ordered him up to Seattle to bring a load of produce, offering a mere $895 for the journey—hardly enough to pay for the gas. And the dispatcher refused to guarantee that Gonzalez would receive a return load for his trouble. If he went, he risked spending more than he would earn. "I said, 'No way. It's not worth it,'" Gonzalez recalled. "'I'm not going.' And he said, 'You fucking Cuban, if you don't go up there now, I'm going to scrape that Trader Joe's decal off your door.'"

Only two years earlier, while the tech bubble was still inflating demand for everything, Gonzalez was making $250 for a one-way haul from San Jose to San Francisco, a trip that could be completed in under an hour. Now, he was being ordered to spend two to three days on the road, there and back, for a sum that might not even cover his expenses. He scraped the decal off the door himself and quit. He sold his truck back to the dealer. It was worth less than he owed in payments, so he sold his house, too—for $207,000—to raise cash to make up the difference.

For Gonzalez, the technology boom had delivered material comfort he and his family had not previously known. Yet once it was over, it was almost as if it the good times had never happened. The debts, on the other hand, remained very real.

༄

In 2000, as President Bill Clinton presided over the last of his annual black-tie dinners for the White House Correspondents Association at a hotel ballroom in Washington, he screened a hilarious mock documentary about his final days in office. Lonely, bored, and increasingly irrelevant, the president makes lunch for the First Lady, watches movies with his dog, and washes the executive limousine. In a memorable segment, he bumps into Stewart, the Ameritrade pitch guy, in the bowels of the White House. Stewart is again photocopying his face. Clinton summons him to the Oval Office, where Stewart initiates the president in the particulars of e-Bay, the online flea market. In the final sequence, Clinton and Stewart pilfer ice cream sandwiches from a basement vending machine and walk off arm in arm.

The sketch brought the house down. It was a hard act for even Jay Leno to follow. I laughed as much as anyone that night, seated with a table of telecom executives amid hundreds of people in tuxedoes and gowns. We were marking the end of a presidency that, on economic grounds, appeared more successful than any in recent memory. More than 22 million jobs had been created during Clinton's tenure. The economy had grown robustly. The stock markets had created vast new wealth, not least for the wireless and Internet industry executives seated at my table. But, a decade later, Clinton's gag with the Ameritrade pitch man seems fitting in a way not intended by the mock documentary:

Clinton and his advisers followed Stewart in an excessive belief in the powers of the New Economy. They made crucial decisions that assumed the abundance of the technology era could be sustained indefinitely.

In the summer of 1996, in the midst of the explosion in employment, the Clinton administration joined with Republicans in Congress to end the days of guaranteed cash assistance for poor people. Clinton had been elected on a pledge to "end welfare as we know it." By affixing his signature to the Personal Responsibility and Work Opportunity Reconciliation Act, as the bill was titled, he delivered on that campaign promise. The act imposed a five-year federal time limit on cash benefits for recipients. It allowed states to set much stricter deadlines, as many did. For poor single mothers, government aid was no longer guaranteed. They would have to go out and get jobs.

In the previous decade, libertarian social critics such as Charles Murray and George Gilder had advanced the idea that liberal social policies aimed at eradicating poverty in the 1960s had been not merely ineffectual but malevolent: they had perpetuated poverty by rewarding the poor for their moral deviance, writing bigger checks to ghetto dwellers having children out of wedlock. This was a powerfully subversive idea. It not only let policy makers off the hook for poverty and joblessness, but contained the implicit imperative that government must scrupulously *avoid* doing anything to address the steady slide backward for millions of people. If government stepped in and, say, adjusted the tax code to collect more from the rich so it could spend more on public education and health care in inner-city neighborhoods, that would interfere with the natural workings of the market, and everyone would be set back. Tax dollars devoted to social programs such as food stamps for the poor, unemployment insurance for the jobless, or child care for single mothers wanting to complete school were worse than wasted. "Trying to eradicate inequality with artificially manufactured outcomes has led to disaster," declared Richard J. Herrnstein and Charles Murray in their highly controversial 1994 book, *The Bell Curve*. "It is time for America once again to try living with inequality, as life is lived: understanding that each human being has strengths and weaknesses, qualities we admire and qualities we do not admire, competencies and incompetencies, assets and debits." Government assistance to the unemployed amounted to sabotage, a willful impediment to the market. Why not save those dollars and instead cut taxes, handing the money back to productive members of society who would invest it and spend it?

Herrnstein and Murray argued that one's station in life was a reflection of naturally endowed intelligence. Therefore, government programs aimed at improving the academic performance of poor, inner-city children were a waste of time and effort, because success was hard-wired. The sort of home in which one was raised, the quality of local schools and health care, were all trifling factors compared to one's innate cognitive ability. Rather than wasting public money on futile efforts to change nature, the government would more wisely end cash assistance for poor, single mothers, which would at least discourage such women from bringing more children with low IQs into the world.

The Bell Curve was widely pilloried as an intellectual fraud crafted with a highly selective use of data. Critics assailed it as a racist cant that implicitly endorsed the notion of a genetic basis to success. Academics generally dismissed it as a trivial bit of attention seeking. Yet the very fact that it was even published and the commotion that its release provoked hinted at the tensions building within American society over social policy and deeper views on the justness of market forces. Those inclined to put faith in the market and shrink the role of government in managing the economy could now cite a seemingly authoritative analysis, laid out in academic prose, that validated the wealth of the successful and the poverty of the downtrodden. Here was an intellectual justification for dismantling the social safety net built up since the Depression and distributing the extra cash to those with a veritable birthright to enjoy it— those who had been smart enough to figure out the merits of being rich.

Such notions operated upon thinking that had long been operative in American society, going back to the Horatio Alger story. "Most Americans believe that opportunity for economic advancement is widely available, that economic outcomes are determined by individuals' efforts and talents (or their lack) and that in general economic inequality is fair," concluded an analysis of national survey data collected in 1969 and 1980 by sociologists James Kluegel and Eliot Smith. Asked to explain the prevalence of poverty, the survey respondents most frequently proffered "lack of thrift or proper money management skills," "lack of effort," "loose morals and drunkenness," as well as the "failure of society to provide good schools." Those who didn't prosper only had themselves to blame.

According to the proponents of welfare reform—the Republicans in Congress who shaped it, and Clinton, who ultimately signed it into law—an entrenched culture of dependency on state aid among the poor had to be traded in for a renewed focus on work and self-reliance. Rather than collect meager monthly welfare checks and staying out of the job market indefinitely, effectively setting their children up for similarly impoverished lives, Americans would be forced to better themselves and their families by going to work. Meanwhile, the federal government would give the states money to pay for programs to temporarily support women making this challenging transition, including subsidized child care, health insurance for poor children, and job training so they could gain needed skills. The days of welfare as an entitlement for anyone poor enough to qualify were over. The market would be entrusted with the fate of America's poor.

The change came amid considerable political wrangling. Republicans in Congress, led by House Speaker Newt Gingrich, sought to twin the time limits on welfare with cuts to food stamps and health insurance for poor children. President Clinton vetoed two such versions of the bill, branding them punitive. The point was to help poor women transition to something better, he argued, not simply to kick them off the welfare rolls. Without support programs, most women, the vast majority of welfare beneficiaries, would sink deeper into poverty.

When the Republicans delivered a third bill with guarantees for food stamps and medical benefits plus increased aid to cushion the transition, Clinton signed off, much to the consternation of liberal advocates for the poor. The then first lady Hillary Clinton, who had worked for the advocacy group Children's Defense Fund, considered its founder, Marian Wright Edelman, to be her mentor. As the president signed the time limits into law, Edelman released a blistering statement accusing him of throwing the poor to the wolves, leaving families with no safety net when hard times returned. The signing "makes a mockery of his pledge not to hurt children," Edelman proclaimed. "It will leave a moral blot on his Presidency and on our nation that will never be forgotten." Her husband, Peter Edelman, swiftly resigned his job in Clinton's Department of Health and

Human Services to protest what he later called "predictably bad public policy."

In her memoir, Hillary Clinton acknowledged that political considerations played a role in her husband's decision to enact welfare reform. "It was preferable to sign the measure knowing that a Democratic administration was in place to implement it humanely," she wrote. "If he vetoed welfare reform a third time, Bill would be handing the Republicans a potential political windfall."

But the decision to sign off also reflected the abiding belief that the extraordinary job growth of the 1990s would be an enduring feature of the American economy. "A long time ago, I concluded that the current welfare system undermines the basic values of work, responsibility, and family, trapping generation after generation in dependency and hurting the very people it was designed to help," President Clinton told reporters at the White House, as he announced his decision to sign the bill. "Today, we have a historic opportunity to make welfare what it was meant to be, a second chance, not a way of life."

As Clinton acknowledged, the legitimacy of that second chance rested on the assumption that there would be enough jobs to sustain the women who were being forced off of government aid. He cast the reform bill "as an opportunity to bring everyone fully into the mainstream of American life, to give them a chance to share in the prosperity and the promise that most of our people are enjoying today," and he sounded confident that the private sector would continue to create needed jobs. "You can't tell people to go to work if there is no job out there," Clinton said.

In the years immediately following Clinton's decision, there were indeed lots of jobs, and welfare reform was widely hailed as a success. By August 2000, the welfare rolls had declined by half, and one-third of parents still on public assistance were employed. As unemployment fell from 6.8 percent to 4 percent between 1991 and 2000, poor families with children saw their inflation-adjusted incomes climb by 50 percent. The percentage of single mothers who were employed climbed from 47 percent in 1994 to 69 percent by 2000, according to an analysis of Census data.

"One of the things welfare reform did is make moms who used to be insulated from the market part of the market," said Ron Haskins, a former Republican aide on the House Ways and Means Committee, who played a central role in writing the bill. But welfare reform was enacted when the market was a nice place to be. The boom in employment was pumped up by the easy money and creative math of Wall Street and Silicon Valley. When the market was no longer so hospitable, the reform's merits seemed questionable. Between 2000 and 2005, income for poor families headed by single mothers slipped by more than 2 percent a year, according to an analysis of federal data by economist Jared Bernstein. During the same period, family income for households headed by single mothers with less than a high school education slipped from $27,000 a year to $25,000—numbers that included both earnings from jobs and government aid.

By 2007, the number of children in poverty reached 13.3 million, up from 11.6 million in 2000.

The biggest consequence of the Clinton administration's belief in the New Economy was its failed oversight of the financial system. Two of Clinton's Treasury secretaries, Robert Rubin and Lawrence Summers, joined with Fed chairman Alan Greenspan to stave off the regulation of the very financial derivatives whose unlimited trading would eventually help bring down much of the financial system. By keeping easy money flowing through the 1990s, Greenspan allowed investment in technology to build to dangerous levels. Though he recognized the bubble in the making, he decided not to raise interest rates to choke it off, as some Fed governors urged. Indeed, he had dropped rates aggressively in the wake of the Asian and Russian crises. "People would stop me on the street and thank me for their 401(k)," Greenspan wrote in his memoir. He saw the run-up in stock prices as a gift from the market, one he had no intention of refusing.

Other economists, including Robert Shiller and the Nobel laureate Joseph Stiglitz, later criticized the policy, arguing that these low interest rates boosted the mania that gripped the markets. But Greenspan was relentless. "A stock market boom, of course, is an economic plus," he wrote. "It predisposes businesses to expand, makes consumers feel flush, and helps the economy to grow. Even a crash is not automatically bad. . . . Only when a collapsing market might threaten to hamstring the real economy is there cause for people like the treasury secretary and the chairman of the Fed to worry."

The crash that ended the tech bubble was indeed terrible. Once investors realized that too much easy money had nurtured more make-believe than real companies, the markets reversed course with a vengeance. The Nasdaq plummeted to 1,300 by August 2002—a drop of roughly three-fourths in a little more than two years. The pullback destroyed $8.5 trillion in stock market value. After the economy dropped into a recession in 2001, it shed more than 3 million jobs over two years.

In a historical context, the technology bubble was just another investment frenzy, the latest in a very long string tracing back to the tulip mania that seized the seventeenth-century Netherlands, where single bulbs sold for sums equivalent to thousands of dollars. "Financial and non-financial bubbles have been part of the history of capitalism," said Alan S. Blinder, a former vice chairman of the Federal Reserve and an economist at Princeton. "Market participants are manic-depressive. This is definitely not new, it's just extreme today."

But the technology bubble was especially costly to the American psyche. Past investment manias had mostly been restricted to the business elite—open only to those with land and capital sufficient to participate; the technology bubble assailed the broader economy. It hurt people invested through 401(k) retirement accounts, their futures tethered to markets gone manic. Between 2000 and 2002, the total value of retirement accounts shrank by one-third. Job losses spread far beyond the executive ranks enjoyed by people such as Bochner, punishing workers throughout the economy as demand for goods and services plummeted.

From 1993 to 1996, Greg Bailey, the Oakland truck driver, worked for a local seafood company, delivering fish to restaurants and markets for $9 an hour. The boom had trickled down to restaurants, giving households the wherewithal to buy crab legs and ahi tuna, and the company was having a hard time finding enough people. "They would literally hire you right off the street," Bailey said.

Then he found something with greater potential, driving a bobtail truck for an electrical and construction supply company. The starting pay was $12 an hour. Bailey delivered endless coils of fiber optics cables from warehouses in Oakland out to South San Francisco, where dot-com companies were setting up offices and wiring themselves to the rest of the Web. The jump in pay was enough to finally allow him to move into his own apartment—a one-bedroom place near Lake Merritt, in the center of Oakland, for $425 a month. He stayed at the company for four years, assuming that a greater payoff lay ahead: the bosses told Bailey and the other drivers that they would eventually vest in a 401(k) retirement plan and claim a share of the company's profits. "They told us that after five years, we would have a nest egg of forty thousand dollars," he said.

But the dot-coms began disappearing. Major Internet companies like WorldCom and AT&T began slowing their purchase of equipment as the realization took hold that too many cables were going down beneath the pavement. By 2000, Bailey's company was seeing business evaporate. The bosses changed their minds about creating the retirement plan. There wasn't enough profit left to share. Disgusted, and feeling cheated, Bailey and many of the others quit, heading into a suddenly lean job market without savings.

Among the crucial lessons of the New Economy was this: once investment make-believe succumbs to reality, it leads not to a state of normalcy but to a paralyzing state of cynicism. After the tech bubble burst, markets became consumed with fear of unknown risks. When investors finally figured out the dangers of betting the farm on the transformative story of the Internet, when they stopped buying the new forms of measurement and started demanding solemn old things, such as profit, they shunned the technology sector, for precisely the same reason it had once been so mesmerizing: no one could figure out how to value anything. It became impossible to sort out the hot air claims of analysts like Henry Blodget and frauds like WorldCom from the brilliant ideas and genuine opportunities that were clearly still there. For years, almost indiscriminately, the market starved technology companies of capital. As investment went into hibernation, the economy ground to a halt in 2001. More than an ordinary end to another ordinary business cycle, money recoiled as if in angry reaction to a con—a foretaste of the financial crisis that afflicted the nation again after the housing bubble burst. Even after the economy resumed growing in 2002, managers remained skittish and fearful of hiring.

"The economy never got its groove back after the tech bubble burst," said Mark Zandi, chief economist at Moody's Economy.com, speaking in 2008. "We're still feeling fallout from the collapse of the tech economy and the accounting scandals. There are still psychological scars for the managers affected. Managers are less interested in taking risks."

But one feature of the tech boom remained, lying dormant until money started moving again: the American willingness to buy into make-believe in the service of soaring economic spirits. Once investment dollars resumed flowing, they pumped up the largest, most perilous investment bubble in generations, making use of a thought even more wonderful than the promise of cyberspace—the enduring solidity of the American home.

4

Full Faith

"China has become banker to the United States."

As the ill fortunes of the technology bust pulled the American economy into a recession in 2001, sowing joblessness and austerity, the Federal Reserve once again dropped interest rates—this time with extraordinary dispatch and aggression. Seven times between January and August 2001, the Fed cut the so-called Federal Funds rate, taking its target down to 3.5 percent. After 9/11, as President Bush exhorted the nation to go out and spend, the Fed opened the credit taps wider still, taking the target rate down to 1 percent by the middle of 2003—the lowest level since 1958.

Low interest rates were directed at easing credit to make more money change hands. Once again, the strategy worked too well. Financial institutions began borrowing huge quantities of money and lending it out, particularly to developers, construction companies, real estate speculators, and home owners. By 2004, even people with poor credit and minimal income were receiving aggressive pitches for mortgages and home equity loans, bringing more and more buyers into the real estate market. Americans pulled swelling volumes of cash from their homes through second mortgages, and they distributed this money to retailers, restaurants, home furnishing dealers, and so on, building another virtuous cycle—but without the virtues of hard-earned wages. Interest rates remained below 2 percent, making mortgages easier and cheaper to obtain and fanning speculation.

Had the United States been any other country, the Fed never could have sustained this easy money policy. Americans were spending other people's money, and the numbers were growing astronomically. Since the mid-1980s, Americans had been buying extravagant volumes of imported products while selling much smaller quantities of American wares to the world. In 1987, American imports exceeded exports by more than $150 billion. By 2000, the trade deficit had ballooned to $422 billion. By the end of 2007, it exceeded $700 billion. Meanwhile, Americans availed themselves of low-interest credit cards alongside their lenient mortgages. Between 1984 and 2006, total U.S. household debt expanded from $1.9 trillion to $12.8 trillion. The financial system lending out all this money was itself using borrowed funds, with its debts swelling to $14.2 trillion by 2006.

Under the forces governing finance on the rest of the planet, this lopsided balance of trade and deepening debt should have made life tighter for Americans. It should have forced households to cut back on their spending and pare their debts or risk losing access to future credit. It should have pressured the Fed to lift interest rates—not lower them. Dollars were flowing out of the country and buying up currencies in other lands to purchase foreign goods. That tended to weaken the dollar and strengthen other currencies. And consumers were spending dollars they did not really have, applying downward pressure on the value of American money.

Money is but a piece of paper that society has collectively agreed holds value. That value depends upon belief in the integrity of the country printing the money and confidence in its ability to honor its debts. Until the 1970s, the value of a dollar was clearly determined: it was tied to gold. A dollar bill was an explicit promise from the U.S. government that it would, in theory anyway, hand over a defined quantity of gold in exchange for that piece of paper. When President Nixon broke with that standard in 1971, he ushered in an extraordinary expansion of credit. The government began creating dollars out of thin air, without reserving any additional gold against them. That made money abundant, increasing purchasing power. It also generated crippling inflation—rising prices for goods—as more dollars chased the same number of goods, a problem that required several years of painfully high interest rates to snuff out. Above all, it shifted the value of a dollar from something tied to a tangible commodity with intrinsic value to something that floated with the degree of confidence that the United States would be able to honor its debts.

Over the past two decades, the United States tested that confidence, continuing to ingest growing quantities of foreign-made goods without sending back American-made goods of equal value. Swelling household debt further increased the pressure on the dollar. If a friend kept asking you to pay his bills while handing you paper IOUs, you would eventually begin to question the value of that paper. Somewhere between a few dinner tabs and infinity lay a point at which you would conclude that your friend had neither the intention nor the ability to settle his debts. Then, those IOUs would seem like worthless pieces of paper, and you would refuse to accept more of them.

The American dollar faced similar pressures. As U.S. households sank deeper into debt and the trade balance widened, trading partners might have grown reluctant to keep accepting green pieces of paper embossed with portraits of dead U.S. presidents in exchange for demonstrably useful things such as oil, sneakers, and electronics. But the reverse happened. Not only did foreigners—particularly China—keep sending goods to American ports and taking dollars as payment, they went one better: they took the dollars they received for their goods and used them to finance the American debt, ensuring that Americans could keep spending. They purchased stunning quantities of government savings bonds. They bought so-called agency bonds, those sold by the government-sponsored mortgage giants Fannie Mae and Freddie Mac, which gave these institutions more money to buy more home loans from banks. That gave the banks more money to write fresh loans, while keeping interest rates low. Foreigners continued absorbing U.S. debt from 2001 right up through 2009—indeed, China dramatically accelerated its purchases—even as the Fed lowered interest rates, which lowered the return on investments held in dollars.

On its face, this defied economic logic. If the savings bank where you deposited your paycheck kept lowering its interest rates, you would eventually think about shifting to another bank with better rates to maximize the value of your money. China, faced with lower interest rates on U.S. savings bonds, might have been expected to begin putting more of its savings in investments priced in British pounds and euros to take advantage of higher interest rates elsewhere. But the Fed managed to drop interest rates, undermining the attractiveness of the dollar, even as the balance of trade worsened, without moderating China's hunger for American debt. This was possible because, for more than half a century, the United States has enjoyed a unique privilege in the global economy: the dollar has functioned as the world's reserve currency, the principal money used in most global commerce, from selling coffee in Kenya to paying Pakistani laborers erecting skyscrapers in Dubai. Come what may, Americans have been able to operate with assurance that foreigners will require dollars, allowing aggressive borrowing without fear of an unruly plunge in the value of the currency.

Since the mid-1980s, the world economy has been governed by a state of codependence. Foreigners have continued to buy American debt even as the trade deficit has expanded for the simple reason that no trading partner can afford the prospect that American consumers will stop spending. When Americans hit the mall to buy a pair of jeans, they are likely to drive there in a Japanese or European car, burning gasoline from Saudi Arabia or Venezuela. The jeans are likely made from cotton grown in India or Texas, the yarn spun in North Carolina or Guatemala, and the fabric stitched in China. The computerized inventory system through which the cashier records their purchase is perhaps the work of engineers in Silicon Valley or southern France, using chips fabricated in South Korea, Taiwan, or Malaysia. And the ship that carries the jeans to an American port was probably built in Japan, with steel smelted using iron ore mined in Brazil or Australia. So even as the Fed slashed interest rates and kept them low, making the dollar a less palatable variety of money to hold, foreign countries—particularly China—kept extending credit, cognizant that any other way risked shrinking demand for their goods.

China was hardly alone in its appetite for American debt. Japan was buying enormous sums, too. So was Saudi Arabia, folding the proceeds of its oil sales into investments counted in American dollars. But China was the fastest-growing—and soon-to-be largest—source of foreign capital. In 2000, China held less than $100 billion worth of U.S. Treasury bills and agency bonds, according to economist Brad Setser. By the middle of 2005, China's holdings exceeded $500 billion. By early 2009, China was reporting nearly $2 trillion in foreign exchange reserves—twice as much as Japan and four times the holdings of Russia and Saudi Arabia. By Setser's estimate, after factoring in the full portfolios of China's central bank, the People's Bank of China, plus those of state banks and China's so-called sovereign wealth fund, which invested money overseas, the real value of China's reserves was $2.3 trillion. Setser said that some 65 percent, roughly $1.6 trillion, was invested in dollar assets.

This dynamic lay at the very center of the global economy, an arrangement the financial historian Niall Ferguson dubbed "Chimerica," for China plus America, describing a virtual country that held one-fourth of the world's population, generated a third of all economic output, and was responsible for more than half of all the growth in the global economy since 2000. This odd "joint venture" served the interests of both countries, allowing both to put off hard policy choices. By plowing the proceeds of its exports into American debt, China ensured that Americans retained the wherewithal to buy increasing volumes of Chinese-made products, guaranteeing employment for tens of millions of people in its multiplying coastal factories. China's purchases of dollars also kept its currency, the yuan, weak relative to the dollar, which kept Chinese-made goods cheap on world markets. By gorging on inexpensive Chinese goods and Chinese credit, Americans found yet another way to preserve their living standards in the face of declining incomes. "In effect," writes Ferguson, "the People's Republic of China has become banker to the United States of America."

If there is one thing Americans have learned from the experience of recent years, it is this: we would do well to gain a deeper understanding of our banker. Much to the nation's detriment, we did not grasp the bizarre machinations that made it profitable for the corner mortgage broker and Wall Street alike to trade in loans made to people who clearly could not afford to buy their homes. China is indeed America's banker and its capital has only grown more crucial in recent years, as the financial crisis has intensified, and as the American economy has sunk deeper into the worst downturn in generations.

The surge of capital from China helped explain why Fran Barbaro kept getting offers from banks to extend new loans against her Boston area home, even as her monthly payments climbed. It explained why her house was worth nearly $1 million by 2006, allowing her to pull money from it much the same way she had once turned her Cisco Systems stock into cash. Money from China was the bedrock reality that would soon enable Willie Gonzalez to become a home owner again, despite his fluctuating income and his itinerant lifestyle. The great influx of capital from China explained the construction boom that would unfold from the gold coast of Florida to the empty desert east of Los Angeles. It explained how American real estate would come to be bought and sold much as dot-com stocks had changed hands in the previous decade. Because China was saving and investing in the United States, Americans felt little compulsion to save at all.

When President Obama took office in January 2009 and swiftly crafted a plan to spend $800 billion by 2011, there was little mystery where the money would come from: the Treasury would have to sell fresh bonds, and many would be purchased by China. Still, it was hard to see how this arrangement could continue forever. How could Americans continue to live in excess of their incomes while importing far more than they exported? Why would China keep taking the winnings from its export trade and investing them in the richest country in history? Why would Beijing in essence direct the national savings toward renovating rich Americans' homes instead of replacing the grimy apartment blocks of its own cities?

These questions have only intensified as the sums involved have grown, and as China has begun to send signals that it may diversify its foreign exchange holdings, taking a little of the money it has been spending on dollar investments and directing it instead into other currencies such as the Japanese yen and the euro. The endurance of Chimerica weighs as one of the great uncertainties hanging over the global economy. If China were to moderate its purchases of American debt even a little, that would likely push up interest rates in the United States while pushing down the value of the dollar and increasing the cost of imports. And if China's appetite for the dollar were to wane considerably, that could prompt other holders of dollar assets to dump them, putting more downward pressure on the American currency, while diminishing American spending.

In myriad and meaningful ways, American economic fate remains dependent on the continued willingness of China to invest in the United States. Yet the American understanding of China—a huge and complex country with its own pressures—has been superficial at best, leaving the United States vulnerable to an unexpected change in the relationship.

Whatever policy makers do from here, they would be wise to understand China more fully than they understood Bear Stearns, Lehman Brothers, and the other names now etched on the memorial stones of Wall Street.

∽

As Americans pulled away from the wreckage of the tech bubble and re-linquished reverence for Silicon Valley, a new thing occupied the attention of the business set: a fascination with China as a transformative force in the global economy, capturing the attention of academic journals and investor conferences. The same business magazines that only a couple years earlier had trumpeted the world-altering genius of technology companies shifted their attention to China. "Get ready for the biggest coming-out party in the history of capitalism," declared a 2001 *Fortune* story about China's admission to the World Trade Organization, which opened new markets to Chinese goods and opened Chinese markets to foreign entrants. "It's all made in China now," the magazine announced the following year, bestowing a shopworn title on the country—"workshop of the world." "No country plays the world economic game better than China," asserted journalist Ted Fishman at the outset of his 2005 bestseller, *China Inc.*, in which he confirmed the emergence of a new superpower. "No other country shocks the global economic hierarchy like China."

In the story being told in corporate board rooms and government offices, union halls and university campuses, China was awakening from a long, self-imposed slumber. It was turning its back on its once-fervent ideological commitment to peasant-led revolution and embracing the revolution of globalization, tying the fortunes of its people to the vagaries of trade. The consequences of this shift were far-reaching. Suddenly, a new appetite was showing up at the world's table, demanding the building blocks of modern industry—iron ore to feed its smelters, oil to power a growing fleet of cars, and coal to generate electricity—raising the prices for each of these commodities along with the price of shipping. A country that had intentionally bottled up its industrial might under the reign of Chairman Mao was unleashing it upon the world.

Workers from Detroit to Milan decried the impossibility of hanging on to their jobs in a global market dominated by China, with its hundreds of millions of peasants eager for factory work. Manufacturers claimed China was manipulating the yuan, keeping it priced too low against the euro and other currencies to make its goods unfairly cheap. Factories from the United States to Sri Lanka complained that they were being squeezed by their customers to produce at "the China price," a term that had become synonymous with "the lowest price possible."

A simplistic tendency to treat China as a monolith colored many accounts, describing a country whose ruling Communist Party never had to answer to public opinion or balance competing domestic interests. Portrayals by American and European journalists and policy makers too often traded in cartoonish caricatures, as if China were a giant gulag where oppressed peasants toiled robotically in fear of Big Brother, a single-minded commercial machine intent on capturing every world market, or a land ruled by a singularly crass materialism. Fear of China was taking on momentum, altering politics in many countries by feeding and reinforcing a generalized backlash against globalization, one laced with a thinly veiled Yellow Peril cant: the indefatigable and ruthless Chinese would prosper at the expense of everyone else. What these portrayals all had in common was the assumption that China's ascendance was a fait accompli. China was indomitable, a natural superpower, a giant emerging from its strictures in a development that was rewriting history.

When I moved to Shanghai to track China's economic ascent for the *Washington Post* in 2002, it seemed as if the New Economy hadn't really died, but merely shifted venues across the Pacific, gaining new props with which to spin tales of another limitless future. Much as Ariba had sold the idea that its network would collect a tiny piece of all business transactions, the multinationals pouring into China—including Citibank, General Motors, Kodak, and Motorola—aimed to prosper by snagging just a small slice of what was potentially 1.3 billion mouths waiting to eat KFC chicken, 2.6 billion feet ready to wear Nike sneakers, and who knew how many teeth available for brushing with Colgate toothpaste. But China's real power was as a manufacturer. China was "absolutely center stage," pronounced the worldwide director of McKinsey, the ubiquitous business consulting company. Walmart alone was buying $15 billion worth of goods a year from Chinese factories, a sign of a world sloping precipitously toward the Middle Kingdom. Indeed, Walmart—with its imperial requirement that any company wanting its business set up an office in its home base in Arkansas—soon located a global procurement center in the southern Chinese boomtown of Shenzhen.

Having just watched one purportedly unprecedented bit of history end in disaster back in the United States as a technology reporter, I was suspicious of the whole conversation. I had seen one Neverland of endless riches exposed as fantasy. As obsession with China mounted, as foreign investment flooded in along with the usual lineup of supporting actors—Wall Street investment bankers, public relations people, dubious analysts, and consultants—I was inclined to try to poke holes in the story. Yet, much like anyone who has traveled in China in recent years, I was amazed by what I saw, the scale and pace of the development. A massive public works campaign was under way, revamping boulevards and public squares in every city and extending rail lines to distant places in a fashion reminiscent of the development of the American frontier. A network of freeways virtually indistinguishable from those in the United States or Europe now linked most of the country. Every provincial capital had—or was in the process of gaining—a new airport. Every coastal city teemed with manufacturing. On the Yangtze River, the Three Gorges Dam, the largest engineering project on earth, signaled that the same cultural ambitions that had erected the Great Wall were still at work. From these vantage points, the story of China's indomitable rise seemed genuine.

China's exports—the source of cash that Beijing was sending back to the United States—was building with seemingly unstoppable momentum. Between 2001 and 2004, China's exports of merchandise more than doubled, expanding from $266 billion to nearly $600 billion. Over the next three years, exports expanded at a better than 25 percent annual clip, exceeding $1.4 trillion by the end of 2008. Exports specifically to the United States grew from $54 billion in 2001 to $252 billion in 2008. China had entire cities geared to dominate global production of certain products—an underwear city, a sock city, a belt city. The organization of these localities centered on amassing the raw materials, the machinery, the labor, the capital, and the know-how to produce at a scale surpassing that of any other competitor on the globe. The country's conspicuous lack of labor and environmental standards, its willingness to steal intellectual property and funnel capital to the most politically connected companies, and the enormity of its population supplied advantages.

In a cavernous factory in the southern Chinese city of Shunde, in Guangdong province, eighteen thousand workers labored for about $6 a day, making microwave ovens destined for the United States, Europe, and other countries around the world. Workers manufactured some forty thousand ovens a day in 2003. In less than a decade, the company running the factory, Guangdong Galanz Enterprise Group, had expanded from a niche maker of household appliances into the largest manufacturer of microwaves on earth, turning out 15 million a year. Galanz made these goods under contract for eighty-eight distinct worldwide brands and, increasingly, under its own name, exporting two-thirds of its production.

Galanz was just one prominent piece of Shunde, a gritty city of about 1 million people whose smokestacks seemed to expand by the day into the surrounding rice paddies. By 2003, the city held 100,000 factories, according to local estimates. They ranged from tiny operations tucked into homes, where families stitched clothing under bare bulbs hanging from the ceiling, to enormous modern combines with first-rate machinery imported from Germany and Japan, such as the plant Galanz operated on the banks of the Xijiao River. Shunde was one of dozens of industrial cities stretching for hundreds of miles in Guangdong province, which had become one of China's most important production centers. Highways teemed with trucks hauling coils of steel, molded plastic, drums of chemicals, and boxes of finished goods, on their way to ports. At every hour of the day, workers labored amid the ceaseless din of pounding metal, the whine of saw blades and the whir of sewing machines, producing T-shirts, stereo cabinets, laptop computers, basketball shoes, baby strollers—seemingly everything the world might buy.

Guangdong was at once inspiring and horrifying, compelling and repellent, promising and sleazy. Above all, it was vivid. Migrant workers were streaming into its cities from every poor, rural hinterland. They emerged from buses and train stations with meager belongings piled into buckets slung from poles across their shoulders or stuffed into plastic sacks, then headed to the factories where they could earn cash to send home to their villages. It was a pilgrimage laced with desperation and opportunism. Workers lived in factory dormitory blocks stuffed eight and ten to a room, sharing reeking toilets with fifty others. They were frequently cheated out of wages, robbed of their earnings, or injured in unsafe working conditions. Yet the earnings they sent home enabled children to stay in school and parents to seek medical care. The horizons of every city in Guangdong—and many other provinces, for that matter—were filling with new villas and high-rise apartments for the factory bosses and the Communist Party officials who handed over access to land and arranged the state financing that was bringing industry to life. High-end Cantonese restaurants with marble lobbies, grand pianos, and Hong Kong chefs beckoned this growing population of nouveaux riches. Five-star hotels glimmered in the center of every city, the headquarters for the foreign businessmen streaming in for a piece of the action. Prostitutes brazenly patrolled the pavement outside, and sometimes even the hallways and elevators inside. At markets and street stalls, petty merchants hawked fake luxury handbags, polo shirts, and watches as well as pirated copies of the latest Hollywood movies. Navigating streets choked with cars, bicycle rickshaws ferried charcoal, plumbing supplies, and live chickens past shopping malls full of designer fashions.

In Zhejiang province, south of Shanghai, a grubby city called Shengzhou had eclipsed Italy as the origin for most of the world's neckties. "Italy has so many famous brands, but they are increasingly made in China," Lou Yuming, the general manager of Zhejiang Jintiande Necktie Group Company boasted in the winter of 2003. Five years earlier, he had taken his first scouting trip to Como, a city of handsome brick houses on stone streets in the lake country of northern Italy. Back then, Shengzhou had only eight computer-controlled looms capable of generating neckties in large-scale production. Since then, the number had swelled to 672, more than doubling Como's stock. Some fifty thousand people were working in Shengzhou's roughly three hundred factories, producing 200 million neckties a year—more than three-fourths of all those sold in the world, according to the Shengzhou Necktie Industry Association.

Where workers in the factories of northern Italy were paid $1,800 a month, their counterparts in Shengzhou were making less than that in a full year. This equation made it possible to churn out neckties destined for store shelves in Los Angeles, Lima, and London for as little as $2 each. Companies in Shengzhou were also able to exploit the power of popular consumer brands without paying licensing fees. In Zhejiang Jintiande's showroom, a manager brazenly laid out ties with Yves Saint Laurent labels, though the plant had no commercial relationship with the French designer. This was technically illegal, yet unofficially tolerated by the Chinese government, which tended not to enforce trademark violations.

The American celebration of Christmas had become a largely Made-in-China affair, from the toys and electronics wrapped in Chinese-made wrapping paper to the ornaments and the trees themselves. By the end of 2003, three of every four artificial trees sold in the United States were produced in the city of Shenzhen and its environs in Guangdong, according to the Shenzhen Arts and Crafts Industry Association. At the Shuitou Company factory near Shenzhen, peasants from across interior China spent their days squatting in front of hissing machinery as they melted chips into moldable plastic and pulled levers that shaped the fluid mass into Christmas ornaments. Women sat barefoot on empty cardboard packing tubes, knives in hand, shaving extra bits of plastic from the finished products before depositing them in an oil drum. Two dozen men fed spools of green plastic into machines that stretched them along conveyors and creased them around a wire and then sliced them into fringes, yielding branches for artificial Christmas trees. Other men fused the branches together, jamming them with their bare hands into the center of a spinning rotor.

China's rise into an export power—generating the finance that was filling American closets with clothes, American living rooms with electronics and furniture, and American wallets with credit cards—rested upon one of the great mass migrations in human history. In parts of Jiangxi province, a major source of laborers for the factories of the coast, virtually everyone from age sixteen to fifty-five was gone for at least half of the year. "My son refuses to call me mother," said Li Meilan, who had left her five-year-old boy behind in Jiangxi with her mother-in-law for most of his life while she and her husband ran a small business in Guangdong. "He calls me 'older sister,' and he says, 'You're not my mother.' It's a very bad feeling." Overall, 150 million Chinese peasants have streamed toward the cities in recent years. These are the people whose labors generated the cash to finance Americans' easy money.

෴

More than the ceaseless march of rural people explained China's breakneck growth and the money it was investing in the United States. A nation that had only recently branded the profit motive as counterrevolutionary was freeing up ordinary Chinese to engage in commerce. It was a hybrid form of capitalism shaped by corruption and state interference; yet some areas of the economy were increasingly open, competitive, and freewheeling.

In Wuhan, a major port city on the Yangtze River that is sometimes likened to Chicago for its strategic position in the center of the country, the textile industry was largely defined by private enterprise. Dolucky Knitwear, whose low, cramped factory was tucked into a quiet, residential area, was a typical exponent of the evolution that had taken place. The factory was overseen by an affable, energetic man named Li Suiming, who had begun working there in the mid-1980s, spending his days hunched over a sewing machine, and his nights in the factory dorm. Twenty years later, Li was the majority shareholder and general manager. His factory was already exporting throughout Asia. In 2004, he set his sights on the biggest market of them all: the United States.

Rail thin and short, Li had begun working at what was then known as the Wuhan Number One Knit Mill, one of hundreds of money-losing state-owned factories in the city. In those days, profit was not in the lexicon. The factory paid everyone about $3.50 a month and the workers made only what central planners dictated: one-size-fits-all, scratchy cotton underwear, the trousers too long for most people, and the tops too short, all of it in a single generic color—navy blue. "What they made was not what the market wanted," Li said. "The product hadn't changed in decades. It was a really old-fashioned color, and the design wasn't at all comfortable to wear. The quality was really lousy."

Li was full of ideas about how to improve the product. His father had been a university graduate, and he himself had nearly completed a specialized trade school in textiles in the mid-1960s, before his studies were cut short by the outbreak of the Cultural Revolution. In the 1980s, as Deng Xiaoping freed the factories in the coastal provinces to experiment with capitalism, Li examined the new types of imported underwear hanging at street markets set up in the alleyways of Wuhan. They were coming in by ship from Shanghai, and by truck and rail from Hong Kong, in an array of colors and in softer materials. "I had the sense that I could make better underwear," he said.

By 1993, the state lifted price controls for many goods—underwear included. Managers became more accountable for their balance sheets. The manager at Dolucky faced a tough situation. The factory was then losing about $120,000 a year. It was subsisting, as most state firms did, on fresh loans from a state-owned bank, the Industrial and Commercial Bank of China. Li offered a proposal that had previously been unthinkable in Wuhan: he approached the managers with a plan to lease an idled production line, with the right to employ the workers as he saw fit. He would hand over 30 percent of the profits to the state managers, and he would hire forty workers laid off from other textile plants. The managers agreed, delighted that part of the failing factory was now someone else's problem, and particularly keen to generate jobs at a time when unemployment was threatening social peace. Over subsequent years, Li took over more and more of the factory, until the whole operation was his.

The first year, Li made men's and ladies' cotton briefs, purely for the domestic market. With no budget to buy fabric, he relied purely on scraps generated by the rest of the factory. But even a slight improvement in the design and the production of varying sizes revealed a great untapped demand for more comfortable undergarments among the people of Wuhan. "There were not so many choices then," he recalled. "If you offered something just a little bit more appealing and at an attractive price, it was easy to sell all your production immediately." Still, he could not reliably get hold of enough scraps from the factory, and he found himself idling production while he waited for more. Upgrading the product with better fabrics required finance. Li employed a connection. His wife's sister worked at the Agricultural Bank of China, a state-owned giant. In 1994, she helped secure a loan for nearly $6,000. He bought woven cotton from a local producer, dramatically improving his product. By 1995, he was earning nearly $4,000 a year.

That same year, a Chinese trading company approached him about making goods for export. He sent a shipment of pajamas to Germany, then another to Belgium. He took on the name Dolucky, the Roman letters lending his product what seemed to him an air of international sophistication. By 1997, Li was exporting nearly three-fourths of his product. By 2004, his entire production was being shipped overseas, and Dolucky was racking up about $3 million in sales.

By then, Li had traded in his bicycle for a new Peugeot sedan. The factory dorm was a memory. He and his wife and son occupied a new apartment in a high-rise looking out over the sprawling city. He had spent about $60,000 improving the factory's machinery. Still, his office remained a monument to thrift, with no air-conditioning to cut the furnacelike summer heat, and an old ceiling fan buzzing loudly. The walls were bare save for a calendar. The primary piece of office furniture was a bench seat scavenged from a passenger van.

In the fall of 2004, Li and his staff set up a booth at a manufacturing fair in Guangzhou to try to attract American buyers. There, they met the president of an American label known as Omega Apparel, who ran his hands over the polo shirts on display and asked for a price—about $2.60 each. In December, Omega placed its first order. In the spring of 2005, a container full of eighteen thousand polo shirts sat atop a cargo ship making its way from the port of Shanghai toward the United States, adding to China's prodigious balance of trade and its growing pile of U.S. investments and dollars.

∽

Why was China taking those dollars and sending them far away, to the U.S. Treasury? Among the key reasons was concern among China's leaders that too much money coursing through the country's economy was exacerbating often corrupt deal-making, fueling increasingly violent public protests.

By the early years of the twenty-first century, the Communist Party's continued nominal allegiance to the prescriptions of Karl Marx seemed almost comical. In Shanghai, the old houses surrounding the party's first meeting place had been torn down to make way for one of Asia's glitziest shopping areas, New Horizons, where well-heeled throngs surrendered stacks of money emblazoned with the smiling visage of Chairman Mao in exchange for crystal martini glasses and Italian lingerie. Cadillac sedans were being manufactured on Chinese soil. In this worker's paradise, nothing could get a peasant thrown in jail faster than attempting to organize a labor union.

With the market relegated to the center of Chinese life, the party's claims to legitimacy rested on two things: nationalism and a drive to elevate living standards. The party was generally succeeding on both scores, and yet the rottenness that defined its exercise of power dominated its image with much of the public. So much development was clearly crooked and tied up in the exercise of state power that a social chasm divided those connected to the party, and those on the outside. As party leaders knew clearly, they had themselves claimed power more than a half century earlier by exploiting a similar class cleavage, riding disgust with the corruption of the nationalist party. Revulsion with corruption had been a major factor in attracting students to the demonstrations in Tiananmen Square in 1989, the last significant challenge to the party's rule. "If we do not fight economic crimes and corruption, we will disappoint the people," China's president Jiang Zemin had declared in 1999. "Serious social disturbance could then arise, and the possibility that people will rise and strike us down cannot be ruled out."

By 2003, much of China's wealth seemed to be coming at the direct expense of its poorest people. In every city and in every village, one encountered stories of developers who had used relationships with officials to clear land for their projects without paying legal compensation. Among the displaced, resentments were boiling over. Peasants were organizing to challenge the seizure of their land. Factory workers were mobilizing to challenge layoffs as managers took control of state-owned companies and shut them down to sell off the pieces at personal profit. Three million people attended seventy thousand protests in 2004, in the midst of China's swift growth, more than eight times the number of a decade earlier. Paramilitary troops were often required to restore order, descending into often-bloody standoffs between peasants and local police.

One particular case brought this home. In early 2002, in Fawang, a village in the northeastern province of Shandong, residents heard an astonishing message over the public address system: the Yancheng town government, which held sway over the area, had allocated the local fields for a golf course. The villagers would no longer be allowed to plant their crops.

Wang Jijing had spent all of his fifty-seven years in Fawang, a loose grid of earthen lanes lined with mud-brick houses, most of them enfolding courtyards, in the center of the fertile Yellow River valley. He and his wife and their two sons, plus their wives and his three grandchildren, all depended on the local farmland for their sustenance. Outside of planting and harvesting seasons, the men journeyed to the city of Jinan, a two-hour bus ride away, to work in construction or to wash dishes in restaurants, earning cash needed to buy clothing, keep the grandchildren in school, and prepare for run-of-the-mill crises.

Wang's household of nine people subsisted on about $2,500 per year, plus whatever food they could coax from their soil. Their land was the insurance policy that allowed the men to leave in search of more. It was less than three acres, but it was under their direct control, the cash from the crops it produced theirs and theirs alone. They planted wheat in the winter months and corn and melons the rest of the year. Now, the land was being stripped from them so rich people could come hit little white balls across the soil. "We just didn't understand what to do, what to make of it," Wang told me two years after the news, as he leaned against the brick wall of a neighbor's house and sat on his haunches. He wore a gray turtleneck sweater and a frayed blue work coat. Wrinkles formed across his forehead as he squinted into a glaring March sun. "We're ordinary people," he said. "We don't know the laws. We don't know whether this is proper or not. I thought, 'No money? No land? How can we live?'"

The first thing the villagers did was protest to the township government, oblivious to the reality that the officials had themselves been given equity stakes in the project by the Beijing-based developer. Township officials told them the matter had been decided at much higher levels, and there was nothing to be done. So nine villagers boarded a bus for Jinan, the provincial capital, where they managed to locate the Ministry of Land and Resources. A sympathetic official there promised to stay the project for at least long enough to allow them to harvest their crop. They also extracted a promise for compensation—about $350 annually per family for the next five years. They got the first payment in September 2002. "Satisfied? Are we satisfied?" Wang considered the question as if asked to comment on whether night and day had been justly apportioned. "We're ordinary people. We have no other options. We are at the mercy of the government."

In June 2003, officials from Qihe County attended a groundbreaking ceremony for Guoke International Golf Villas, each one carting away a new color television set as a gift, the villagers recalled. The next day, the tractors returned along with bulldozers, hacking away at the remaining wheat and leveling the land. Nine villagers traveled to Beijing to demand an investigation. Other villagers visited Beijing three times more during 2003. But each journey proved futile. They waited for hours outside government offices for an audience, each time receiving the same dispiriting word: go back to the province and take up the matter there. What the villagers had little way of knowing was that the developer had the highest backing of the provincial government. Officials had aggressively courted Guoke's president as part of a campaign to boost the local economy. The party secretary of Qihe County had been among the most forceful proponents of the local development campaign, dispensing 2.5 acres of land to any developer willing to sink $375,000 or more into a project in the area. By the year the golf course arrived, the county had attracted some $12 million in investment from fourteen different projects.

The golf course development included 215 villas with marble floors, crystal chandeliers, and private lawns behind white picket fencing. Alongside the villas and the golf course, the plans called for a three-hundred-room five-star hotel with a spa. The first phase of construction alone would cost $225 million. Subsequent phases were to add another 585 villas.

Nobody outside the players themselves knew what Guoke had paid for the land, but it certainly wasn't much. "Of course the price was not very high," said the head of sales at the villa compound, Jin Hao. "The local government gave us the land as a way to attract capital."

With the project seemingly unstoppable, Wang's family opted to extract from it what they could: Wang's son, Wang Guangwu, started working for the construction company. In place of growing wheat and melons, he would turn it into fairways. He was supposed to be paid upon the completion of each villa. But several months later, with dozens of houses completed, Wang and many of the other workers had yet to receive anything. When they complained to the construction boss, he offered only vague promises. So, in January 2004, Wang Guangwu and nine other men took the bus to the county seat and complained to land bureau officials. The government's response was swift: the men were all arrested and lodged in the county jail without being formally charged. "They won't say what he did," said Wang Guangwu's wife in March 2004, then tending to her two children alone. "They won't even let me see him." She fell to the ground and wept.

On the other side of the brick wall separating the village from its former fields, an alternate universe had taken shape. Some 415 villas stood on lanes named after seasons and trees and constellations, many of them dotted with cypress trees, around the completed eighteen-hole golf course. They were fronted by Roman columns and patches of lawn, the landscape strewn with statues of rabbits, cactus, and mushrooms. A bronze statue sat in a still pool of water—a busty woman, naked save for a tunic reaching below her belly button. A black Audi sedan with military license plates pulled beneath the archway as the security guards stepped smartly aside. A Buick sedan followed closely behind, disgorging local officials. They stood in the driveway in their black suits, changing into white leather golf shoes.

On his side of the fence, Wang stood in his courtyard, where black rubber galoshes lay in the dirt, next to an aluminum pot with leftover rice. A rusty bicycle sat propped up against the red bricks of his house. He wondered what his family would do to support itself when the compensation money ran out. He wondered when his son would be let out of jail. He wondered what there was to do for a fifty-seven-year-old man who had lived through Chairman Mao and the Great Leap Forward, the Cultural Revolution, and now this—a strange new era in which men in suits and tasseled golf shoes rode electric carts across what had been his wheat field.

"I'm already so old," Wang said. "What am I supposed to do, get a part-time job? Nobody will want me. What can I do? Looking at these houses, I feel like my life has no future."

The struggles of people like Wang were not lost on China's leaders, who were increasingly keen on stamping out corruption before it devoured the country along with whatever shred of legitimacy remained for the party. As corrupt deal-making turned Chinese fields into fairways, sowing social strife, China's leaders felt greater compulsion to send the country's national savings far away.

❦

Yet, even worse than peasants like the Wangs losing their land was the prospect that no jobs would await them on their inevitable march to the city. Sending finance across the Pacific, which enabled Americans to keep buying Chinese goods, helped generate that work. So did the development projects that were displacing peasants.

So rice paddies kept getting turned into factories throughout Guangdong, other coastal provinces, and increasingly the interior. Wheat fields were transformed into fairways and office parks. The muddy banks of the Huangpu River in Shanghai sprouted more skyscrapers.

The only real losers were the ultimate source of the capital—the Chinese public whose savings stocked the state banks that were directly on the hook for the loans to local developers. Because China's stock and bond markets were in their infancy, bank loans were the dominant source of finance for businesses.

The central government was well aware of the danger. China's supreme leaders talked openly of the need to reform state banks by holding them accountable to the bottom line lest they squander too much capital and trigger a crisis. China's former premier, Zhu Rongji, told the National People's Congress in 2003 that the government had to be "extra careful about the rapid increase of investment in real estate." The year before, a fresh $95 billion had surged into property. Overall, the country's banks had about one-tenth of their $1.6 trillion in outstanding loans tied up in real estate. If things went bad—if too many towers remained unsold—China's banks would confront heavy losses.

In the city of Shenzhen, a full-blown real estate frenzy was under way, fueled by available finance and a reach for opulence. SEASIDE LIFESTYLE, proclaimed a sign at the entrance to Paradiso, a complex of eleven high-rise towers still being erected that was to have two thousand–plus apartments, as well as restaurants, tennis courts, and a clubhouse. On the thirty-third floor of one tower, a penthouse was on offer for $450,000, boasting tropical hardwood floors and marble bathrooms. Palm trees fringed the swimming pool downstairs, and elephant statues stood guard over the Jacuzzi. In the adjacent spa, orchids floated in ceramic bowls. So much luxury, looking out on the South China Sea.

The trouble was the view in the opposite direction, toward the rest of the city. The horizons were crammed with half-built towers draped in scaffolding and banners promising cheap finance. In the Futian district, a veritable Manhattan's worth of real estate was going up in one shot. Investment was being propelled by a $2.4 billion plan to turn the area into a fresh urban center, with a new city hall, the largest exhibition space in all of Asia, and an enormous shopping mall. Already, the market was showing signs of extreme overbuilding. Nationally, more than a quarter of all office space was vacant and prices were beginning to fall. Nearly one-fifth of the housing stock was unoccupied.

The developer of the Paradiso, the China Vanke Group, was increasingly bothered by the glut coming on the market. "There is a tendency toward a bubble if the central government doesn't take steps to cool off the economy," said Vanke's chairman, Wang Shi, during an interview at the company's headquarters. "If the current problem cannot be solved properly, then there is risk this will lead to very, very serious problems later on."

History was not comforting. In the early 1990s, China had suffered a disastrous real estate bubble that caused several lenders to collapse when overbuilding caused prices to plummet. And real estate investment had been at the center of the Asian financial crisis of 1997 and 1998. "Financial reform is the most difficult and the most crucial part of our overall economic reforms," Premier Wen Jiabao said. "As is known to all, the financial sector in China has been plagued by many problems. The biggest problem is the fairly high proportion of nonperforming loans from banks. There exists significant risk."

Month after month, directives were issued to the banks that they take a closer look at the real estate projects they were backing; that they scrutinize the credit of the buyers signing off on the mortgages. Yet the boom went on, largely unhindered, adding more vacant properties to the expanding metropolis of Shenzhen. For the local developers and the local officials at the branches of the state banks, the boom was simply too lucrative, even as it increased the overall strains on the Chinese financial system. "Every compound has lots of empty units," said Zhou Xiaohua, a real estate agent. At one complex, City's Elite Homestead, a saleswoman scoffed at the suggestion that the banks were tightening up and being more selective about their lending. "Basically, anyone can get a loan," she said. "If we introduce you to the bank, you can get a loan. It's fair for everyone. It's just a formality."

China's central bank, the People's Bank of China, had no power to fully alter this dynamic. It did not run the country. It did not even run economic policy. Directives from the central government were frequently ignored by state and local governments that pursued their own interests. But the central bank did have great influence over one crucial area. It decided what happened to most of the money that China collected from its exports.

჻

China was booming in large part because its companies were making huge volumes of products desired by consumers around the world. The private sector was taking root, even as it contended with the built-in advantages of state-owned companies and a potential real estate glut. But naive foreign investors were prone to getting fleeced by upstart Chinese companies, and if enough returned home with bad experiences, that could dissuade future comers, lessening economic growth. The banks lent so indiscriminately that one could not discount the possibility of a financial crisis, despite China's enormous hoard of foreign exchange reserves. Crippling electrical shortages in much of the country forced factories to shut down during peak hours. China clearly had a homegrown need for capital.

Yet these growing pains of development were part of what motivated the people in control of China's economy to invest so much of the nation's savings overseas. China had to buy larger and larger volumes of dollars to manage its exchange rate, keeping the yuan at a low value compared to the euro and other Asian currencies as a boost to its exports. These purchases amounted to a cautious form of financial management. In a society still short on capital, Beijing was intent on preserving what it had.

China's rapid development and trappings of wealth were concentrated in discrete areas, and they were the product of a highly unstable form of capitalism, built on often corrupt deal-making and personal relationships, that lent itself to precipitous booms and busts. Recent growth had been fueled by surges of foreign investment into places like Guangdong and the industrial zones around Shanghai. China's leaders had seen how quickly foreign investors abandoned the region in the Asian financial crisis of the late 1990s. No one could be sure how long the good times would last. The success of companies like Galanz and Dolucky had increased calls for protective tariffs against Chinese goods from Washington to Brussels. If a trade war broke out and large markets suddenly began turning away Chinese products, that would throw people out of work in Shunde and Shenzhen and many other factory towns. China's recent history had delivered the message that awful times could sweep in quickly, so China amassed its pile of dollars as security. "I know very well how uneven our development has been," Premier Wen Jiabao said in the fall of 2003. "Yes, it is true that in the coastal areas in the east, skyscrapers overwhelm you. However, in large areas of the countryside, people are still living in shabby houses with thatch roofs and still use oxen to till the land. Thirty million people are still below the poverty line." He employed an analogy to describe the potential impacts of this growing gap between rich and poor, one that hardly spoke of supreme confidence in the future: "It's like a human being who has one long leg and one short leg. If one leg is longer than the other, this person is bound to stumble and fall. And a country with one leg longer than the other will also stumble and fall."

On some evenings in Shanghai, I strolled along the Huangpu River, which divides the city in two. The original districts stretched westward. On the eastern bank, a new city had taken shape—a sprawling empire of factories, office towers, and exclusive suburban-style villas, many with swimming pools and golf courses and placards on their front entrances bearing names such as Oasis Garden and Richgate. Barges piled high with coal slipped up the black waters of the river, one after the other, in a silent, ceaseless procession. Deck hands leaned back against iron railings as their laundry flapped in the breeze behind them, taking in the sight of the nightscape unfolding ahead—high-rises bedecked with video billboards touting cell phones and financial services; streets choked with cars; nightclub balconies pulsating with light. On the eastern river bank, where a financial center had come to occupy what had been muddy farmland barely a decade earlier, Chinese tourists posed for snapshots in front of the Pearl Tower—a pair of pink orbs skewered by a futuristic television antenna rising higher than the Empire State Building.

In a sense, Shanghai and its famed riverfront amounted to a meticulously crafted display piece for the world, forged by its overseers to elicit a sense of awe, cementing the reality that China had arrived as a modern power. It spoke of how China would not be held back; that it was open for business and a land to be reckoned with.

But the Shanghai nightscape was a false billboard. It announced that the city was a modern financial center, yet China's leaders themselves did not fully believe its message. They were cognizant of the corruption that—far from merely infecting Chinese business—often seemed like the very fabric of commerce. Major projects, including many of the skyscrapers visible from the Shanghai waterfront, were constructed with a hefty dose of finance from state banks, the loans procured with the aid of local party officials who shared a cut. Land use permits often required bribes, as foreign investors who had erected joint ventures with Chinese companies routinely acknowledged (so long as you kept their names out of print). Sometimes, this meant cash payments. Other times, it meant generous gifts given to the daughter of a party official at her wedding, or a getaway to Hong Kong or the casinos of Macao for an official and his mistress. Many of the towers crowning Shanghai were money losers, the bank loans never repaid. Projects often came into being purely as excuses to make money change hands so well-positioned fingers could extract some. In the sort of capitalism that had been operative in China over the last two decades, profit need not result for a deal to make abundant economic sense for nearly everyone involved. This mode of business had left China's banks with a trove of bad loans estimated to reach some $500 billion by 2003.

"Certain power-concentrated, capital-intensive, lucrative and highly competitive sectors are often ridden with corruption," acknowledged Wang Zhenchuan, deputy procurator general of a Chinese government agency tasked with cracking down on corruption, in an extraordinarily candid interview with the Chinese financial magazine *Caijing*. "Certain key positions have become corruption disaster areas. As in recent years, many directors and deputy directors of local transportation departments have been under investigation for bribery. Many officials in urban planning and construction areas are found guilty of bribery, too, including those heading local, state land and planning departments."

Even the private sector, though increasingly vibrant, was dominated by companies that had been hived off from state-owned enterprises, with managers typically taking control by buying the shares for next to nothing. "Ordinary people in China often say that 'privatization' really means power stealing wealth," said Kuang Xinnian, a literature professor at Qinghua University in Beijing.

This messy backdrop was crucial to understanding why China's leaders were sending so much of the national savings far away. In essence, the party delivered China's savings to the United States to keep it free of the depredations of China itself, using the U.S. Treasury as a safe deposit box. Beijing put the money out of reach of the nation's corruption-laden, capital-wasting, patronage-infested financial system. China's leaders understood clearly that a dollar invested inside China was a dollar that might well be lost, squandered, or stolen a thousand different ways—raked off by connected bureaucrats, shipped to private bank accounts in the Cayman Islands, gambled away in the casinos of Macao, or invested in largely empty skyscrapers bearing the names of insolvent state-owned companies. By contrast, giving the money to Uncle Sam seemed significantly less risky, because the American government stood behind those bonds.

Fearful that the banks would generate disastrous overinvestment at home and waste capital on money-losing projects, the People's Bank of China squirreled away trillions of dollars beyond reach of the financial system, entrusting those funds to the American Treasury, to Fannie Mae and Freddie Mac. Rather than risking a disastrous investment bubble at home, China's leaders sent much of their nation's savings across the Pacific, where their American counterparts lent it out to Fran Barbaro and Willie Gonzalez and where American banks wrote mortgages to nearly anyone who asked.

5

Home Rich

"If you were alive, they would give you a loan."

With the tech boom history, and his eighteen-wheeler truck and house sold off, Willie Gonzalez had to start over. In the late summer of 2002, he began selling cars at a lot in Modesto. The owner introduced him to a friend from Utah, who needed a good salesman at his own lot in a town south of Salt Lake City. Gonzalez liked the thought of cheaper, quieter living in a new place. He and Ibis visited and they felt comfortable. By fall, they had moved down with the children.

Easygoing and confident in manner, Gonzalez was a star on the lot. He had a way of relating to customers that seemed authoritative and yet somehow disinvested from their decisions, creating the closest thing to a pressure-free atmosphere that a car buyer might hope to find. In his second month, he racked up $9,500 in commissions.

It was not merely his manner that explained his success. Gonzalez also displayed intuitive dexterity in tapping into the surge of credit coursing through the country, eventually finding its way to Riverton Chevrolet in Springville, Utah. He specialized in selling cars for no money down, using long-term loans that stretched out the payments, making people feel capable of carrying purchases that would otherwise have been beyond them.

"I'd convince people to buy used, save them some money, and

convince them to sign up for an eighty-four-month-car loan," he says. "They used to call me '84 Willie.'"

A customer would want a new Suburban but lacked the required $15,000 down payment. Gonzalez would focus on the size of the monthly payment they were willing to make, and then work toward that end point, using no-money-down financing for a vehicle with thirty thousand or so miles on it. The customer drove off the lot in a car that felt virtually new, and he or she did so without writing a check or opening a wallet. Only in Chimerica.

But even as Gonzalez again found himself bringing home good money, he and his family did not take to Utah's winter. And with his mother ailing back in Miami, Gonzalez felt a tug to be near her. In May 2003, he and his family drove back to Florida, resuming their lives there.

At first, they stayed with Gonzalez's nephew, who made his living as a handyman. One day, Gonzalez and his nephew built a wooden fence together. Then Gonzalez started painting houses, and just like that, unwittingly, he found himself riding the next great investment wave surging over the American landscape. Real estate was changing hands. Housing construction was exploding. The highways were full of commuting contractors, workmen packed into the beds of their pickup trucks amid cans of paint, two-by-fours, and tools. Already sprawling, greater Miami was stretching south and north and west.

"I started off in South Miami painting one house," Gonzalez said. "Before I was done, one of the neighbors would say, 'You want to do the same for me?'" Soon, he was bringing in $2,500 a month, cash in hand, making other people's houses shine with fresh color. By April 2004, he bought his own house, taking a major step toward restoring the stability he felt back in California, the last time money flowed with ease.

The house sat in Cutler Bay, just south of Miami—a three-bedroom, two-bathroom red-painted stucco in a solidly middle-class neighborhood of shaded porches, American flags, and barbecues out back. The streets were lined with palm trees. Children pedaled bicycles down the pavement. Guava, avocado, and banana trees flowered in the backyard.

The new house cost $187,000. It was a real stretch, even with the cash Gonzalez was bringing in regularly. But finance was abundant—for "84 Willie" and the rest of the nation. He wrote a check for $4,000—a mere 2 percent down. Then he used credit cards to buy furniture and other home furnishings.

Lenders and consumer credit counselors if asked would typically have said this was a reckless move that was likely to end badly. Gonzalez was taking on monthly payments of more than $1,600 a month, which was more than half of his monthly income. But credit counseling brochures were being buried under an avalanche of come-ons for cheap mortgage finance. Gonzalez felt at ease and even responsible about the transaction. As he saw it, he was simply putting a decent roof over his family's head. Home prices were going up, which meant he was effectively saving simply by jangling the keys to his front door. If he ran out of money to pay the credit card bills, or if his income unexpectedly dropped off, he could easily take advantage of the inevitable increase in value by arranging another, slightly larger mortgage, the same way millions of other families were doing. Just pull a little money out of his address. Refinancing felt natural, like plucking a guava from the tree in the backyard, knowing that more fruit would soon grow. "I wasn't concerned," Gonzalez said later, in the summer of 2008, after it all turned out so differently and he tried to stave off foreclosure. "I knew I'd be able to pay it. I knew when I bought the house that I'd be able to refinance." That truth had currency in Cutler Bay. It had embedded itself into the collective assumptions of American financial planning—a term that was beginning to be an oxymoron. In millions of households, the plan had become elegantly simple: buy a house, watch it climb in value, and pull money from it as if it were an ATM machine, one that never required a deposit.

Once, American families had saved money to buy a house. In this new era, Americans bought houses on credit and convinced themselves that this *was* saving. On the strength of this wonderful thought, Cutler Bay, Miami, and communities across the nation were all being lifted up to a vast new territory where bills seemed to never come due and spending could go on forever.

✑

In the post-tech bubble economy, the fortunes of the United States were built on real estate. China kept sending larger sums of money, enabling the Fed to keep interest rates low. The resulting cheap credit enabled banks to lend money aggressively, which sent housing prices up. That brought speculators into the market and enticed developers to finance a wave of construction that made the economy hum.

Once again, a surge of investment rippled through the economy. Financial services jobs expanded, from mortgage offices in every town to trading perches on Wall Street. Construction jobs proliferated, as the pace of building intensified. Real estate agencies expanded, deploying armies of people to sell the inventory being created. Retail jobs multiplied, especially at home improvement and furniture stores. Electricians scrambled to meet orders for the wiring in new homes. Plumbers laid down pipes and installed sinks in new kitchens and bathrooms. As people began to borrow more against their homes, they distributed their dollars to travel agencies and airlines, to hotels and restaurants, to golf courses and car lots and landscapers. By the first half of 2005, in the midst of the boom, economists estimated that roughly half of all economic activity was tied to housing, either through home-building, the purchase of housing-related goods like furniture and appliances, or spending unleashed by people borrowing against the increased value of their homes.

Greg Bailey was not picking out any home furnishings or signing mortgage papers, yet he, too, felt the effects of the boom. Suddenly, there was more work, and at higher wages—albeit the same sort of repetitive, back-straining work he had known for most of his adult life, his days passing in an exhausting tableau of bending, lifting, driving, and trying to stay awake.

After his bosses at the fiber optics company canceled their plans to provide retirement savings accounts and he quit, he made an aborted effort to become an electrician. Next he worked for a couple of years driving a bus outfitted for paraplegics, earning $12 an hour. Then he got a better job still, one that paid $14.50 an hour. In 2005 and 2006, the heart of the housing boom, he worked for a company called Penske Logistics, installing Whirlpool washing machines and refrigerators in homes throughout northern California.

From the Bay Area to the Central Valley, the housing boom was exploding with particular force. Formerly undeveloped parcels on the outer edges of suburbia were rapidly being covered with new subdivisions and condos. All those homes required refrigerators, along with washers and dryers. People in existing homes were availing themselves of home equity loans to renovate kitchens and basements, putting in new appliances. Bailey was the guy who showed up at the front door with the goods. He worked seventy hours a week, from five in the morning until seven at night, sometimes driving 150 miles to get to a single job, pausing only for a quick bite or an energy drink, installing as many as six washers a day.

Once, he and his partner installed an eight-foot-high Sub-Zero refrigerator that weighed nearly one thousand pounds into a house—just two guys, some rope, and a dolly. One Christmas Eve, the dispatcher sent him on a job all the way down to Pebble Beach, the ocean-side resort near Carmel, where he had to deliver a small refrigerator. "It was pouring rain," he recalled. "I couldn't see. I mean, it was totally black." He squinted through the windshield, trying to make sense of the shadows and smudges through the glare of oncoming headlights. Fearing for his life, he pulled over and called the dispatcher and announced that it was too dangerous. He was turning back. But the dispatcher ordered him to continue. "That job was crazy," he said.

For the second time inside a decade, an investment bubble lay at the center of a dramatic increase in economic activity. This one was generated by absurdly easy finance and the American embrace of home ownership, which rationalized a departure from traditional financial constraints. As Chinese investments flooded the economy and mortgages got cheaper, more and more Americans craved a home of their own. It seemed that demand for housing was virtually limitless. On the strength of this idea, banks themselves took advantage of low interest rates, borrowed from other banks, wrote mortgages of increasingly lenient terms, and then sold those loans to raise money to write more. In such fashion, total U.S. mortgage debt more than doubled, from $6.3 trillion at the beginning of 2000 to $13.3 trillion by the end of 2006. Over the same period, housing prices across the country rose by 86 percent. Wall Street borrowed against the stream of mortgage payments to generate complex new investments tied to housing, bringing in even more finance to write more loans.

The economy became governed by a new exercise in make-believe, the notion that housing prices could collectively never fall. This played directly to the fears still lingering from the fiasco of the New Economy. The commodity at the center of this new boom was something comfortingly solid, easily measured, and of intrinsic benefit. In the late 1990s, as Ariba's stock price multiplied, the very architecture of business would have had to be redrawn to validate its valuation. For real estate prices to make sense—and therefore the trillions of dollars in mortgage-related investments attached to homes—the only requirement was that American families continue to behave much as they had for generations, aspiring to own a garage, a yard, a den.

Property has always held special allure in the American psyche, but the carnage in the stock markets as the tech bubble burst seemed only to affirm its worth more deeply, reinforcing conditions for yet another bubble. In 2003 and 2004, the economists Robert Shiller and Karl Case asked recent homebuyers whether experiences in the stock market had contributed to their decision to buy real estate. Most said no, but of the 26 percent who said yes, an overwhelming percentage said their stock market experiences had encouraged them to buy homes. "Stock market shares are too volatile in values, making the risk higher," one respondent explained in a written comment. "Buying a house & land retain better investment value because land will not be depleted over time." "Diminishing returns & huge losses," another person explained. "Looked for alternative use of capital." No one could live in worthless shares of technology companies. But a house was a roof overhead, whatever its paper value. Real estate fever seeped deeply into the culture. TV reality shows traced the exploits of adventurous souls making their living by flipping properties. Dinner parties again buzzed with talk of easy money, this time centered on the lowest mortgage rates and the fastest-appreciating neighborhoods for speculative homes. Just as in the days of the technology boom, the sidelines began to seem a place only for people who had an aversion to wealth. Real estate speculation came to seem not like gambling, but more like picking up the money just lying there for the taking. A gold rush was playing out across every suburban cul de sac. "The market isn't acting rationally," said Christopher Thornberg, a UCLA economist, quoted in an article in *Fortune* magazine in the fall of 2004. "It's now an emotion-driven market where people are buying on the expectation of future appreciation."

Starting in the 1970s, the average American home was worth about seventeen times the annual rent for a comparable place. By the end of 2005, that ratio was up to an all-time peak of twenty-five times. During most of the 1980s and 1990s, the national average sales price of a home remained below six times the average per capita after-tax American income. By the peak of the boom in 2005, the average house cost nearly eight times the average income. That year, Robert Shiller re-leased an updated edition of his book, *Irrational Exuberance,* in which he cited similar numbers to argue that housing prices had risen well beyond historic norms. He warned that the same psychological mecha-nisms that had pumped up technology stocks had gravitated to real es-tate. "The bad outcome could be that eventual declines would result in a substantial increase in the rate of personal bankruptcies, which could lead to a secondary string of bankruptcies of financial institutions," Shiller warned. "Another long-run consequence could be a decline in consumer and business confidence, and another, possibly worldwide re-cession. This extreme outcome—like the situation in Japan since 1990 writ large—is not inevitable, but it is a much more serious risk than is widely acknowledged."

But just as creative analysts had invoked a New Economy as justifica-tion for otherwise impossible stock values, the real estate and home-building industries—joined by policy makers—conjured fresh models that aimed to make sense of stratospheric housing prices. Land was a commod-ity in finite supply, they argued. Financial innovation lowered the risks of mass default, enabling more loans. In a piece in the *Los Angeles Times* in 2003—a year in which local housing prices jumped by one-fifth—Susanne Trimbath, an economist at the Milken Institute, derided those worrying about a real estate bubble for focusing only on home prices and not on the clear shortage of homes. "They apparently lack the ability to consider two pieces of information in unison," Trimbath wrote. In an argu-ment reminiscent of the old talk that technology had tamed the business cycle, Trimbath suggested that the importance of housing as an ascendant source of economic growth made it impervious to the old ups and downs of the market. "It could mean we've seen the end of the boom-bust cycle in real estate," Trimbath declared. "This could signal a fundamental change in the way we analyze the U.S. economy, with housing becoming the sec-tor to watch all the time." Those paid by the housing industry were even more sweeping in their assurances. "We have driven a stake through the heart of the housing bubble story," Robert Kleinhenz, senior economist for the California Association of Realtors, said at a real estate investment con-ference in the San Francisco Bay Area. "There are fundamental reasons why home prices in general keep rising."

The ultimate voice of authority belonged to the man in charge of the money supply, Fed chairman Alan Greenspan. Never wavering in his belief that housing prices were solid, he kept interest rates low, deflecting calls that he try to snuff out excessive speculation with rate hikes. He pointedly dismissed suggestions that the same fantastical thinking about technology had been transferred to the home. "Any analogy to stock market pricing behavior and bubbles is a rather large stretch," Greenspan said before a gathering of bankers in Orlando in March 2003. "First, to sell a home, one almost invariably must move out and in the process confront substantial transaction costs in the form of brokerage fees and taxes. These transaction costs greatly discourage the type of buying and selling frenzy that often characterizes bubbles in financial markets. Second, there is no national housing market in the United States. Local conditions dominate, even though mortgage interest rates are similar throughout the country. Home prices in Portland, Maine, do not arbitrage those in Portland, Oregon. Thus, any bubbles that might emerge would tend to be local, not national, in scope."

This was not only wrong, it was disastrously wrong. A national bubble was already forming. And the academic literature had already shown that housing bubbles tended to be roughly twice as costly as stock market bubbles when they popped. Greenspan fundamentally misread the degree to which financial engineering—cheap and abundant real estate loans—was driving home prices higher across the country. His decision to keep pumping easy money into the market would ultimately become his legacy.

෴

Still, the responsibility for the housing bubble cannot be hung on any single person or institution. The bubble was the product of years of government policies that aimed to make it easier for more Americans to own houses. It stemmed from the nation's continued reverence for unsupervised markets, which allowed financial institutions to pour near-limitless quantities of money into home loans largely clear of government oversight. And it was once again an outgrowth of Wall Street and Madison Avenue, which systematically transformed the home from a mere place to live into an all-purpose financial instrument.

Through multiple administrations, the federal government had long promoted home ownership as a social good. In 1997, President Clinton persuaded Congress to eliminate capital gains taxes on the profits from most home sales, a move that significantly encouraged more buying and selling, according to subsequent studies. Clinton's secretary of housing and urban development, Henry Cisneros, loosened conditions for first-time home buyers to qualify for government-insured mortgages, lowering the requirement for stable incomes from five years to three years. That brought more buyers into the market, lifting prices and—in the logic of markets—validating the policy.

In 1999, with evidence mounting that diminished standards were attracting unsavory lenders into real estate, Democrats in Congress sought passage of a bill that would have penalized lending with excessively high rates of interest and fees, typically marketed to people with tarnished credit histories. Republicans squelched the bill, arguing that it would prevent legitimate lending. "Don't apologize when you make a loan above the prime rate to someone that has a marginal credit rating," Phil Gramm, the Texas Republican then chairing the Senate banking committee, told bankers in 2000. "In the name of predatory lending, we could end up denying people with moderate income and limited credit ratings the opportunity to borrow money."

When George W. Bush took office the following year, he laid out expanding home ownership as one of his primary goals, particularly among minorities. This aspiration was a key piece of Bush's Ownership Society, and it drew broad support in Congress. In 2002, Bush explicitly challenged lenders to create 5.5 million more minority home owners by the end of the decade. "Part of economic security is owning your own home," Bush said in Atlanta, as he unveiled his plan. But the Bush administration relinquished to the markets the conditions in which that goal would be advanced, limiting the sort of regulation that might have prevented—or at least limited—the conflagration already gathering force.

The White House and members of Congress from both sides of the aisle pressured the government-sponsored mortgage companies, Fannie Mae and Freddie Mac, to lend more widely, dropping their standards in the process. These two companies made finance available to banks by buying mortgages that conformed to its lending guidelines, thus giving them fresh capital to make more loans. Fannie was already working toward a goal of buying $2 trillion in loans from low-income, minority, and risky borrowers by the close of the decade. To meet that goal, the company had to essentially buy whatever came in the door, without spending a lot of time making sure borrowers would be able to make their payments. "We didn't really know what we were buying," Marc Gott, a former director in Fannie's loan servicing department, told the *New York Times'* Charles Duhigg. "This system was designed for plain vanilla loans, and we were trying to push chocolate sundaes through the gears."

According to internal documents released by a congressional panel, by 2004 senior executives at Freddie were already concerned that the company had significantly lowered its standards in pursuit of expanded home ownership. In a memo to chief executive Dick Syron, Freddie's chief enterprise risk officer, David A. Andrukonis, warned that the company was risking damage to its reputation by purchasing mortgages that did not require borrowers to prove their income. Such loans appeared "to target borrowers who would have trouble qualifying for a mortgage if their financial position were adequately disclosed," Andrukonis wrote. He concluded that such loans appeared to be "disproportionately targeted towards Hispanics," adding: "The potential for the perception and the reality of predatory lending with this product is great."

As the sense took hold that it was open season in real estate—with Wall Street delivering capital, Fannie and Freddie guaranteeing loans, and the regulators staying out of the way—banks began handing out mortgages to nearly all comers. When they ran out of creditworthy people to lend to, they began lending to those with credit troubles, issuing so-called subprime loans. "When money is free," George Soros, the world-famous hedge fund manager would write later, "the rational lender will keep lending until there is no one else to lend to."

This tendency was amplified by the perverse compensation system at play: the riskier the loan, the higher the fees. Companies such as Countrywide Financial Corporation, the nation's largest mortgage lender, unleashed considerable marketing machinery toward writing subprime loans. The fees on these loans were so high that mortgage brokers were soon marketing them to everyone, even those who could qualify for mortgages at much better terms. By 2005, subprime loans made up more than one-fifth of all mortgages issued, with annual lending reaching $625 billion, up from $145 billion in 2001. More than a third of those loans were for more than the purchase price of the house, meaning that people were taking money out of their homes even before they were moving in.

Of greatest concern, the financiers were writing loans without verifying the incomes and credit histories of borrowers, and often without receiving down payments. Between 2000 and 2006, the percentage of subprime borrowers who did not fully document their incomes and assets swelled from 17 percent to 44 percent. And if subprime was the clearest area of deviance, lending standards were loose for nearly every segment of the population—the rich, the middle class, and the working poor.

"The game was certainly different than it ever was before," said Nan Lanros, a real estate agent in Palm Springs, California, the desert enclave of the moneyed set. "It was like they took the words 'No,' 'Denied,' and 'Can't Qualify,' completely out of the lenders' vocabulary." Nearly anyone could walk into a mortgage broker's office and secure finance, she said, with the required documentation often fudged to meet whatever criteria were at issue. A customer "could be a postal worker that fell in love with an $800,000 house," Lanros said. "It didn't matter. The borrower would give them true and accurate information as far as income, correct social security number. After the borrower left was when the fraud would start. Once the loan agent started to work on the file he had license by his own company to twist the facts as much as needed to get the loan through. The borrower might end up being an astronaut! Whatever it took to make the numbers work."

In the olden days of American finance, none of this would have made any sense. Why would a bank knowingly lend money to people without jobs or income? The bank would then get stuck with the inevitable losses. But in the new game governing Wall Street, it made trillions of dollars' worth of sense. Countrywide and the other mortgage giants were selling most of the loans they made to Wall Street. Even if the borrowers failed to pay up, that would be someone else's problem. Following the practice mastered by Salomon Brothers during the S&L fiasco, investment banks were pooling mortgages together with millions of others, slicing them into pieces, and then selling them off as an array of different investments to buyers around the world—to pension funds in Buffalo, municipal investment funds in Norway, and banks in China—thus raising more money to make more loans. The investors buying these loans were eager for the riskier batches and would pay a premium for them, because they came with interest rates that started low but then

reset higher, and other lucrative goodies such as penalties for early payment, seemingly guaranteeing greater profits in the years ahead. Batches
of subprime loans were two and three times more profitable for Countrywide to sell than loans made to more creditworthy households. As a
result, Countrywide and other mortgage companies paid higher commissions to its salespeople when they brought in riskier, more expensive
loans, encouraging them to stick the customer with the very sorts of obligations that would get them in trouble and eventually spawn a financial
crisis.

Washington Mutual, another home loan giant, relied on wholesale
mortgage brokers as a pipeline for its most lucrative loan—the option
ARM, for adjustable rate mortgage—which gave customers the option of
how much to pay in any given month. The loan began with a tiny rate
of interest, as little as 1 percent for the first two to five years. But what the
mortgage brokers frequently did not bother to explain—or the borrowers
did not understand—was that the minimum payment was even less than
the interest due on the loan. A borrower who opted to make only minimum payments was each month borrowing more against the value of their
home, increasing their principal balance. Once that balance reached 110
or 115 percent of the value of their house, that triggered the end of the promotional rate, doubling or even tripling the required monthly payment.

The option ARM was an appropriate loan for a speculative buyer
who was planning on renovating a property and then quickly selling it. It
made sense for someone with variable income, like an attorney who only
got paid when a big case came through. For almost everyone else, it was a
ticking time bomb. But WaMu, as the bank was known, marketed such
loans to practically everyone, enticed by the money it could make reselling them. It targeted option ARMs at first-time homebuyers. It touted
them to retirees on fixed incomes, who would have been better served by
a fixed-rate mortgage. WaMu's wholesale lending channel paid brokers 2
and 3 percent commissions for such loans, while sending monthly re-
tainer checks to those who delivered particularly high volume.

When mortgage brokers explained the details of the option ARM to
their customers, they typically offered assurances that no day of reckoning would ever come. Another infusion of cheap credit could always
stave it off. If the payments increased, the customer could just refinance
the mortgage, fold the old balance into a larger loan, and start over with

a new teaser rate. It was a sweet deal for everyone. WaMu claimed extra business by refinancing millions of mortgages, collecting more fees in the process. The home owner got the keys to an otherwise unaffordable castle. The mortgage broker got commissions.

There was just one detail upon which an ultimately happy outcome rested: home prices had to keep rising. If home prices stopped going up, then millions of home owners with option ARMs would be unable to re-finance their mortgages because not enough value would remain in their homes against which to borrow. Then, they would be stuck with vastly increased payment obligations. "I saw it as a death trap," said Barbara Fronek-Cooper, who worked in the underwriting department at WaMu's loan processing center in Downers Grove, Illinois, in 2005 and 2006, where she mostly handled option ARMs. "I knew exactly what was going to happen once those loans were going to mature."

Mortgage brokers say they, too, understood the implications of what they were selling. "It was just criminal and in my head I knew it, but I was happy to take the checks," said a southern California mortgage broker who spoke on the condition he not be named because he still worked in the industry. "You can make three [percentage] points on the back and the customer won't have a clue. That's like putting crack out on the street. The brokers made out like bandits."

⌒

As Fran Barbaro reached for a ringing telephone one day in 2004, she simply knew she needed cash, and the telemarketer on the other end of the line was offering a reliable way to get some. She was happy to listen to the pitch.

For the past few years, Barbaro had been living on her wages from various technology consulting jobs, the embers of her stock portfolio, and sundry credit cards. During months when she could not work because of her illness, she was running up credit card balances that had spiraled be-yond her ability to pay. Her only remaining asset of value was the house on Juniper Road, by then worth nearly $1 million. The finance company on the line was offering to turn some of that paper gain into money.

The telemarketer offered up a loan that would pay off Barbaro's pre-vious mortgage and give her extra cash to pay off her credit card bills. It would begin at a very low rate of interest that was supposed to last for two years, yielding an initial monthly payment of $2,600. "It seemed okay," Barbaro said later. The bank tacked on a $44,000 home equity line of credit, essentially a checkbook that drew funds from the value of her home. She provided the requisite information—her income, her Social Security number, her date of birth. The whole thing was over in ten minutes. When the loan documents came in the mail from Washington Mutual, she tossed them in a drawer, the fine print not worth fussing over. The point was the bold print on the monthly invoice, the amount due— a number that was once again manageable. She had no income and she had debts to pay. She needed the deal. "I was absolutely at the mercy of everybody," she said later.

WaMu was all about rescuing people from their short-term situations and satisfying their needs of the day, be it special after-school classes for children, a new home, or just keeping a collection agency at bay. Within the real estate industry, WaMu had a well-earned reputation as a company that would do whatever it took to get loans approved. The WaMu underwriters who were supposed to abide by lending requirements frequently fielded angry complaints from sales people when they did not process problematic loans. Appraisers were accustomed to hearing from sales people with regularity, demanding that they place high-enough values on homes they assessed to justify hefty loans. "It was the Wild West," said Steven M. Knobel, a founder of a New York appraisal company, Mitchell, Maxwell & Jackson, that did business with WaMu until 2007. "If you were alive, they would give you a loan. Actually, I think if you were dead, they would still give you a loan."

Inside its offices, the bank's foot soldiers received unrelenting pressure to process as many applications as they could. At WaMu's San Diego loan processing office, Sherri Zaback, who reviewed incoming files, recalled a 2005 loan application from a borrower in Los Angeles who listed his profession as "gardener" while claiming monthly income of $12,000. The system merely required that she verify the borrower had a business license. Even then, she came up empty. When she took the file to her boss, he arranged to photograph the borrower's truck emblazoned with the name of his landscaping business. The photo went into the file. Approved.

Another time, Zaback tried to confirm the assets of a borrower whose application included a letter from a bank showing a balance of

$150,000. When Zaback called the bank, they told her the real balance was $5,000. "You could see where the numbers had been added to the letter," Zaback recalled. "This was serious fraud." She took the file to her boss, saying she no longer wanted to work with this particular loan officer. His reply: "Too bad."

When I interviewed her boss, John David Parsons, in December 2008, he wore an orange prison jumpsuit and spoke through wire-reinforced glass at the Richard J. Donovan Correctional Facility southeast of San Diego, near the Mexican border. He was serving a sixteen-month sentence for theft following his fourth arrest in four years, all involving drug charges. Parsons had supervised a team of loan processors in San Diego at the height of the boom, from 2002 through 2005. All the while, he was regularly snorting methamphetamine, he acknowledged. Zaback said his drug use was known within the office. On her first day at work, she saw him with drug paraphernalia on his desk. "In our world, it was tolerated," she said. "Everybody said, 'He gets the job done.'"

At WaMu getting the job done meant honoring the spirit of the company's advertising slogan, which was prominently plastered on the walls of its offices — "The Power of Yes." Parsons lived it. "I'd lie if I said every piece of documentation was properly signed and dated," he said, speaking into a telephone that connected us through the glass. "If a deal doesn't close, nobody gets paid. There was pressure to make all the fucking loans you can."

His methods were not unusual, he said. Taking the photo of the gardener's truck was a trick he had learned from his boss a year earlier, he said, when a mariachi singer with a high reported income and no business license sought a loan: the singer donned his mariachi outfit and stood in front of the home for a photo. Approved.

As President Bush's calls for expanded lending to minorities filtered through the mortgage world, some WaMu branches focused aggressively on Latino borrowers. In Downey, a heavily Latino community southeast of Los Angeles, the local WaMu branch specialized in lending to recent immigrants who spoke little English, targeting them with option ARMs, according to a former employee who spoke on condition he not be identified because he remained in the mortgage industry. According to the employee, the Downey branch became one of the leading WaMu profit centers by inviting real estate agents to bring in loan applications for their clients and enabling these agents to collect hefty "referral fees." Fees paid directly from WaMu to the agents would have been illegal, so WaMu arranged to have the commissions paid by the buyers as part of the costs of closing on their houses—just another item added to a stack of paperwork that most people did not bother to scrutinize.

The former employee said that buyers were generally oblivious to the fees being captured by their realtors. The realtors would take their clients to see properties and promise to arrange the financing so that the monthly payments would run as little as $1,000 a month. The real estate agents generally did not bother to explain that the initial payments would soon reset higher. "Most of the buyers didn't understand how this worked," the employee said. "They thought the minimum payments would just continue. A lot of the people didn't speak English and their realtor was their trusted friend. The realtors would sell them on a minimum payment, and that was an outright lie."

According to the former employee, the architect of this strategy was a man named Thomas Ramirez, who headed a sales team of more than twenty agents at the Downey branch. When I called him, Ramirez confirmed that his team enabled realtors to collect commissions, though he rejected the notion that customers had been cheated. The fees collected by real estate agents were fully disclosed to buyers as part of the closing costs, he said. "I don't think the bank would have let us do the program if it was bad," Ramirez said.

Ramirez's innovation proved so successful that his team closed nearly $1 billion worth of loans in 2004, he said. His performance made him a perennial entrant in WaMu's President's Club, which brought recognition at an awards ceremony typically hosted by top WaMu executives at tropical venues such as Hawaii, along with bonuses and increased commissions. As real estate agents arrived in Downey from all over southern California, bearing six and seven loan applications at a time, WaMu took over an entire building next to the branch and filled it with loan processors, underwriters, and appraisers—all of them dedicated to the Ramirez team.

By late 2004, other branches throughout California were copying the practice of paying referral fees to real estate agents, the former employee said. In 2006, as federal authorities probed WaMu's lending practices, headquarters largely banned the practice, fearing that the commissions could be construed as illegal payments from the bank to realtors, the former employee said.

But WaMu allowed Ramirez's team to continue the practice, the agent said. It was simply too lucrative to shut down.

౷

The sort of lending WaMu, Countrywide Financial, and the other banks were doing could remain lucrative only so long as investors were willing to buy the loans they were writing with reckless abandon.

How was Wall Street able to peddle so much trash for so long?

The Neverland of permanently rising house prices was so profitable for everyone involved that no one wanted to come home. The people who worked inside Wall Street's investment banks became expert at pooling and slicing mortgages into the right sorts of bundles, apportioning the loans to gain the favor of ratings agencies such as Moody's and Standard & Poor's. Their seals of approval gave investors assurance they were buying something solid. In turn, the ratings agencies assisted in the financial alchemy, receiving lucrative fees from the very Wall Street institutions whose investments they were supposed to dispassionately assess and counseling the banks on how to engineer their mortgage-backed investments to garner the best ratings. This blatant conflict of interest did not seem to trouble anyone until after the system collapsed, much as the Pollyanna pronouncements of market analysts working for investment banks during the tech bubble drew little concern before the meltdown.

Selling pools of loans only got easier and more lucrative as Fannie Mae and Freddie Mac began buying riskier notes from mortgage companies. Between 2005 and 2008, Fannie alone purchased some $270 billion in loans to high-risk home owners, more than triple its purchases in all earlier years combined, according to company filings and industry data.

Much like the tech boom's transcendent arithmetic, the profits flowing from real estate in the 2000s fostered a belief that a new wealth-generating fantasy had become reality. Everyone involved was seemingly getting ahead, from the home owners pulling cash from their houses, to the real estate and mortgage brokers generating the loans, to the people on Wall Street taking home seven- and eight-figure bonuses for expanding their businesses. Rising prices validated the market's and the debtors' assumptions about the solidity of the American home and the perpetual shortage of houses. More investment made prices go up further still, a lucrative feedback loop. The fact that American mortgages were being sold as far away as Scandinavia and China lent a sense that the system was spread so wide and involved so many different players that it could not possibly fail.

"The risks inherent in mortgage lending became so widely dispersed that no one was forced to worry about the quality of any single loan," writes Mark Zandi, chief economist at Moody's Economy.com in his lucid history of the mortgage crisis, *Financial Shock*. "As shaky mortgages were combined, diluting any problems into a larger pool, the incentive for responsibility was undermined. At every point in the financial system, there was a belief that someone—*someone else*—would catch mistakes and preserve the integrity of the process. The mortgage lender counted on the Wall Street investment banker who counted on the regulator or the ratings analyst, who had assumed global investors were doing their own due diligence. As the process went badly awry, everybody assumed someone else was in control. No one was."

In the end, the mortgage mania proved a recipe for broad distress. By the fall of 2008, one-tenth of all home owners nationally were behind on their loan payments or in foreclosure. The trouble was increasingly afflicting a broad spectrum of Americans. Among those with option ARM loans, nearly one-fourth were at least two months behind on their payments, up from 5 percent a year earlier. Among those who had fallen into delinquency, subprime borrowers were by then a minority, outnumbered by those in trouble with prime loans, which were extended to people with ample income and good credit, according to a *Washington Post* analysis. A new term was coined: *jingle mail*. With so many houses worth less than people owed banks, many just mailed in their keys in lieu of a payment and walked away.

Between 2000 and 2007, the number of Latino households that owned homes had increased by 2 million, reaching 6.1 million. The Latino home-ownership rate had jumped from 45 percent to 50 percent over the same period. But by late 2008, as foreclosures mounted, the rate sagged back below 50 percent.

This reckless mode of mortgage finance devastated ordinary shareholders and their pension funds and other investors who had loaded up on mortgage-backed securities. When Countrywide sold itself to Bank of

America in January 2008 in a \$4 billion deal, its shares were worth less than one-fifth of their peak value. When WaMu disintegrated in September 2008 under the weight of \$11.5 billion in bad loans, regulators seized it and sold it to JPMorgan Chase for less than \$2 billion—far less than the \$40 billion its shares had been worth at the market's peak.

Yet, the very lending that wiped out shareholders, devastated the financial system, and sent the economy into a terrible recession was richly rewarding for the people at the helm of those companies. Before the stock markets figured out how and why banks were seeing such a dramatic expansion in their mortgage businesses, they bid up the shares of those showing the biggest loan volumes, boosting paydays for executives who collected stock options. From the middle of 2006 through the middle of 2007, Countrywide's chief executive, Angelo R. Mozilo—the son of a butcher from the Bronx and a member of the Horatio Alger Association's Hall of Fame—secured \$129 million from the sale of the company's shares. Between 2001 and 2007, Washington Mutual's chief executive, Kerry Killinger, received compensation of \$88 million. Even after the country's real estate mania ran out, these executives kept the cars, the mansions, and the jewelry while millions of ordinary families who had borrowed from their companies loaded their belongings into storage containers and met the harsh reality of foreclosure.

6

Locked Out

"Financial weapons of mass destruction"

Banks poured so much money into real estate during the bubble years that the inevitable drop in home prices was sure to be wrenching, leaving many financial institutions nursing losses on investments linked to mortgages. Too much fairy dust had fertilized too much construction, resulting in too many vacant homes. When the market figured this out in 2006, prices began to fall. As home owners suffered drops in the value of their properties, they lost the ability to refinance their mortgages, forcing them to make higher monthly payments when their introductory rates ran out. By the summer of 2007, millions of people had stopped paying, and the financial system found itself confronting a very expensive problem.

But there was a crucial element that turned the housing bubble from just another costly investment mania into a disaster potent enough to wreck the financial system: extraordinary quantities of borrowed money. Financial institutions had been using their mortgage-linked investments as collateral to borrow trillions of dollars and then investing those funds back into writing more mortgages. That meant that a single stream of payments from one home owner on one mortgage was effectively backing twenty to thirty more loans. Once home owners stopped making their payments in significant numbers, the entire system was vulnerable to losses, because this brought down the value of all investments linked to mortgages.

Then it emerged that the mortgage crisis itself lay at the tip of a much larger financial problem that had taken root in the atmosphere of faith-based regulation. Wall Street's financial institutions had been buying and selling unfathomable quantities of derivatives—those inscrutable investments, championed by Long-Term Capital Management before the Asian financial crisis, whose value fluctuated with movements in other investments—without setting aside adequate funds to cover potential losses. Many of these derivatives were tied to the value of mortgages. By the summer of 2007, with housing prices falling, trillions of dollars' worth of derivatives were going bad at once. Banks demanded payment from other banks that lacked the needed cash to settle up, and the figment of permanently rising housing prices gave way to the horror of a systemic meltdown.

There were supposed to be limits on how much capital a given institution could put at risk, requirements that lenders reserve cash to cover investments that might go bad. This was a basic principle of modern banking, a key to ensuring confidence. But in an era in which Wall Street was king and the market was practically God, regulators felt little inclination to stop the lucrative fiesta over such niggling details. The financial institutions mesmerized regulators with a range of exotic investments that supposedly limited risk by spreading it around. The most important of these would-be risk-management tools was a variety of derivative called a credit default swap. Despite its forbidding name, this swap was a straightforward transaction: one company paid another to promise to make good if it got stiffed on a particular investment. Imagine you paid your neighbor a fee for the right to use his garden hose should your house catch fire. Your neighbor pocketed money for doing nothing more than making a promise, while you took comfort that your house would never burn down because someone else was obligated to come running at the first hint of smoke.

The credit default swap was like an insurance policy against failure, except no one used the word *insurance*. That would have triggered regulation by a state board or a federal body, which would have required that the institutions selling such policies actually set aside enough money to make good on their obligations, if called. Technically, the credit default swap was just a private contract between two willing parties. It was an irresistible transaction during the housing boom. The heads of big banks collected bonuses and stock options for growing their mortgage businesses as quickly as they could, and the swaps enabled them to expand almost without limit. By buying swaps, they could justify investing huge amounts of money in mortgage-related investments, far more than would have otherwise seemed prudent, because someone was required to reimburse them if their bets went bad. Instead of keeping their money on the sidelines, they could bet more, swelling the risks that would soon pull the financial system to the edge of the abyss.

The institutions that were selling such policies—companies such as the American International Group, Inc., which by March 2009 had received a taxpayer-funded bailout worth roughly $170 billion—wrote as many of these policies as they could, because it seemed like free money. They were convinced by supposedly sophisticated computer models and wonderful thinking that housing was such a solid bet that prices could never fall, so mortgages could not go bad en masse. In the Neverland of permanently rising house prices, the swaps seemed like a way to collect money for insuring against the possibility that the sun would not rise tomorrow. By the end of 2007, the notional value of credit default swaps—that is, the value of the assets they supposedly insured—exceeded $62 trillion, according to the International Swaps and Derivatives Association. That was larger than the value of the annual economic output of the planet.

When housing prices fell in 2007, and mortgages began going bad in large numbers, the Wall Street bankers picked up their phones in unison, seeking out payments from the institutions responsible for covering their losses via their credit default swaps. And then they figured out that no one had actually provisioned for this unfortunate day. It was as if your neighbor—unbeknownst to you, and unwatched by any regulator—had been collecting payments from everyone on the block for the same promise to use the same hose in event of a fire. Indeed, he had been collecting payments throughout town and across neighboring states. What happened if more than one person had a fire at the same time? And how much more likely was fire if everyone began lighting tiki torches and setting off fireworks, thinking that the neighbor's garden hose stood at the ready? Now suppose that everyone on the block—confident in their hose contracts—dispensed with smoke detectors, sprinkler systems, and fire extinguishers, and that community leaders, certain that the threat of fire itself had been tamed by your neighbor's brilliant civic spirit, dismantled the fire department. This is essentially what the people in charge of the American economy did in allowing unfathomable quantities of capital to flow into real estate and derivatives that supposedly limited the risk of these investments while failing to make sure that enough was set aside in reserve to cover the bets. They dismantled the fire department, deeming it a relic of more dangerous times.

Then they sat back and watched Wall Street build a bonfire big enough to burn down the whole neighborhood.

જી

Alan Greenspan consistently championed swaps as a comforting innovation that helped spread the risks of the financial system, making capitalism safer for everyone.

"Proposals to bring even minimalist regulation were basically rebuffed by Greenspan and various people in the Treasury," recalled the Princeton economist Alan S. Blinder, who served with Greenspan as a vice chairman of the board of governors at the Federal Reserve. "I think of him as consistently cheerleading on derivatives, as arguing consistently that they were extremely valuable risk hedging instruments and if we interfered, we would disrupt the market. The government's heavy hand of regulation, if it were to descend upon them, would cause all these pernicious things."

In the end, the swaps spread risk only in the sense that a problem in one place quickly became a problem for everyone, prompting the $700 billion bailout of the financial system, followed by the creation of a public-private partnership in 2009 that seems likely to cost taxpayers hundreds of billions more. Risk had become socialized, with the American taxpayer stuck covering the losses. The profits remained private, rewarding the executives running the system beyond their wildest dreams.

None of this was unforeseen.

Warren Buffett, the widely admired money manager, once called derivatives "financial weapons of mass destruction." In the early 1990s, the hedge fund manager George Soros proclaimed that his company avoided derivatives such as credit default swaps "because we don't really understand how they work." In 1992, Congress began investigating the dangers in their unregulated trading. Representative Ed Markey, a Democrat from

Massachusetts who chaired the House subcommittee on telecommunications and finance, asked the General Accounting Office to study the risks. In May 1994, the GAO released its report. It identified "significant gaps and weaknesses" in the regulatory oversight of over-the-counter (OTC) derivatives, meaning those sold privately between two companies. The report noted that the worldwide volume of derivatives in circulation at the end of 1992 exceeded $12 trillion in terms of the value of the investments to which they were linked.

The day after the report was released, the comptroller general, Charles A. Bowsher, went to Capitol Hill to testify in front of Markey's subcommittee. He warned that a financial crisis could result from continuing to allow the market to grow without oversight. Many large institutions had already lost substantial amounts of money on complex derivatives, and many had become so interlaced that if one ran into trouble, it could drag down others, Bowsher said. "The sudden failure or abrupt withdrawal from trading of any of these large U.S. dealers could cause liquidity problems in the markets and could also pose risks to others, including federally insured banks and the financial system as a whole," he testified. "In some cases intervention has and could result in a financial bailout paid for or guaranteed by taxpayers." Bowsher called on Congress to bring "currently unregulated" affiliates of investment banks and insurance companies that were trading in over-the-counter derivatives "under the purview of one or more of the existing federal financial regulators."

Later that year, Markey introduced a bill requiring dealers of derivatives to register with the Securities and Exchange Commission, while directing the commission to draft rules requiring that they reserve adequate funds against losses. On May 25, 1994, Greenspan came in front of Markey's subcommittee to offer assurances that the "risks in financial markets, including derivatives markets, are being regulated by private parties." He was joined by Arthur Levitt, chairman of the Securities and Exchange Commission, who concurred that regulation was not required.

When questioned, Greenspan spelled out precisely how derivatives could actually amplify a crisis, because they tied together the fortunes of many institutions. "The very efficiency that is involved here means that if a crisis were to occur, that that crisis is transmitted at a far faster pace and with some greater virulence," he said.

"Like a quickly spreading flu bug?" asked Lynn Schenk, a California Democrat on the panel.

"Yes," Greenspan replied.

But he called the chance of a crisis "extremely remote," and, above all, something legislation should not try to prevent.

"Were we to endeavor to do that, we'd end up with a stagnant economy," Greenspan said. "Risk is part of life."

The subcommittee did not pass the bill. The following year, the Republicans took over Congress, bringing a sharply deregulatory bent, and the bill disappeared.

Greenspan ruled Washington with his authoritative mien, his apparent grasp of the intricacies of global finance, and his frequent use of impenetrable economic jargon, particularly in technical areas such as derivatives. "It's like dealing with a professor of a complex subject that you're supposed to know something about," Levitt said in the fall of 2008. "I always felt that the titans of our legislature didn't want to reveal their own inability to understand some of the concepts that Mr. Greenspan was setting forth. I don't recall anyone ever saying, 'What do you mean by that, Alan?'"

In the mid-1990s, the Commodity Futures Trading Commission, another regulatory body, launched an official inquiry into whether derivatives should be governed by rules requiring that trades be disclosed publicly, with capital set aside in reserve. "The market was completely opaque," the commission's chair, Brooksley Born said years later, in an interview published in *Washington Lawyer* magazine. "Neither the commission nor any other federal regulator knew what was going on." She called the market "a nightmare waiting to happen." Born immediately came under attack from Greenspan, then Treasury secretary Robert E. Rubin—a Wall Street icon, who would later take a top executive position at Citigroup—and Rubin's deputy, Lawrence Summers. They accused her of risking havoc throughout the financial system by injecting legal uncertainty in derivatives contracts.

"Greenspan told Brooksley that she essentially didn't know what she was doing and she'd cause a financial crisis," recalled Michael Greenberger, who was then director of trading and markets at the commission, and who attended meetings with the principals. "Brooksley was this woman who was not playing tennis with these guys and not having lunch with these guys. There was a little bit of the feeling that this woman was not of Wall Street."

In the spring of 1998, Summers called Born and reprimanded her, according to Greenberger, who was in the office at the time. "He said, 'You're going to cause the greatest financial crisis since the Great Depression if you regulate this,'" Greenberger recalled.

Summers initially refused to discuss that conversation, angrily asserting that journalists were engaged in a "jihad" to blame him and his colleagues for the derivatives crisis. Days later, Summers said he could not recall the conversation with Born, but acknowledged that he had agreed with Greenspan and Rubin that her proposal was "highly problematic." When Born's commission went ahead, Greenspan and Clinton's Treasury officials turned to Congress. They lobbied the Republican leadership for legislation that explicitly walled off derivatives from the commission's regulatory purview. They did not pause in their pursuit of deregulation even as Long-Term Capital's near collapse in the summer of 1998 put the spotlight on how large areas of the financial markets operated beyond oversight while posing risks to the whole system. At a Senate hearing in February 2000, Senator Tom Harkin, an Iowa Democrat, asked Greenspan what might happen if Congress enacted the deregulation bill. "With an exclusion, we have washed our hands of it," Harkin said. "I mean, that is a lot of risk out there. . . . If you have this exclusion and something unforeseen happens, who does something about it?"

"It is largely counterparty surveillance which is our primary source of regulation," Greenspan replied, meaning that the banks could be trusted to scrutinize one another. He implored Congress not to allow good intentions to spawn damaging policies that would sap vitality.

"There is a very fundamental trade-off of what type of economy you wish to have," Greenspan said. "I mean, you can have huge amounts of regulation and I will guarantee nothing will go wrong, but nothing will go right either."

In the last hours before Congress adjourned for Christmas in 2000, Senator Phil Gramm, the Texas Republican who chaired the banking committee, took the bill deregulating derivatives trading and attached it as an amendment to an eleven-thousand-page appropriations bill. Clinton signed it into law, one of the final times he would wield the presidential pen. A five-thousand-word White House press release about the signing contained a lone paragraph on the derivatives measure buried within the bill, asserting that it would "provide regulatory relief for investors."

⁖

More than reverence for market forces explains why Greenspan, Rubin, Summers, and Levitt worked so hard to deregulate the financial instruments at the center of the financial crisis. They safeguarded the freedom of financial institutions to continue their make-believe because that amounted to a highly profitable business on Wall Street, and the American economy was increasingly dependent upon the industry for its sustenance.

In 1950, manufacturing was still responsible for nearly one-third of U.S. economic activity, while financial services comprised only about one-tenth. By 2003, the balance had grown lopsided in the other direction, with manufacturing shrunken to a mere 13 percent of the economy and finance swollen to roughly 20 percent. Over the same basic time frame, jobs in finance grew steadily, reaching 8 million by the middle of 2003—more than four times the number in the early 1950s. By comparison, more than 14 million manufacturing jobs remained in 2003, but that was about the same number that the country boasted in the 1950s.

Greenspan, Rubin, Summers, and Levitt were all keenly aware of the importance of financial services jobs to the economy. Growing ranks of Washington lobbyists working for the industry were skilled at delivering reminders. These were high-wage jobs, in an area in which the United States had significant advantages. "The nation's financial system is at the heart of our economy," Rubin told the Senate banking committee in 1998, as he urged passage of a bill that repealed the last vestiges of the Glass-Steagall Act, which had long divided Wall Street investment banks from those that took deposits from ordinary people. The change enabled Citigroup to buy the insurance giant, Traveler's. The following year, Rubin took a senior executive job at Citibank, where he earned $126 million over the subsequent decade.

Policy makers were inclined to cater to the desires of the money masters, fearful that too many rules would send them fleeing to more lenient venues such as London and Hong Kong, taking capital and jobs out of the United States. The rules aimed at regulating derivatives in the mid-1990s were portrayed by Wall Street as a threat to its competitive advantages. "The consequence of such action would be U.S. OTC derivatives market activity moving to off-shore markets in Europe or Asia, detrimentally affecting the U.S. economy and diminishing the competitive position of the U.S. as the dominant financial center," warned George M. James, a managing director of the Wall Street investment giant Morgan Stanley, in testimony on Capitol Hill back in July 1998.

Summers echoed those threats, asserting that the very process of considering regulations could scare away business. "The American OTC derivatives market is second to none," he told a Senate panel. "In a few short years, it has assumed a major role in our own economy and become a magnet for derivative business from around the world. . . . We've seen reports of software companies developing products to support OTC derivatives choosing to domicile their businesses in the United Kingdom rather than the United States because of a perception that the U.S. regulatory environment is inhospitable and unstable."

As the financial crisis intensified in the fall of 2008, and as credit default swaps emerged as a central source of the trouble, I called Rubin to seek his reflections on the wisdom of deregulation. He insisted that he had always favored regulating derivatives, but saw no way to impose rules amid the prosperity of the 1990s. "There was no political reality of getting it done," he said. "All of the forces in the system were arrayed against it. The industry certainly didn't want any increase in these requirements. There was no potential for mobilizing public opinion."

Freed of regulatory oversight, the notional value of credit default swaps expanded from $1.6 trillion in the middle of 2002 to $45 trillion by the middle of 2007, when the financial crisis began. By 2008, the notional value of all financial derivatives had reached ten times the worth of the world's total annual economic activity, a level of absurdity that beggared the traditional conception of managing risk. In the financial world, investments are supposed to be "secured" by something real. Home owners pledge their houses as collateral for their mortgages. If they fail to pay, the banks can seize the houses and sell them to recoup what they can. But in the profitable world of derivatives, Wall Street was selling investments secured by nothing more than the wonderful thought that no one would ever need their money back. As the journalist John Lanchester put it in an essay in the New Yorker, "the market for products that derive from real things" had become "unimaginably vaster than the market for things themselves."

As soon as the day came that investors exercised their derivative contracts, demanding payment from the financial institutions that had been selling credit default swaps, crisis was inevitable. Greenspan had said repeatedly that such a day would never come: the people running the banks would never put themselves in the position where they were depending upon other institutions that did not have the money to meet their obligations. Bankers would scrutinize the balance sheets of their trading partners, and this would discipline the market. But when banks started demanding payment from other banks, they quickly discovered that the whole system had been trading with make-believe currency, without setting aside real dollars. There was nowhere near enough money on hand to pay up on the swaps. The only source of real money available to shore up balance sheets and stave off catastrophe was the American taxpayer.

"If there's one person to blame all of this on, it really is Alan Greenspan," said Frank Partnoy, a law professor and expert on the regulation of financial markets at the University of San Diego. "Clearly, derivatives are a centerpiece of the crisis, and he was the leading proponent of the deregulation of derivatives."

What is striking is the degree to which Greenspan carried an antiquated, even naive confidence in how banks would behave in a modern economy, despite a compensation structure that clearly rewarded risk. His belief in what he called "market regulation" amounted to a conviction that the overseers of Washington Mutual, Countrywide, AIG, and other institutions would have greater incentive to ensure they managed their money responsibly than any bureaucrat ever could. This notion was consistent with Greenspan's libertarianism, but it rested upon a view of human nature that seems almost sweetly quaint, as if the financial marketplace was just an overgrown small town.

"It is remarkable how much trust we have in the pharmacist who fills the prescription ordered by our physician," Greenspan told a conference of legal scholars at Georgetown Law School in the fall of 2008. "Or the trust we grant automakers that their motor vehicles will run as certified. We are not fools. We bank on the self-interest of our counterparties with whom we trade to foster and protect their reputation for producing quality goods and services."

The philosophy that Greenspan applied to Wall Street was akin to dismantling the Food and Drug Administration, figuring one could count on the decency of the corner pharmacist to protect Americans' health, and never mind that the modern-day pharmacist was likely part of a conglomerate that bought and distributed its products as part of a globalized supply chain answerable to stock market investors, with the interests of the customer but one consideration among many. The banking system was run by chief executives such as WaMu's Kerry Killinger, who could sell stock options today and remain stunningly wealthy long after the decisions that pumped up their stock prices led their companies to ruin. People on Wall Street got paid bonuses for saying yes to deals. Nobody got paid for saying no. The long-term interests of a given institution and the immediate-term interests of the people running it often pulled in opposite directions.

Greenspan either missed this truth or willfully pushed it aside in pursuit of a libertarian utopia, helping deliver a financial disaster. He allowed leverage to build up to deadly proportions on Wall Street, while the very people he counted on to behave decently effectively looted the financial system, a fact he came around to himself, long after it was too late. "Those of us who have looked to the self-interest of lending institutions to protect shareholders' equity, myself included, are in a state of shocked disbelief," he told a congressional panel in October 2008.

৲৲

Shocked disbelief pretty much captured Fran Barbaro's reaction in June 2006 as she tore open the envelope from Washington Mutual and looked at her monthly mortgage bill. The balance was climbing, not going down. It had been $760,000 a few months earlier. Now it was suddenly $819,000.

"I called the bank," Barbaro recalled. "'What the hell is going on?' They said, 'You have a negative arm.'" It was the bank's shorthand for a negative adjustable rate mortgage, or an option ARM. "I had no idea what this was."

Every month, as she had made her minimum payments, Barbaro had been borrowing more. Her bill was not in error. Her loan amount was expanding.

In fact, Barbaro's loan balance had risen so high that it exceeded the total value of her house, which had fallen in recent months. That triggered the automatic cancellation of her low introductory interest rate, forcing her to start paying off some of the principal—a significant change to the arithmetic. Her bill was $3,300 that month, up from the initial $2,600. Soon, it would climb above $4,000.

It was more than she could manage. Her stock portfolio was gone. She owed some $200,000 in taxes for pulling funds out of her retirement early to pay bills during much of 2005 as she recuperated from surgery. She had "a little bit" of credit card debt, with interest rates reaching 22 percent.

Barbaro did not seem typical of the home owners whose distress was already beginning to capture headlines. She was white, and did not live in a predominantly minority community targeted by predatory lending operations. She was not a first-time home buyer or someone unfamiliar with the details of a business transaction. Indeed, she negotiated deals for a living, often on behalf of large companies. She was not the sort of person one might think would find herself at the mercy of the financial system. And yet, that's precisely where she was.

Barbaro tried to persuade the bank to negotiate a fresh deal that would bring her payments back to a manageable level. But when she called the number on her mortgage bill, she learned that refinancing was no longer an option; she owed too much and her house was not worth enough. No one at the WaMu phone center had the authority to alter her existing loan, because they could not even figure out who owned it. WaMu had sold it long ago, and was now merely servicing her mortgage, mailing out the bill and collecting the payments. The current owner of the note was some other institution, and no one seemed able to provide her with a name.

Barbaro's mortgage was part of a web of finance so complicated that no one could unravel it. Housing prices were plummeting, falling by 25 percent in the nation's largest twenty markets between May 2006 and November 2008. Her place on Juniper Road had been tapped dry. So had homes across the country. And as more home owners fell behind, Washington Mutual, Countrywide, and a host of giant banks found themselves stuck with the loans they had been writing and selling. No one wanted to buy them anymore. They began writing off tens of billions of dollars in losses. Much as the end of the technology boom had turned all tech stocks radioactive, so it was with investments linked to mortgages. Though the vast majority of American home owners still made their mortgage payments, meaning that mortgage-backed investments clearly had value, the markets reacted as if no one was paying and these holdings might as well be worthless. The very complexity of the financial system—an attribute once seen as reassuring, with its risks supposedly spread—meant that no one knew what anything was worth. The market for investments linked to mortgages shut down.

Unable to sell their loans, the banks belatedly became interested in the creditworthiness of their customers. At WaMu, "the Power of Yes" gave way to scrutiny, requirements for documentation, and widespread loan rejection. Banks stopped writing option ARMs and many other types of lenient mortgages. They started demanding traditional down payments. Their newfound reluctance to lend took buyers out of the market, sending house prices down further and sending more home owners into default—a downward spiral. Economists nudged up their estimates for the ultimate toll of the losses in the financial system. A trillion dollars was the accepted wisdom in early 2008. By that summer, many said $1.5 trillion would be gone before the reckoning was done. Before the end of 2008, Nouriel Roubini— an economist whose early warnings of mayhem were dismissed—was putting the damage at $3 trillion, or roughly the annual output of Great Britain. And by February 2009, Mark Zandi, the Moody's Economy.com economist, saw a one-in-four chance that the losses to the financial system would eventually reach $3.7 trillion.

Barbaro was hardly the only American who had tossed her mortgage papers into a drawer without taking note of the particulars: in essence, Wall Street had done the same thing. As the losses mounted along with a sense of vulnerability, Wall Street banks puzzled over the inscrutable terms of the multibillion-dollar bets they had been making, just as Barbaro felt the need to go rooting back through the drawer to find her mortgage contract. The fine print was coming into focus across America, and its terms were crippling.

The mortgage game had worked wonderfully, so long as everyone believed that real estate prices only went up. But once prices started to fall, imagination became a lethal instrument. The people in charge of money saw danger lurking everywhere. What they could not measure and assess and easily verify they shunned as hazardous. Credit locked down.

As Barbaro worked her way through the hierarchy at WaMu, the most she could extract was an offer of "forebearance"—three or four months free of payments in the hopes that she could then get her finances straightened out and resume paying. But that was a nonstarter. She was earning about $5,000 a month, and her debt payments alone absorbed $4,400.

Her only chance to keep the house was to drastically cut her expenses and try to get more consulting jobs, building up enough savings to allow her to again make the payments. So Barbaro rented out her house to another family for $3,000 a month. She put her clothing in suitcases, put books and toys for the her sons into boxes, and moved into the basement apartment at her parents' house.

She put the boys in the sole bedroom. She lay on the fold-out bed in the living room. Many nights passed sleeplessly, filled with the sounds of nibbling and water dripping as she tossed and turned: three rabbits occupied three cages lined up against the wall beside her. She had bought them to try to console her younger son, Gabriel, then ten, when they moved away from Belmont Hill.

"He was just so depressed that we had to leave the house," Barbaro said. It had been his home for his entire life. Barbaro had figured they might stay there forever, or at least until she got her boys off to college.

But as she lay in the dark in the basement of her parents' house, her belongings stacked around her, the Belmont house seemed far away. It had lost its currency as a financial instrument, reverting back to its primal state as a mere place to live. It would take an awful lot of austerity, a good deal of pleading, and a fair bit of luck for Barbaro and her children to occupy it again.

7

Lost Work

"Every day, I'm losing a piece of myself."

A sense of stifled anguish hovered over the job center. Beneath buzzing fluorescent lights, between walls covered with fliers offering debt management workshops and job training programs, dozens of people sat quietly at cubicles, peering at computer screens in the hopes of changing their current status: unemployed.

It was early February 2008, much closer to the beginning of the recession than the end, and Greg Bailey's long frame was squeezed into an office chair, his knees scraping the desktop as he leaned forward for a better look. No matter how he arranged himself or manipulated the cursor across the screen, the view remained essentially unchanged. There were jobs in stockrooms that paid $8 an hour—barely half of what he had been making three years earlier, when he was still driving a truck for Penske, hauling refrigerators around the Bay Area. The best possible advancement from one of those positions would be a job driving a forklift for $12 an hour. That was still less than he used to make, and short of what he needed to help support his nine-year-old son, Jordan. ("We're doing algebra," Bailey said. "I think he'll be something for math.")

Bailey needed no advanced mathematical skills to grasp his predicament. Any of the jobs listed would put him way short of the money he needed for his own apartment, so he could stop shuttling between his girlfriend's place, where acrimony reigned, and his mother's, where crack cocaine remained the dominant motif of daily life.

"I've got to find my own place," he said wearily.

So, here he was again, in downtown Oakland, on the ground floor of a nondescript office building, at the Private Industry Council, a nonprofit employment center. His eyes were red and tired. He was still looking, and he was surrounded by growing numbers of other people, all in a similarly dispiriting position.

"I can't find anything," he said.

Across the nation, plunging real estate prices and rapidly disappearing credit were occasioning much talk that a new era was at hand, one in which Americans would again have to work for a living. In place of home equity loans, stock winnings, credit cards, and assorted financial shenanigans, people would again have to depend on their jobs for sustenance. Yet just as work was supposed to resume its rightful place at the center of household finance, paychecks were getting increasingly elusive.

As an African American man, Bailey's experience was particularly difficult. Yet it reflected the dominant trend throughout the economy. When I met him in Oakland that February morning, the national unemployment rate was rapidly increasing. It would climb from a relatively modest 4.8 percent to 7.6 percent in January 2009, its highest level in seventeen years. Many economists expected it would reach double-digits by 2010, a rate not seen in a quarter-century.

It had been six months since Bailey graduated from his biotechnology training program, a seventeen-week course that was supposed to have set him up for an entry-level job in an industry with considerable prospects. He had opted to enroll in the program back when he was still delivering appliances, after that rainy Christmas Eve drive down to Pebble Beach, when he had nearly turned around for fear of having an accident. "That's when I knew I didn't want to do that anymore," he said.

He had read about the growth of the biotech industry in the local newspaper, and he had seen the sleek campuses with their lettered signs out front. One company, Chiron, had a laboratory right near his grandmother's house. He had heard about the money you could make there—$17 or even $18 an hour to start—with excellent advancement potential.

Bailey searched for local biotech training programs on the Internet and found one at the Regional Technical Training Center, a state-approved organization that aimed to give low-income people job skills that would lift them to better-paying work. The RTTC cast itself as a pragmatic enterprise, a conduit to real jobs. "Our approach is unique," it boasted on its Web site. "We work directly with industry to determine exactly what employee skills they need right now, and what skills they anticipate needing in the future. It had "placed 95 percent of its students with Bay Area firms," the site said.

Bailey attended an orientation at the Private Industry Council, which administers state and federally funded job training programs. There, he learned that if he left Penske he could qualify for a year of unemployment benefits, plus food stamps and a card that allowed him to ride the commuter rail network for free while he attended the biotech training program. His tuition would be paid by the state. After four months, he would graduate with the skills needed for a significantly better job.

"The opportunities were almost endless," he said.

He started the RTTC program in June 2007, attending class every weekday for six to seven hours. He conducted biology experiments in the lab, learned how to handle test tubes and solutions, and listened to lectures. His classmates comprised an eclectic group—thirty-seven people, almost all of them older than Bailey. Many had not worked for years. What they shared was the expectation that they would soon have a job that would allow them to earn a stable living. "They always told us that they had access to jobs, and did job placement," Bailey said. "They said they would have people coming to look for us."

He began seeking out jobs even while he was taking classes, regularly attending sessions on campus with speakers from area biotech companies who offered tips on how to apply. After graduation, one classmate quickly secured a job at Bayer for $14 an hour through a temp agency. But Bailey had his sights on a regular, full-time job. As his search came up empty, he was beginning to question the merits of his program. "Even the entry-level jobs want you to have a bachelor's degree in something," he said. "It could be English and you could be a dishwasher, but you need that degree."

A month after graduation, Bailey was at a job center in East Oakland when he ran into six of his classmates. "I was like, 'Oh man, you're all here, too,'" he said. "We started looking at anything at that point. It was kind of getting depressing."

Bailey was generally not one for moaning about his situation. He was, if nothing else, a survivor, and he held fast to the idea that things would work out in the end. "It seemed like a good field," he kept saying, as if reassuring himself that it wasn't stupid to have gone through the biotech program; that it was just a matter of being patient and persistent. "It sounded great. The opportunities were almost endless. I still feel that way. It's just the opportunity to get in."

He had applied for about thirty jobs and had yet to receive so much as a call for an interview. "I've tried everything," he said. "I've talked to security guards. Everybody wants you to just put in an application on the Internet. It just disappears."

In truth, though, there was a small measure of relief in this familiar disappointment. A call for an interview would amount to a test for which he felt starkly unprepared—not in his skills, or his intelligence, which, despite his exhaustion, remained evident, but in his wardrobe. "I don't think I have the right attire for an interview," he said. "I got one suit, and it's green and I don't think that's appropriate."

He imagined getting some sort of other job first, a better-paying truck-driving job or a warehouse position, so he could get himself set up in an apartment, get the right clothes, gain some confidence, and then stride into the interview in proper fashion, because this might be his last chance at escaping from the exhausting, low-wage physical labor that was never supposed to have been his life in the first place. He was intent on using this chance with great care, to maximize his odds of success.

So he made his peace with dropping his aspirations for a while longer. He applied for the night job at Walmart, in the rough part of town. He applied for warehouse work, truck-driving jobs. He looked for anything.

What he got was an up-close lesson in the sorry state of the economy. The job market was going from lean to mean. Every kind of position was growing scarce—even low-paid jobs at undesirable workplaces.

In March, Bailey began going regularly to a staffing company in Oakland, where hundreds of men congregated, most of them homeless, waiting for odd jobs. He could make $8 an hour—cash in hand at the end of the day—painting houses, unloading trucks, whatever needed doing. But it was no sure thing. He typically got there at four o'clock in the morning, an hour before the place opened, so he could claim one of the first spots.

Sometimes, a call would come in for a needed body and he would be dispatched for a few hours. More often, he would wait until nine, watching the news, reading the paper, before giving up and going back to the job center, on the ground floor of an office building downtown.

He was quarreling with his girlfriend and avoiding her apartment. The situation at his grandmother's house had disintegrated to the point where he could bear it no longer. His grandmother had looked after the place with care before she passed away in 2006. The porch was now rotting, the roof was sagging, and the shrubbery was ragged and untended. His mother and a regular assemblage of addicts occupied the rooms. Outside, emaciated figures loitered in the street. This was no way to prepare for a job interview, no atmosphere for a man trying to rebuild his life.

"I couldn't get any sleep," Bailey said. "I couldn't focus on what I was trying to do. I'm like, 'What are you guys doing to my grandmother's house?' It was absolutely unbearable."

In early April, he checked into a homeless shelter just over the Oakland line in Berkeley. He occupied a bunk bed in a room with seven other men, using earplugs to cut the sounds of snoring. He endured a bedbug infestation. The bathroom had three showers for fifty people. The food was unappealing. "The first night there, they gave us this green stuff," Bailey said. "I didn't know what the stuff was, just that it was green."

But he was grateful to be there, and encouraged. "It was some peace of mind," he said. "I didn't have to worry about being over at my mom's, and I could focus on what I was going to do." His nights secured, he spent his days at the job center, sometimes attending classes that offered tips on how to handle a job application or write a résumé. He showed up on time, with pen and paper to take notes. He met with a counselor there, who advised him on new listings and encouraged him to keep looking.

Among the most shopworn metaphors in a land that subscribed to the Horatio Alger story was that the job market was supposed to be a ladder. Bailey had been straining to climb it for two decades, and he had made so little traction that securing a bunk at a homeless shelter felt like progress.

༄

Bailey had plenty of company in frustration. By January 2009, more than 2.6 million Americans had been officially unemployed for six months or longer, double the number from a year earlier. As layoffs accelerated in the face of diminishing business prospects, people lined up at the front door of the Private Industry Council to use the computers and enroll in training programs.

"You've got more people now looking for the same jobs," said Gay Plair Cobb, the Private Industry Council's chief executive. "There's more competition for every job."

As Bailey scanned job listings, so did Johnson Ching, who had been laid off six months earlier from his job as a mortgage processor at Washington Mutual, a position he had held for five years, earning $20 an hour plus benefits. His unemployment benefits were set to run out the following week, leaving him and his twelve-year-old daughter dependent on his wife's wages from her medical billing job.

Born and raised in Hong Kong, Ching and his wife had come to the United States seeking a better future for their daughter. When he found a job in the mortgage industry, he assumed he had hooked into something solid. "Everybody in the United States needs a home, so I figured the mortgage industry was safe," he said. Since his layoff, he had unsuccessfully applied at other mortgage companies. He had looked for data entry jobs, but kept hearing that he needed experience, which seemed to him ridiculous.

"All you need to know how to do is open a computer and start typing," Ching said. So he was taking classes at a community college, through a state grant, training to become an accountant.

Maria Espericueta was also in training. Three months earlier, she had been laid off from her job assembling packaging at a car parts factory, where she earned $11.30 an hour. Without a paycheck, she could no longer pay the mortgage on her house in East Oakland, and she had recently surrendered it to foreclosure. She was living at her son's apartment while she tried to start over.

Espiricueta was in her early fifties, a Mexican American who had arrived in the United States more than three decades earlier. Back then, hard work alone had seemed sufficient to begin modestly and get somewhere better, she said, but not anymore. She was being turned away from temp agencies and fast-food restaurants alike, because she was not familiar with the technology that now ruled the workplace. "I don't know nothing about computers," she said. "Everything is computers now."

She was willing to take even a minimum-wage job at the hamburger chain where she had worked fifteen years earlier. But even they had computers. With nothing else going, she had enrolled in a government-funded course, learning computer skills and résumé-writing.

At the job center, and across the nation, training had become the mantra, seemingly the solution to all employment problems. Take the jobless, teach them new skills, and watch them thrive—as if unemployment reflected not a shortage of opportunities but a mere mismatch. "The jobs are there, but the people to fill the jobs are not," said California lieutenant governor John Garamendi. "The current demand for skilled individuals in medicals fields, in biotech, for people capable of welding—there's a demand for these people."

But here was Greg Bailey, freshly trained, ready for work, and soon headed for a bed in a homeless shelter. Here were Johnson Ching and Maria Espericueta. Here was Thomas Leach, another African American man at the job center the same day. He had completed a training program in wastewater management two years earlier. Tall, outgoing, and amiable, Leach had a tie knotted smartly around his neck. He carried the certificates from his program in a laminated sleeve, ready for presentation. He, too, was still looking for work.

Forty-three, Leach had spent most of his adult years working as a carpenter, making between $8 and $12.50 an hour. "It pays the bills," he said. "But it's not the lifestyle I'd like to be living." He had settled on the wastewater treatment program through a strategic process. His friends were getting thrown out of manufacturing and construction jobs, so he ruled out those industries. "I was trying to find something steady and that was going to last," he explained. "I figured water was the one thing people would always need." Working at a wastewater treatment plant meant working for the government, an employer seemingly insulated from the ups and downs of the economy. It meant working outside, which he found appealing. "I figured it's out in nature," he said. "You get birds migrating to water."

In 2003, Leach enrolled in correspondence classes at Sacramento State University, pursuing an associate degree through a three-year program. But in the two years following his graduation, he had applied for forty different jobs at wastewater treatment plants in nine different counties and had not received a single offer. He was living in Emeryville with his mother, still working odd carpentry jobs to bring in money.

Leach was a man of astonishing resolve. "Thank God I got skills to pay my bills," he said. "I'll get something sooner or later. I just wish it would come a little sooner." He seemed certain of his eventual success, despite the disappointment all around him. "I will be moving up," he said, not boastfully, but more like a preemptive against unwanted pity.

He was correct, as it happened. Later that week, he was called to interview for a job at a wastewater plant in Santa Rosa, a fast-growing city north of San Francisco. The following week, he was hired. He would work four ten-hour days a week, earning $20 an hour to start, plus state-provided health and pension benefits. The advancement possibilities were substantial: plant supervisors earned between $80 and $90 an hour. It was nothing short of a triumph, a moment to celebrate, a step through the portal to middle-class life.

"The future looks extremely lucrative," Leach said, savoring it.

Yet if this was what it took for a highly intelligent, confident man with enormous drive to find a decent job—five years of struggle and a multitude of rejections—where was the hope that such an outcome could be widely replicated?

It did not take an economist to recognize that a lot of people at the job center, diligently seeking to acquire new skills, could count on disappointment.

✺

In a small classroom off the main floor of the Private Industry Council job center, another sort of training was under way. A half dozen people sat at linoleum-covered desks, listening to an instructor counsel them in how to safeguard and improve their credit. It may have seemed a peripheral use of their time, an activity that had nothing to do with finding work. But companies were increasingly running credit checks on job applicants and rejecting those with troubled histories.

"They figure, if you can't handle your debts, then you can't handle your job," said Anne Chan, one of the job center staff. It made for a cruel Catch-22: at the very moment that people needed paychecks to dig themselves out from unsustainable debts, the debts themselves were preventing some from getting jobs.

Dorothy Thomas sat at a desk in the front row, nodding as the instructor, Judy McGourty—a lone white woman in a room full of blacks and Latinos—described strategies to improve credit scores.

"My credit is just so in a shambles," Thomas told her. "It's just chronic bad, bad, bad."

Thomas had been out of work for a year, living in the house on "Crack Avenue." She had recently gotten all the way to an interview for an administrative position at a hospital in nearby Alameda. But then they ran a credit check and discovered that she had failed to pay an old cell phone bill and a couple of utility bills. That was the end of that.

"They just say that they have found a more qualified candidate," Thomas told the class, as McGourty listened sympathetically. "Your livelihood now depends on your credit. I just never thought that my credit would prevent me from getting a job."

She told McGourty the story of raising two girls with limited means, how she had damaged her credit by trying to provide for them. "I put two kids through college," Thomas said, choking back tears. "All I was focusing on was rent, electricity, food. Just the basics. And tuition. Other bills lose their importance."

"What you just told me, I want you to tell your employer," McGourty said.

"I did," Thomas replied, her voice cracking. "They didn't care. They're saying that credit is a reflection of your character."

At the house, her electricity was about to be cut off for lack of payment. Foreclosure loomed, and Thomas had no idea where she would go when that day came. She had nearly lost her cell phone—her only link to family and friends—before her older daughter, Shawn, paid the bill for her.

Twelve months without work. Twelve months of putting in applications at medical clinics, billing offices, customer service call centers, only to face rejection. "If you had told me before that a person could look for a year and not find a job, I'd have said they were just lazy," Thomas told the class. "Every day, I feel like I'm losing a piece of myself."

A sign taped to the classroom wall offered counsel: PRODUCTIVE EMPLOYEES WHO ARE PUNCTUAL, COOPERATIVE AND COMPETENT WORKERS FIND AND KEEP JOBS. But who could be punctual with neither a car nor bus fare? Who could show up at all?

"Sometimes, when you don't work, you don't even have money to go and look for a job," Thomas said as we spoke after the class. She had already had to skip three interviews because she lacked the $12 she needed for round-trip train fare. And she figured employers could sniff out the people who lacked reliable transportation. "You want to give them the impression that you can get there," she said. "If they think you don't have a car, that scares them."

Thomas thought about asking Shawn for more money, but a teacher's salary could only stretch so far. And it was humiliating to rely on her daughter. "I've been a rock for my family," she said. "Can you imagine what they would say if they could see how far I've fallen?"

The very composure that had carried her through her life—through the hallways of a forcibly integrated school in Oklahoma, through office corridors alongside people with elite degrees and expensive clothes—was slipping away. The poised and beautiful young woman who had sold makeup at a department store counter had become a middle-aged woman bulging out of a pair of sweatpants, her face sagging with exhaustion, her hair matted and unwashed for lack of regular access to a shower, and crudely tied up. Each day that her phone did not ring, each fresh rejection, intensified her fear that she would never get another job.

"Is it my age?" she asked. "I'm starting to lose all my confidence. Is it because I've gained weight?" She had been visiting a nearby church food bank for aid. "They give us cakes and cookies," she said. "That's full of fat. And then you wonder why poor people are fat! They're not giving us fruits and vegetables and alfalfa sprouts."

Her outpouring of dismay rested on the surface of a much deeper frustration. Thomas seemed to feel like the victim of a mistaken identity, as if it were only a matter of finding the right document, or uttering the right sentence, to set it all straight. She strained to cut through the impression she feared she was making—another unemployed, middle-aged black woman at an Oakland job center. She riffled through a folder, proffering her résumé, her job applications—evidence that she was comfortable in the white-collar world, that Crack Avenue was merely her accidental address. "I'm articulate," Thomas said, as she shifted suddenly from the colloquial voice of the rough streets into the smooth, receptionist voice of gleaming offices. She pantomimed answering the phone. "How may I direct your call?"

"I'm a positive person," she said, clinging to those words as she shook with frustration. "When you get discouraged, it's hard to recover. People who aren't poor, it's as if they think we don't know what our lives are like and what's happening to us. But we know. We know. Poverty is like a prison without bars."

⌇

African Americans, as a group, have long struggled with joblessness. Single mothers have a hard time paying their bills. Opportunities tend to be scarce for recent immigrants, people who speak less-than-perfect English, and those without college degrees—most of the unemployed at the Oakland job center. But as the recession intensified, almost no one was safe. In his classic study *When Work Disappears*, the sociologist William Julius Wilson argued that morally loaded judgments about poverty distracted many Americans from the economy's steady bleeding of low-skilled jobs. That bleeding hit African American communities harder than most. But "if inner city blacks are experiencing the greatest problems of joblessness," Wilson writes, "it is a more extreme form of economic marginality that has affected most Americans since 1980."

Indeed, by early 2009, the unemployment rate among white college graduates was 6.4 percent, up from 3.8 percent a year earlier, the highest level in more than a quarter-century. Among Asian college graduates, the unemployment rate had spiked to 4.9 percent, up from 1.9 percent a year earlier. Joblessness itself had become a source of more joblessness: as people lost wages, they spent less, depriving shopping malls, restaurants, and auto dealers of sales receipts, and prompting more layoffs. Layoffs, falling housing prices, and the financial crisis all became mutually reinforcing. As people lost paychecks, they failed to make their mortgage payments, which turned more loans bad, intensifying the strains on the financial system. As more foreclosed homes landed on an already glutted housing market, property values fell still more, further reducing spending power. More than half a million retail jobs disappeared in the course of 2008. Some twenty-three thousand accounting and bookkeeping jobs were eliminated. By January 2009, there were fifteen thousand fewer legal services jobs in the U.S. economy than there had been a year before. Architects and software developers were drawing unemployment checks. People who disdained government aid as a matter of principle were living off it. People who were already out of work were staying out of work longer.

In February 2008, I met Nicole Flennaugh, an African American woman who had graduated from Mills College, an elite institution. Two years after being laid off as a customer service representative at the Educational Testing Service—best known for administering the SATs—she remained without work. She had been getting by with occasional stints as an office temp to support herself and her two daughters, ages sixteen and four.

Flennaugh had not been particularly worried back when she was laid off. She had her college degree and years of office experience. Then thirty-six, with an air of responsibility, she had been paid $17 an hour plus health benefits at ETS, which seemed to indicate her value in the workplace. And it wasn't as if she had been singled out for elimination. The testing service had closed the whole office, laying off roughly two hundred people. They gave everyone two months' notice, which seemed plenty of time to find another job. "And then we realized there weren't any jobs," Flennaugh said. "Ever since then, it's just been downhill."

Flennaugh had married just after graduating from college in 1992. Her husband had been the primary breadwinner—an iron worker—but he had died of bone marrow cancer nearly three years earlier, leaving her with a small insurance policy, a meager retirement fund, and a new life as a single mother. The testing service job had been perfect for her, a reasonable adjustment to her new circumstances. Her sister looked after her younger daughter while Flennaugh spent her weekdays in the office. Every two weeks, she received a check for $1,200, plus overtime and bonuses. But over the past few months, she had found herself having to figure out a way to pay bills with a $212 weekly welfare check. She had recently worked a two-day stint with a friend in the administrative offices of a hospital for $16 an hour, and she remained on call for future assignments.

"I can't complain," she said. "Compared to nothing, it's okay." Mostly, she sat in offices, typed letters, or made copies for $8 to $12 an hour as a temp, as she had the previous week. For this, her mother had paid tuition at Mills? "I felt like a jackass," she said. "Just sitting there and counting paper clips. I feel bad, because my mom wasted her money. Because I can't find anything. I've been to college and have had all these experiences and I still can't find a job. I've literally sat and cried, but my friends with double degrees are doing worse than me. It's the economy. It's really bad."

In Boston, Fran Barbaro was without work, a fact that was threatening to derail her personal recovery. In June 2008, she had managed to move back into the house in Belmont Hill. She finally got WaMu to renegotiate her mortgage after she threatened to file for bankruptcy. They gave her an interest-only mortgage that dropped her payment down to $1,500 a month, with a $60,000 balloon payment due after five years. But the following month, she lost her job at a local software company. "I've been going crazy looking for a job," she said in September.

She had applied at technology companies. She had recently joined a telemarketing firm in New Hampshire that allowed her to make calls from home for $20 an hour, but they could not turn up enough business and laid everyone off. She was living on unemployment benefits of $650 a week, plus $400 a week in child support. "What are we doing here?" she said. "What's going to happen to me and the kids? I have no plan. My plan is to get a plan."

Andrea White, a thirty-six-year-old African American in Columbus, Ohio, had a master's in business administration. In theory, that should have made it easier for her to find work after she lost her job as an advertising sales person at a local television station in January 2008. But eight months later—in the middle of a year in which the economy would lose nearly 3 million jobs—White's advanced degree seemed to be working against her. There were few good jobs in Columbus. She was visiting temp agencies to try to line up receptionist work so she could at least bring home needed dollars, and she was hearing a dreaded word: overqualified. "I've contemplated not even mentioning that I have a master's or even a bachelor's degree," she said.

Her husband was still bringing home $40,000 a year from his job as a quality control manager at a plastics company. But things were so tight that they had recently sold off their furniture for cash. That meant explaining to their two girls, seventeen and twelve, why the living and dining rooms were suddenly empty, and why—for the first time—they were not getting new outfits for the new school year. They were putting off a needed transmission job on White's car, which limited her job search. "I can't drive on the freeway," she said. "So I have to look for work that's in my area."

By the start of 2009, she was still without work, and her husband's plant was idling production for weeks at a time, cutting into his paycheck. They filed for bankruptcy. Her car was repossessed. Her older daughter was accepted to three universities and was awaiting word on her admission to Brown, her first choice. Where she enrolled hinged on the availability of scholarship money.

In the Piedmont country of North Carolina, Howard Dempsey had spent nearly a decade at a Freightliner factory, assembling the sorts of tractor trailers that Willie Gonzalez had driven back in the late 1990s. It was the classic sort of manufacturing job through which a hardworking person with a high school diploma had long been able to earn a middle-class living. He had brought home $22.30 an hour, plus health insurance—enough to buy a house for his family and plan for college for his two children, with a third on the way. But in June 2008, with product no longer moving thick on the highways and truck sales down sharply, Freightliner shut down half of its enormous plant in Cleveland, North Carolina—the largest tractor-trailer factory in North America. In one shot, it eliminated half of the factory's three thousand jobs, Dempsey's among them. His wife was still working at a local hospital, bringing home $14.25 an hour, but she was about to go on maternity leave.

"Once I lose my health insurance," he said, "I don't know what we're going to do. We've got to rethink college and see how we're going to pay for that. It's kind of tough when you've got to tell your family that a lot of things are going to change and the things we're used to are basically going to stop."

～

Standing in line to enter a job fair in Columbia, South Carolina, in December 2008, Lori Harris was growing despondent. Forty-seven, she had graduated from an associate degree program in medical assisting a year earlier and was paying $95 a month toward $23,000 worth of student loans. A year's worth of searching had yielded one job offer, as a medical technician dispensing pills to patients. It paid $7.50 an hour with no health insurance, as if the proper handling of prescription drugs had no greater societal importance than burgers and fries. "I said forget it," Harris said. "I was like, 'Is it worth going to college? Did I waste my time?'"

She was living with her boyfriend, who was supporting her, and not always cheerfully. She had no health insurance and could not see a specialist for a torn rotator cuff. Harris, who is white, openly derided African Americans. "They don't want to work for a living," she said. "They just collect welfare." And yet, for the first time in her life, she had recently applied for food stamps. "I tried to better myself," she said, "and I'm getting nowhere with it."

The job fair was a window into the punishingly weak market. A half hour before the doors opened, the line snaked into the parking lot, more than one hundred people long. Inside, the offerings were slim — career advising services for a fee; jobs that paid only commission. Soldiers stood in desert fatigues recruiting for the army. At a booth for the U.S. Border Patrol, an officer in an olive green uniform stood next to a screen displaying video footage of terrified people running frantically through garbage-strewn patches of desert, chased by helicopters and jeeps. Starting pay for the border patrol was $36,000 a year, he told would-be applicants. But no one over forty was eligible, and every newcomer was required to start near the border.

YOU WANT A JOB THAT MAKES YOU SMILE, proclaimed a placard for Wendy's, the fast-food chain, which listed the benefits of working at its restaurants, among them FREE UNIFORMS. An air-conditioning company sought production technicians, but the pay was less than $10 an hour. A collection service that specialized in overdue medical bills — a rare growth spot in the economy — was hiring aggressively. "There's a lot of money to be made," the recruiter told anyone who stopped at his booth. "The more you do in collections, the more you make."

Frank Kelly, a fifty-two-year-old white man with management experience, surveyed the floor and wondered how much further down he would slide. Back in the 1990s, he had earned $65,000 a year writing computer manuals for IBM in upstate New York. After he lost that position in the downsizing of that era, he took a job as a supervisor at a lab that tested raw materials at a automobile brake pad factory in Orangeburg, South Carolina, earning about $55,000 a year. But in October 2008, amid Detroit's widening distress, he had been laid off again. Now, he was standing in front of a booth in a suit and tie, waiting to hand his résumé to a pet food company.

The damage was not confined to those losing jobs. Working hours across the country were being cut as well, a stealth force of retrenchment operating below the surface of the national unemployment rate. By January 2009, some 7.8 million Americans were working part-time because their hours had been reduced due to weakening business, or because they couldn't find full-time jobs—a jump of more than 3 million in a single year. By April 2009, the so-called underemployment rate—which lumps together jobless people with those who have given up looking for work, and those working part-time involuntarily—had shot up to 15.8 percent, its highest level since records began being kept in 1948.

In St. Joseph, Michigan, Marvin Zinn, a clerk at a Walgreens drugstore, had seen his take-home pay drop from about $650 every two weeks to $550, when I spoke to him in the fall of 2008. He had run up nearly $2,000 in credit card debt to buy food. He had quit using his cell phone and put off dental work. He was no longer attending church, he said, "because I can't afford to drive."

In Denver, Ron Temple reluctantly assented to his own loss of hours as an airport baggage handler for United Airlines, rejecting the alternatives: a shift to another city or an indefinite furlough without pay. Temple had worked for United for a decade, earning more than $20 an hour, plus generous health and flight benefits. The loss of pay was a harsh blow, but he saw no alternative. He could not move, because he could not sell his house. Similar homes near him were selling for about $180,000, and he owed the bank more than $200,000. In July 2008, he reluctantly traded in his old shift—three in the afternoon until midnight—for a shorter shift running from 5:30 P.M. until 10 P.M. His take-home pay shrank from about $1,400 every two weeks to about $570. By the end of the month, he and his wife were having trouble making their mortgage payment. He had recently brought home groceries from a church that sold them low-cost to people in need. "That's the first time in my life I've had to do that," he said.

Temple had been searching for another job to make up lost ground—applying for a cashier's position at Safeway, a clerk's job at Home Depot, and more than a dozen others—but the market seemed hopeless. He could no longer afford to drive in search of work, and he could not search online at home because he had lost Internet service after failing to pay the bill. On a recent day, he had bicycled to a Starbucks with his laptop to ride the coffee shop's free wireless connection.

For those just starting out in the job market, things were especially bleak, and education was no antidote. During the first half of 2008, more than one-fourth of college graduates under age thirty were employed in jobs that did not require their degrees or skills, according to an analysis of Labor Department data by the Center for Labor Market Studies at Northeastern University.

And the summer of 2008 saw the worst job market for teenagers on record. So many adults were desperate for any sort of job that many were filling ranks typically occupied by teenagers. "When you go into a recession, kids always get hit the hardest," said Andrew Sum, an economist at the Center for Labor Market Studies. "Kids always go to the back of the hiring queue. Now, they find themselves with a lot of other people in line ahead of them." Chick-fil-A, a national fast-food chain of chicken restaurants based in Atlanta, had traditionally relied on fourteen- to nineteen-year-olds for 70 percent of its workforce. That percentage dropped in 2008 as adults became so eager for jobs that they began applying there in greater numbers. Adult workers "have lost jobs in this economic downturn and begun to seek employment in our stores," said Andy Lorenzen, the company's senior manager for human resources.

⌇

The recession and the financial crisis were making choices particularly disheartening for single mothers who were losing access to government aid just as they needed it most. The logic of welfare reform was increasingly up for reexamination, even among experts who had supported the landmark legislation. Welfare reform was supposed to be a transition from a culture of unhealthy dependence on meager government money to ample futures defined by work. But where was the future if there weren't enough good jobs?

Several states, including Texas, were imposing timelines for welfare payments that were as short as a year. With eligibility tightened, growing numbers of poor single mothers were falling through the cracks—neither earning enough in the workplace to cover their basic needs nor receiving aid or education from the government. And, even as the job market collapsed in 2008, eighteen states managed to cut the size of their welfare rolls—a clear indication that the social safety net was no longer in place. Nationally, the welfare rolls remained at their lowest level in more than four decades, according to an analysis by *New York Times* reporter Jason DeParle. Among the dozen states with the largest increases in unemployment, eight had either reduced or maintained the size of their welfare caseload. Michigan, where unemployment was already above 9 percent, cut its caseload by 13 percent.

Critics of welfare reform claimed vindication for their decade-old warnings that trimming the program had been a dangerous idea. Even proponents such as Ron Haskins, the former Republican congressional aide who had helped write the bill, were questioning the merits of the change. "There is ample reason to be concerned here," Haskins told DeParle. "The overall structure is not working the way it was designed to work. We would expect, just on the face of it, that when a deep recession happens, people could go back on welfare."

Haskins singled out for criticism the decision to allow the states to determine the contours of available aid. "When we started this, Democratic and Republican governors alike said, 'We know what's best for our state; we're not going to let people starve,'" explained Haskins, now a researcher at the Brookings Institution in Washington, D.C. "And now that the chips are down, and unemployment is going up, most states are not doing enough to help families get back on the rolls."

In Austin, Texas, Crystal Bates, a twenty-seven-year-old single mother of two boys, had begun drawing a welfare check in January 2007, when she separated from the father of her second child, fleeing an abusive relationship. After several months in a domestic violence shelter, she had moved into a rental apartment of her own. At the state welfare office downtown, her case worker urged her to get a job as quickly as possible, warning Bates that she would soon lose her benefits because Texas had imposed a one-year deadline. Bates had hoped to go to nursing school so she could make a decent living. She had attended some college and felt confident that she would thrive in the classroom. She was cognizant that education was the source of much prosperity. But the state of Texas was telling her that she had to go to work immediately, in some capacity, or risk being cut off and left to raise two children with no income. So she took the first job she could get, as a cashier at a grocery store. She earned $8 an hour, hardly enough to bring home groceries. By working, she lowered her welfare check from $236 a month to $120.

Keeping that check required monthly visits to see her caseworker. That entailed taking a day off from work—something her bosses did not cheerfully accommodate—and then heading downtown by bus with her two kids in tow to sit in a stuffy waiting room, often for hours. Sometimes her paperwork was pronounced lost and she had to fill out the forms again. Sometimes her benefits were mysteriously canceled. Sometimes, she was introduced to a new caseworker and had to start over—all this for $120 a month.

"It's almost not worth it," she said. "It's not set up for somebody who really needs the program." But she endured it, because staying on welfare was the only way she could qualify for free child care, one of the key supporting programs that President Clinton had insisted on in exchange for approving welfare reform.

In February 2008 Bates hit the one-year limit for cash assistance for someone of her age and educational background. Gone was the free child care. She had to shell out for child care herself, $135 a month, and it was only available until six o'clock in the evening. That made it hard for her to apply for clerical jobs in health care, which would have paid more and given her a shot at advancement. They generally required night and weekend work. And that made it virtually impossible for her to go back to school and pursue a career in nursing. "I'm kind of stuck," she said, offering up a pronouncement with no obvious counterargument.

Bates was among the millions of poor women who would have preferred to be in school, trying to build a foundation for a better future, but were instead contending with scant job offerings. Education was among the clearest differences between the old welfare scheme and the new one. In 1997, 12 percent of welfare recipients were attending college classes, according to a survey by the Urban Institute. By 2002, the percentage had dropped to 7 percent.

"Women are being hounded out of school," said Diana Spatz, a former welfare recipient and single mother, who founded LIFETIME, a California-based group that campaigns for more education for welfare recipients. "The pressure to work first is so severe."

But what were they being hounded out of school to do?

More than 35 percent of welfare recipients were black, and 41 percent had less than a high school diploma, according to the Urban Institute. By January 2009, less than one-third of African American adults with less than a high school diploma were employed. Some 31 percent of other welfare recipients were Latino. Among adult Latinos lacking a high school diploma, the unemployment rate was 54 percent. Among blacks and Latinos, these employment ratios had changed little in the decade-plus since welfare reform. In other words, the people who had most depended upon welfare and were being forced into the job market to support their children were the same people who were generally having the hardest time getting jobs.

"The labor market for low-income women is so poor that it's almost a hoax," said Randy Albelda, an economist at the University of Massachusetts in Boston.

∽

The terrible job market was clearly a function of the recession and intensified by the financial crisis, but it was landing atop many years of lean offerings. Long before the onset of the acute economic troubles that assailed Americans at the end of the real estate bubble, chronic problems had made jobs scarce for millions of working people—particularly African Americans, Latinos, younger workers, and less educated people.

This reality ran counter to the way economists tend to see the ebbs and flows of national fortunes. Through the lens of traditional economics, the tough times represented no more than the temporary downside of the same predictable cycle that had always governed capitalism. Seven years of expansion had come to an end, and businesses were pulling back, making it harder to get a job. Eventually, after the usual period of retrenchment, conditions would surely improve and businesses would expand. Banks would lend anew and companies would resume hiring. Then wages would start filtering through the economy, resulting in more spending, creating more jobs—another virtuous cycle. Looked at this way, Greg Bailey, Dorothy Thomas, Fran Barbaro, and millions of other jobless Americans were simply unlucky to be living through a particularly rough patch, but if they waited a bit, better times were on the way.

This was a harder argument to make in the twenty-first century, however, than it had been in generations past. Faith in the replenishing ways of the business cycle had been shaken by two decades in which economic growth had been remarkably poor for many working Americans. There was some truth to the talk of a New Economy, it turned out—just not the truth championed by its proponents. In the real new economy, the ups and downs of the business cycle had been flattened, in the sense that the ups were barely perceptible.

The recession that began in December 2007 ended an expansion that was among the weakest on record. While millions of working people were sliding backward, the economy itself had been growing at enviable rates. Between 1991 and 2005, overall national income rose in the United States by a whopping 45 percent. That was triple the pace in Japan and more than double that of Germany. The previous seven years of economic growth had been good for corporate earnings and people in executive positions, but poor for those dependent on paychecks. The benefits of increased economic output simply did not find their way into the pockets of many workers. Incomes actually fell for most Americans in terms of the purchasing power of their dollars. Indeed, by 2006, nearly one-fifth of adults employed in the private sector were working for wages considered to be poverty level—$9.83 an hour—or less, according to Paul Osterman, a labor expert at the Massachusetts Institute of Technology. Among people working in low-wage jobs from 1995 to 2001, two-fifths of those who remained working saw their earnings either stagnate or drop in those years.

By the end of the previous economic expansion, in 2000, the median American family earned about $61,000 annually, after accounting for inflation. In 2007, before the economy turned down again, the median family had seen its earnings contract to $60,500. For the first time since the government began keeping records more than a half century earlier, an expansion had ended, with most Americans effectively sliding backward.

The people who had benefited significantly during these years comprised a uniquely elite slice of American life. Those with doctorates and advanced professional degrees—3.4 percent of the workforce—were the only group that saw their take-home pay increase, after accounting for inflation, between 2000 and 2006. At the same time, corporate profits as a percentage of national income swelled close to the highest level in sixty years.

For the vast majority of Americans, job growth was strikingly weak over the past decade. Between 1992 and 2000—back in the years of the technology boom—the economy gained 22 million jobs. Over the next eight years, the economy added a meager 8 million. Far from an aberration, this was merely the continuation of a trend that dated back three decades. In the 1950s, '60s, and '70s, American payrolls grew between 3.3 and 3.6 percent a year when the economy was expanding. In the 1980s and '90s, the pace dropped off, with private jobs increasing by 2 to 2.8 percent during years of growth—even as Wall Street and Silicon Valley juiced demand with huge sums of borrowed money. In the most recent expansion, payrolls had increased by a meager 0.9 percent annually.

Even that tepid growth took much longer to materialize than in decades past, as companies remained cautious in their hiring longer after the economy stabilized. Before 1990, it took an average of twenty-one months for the economy to gain back the jobs that it shed during a recession. Yet after the recessions in 1990 and in 2001, thirty-one and forty-six months passed, respectively, before employment levels recovered to close to their past peaks. This was not so much because layoffs were continuing, but because companies had become extraordinarily conservative in their hiring—a phenomenon the Goldman Sachs economist Ed McKelvey referred to as "a hiring strike."

Some 34 million people were hired into new and existing private-sector jobs back in 2000, at the tail end of the last expansion. A year later, in the midst of recession, hiring had fallen off to 31.6 million. As late as 2003, with the economy again expanding, private-sector hiring continued to fall off, to 29.8 million. America was experiencing a jobless recovery. Economic activity was picking up. The recession of 2001 was over. But it wasn't translating into more work. Between 2001 and 2003, while the economy was technically growing, more than one-third of people who lost their jobs failed to find work. Among those who found full-time jobs, earnings dropped 14 percent compared to their previous positions.

The hiring strike reversed what had been a steady march toward economic progress for many communities. Since the 1960s, the percentage of Americans of working age who were employed had been steadily rising. During recessions, the percentage fell below the peak reached in the previous expansion, but then reached a new peak once the economy resumed expansion. Among people ages twenty and older, the employment level swelled from about 57 percent to 66 percent between 1963 and 2000. But after the recession in 2001, that pattern failed to hold. By 2003, the percentage of those with jobs had dipped to 64 percent, and it never regained its previous peak before falling again in 2007. By February 2009, fewer than 63 percent of such people were employed, the lowest level since 1987.

This trend held for nearly every demographic group—men and women; whites and Asians; people in their early twenties and people in their early fifties. All suffered falling rates of employment in 2007 and 2008, with only 74.5 percent of white, college-educated people employed by February 2009, the lowest level in six years. But the phenomenon was particularly severe for black men. By early 2009, only 55 percent of working-age African American men were employed, the lowest level since 1983. The market was particularly bleak for lesser-educated black men. One study found that, since the 1980s, the share of working-age black men had dropped by 21 percent among those lacking a high school diploma, and by 10 percent among those with only a high school degree. Latinos suffered a similar reversal.

Those who were jobless were staying out of work longer than ever. From the 1940s through the 1970s, unemployed Americans generally remained jobless for an average of eight to twelve weeks. During recessions, the average duration of unemployment lengthened to about seventeen weeks. But beginning in the 1980s, the average length of joblessness regularly exceeded twenty weeks during recessions. And during the last decade, it never dropped below 12 percent. In short, unemployment had become ever more difficult to escape.

☙

"I can't find anything," Greg Bailey had said the first morning we met, long before the worst of the recession and long before I knew the extent of his efforts and just how meager opportunities were for people like him. I could not immediately determine whether his experience testified to the weakening job market then already visible in the national data, to his own unique circumstances, or—as is usually the case—some combination of the two. Why couldn't Greg Bailey get a job? It was a complicated question, one that involved his personal family history, choices he had made amid crises, a certain amount of bad luck. But why couldn't people *like* Greg Bailey get jobs? Why was it so hard for those without college degrees or money for cars or suits? The more I looked at the data, the more obvious the answer became: there just weren't enough good jobs. The options were diminishing. What work presented itself frequently did not pay enough to cover basic human needs. Bailey might just make it, get a job in biotech and wind up like Thomas Leach, on the path to his own home, a car, a semblance of economic security. Or he might fall backward into disaster. Either scenario seemed utterly plausible. This said less about him than it did about an economy in which millions of people were being left behind.

The weakness of hiring and a loss of jobs overall is commonly blamed on global trade—and with some legitimacy. By transferring labor-intensive work to factories in Asia and Latin America, where people can be hired much more cheaply, U.S. manufacturers have tended to focus domestic plants toward making higher-value goods that use sophisticated machinery. This has resulted in increased wages for many manufacturing workers while cutting the overall number of jobs. Service industry companies have taken advantage of telecommunications links in transferring work to low-wage countries as well, setting up customer service and software development centers in India and the Philippines and billing and payroll offices in China. This has increased profits for companies able to make use of overseas labor while generating white-collar jobs in the United States—and a reduction in the number of American jobs overall. At the same time, the continued influx of lower-skilled immigrants to the United States has pushed down wages for people at the bottom of the economy.

But while trade and immigration offer a partial explanation for the lean job market and the paucity of wage growth, other factors appear to play much greater roles. A widely cited 1992 study found that trade and immigration explained at most one-fifth of the gap in wage growth dividing highly skilled and lesser skilled American workers. In the much admired 2008 book, *The Race Between Education and Technology*, labor historians Claudia Goldin and Lawrence F. Katz argue that the growing inequality in American wages is above all a function of faltering educational achievement. For the first half of the twentieth century, growing numbers of Americans eagerly pursued a high school diploma, correctly deducing that it afforded entry to higher-paying industries that made skillful use of modern technology. Waves of new high school graduates found their way into the white-collar ranks and into the blue-collar jobs that still paid enough to support families. But by the late 1960s, the pace of educational expansion slowed considerably, and so did the growth of opportunities for many Americans.

The expansion of the high school ranks had been an equalizing force in American society, spreading the promise of higher earnings to more people as graduation rates climbed from a mere 10 percent in 1910 to about 70 percent by 1970. But as my *New York Times* colleague David Leonhardt elucidated, drawing on Goldin and Katz, the rise of the college degree as a determinant of economic success has worked the opposite way: it has sown economic inequality, for the simple reason that not enough people have gotten through college. Between the early 1950s and the early '80s, the share of young Americans who graduated from college increased from 7 percent to 24 percent. Yet in the three decades after that, the share increased only to 32 percent, and virtually all of that increase was among young women. "For the first time on record," Leonhardt noted, "young men in the last couple of decades haven't been much more educated than their fathers were."

Goldin and Katz argued that the slowdown in educational attainment delivered a slowdown in economic growth, skewing opportunities among American workers: better-educated people captured an increasingly disproportionate share of the spoils of economic growth. Just as education enabled workers to exploit technology in the early twentieth century—back when a high school graduate could gain a job making mechanized tractors for John Deere and Company—today's college graduates have a better shot at the higher-paying, technology-intensive industries that excel in the modern economy. Yet, as Frank Kelly, Nicole Flennaugh, Andrea White, and Fran Barbaro's stories illustrate, a college degree guarantees nothing, even as it increases the odds of success.

Back in the heyday of American manufacturing after World War II, a worker in a factory that made, say, industrial pumps might just as easily be hired by a plant that produced auto parts. The skill set was nearly universal. If you knew how to turn a wrench and operate machinery, a factory could generally put you to work. Companies could hire aggressively when they needed to, slow production and furlough their workers when orders dried up, and still feel confident that they could hire sufficient numbers of skilled people as business improved. In the modern-day economy, however, factories are governed by highly specialized machinery and computers, requiring training that can last weeks or months before a worker may be deployed on the line. Even in service industries, many jobs involve proprietary software and systems, and unique approaches to marketing. That makes companies inclined to hang on to people they have bothered to initiate, and disinclined to hire anyone else. Managers are fearful of not finding enough skilled people when they need them, making them reluctant to fire. And they are worried about getting caught with too many workers when business is bad. Much as manufacturers have embraced "just-in-time" management of their inventories—buying parts to fold into production just as they are needed, as opposed to stockpiling in warehouses—companies in many industries have taken a similar approach to hiring. They try to stay as lean as possible at all times while having needed people on hand. "Companies today would rather not go through the process of dumping someone and hiring them back," said Dean Baker, codirector of the Center for Economic and Policy Research in Washington, D.C. "Firms are going to short shifts rather than just laying people off."

The changes in employment were also a manifestation of the steady tilt away from manufacturing and toward service industries—particularly financial services. The traditional business cycle, as conceived by economists, is integrally connected to the factory floor: an increase in production historically requires more people, while a slowdown results in layoffs. Unemployment insurance was created in the 1930s precisely to smooth out the peaks and valleys of industrial production, allowing plant managers to furlough workers and then bring them back as needed. Service industries, by contrast, tend to rely on many more part-time and contract workers, giving managers ample means of adjusting to changes in businesses without hiring or firing.

This tendency reflects and has been enabled by the steady decline of union representation in recent decades, which has freed companies to manage their staffing as they see fit, without having to heed labor contracts. It is also the product of Wall Street's ascendancy. As money managers exerted greater influence over stock markets in the 1990s, they applied greater pressure to companies to cut costs as a fillip to short-term earnings. This boosted stock values and sowed greater insecurity within the labor force.

Bartlett Manufacturing Company, which makes circuit boards for computers, encapsulates how and why jobs were becoming scarce long before the current credit crisis. In the 1990s, as the economy boomed, so did Bartlett's orders. By 2000, the company employed about two hundred people, mostly in blue-collar assembly jobs at its original factory near Chicago, with another fifty or so at a new plant near Albuquerque.

Most of those jobs paid $10 to $11 an hour. By the end of 2001, with the United States gripped by recession and orders flowing to new, lower-cost factories in coastal China, business had dropped by two-thirds. Bartlett shut down its Albuquerque plant and laid off more than one hundred workers in Chicago, bringing its total workforce down to eighty-seven. But even when business improved in 2004 and 2005, the company added no workers. "We improved our process through automation," the company's chairman, Douglas S. Bartlett explained.

Long before the headlines spoke of economic distress, millions of Americans had grown accustomed to declining fortunes. As Greg Bailey, Dorothy Thomas, and Fran Barbaro searched for jobs, they might find some small solace in the fact that their difficulties were shared by millions of working families faced with a permanently lean job market. Their difficulties were being intensified by cyclical problems that would eventually improve when the economy resumed its inevitable expansion. But the fundamental problems were likely to endure and perhaps intensify, absent fresh government policies aimed at generating jobs. A disposition against hiring had become embedded in the basic workings of American business.

PART II

Rebuilding the American Economy

8

Waking Up to the New Thrift

"People are too scared to spend."

L ong after it should have been obvious that a genuine financial crisis
was assailing the United States, the policy makers who might have
eased the damage and the pundits who might have better prepared the citizenry instead remained convinced—in their public pronouncements—
that the troubles in real estate were contained. They took comfort in an
aspect of the national character that seemed immutable: no matter what,
Americans would always find a way to spend money. Even if the real estate
market was troubled, the economy would be okay, because consumer
spending made up 70 percent of the nation's economic activity. They be-
haved as if the streets of Neverland U.S.A. were somehow walled off from
the rest of the American economy.

The new Fed chairman, Ben Bernanke, who replaced Alan
Greenspan in February 2006, offered frequent assurances that the mortgage crisis would not damage the broader economy. In a speech in June
2007, as markets recoiled at news of subprime losses, Bernanke proclaimed that the troubles appeared isolated and suggested that housing
prices were likely to stabilize. "Fundamental factors—including solid
growth in incomes and relatively low mortgage rates—should ultimately
support the demand for housing," Bernanke told a gathering of finance
experts in South Africa. "At this point, the troubles in the subprime sector

seem unlikely to seriously spill over to the broader economy or the financial system."

Bernanke's contentions echoed in some quarters of the media. In a column in the *New York Times* two months later, as the stock markets reacted viciously to subprime mortgage losses, economist Ben Stein ridiculed sellers as modern-day Chicken Littles who had lost all perspective. The value of total outstanding mortgages then exceeded $10 trillion. Subprime loans made up only $1.35 trillion, and a meager 5 percent of them were in foreclosure, Stein noted, estimating that total subprime losses were unlikely to exceed $67 billion. But the stock markets had in the previous weeks excised more than $1 trillion in value. "These subprime losses are wildly out of all proportion to the likely damage to the economy from the subprime problems," Stein concluded. "This economy is extremely strong. Profits are superb. The world economy is exploding with growth. . . . The sell-off seems extreme, not to say nutty. Some smart, brave people will make a fortune buying in these days, and then we'll all wonder what the scare was about."

What Stein and policy makers failed to grasp—or at least were unwilling to acknowledge—was the degree to which real estate and the economy had become almost one and the same. As housing prices declined, millions of home owners were prevented from borrowing against their homes. And that helped impose an end to the unbridled American consumption upon which so much economic growth depended. The subprime problem was the first piece of a much larger mortgage crisis, which was itself the mere tip of a massive derivatives crisis that had been built up through a quarter-century of largely unregulated trading. As these problems erupted over the subsequent months, a scenario Stein blithely dismissed—"a devastating recession (very unlikely)"—punished the country. Far from hysterical, the markets were, by late 2007, rationally deducing that unpleasant surprises were coming.

By October, the financial world was choked by a crippling fear, as Bernanke finally acknowledged in a speech to the Economic Club of New York. The chairman suggested that bigger subprime losses almost certainly lay ahead as more loans reset to higher rates. Yet he continued to maintain that there was little reason to worry about a substantial downturn. "Direct evidence of such spillovers onto the broader economy has been limited," Bernanke said. Most strikingly, he vouched for the solidity of the financial system, suggesting that plenty of money had been set aside to handle future losses. "Fortunately, the financial system entered the episode of the past few months with strong capital positions and a robust infrastructure," he said. "The banking system is healthy."

If Bernanke was trying to reassure the markets, this was an excellent rhetorical offering. It was also ridiculous. The idea that the banking system was healthy was pure make-believe. The banking system was a black box, with many of its most important transactions unseen by the Fed chairman or any other regulator. In the most generous treatments of Bernanke's assessment, he genuinely did not know the extent of the losses that were already mounting in the financial system. The part that mattered was the shadow banking system, the vast and wild realm that operated outside of bank balance sheets, in which unfathomable quantities of derivatives such as credit default swaps had been traded for years. The public had no way of knowing how much money had been wagered on such trades, or how much money had been set aside to cover investments that went bad, thanks to the deregulatory efforts of Greenspan, Robert Rubin, Larry Summers, Arthur Levitt, and Republicans in Congress. As a result, Bernanke was in no position to offer meaningful assurances about the sanctity of the financial system.

Through 2006, the housing market falling and the mortgage crisis rising, Bernanke's Fed had lifted interest rates, concerned about the possibility of inflation. The move was intended to apply the brakes to economic activity, at exactly the wrong time. Not until August 2007 did the Fed begin cutting rates, unleashing an extraordinary expansion of credit that continued through 2008. Many economists faulted Bernanke for being slow to recognize and attack the trouble. "Bernanke did not see the magnitude of the housing recession," said Robert Shiller, the author of *Irrational Exuberance*, who warned of the tech and housing bubbles. "Bernanke was caught asleep at the wheel," Dean Baker, an economist at the liberal Center for Economic and Policy Research in Washington, D.C., said. "There was a colossal failure of economic policy."

Perhaps no one worked harder to reassure the markets that they need not worry about the implications of the mortgage crisis than Hank Paulson, the last Treasury secretary in George W. Bush's administration. A product of Wall Street, Paulson understood market psychology as well as anyone, having headed the investment banking giant Goldman Sachs before taking over the Treasury. He was certainly in a position to grasp the extent to which the financial system had been powered by a collective belief in the sanctity of the markets. That belief was not going to collapse on his watch.

"Credit issues are there, but they are largely contained," Paulson told reporters in early March 2007, long before the worst of the subprime losses. In August, as the markets gyrated wildly amid fears of a broader unraveling, Paulson scoffed at the suggestion that the United States had a problem. "The fundamentals of the economy are very solid," he told CNBC.

Paulson was, of course, taking his direction from President Bush, who continued to exude confidence that the markets could be trusted to sort out problems for themselves. "Our economy obviously is going through a tough time," President Bush said in a speech at a New York hotel in March 2008, in what proved to be the fourth month of the recession. "In a free market, there's going to be good times and bad times." In July, as worries grew about the health of Fannie Mae, Freddie Mac, and the Big Three automakers, Bush pointedly rejected the prospect of bailouts as antithetical to an economy ruled by the market. "Should the government bail out private enterprise? The answer is no, it shouldn't," he said at a news conference, adding there was little reason to worry because the economy "has demonstrated remarkable resilience."

What policy makers either failed to understand or were afraid to say out loud, lest they disrupt the make-believe, was the degree to which real estate had become a central artery of finance for much of the economy. They did not grasp the importance of people like Marshall Whittey, a man who neatly illustrated how and why the economy was in serious trouble.

⁓

I met Whittey in November 2007 in Reno, Nevada. After several years of dramatic increases, housing prices in Reno were plummeting. Whittey, an easygoing, wisecracking thirty-three-year-old, gave me what amounted to a guided tour of ground zero: many home owners in Reno were tapped out, and their spending seemed certain to dry up in coming months, a very bad sign for the broader economy.

Though Reno is best known for its casinos, it had diversified in recent years, using low taxes to entice major technology companies such as Cisco Systems and Microsoft to locate offices there. As home prices in the major cities of California spiraled beyond the reach of many families, cheap and abundant land over the border in Nevada exerted a magnetic pull. Families had been selling their California homes for spectacular gains and starting over in Reno, pouring their winnings into huge spreads on hillsides surrounding the city. Ranchlands that only a decade earlier remained a moonscape of sunbaked soil dotted with sagebrush had been given over to golf courses and brand-new Spanish-style homes topped with ceramic tiled roofs on streets with names like Painted Vista Drive and Rio Wrangler. As speculators jumped in, home prices more than doubled between the spring of 2002 and the fall of 2005. That year, Washoe County handed out building permits for almost $1 billion worth of new residential real estate, nearly doubling the level registered in 2000.

Born and raised in Reno, Whittey was perfectly positioned to capture a sweet piece of this speculative surge. He worked as the installation manager at Creative Design Interiors of Nevada, a wholesale dealer of carpeting, tile, and hardwood flooring. As national home builders descended upon Reno, turning the dry soil into ranch houses and irrigated squares of lawn, Whittey's company took care of the floors. He had begun as a sales manager earning a mere $30,000 back in 2004, when the business was a start-up. More recently, he had netted many times that in commissions alone.

Whittey was also playing the real estate game directly. Like most of his friends and neighbors, he saw a home as something to be traded for profit and borrowed against to enable purchases. He bought his first house in 1999, a modest place in a gated community, for $130,000. Five years later, he sold it for $280,000. Then, he bought a Spanish Colonial on a cul-de-sac in the newly developed Curti Ranch subdivision of South Reno, an area where coyotes and wild horses had roamed when he was a boy. The house sat among thousands of others, on a then-1,000-square-foot lot looking out toward the Sierra Mountains, near one of the largest shopping malls in Reno—a classic slice of Western-style suburbia. He paid $350,000, putting $100,000 down and borrowing the rest at a fixed rate of interest, 6.5 percent for thirty years, giving him a $2,000 monthly payment.

By 2006, Whittey's home was worth about $500,000. Rather than leave the extra value just sitting there, he turned it into cash. He took out a new mortgage for $375,000, paying off the first loan and pocketing the difference—$125,000. That raised his monthly payments to $2,700, but more to the point, it enabled him to spend far in excess of his paycheck.

Whittey and his girlfriend, Holly, regularly went on shopping sprees during which they dropped $1,000 at a time on new iPods, designer blue jeans, and sporting goods. His walk-in closet was filled with three dozen pairs of shoes and untold accessories. He and Holly got massages two and three times a month at nearby spas. They went out for dinner as often as four times a week—frequently at steakhouses inside the casinos, or at a nearby Italian restaurant where they enjoyed wines in excess of $80 a bottle. Whittey furnished his house with tile and hardwood floors from his company. He put a forty-two-inch flat-screen plasma television in the bedroom, and a fifty-inch set in the living room, alongside a cabinet full of stereo equipment. Snowboards and mountain bikes filled his garage. Granite countertops occupied the kitchen. "If I wanted it, I'd just go and buy it," he said. "You want to talk frivolous? I bought a new truck just 'cause I didn't like the color."

When Marshall and Holly were married in May 2007, they reached into the extra money from the house to finance a $35,000 wedding at a sumptuous estate in the Napa Valley. They honeymooned at a beach bungalow on the South Pacific island of Bora-Bora.

For Whittey, the cash was there for all of these purchases, and more seemed to be on the way. He had bought into a speculative house that his friend was building, borrowing $550,000 from a willing bank, putting no money down, and looking forward to selling it for far more.

But by November 2007, the surge of money was moving in reverse. Housing prices had plummeted, making his own home worth about $375,000, or about what he owed the bank. A neighbor had just surrendered his place to foreclosure. Construction had ground to a virtual halt. At work, Whittey's commissions were down sharply. He was carrying credit card debt of about $6,000 and not even trying to pay it off while he shoveled available cash toward the "spec" house. He owed $580,000 on the new property, as construction costs absorbed more than he had budgeted. Yet the house was likely to fetch no more than $480,000 once it was done, meaning that a very unpleasant negotiation with the bank was destined for

Whittey's future. He was struggling to make his payments—$3,800 a month on the spec house, plus the $2,700 a month on the place where he lived—and still keep groceries in his fridge and gas in his truck.

Whittey was laid-back and boyish—in his appetite for gadgets, his casual dress, and the easy way he seemed to amble through life. His cell phone constantly rang or vibrated with text messages, bringing invitations for drinks, games, movies. And yet, he had become an involuntary convert to an old-fashioned mode of living: he had to limit his spending to what he brought home from work, a shrinking quantity of money. "We just don't go out at all anymore," he said. "I don't buy clothes the way I used to. I'm feeling the crunch. And it will only get worse."

Throughout the Reno area, and across much of the United States, people like Whittey were receiving an abrupt introduction to the New Thrift. Even people who had remained fairly conservative in their financial management were now tightening up, taking a fresh look at their priorities.

Eric and Stephanie Lerude, both in their mid-forties, lived with their two sons in a 2,800-square-foot house built in the 1960s in an older part of Reno that felt removed from the casinos downtown and the spreading "edge city" of suburbia. Theirs was a neighborhood that could have been plucked from a small town in the Midwest or New England. Wicker furniture sat on porches, basketball hoops dotted driveways, and orange leaves crowned the tops of the cottonwood trees lining the quiet streets. Eric, a local lawyer, organized relay races in his spare time. Stephanie had started her own business designing promotional products, such as customized tote bags bearing company logos. They had bought their home five years earlier for about $440,000, a manageable sum, and had financed it conservatively, putting down about 30 percent and borrowing the rest via a thirty-year fixed mortgage, locking in a payment of about $2,000 a month. Shopping for status symbols was not their sport.

"We don't keep up with the Joneses," Eric Lerude said. "That's not how we live our lives." Yet like Marshall Whittey, they had indulged in some of the easy money that was coursing through Reno. Just two years after they bought their home, it was worth some $650,000. They decided to take out a home equity line of credit, opening up an account that allowed them to borrow as much as $85,000. They immediately took out

$60,000, investing most of the money in three commercial properties. They bought a used car, a Subaru Outback.

By the fall of 2007, the Lerudes' home was worth about $540,000, and they were worried about local business prospects. They had to cut back. "We're both self-employed in what I hear is an unstable economy," Stephanie Lerude said. "A large percentage of my clients are mortgage brokers or realtors or developers. There's instability there." The family decided to scrap its usual annual vacation. They relinquished thoughts of a modest renovation for their kitchen, replacing an electric stove with a gas range. "We're in a downsizing mode," Stephanie said. "We're trying to do less."

All this austerity was rippling out, diminishing business prospects throughout the metropolitan area. At the Meadowood Mall, in the southern reaches of town, the parking lot was mostly empty, and so were the air-conditioned corridors inside. "We're dead," said Cendy Rodriguez, manager at a Lane Bryant, the plus-size women's clothing store. "I've worked at big box retailers my whole life. This is insane. This morning, we didn't have a sale until noon."

On South Virginia Street—a wide ribbon of pavement flanked by strip malls and car dealerships—salespeople in the showrooms stood listlessly. "It's probably the worst month I've ever had, and I've been selling cars for six years," said a saleswoman at a Volkswagen dealership, Ruthie Thompson. The hardest thing was getting people to qualify for car loans. So many buyers were walking in with battered credit scores. "We've had to really struggle with grinding banks, grinding more money of them," Thompson said. "We're calling and asking for favors, trying to find every possible thing. We're seeing a lot of customers who can't come up with the money."

At the Flowing Tide, a casual watering hole favored by workers at technology companies in South Reno, even a Friday evening was quiet. "Three years ago, you couldn't get a seat," said Shawn Linch, the general manager of a construction company. "Now, no one's coming here. No one's spending any money."

Whittey sat there on a bar stool set at a round table with a couple of friends, both in their mid-thirties, both employed in the mortgage industry. Only months earlier, a gathering of this crowd had a devil-may-care air to it, with glasses lifted in celebration of flipping houses or selling floorboards. It might have been a prelude to a $300 bottle of liquor at a VIP lounge in one of the casinos. On this night, over draft beer, the conversation was more like a wake. "People saw an opportunity to live a type of lifestyle they couldn't afford," said Brian Baca, a wholesale mortgage banker. "People's monthly nut grew, and their income stayed the same."

Next door to Whittey's office, Sierra Nevada Spas & Billiards seemed like a museum for a past age of plenty. Hand-carved teak billiard tables carried prices in excess of $10,000. Hot tubs with room enough for whole families fetched more than $16,000. Many models had been reduced by thousands of dollars. "We're way down," said the manager, Ezra O'Connor, presiding over the lifeless shop floor. He estimated that business was off somewhere between a third and half compared to the previous year. "People are just not wanting to spend money. We don't get half the customers that we used to. And it's not just us. We're selling stuff at contractor prices just to get them out."

He excused himself as the front door opened and a man in a plaid shirt stepped inside—a potential customer. In fact, the man was a sales representative for American General Financial Services. He was going door to door, seeking to gin up fresh business by offering low-interest financing. "I get more sales people in here than customers," O'Connor sighed.

The salesman, Robert Cano, was accustomed to being turned away.

"Everybody is freaked out because their house is dropping in value and they're in debt," he said. "They don't want to take on any more debt. They just want to pay off what they owe."

∽

A major reason policy makers and pundits were so sanguine that the economy would weather the real estate downturn was because of their justifiable faith in the indomitable nature of American spending. So many premature obituaries had been written for the American consumer. Each time trouble emerged, so did some new source of finance—and spending continued. The recession that followed the collapse of the technology bubble did not dent consumer spending. Neither did the terrorist attacks of September 11, 2001, as President Bush urged Americans to spend as a patriotic act. Buy a DVD player and take a vacation, or one might just as well declare victory for Osama bin Laden. "Get down to Disney World," the president said. "Take your families and enjoy life the way we want it to be enjoyed." The wars in Afghanistan and Iraq had not dented American spending. Even as wages declined for most workers, consumer spending continued to increase, month after month, quarter after quarter, propelled by the sophisticated array of mechanisms that allowed people to buy now and pay later.

It had long been fashionable to describe the American reliance on credit as a kind of psychological ailment, a perversion of traditional ways of thrift and careful savings that had supposedly once ruled household finances. "Rather go to bed supperless than rise in debt," wrote Benjamin Franklin, whose ideas have retained almost biblical currency over the centuries, though they have been widely disregarded. "People have changed their view of debt," grumbled the economist John Kenneth Galbraith in his 1958 book, *The Affluent Society*. "Thus there has been an inexplicable but very real retreat from the Puritan canon that required an individual to save first and enjoy later," which was being "overwhelmed by the massive power of modern merchandising." Galbraith warned that the consequences of continued dependence on debt would be "considerable and disagreeable."

But many of the criticisms of consumer credit rest on a largely mythologized view of American history. Many generations before the advent of home equity loans and zero-interest mortgages, Americans were well accustomed to buying on credit.

In *Middletown*, the classic study of Muncie, Indiana, in the mid-1920s, the sociologists Robert S. Lynd and Helen Merrell Lynd, found an explosion in the use of installment payment plans as families brought home the accoutrements of modern living. The standards of lending were often so lax that the members of Washington Mutual's subprime mortgage operation might have felt at home. "Today Middletown lives by a credit economy that is available in some form to nearly every family in the community," the Lynds wrote. "The rise and spread of the dollar-down-and-so-much-per plan extends credit for virtually everything—homes, $200 over-stuffed living room suites, electric washing machines, automobiles, fur coats, diamond rings—to persons of whom frequently little is known as to their intention or ability to pay."

No longer did the construction of a house simply entail paying a carpenter to do the work. "The contractor is extensively financed by the banker," they wrote, "and this more and more frequently involves such machinery as 'discounting second-mortgage notes.'" The Lynds noted the growing prevalence of families buying homes on a so-called "contract for deed plan whereby one pays for his home by the month at a rate approximately 50 percent higher than the rent for such a house would be." The risks to the homebuyer, should they fall behind in their payments, were severe. "If one misses two months' rent in succession the home automatically reverts, with all improvements that the buyer may have put into it, to the holder of the title."

The system proved disruptive to Muncie's social fabric, prompting the Lynds to add a footnote that could describe America in 2009: "Untrained in such matters as the amount a family can afford and coaxed by constant pressure to buy, it is not surprising that ventures in home ownership not infrequently end in shipwreck."

By 1926, two out of every three cars sold in the United States were paid for with credit. By the end of the decade, the phrase "Buy Now, Pay Later!" had become fully incorporated into the American vocabulary.

The 1950s were a watershed in the development of consumer credit. First, growing numbers of Americans availed themselves of layaway plans and other loans that enabled them to bring home household goods then remaking domestic life. This embrace of credit definitively lifted the fear and caution still lingering from the Great Depression in many households, as recounted by Joseph Nocera in his history of consumer credit, *A Piece of the Action*. "For the burgeoning middle class, seeking a loan was no longer an act of desperation but one of cautious optimism, no longer primarily about need but about want," Nocera wrote. "Televisions, refrigerators, new models of automobiles, and a dozen other modern conveniences. People wanted these things. The logic of the Depression said they should go without until they had saved the money to buy them. But Americans were tired of going without. So rather than wait and save, they took out personal loans or bought on the installment plan. And when they saw that nothing bad happened as a result, they did it again."

In 1958, Bank of America unleashed the first credit card in California, the origins of the modern-day Visa card. The same year, American Express distributed its first credit cards. The new product permanently altered the terms of American transactions and exponentially increased the ability of consumers to tap immediately into a vast pool of credit. Over the three decades that followed, the national consumer debt load swelled from $45 billion to $666 billion, a sum equivalent to $7,400 per household.

In a useful social history of consumer credit, *Financing the American Dream*, Lendol Calder seeks to refute what he calls "the myth of lost economic virtue," the notion that dependence on debt represents a departure from national tradition. Calder asserts that debt has itself delivered its own virtue: as Americans have made purchases under installment plans and secured houses through mortgages, this has imposed restraint in spending, forcing households to live under a budget. "Installment financing saddles borrowers with a strict schedule of payments," Calder writes. "To satisfy their obligations, modern consumers are forced to commit themselves to regimens of disciplined financial management. In this way, consumer credit has limited the hedonistic impulse within consumerism, while preserving the relevance of traditional values such as 'budgeting,' 'saving,' 'hard work,' and even 'thrift.'"

It seems impossible to dismiss that characterization fully, even in the wake of the mortgage fiasco. No doubt, generations of Americans have opted to skip soon-to-be-forgotten restaurant meals because of the pressing need to make car payments. The tyranny of the mortgage payment has clearly taught some people how to budget. But one cannot contemplate Fran Barbaro sleeping amid rabbit cages in the basement of her parents' house, or peer into Marshall Whittey's wardrobe, with its thirty-five pairs of shoes, without reexamining Calder's portrayal. He argues that consumer credit has been a valuable tool in spreading American prosperity, something that seems beyond challenge. Yet it seems equally clear that, somewhere between the thirty-year, government-backed, fixed-rate mortgage, which put so many families into homes, and the WaMu option ARM, which put so many into foreclosure, Wall Street, Madison Avenue, and the mortgage brokers on Main Street turned consumer credit into a financial cancer.

The key to Calder's belief in the virtue of credit is the assumption that consumers will steadily pay back their debts according to a rigorous schedule. The devious genius of the forms of finance that proliferated during the housing boom was how it invited consumers to keep spending regardless of their debt loads, without having to worry about repayment.

Because the new wave of spending was tied to a seemingly bottomless reservoir of value, the American home, it did not feel like debt. "People have come to view credit as savings," said Michelle Jones, a vice president at the Consumer Credit Counseling Service of Greater Atlanta.

This idea did not arrive from nowhere. It was the product of a concerted campaign conducted by banks over many decades to convince Americans that it was okay to take out a second mortgage and spend the proceeds. Consider the catchy new euphemism for a second mortgage: in its new incarnation, it was a home equity loan. That phrase had been around since the Depression, when it popped up in classified ads. But not until the early 1980s did it enjoy wide usage, as federal authorities loosened regulations to allow ordinary commercial banks to offer second mortgages and loans with extraordinarily lenient terms. The banks unleashed a wave of advertising aimed at reassuring home owners that borrowing against the increased value in their properties was a fine and grown-up thing to do. "There's got to be at least $25,000 hidden in your house," Citibank proclaimed in ads touting home equity lines of credit. "We can help you find it." A 2006 campaign by PNC Bank featured a wheelbarrow with the caption, the "easiest way to haul money out of your house." An ad from CIT Financial promised, "You don't have to sell your home to get $10,000, $30,000 or even more in cash. You don't even have to walk out the door."

Between 1990 and the end of 2007, the outstanding balance of home equity loans swelled from $214 billion to more than $1.1 trillion. By the middle of 2008, Americans were on the hook for $2.56 trillion in consumer debt overall, an increase of 22 percent since 2000 alone. Debt-financed spending made household finances that much tighter, requiring even more reliance on debt to pay the bills. By 2008, Americans were surrendering 14.5 percent of their after-tax income to banks and other financial institutions in making payments on their credit cards, car loans, mortgages, and home equity loans, up from 11 percent in 1993.

This explosion in debt both reflected and enabled the abandonment of savings. In 1984, Americans still saved more than one-tenth of their collective income. A decade later, the rate had dropped by half. By early 2008, the savings rate was negative, meaning that, on average, Americans were spending more than their after-tax incomes. For the 34 million American households that had borrowed against their homes through a refinance or a home equity loan sometime during the housing boom, the savings rate was running at negative 13 percent by the middle of 2006. These people—which is to say roughly one-third of all households in the United States—were borrowing heavily just to finance their day-to-day lives.

To some extent, they had no alternative. Many of the 4 million factory jobs lost over the course of the 1990s and 2000s had paid wages enough for middle-class lives, including health benefits. Many of those put out of work had since taken jobs as cashiers, salespeople, handymen, or janitors for a fraction of their previous earnings, and typically with no insurance. Companies struggling to compete in a global economy and under pressure from Wall Street to cut costs had downgraded their health benefits or scrapped them outright, forcing employees to reach into their own pockets for a greater portion of medical costs. The share of Americans who worked at least twenty hours a week and had health insurance slipped from more than 70 percent back in 1980 to about half in 2005. When Americans got sick, they increasingly had to use credit to pay for medical care—or simply go without.

The Yale political scientist Jacob Hacker coined a useful term to de scribe this refashioning: *The Great Risk Shift.* In his 2006 book bearing that title, Hacker argued that the traditional social compact governing American life has broken down, leaving families vulnerable to disaster when their income drops or illness descends. In decades past, Americans were guaranteed the basics of economic security—steadily increasing wages, health care benefits, and pensions from their jobs; Social Security; and a decent government-provided education. But as companies rolled back benefits and health care costs climbed, the burden has shifted largely to individuals, sowing vulnerability.

Working families priced out of the downtowns of gentrifying cities marched steadily to outer suburbs to find affordable homes and better schools for their children. Many took on bigger mortgages than they could handle in the process. The cost of a college education soared— along with the financial penalties of not getting one—with tuition more than doubling in inflation-adjusted terms since 1980. At the same time, increased tuition costs vastly exceeded available financial aid. Three decades ago, federal Pell grants, the primary aid for low-income students, paid for nearly three-fourths of the average cost of a college education. They now cover about one-third of the cost. Those leaving public colleges with loan debt surged from 25 percent of all graduates in 1993 to nearly 60 percent by 2003. Among graduates from private colleges, the share of those in hock jumped from 40 percent to 70 percent over the same period. No wonder so many parents felt compelled to take out second mortgages to send their children to college, and no wonder so many students began to graduate with large debts, contributing to a stunning embrace of credit cards by younger people.

Still, it would be ridiculous to dismiss extravagance as a source of the American debt crisis. One can see it in the proliferation of spas and luxury cars, the spread of plastic surgery and six-figure weddings. Credit counselors who staff hotlines for strapped consumers speak of how ordinary people have come to see a flat-panel television as a basic necessity. In Oakland, Dorothy Thomas herself acknowledged that part of her trouble stemmed from not being able to resist "a cute pair of shoes." Yet to focus solely on indulgence is to miss the full picture: for millions of Americans, living within their means has meant living on not enough.

As much as any other factor, the home equity loan served as the crucial stopgap for American families. The loans and their cousins—home equity lines of credit, which gave the borrower a checkbook or a credit card to draw against their home value, and refinanced mortgages, which gave the borrower cash—linked spending power to the eminently responsible act of owning a house. The assurance that he could pull money from his house emboldened Willie Gonzalez to take on more debt than he could manage and still feel he was behaving conservatively. It gave Fran Barbaro the false sense that her finances were in order, even as she exhausted her life savings.

Economists tend to believe in something called "the wealth effect." The more wealth a household builds up, the more willing that household is to spend and the less pressure it feels to save. The home equity loan tapped into this psychological vein. The housing boom increased the value of American residential real estate by something on the order of $8 trillion. Estimates vary wildly as to how much extra wealth gets turned into spending. But under even the most conservative estimate—with five cents of every dollar spent—the housing boom propped up U.S. consumer spending by $75 billion a year, enough to raise the economy's economic growth rate by half a percentage point.

Between 2004 and 2006, Americans pulled roughly $840 billion a year from their homes through house sales, home equity lines of credit, and cash-out mortgages. These so-called home equity withdrawals financed as much as $310 billion a year in personal consumption during those years. By the end of 2006, this gusher of cash comprised a startlingly large percentage of after-tax income in many areas of the country, particularly those in which real estate prices had risen most dramatically—23 percent in the Phoenix area, 22 percent in Las Vegas, 21 percent in the Oakland area, and 20 percent in many parts of Florida. Nationwide, home equity withdrawals made up 9 percent of all disposable income.

By late 2007, as Whittey commiserated with his friends in Reno, the pullback was already clear in the data. Home equity withdrawals had fallen to 8 percent of local disposable income, down from 17 percent a year earlier. By the first half of 2008, home equity withdrawals nationally fell off to an annual pace of about $400 billion—less than half as much as during the heyday of the housing boom.

And by the fall of 2008, American consumers did what experts said they could not: they cut back. Between July and September, consumer spending dropped for the first three-month period in seventeen years, and by the largest percentage—a 3.1 percent annual rate—since the middle of 1980. The very culture of American consumer spending seemed to have been altered.

∽

In Elk City, Oklahoma, a small town about 120 miles west of Oklahoma City, Elena Gamble had gotten accustomed to relying on small consumer loans from the loan shops in town when she needed a new pair of pants or pocket money for the weekend. She had tapped credit cards beyond her means of paying. It was all about keeping up appearances, living like the neighbors. "We live in a small town, and everybody looks at your clothes and what you drive and where you have your hair done," she said.

She earned $2,600 a month as a grievance counselor at a local prison. Her husband brought home $2,000 a month as a prison guard. But their debts were beyond them by early 2008, some $10,000 at high interest rates. They were no longer going out to eat, beyond the occasional meal at

McDonald's. They had canceled their Internet service. Their car had recently been repossessed. "What we say now is, 'If we can't afford it, we can't buy it,'" Gamble said.

It seemed more than a change to her household finances. It was part of a new mind-set, as if Americans had reached a cultural inflection point. Gamble looked across the street and spotted a Cadillac parked in front of a modest home. Only months earlier, she would have felt a twinge of jealousy, she confessed. With her bills piling up, what she felt instead was pity. "I say, 'Oh my, you're living here and driving that? There's got to be something wrong,'" Gamble said. "'You're in debt, and you're in trouble.'"

In Leesburg, Virginia, about forty miles northwest of the nation's capital, Lisa Merhaut, forty-four, had a six-figure income at a nearby telecommunications company and no end of credit. But she and her family had run up credit card debts that had gotten beyond them, and they were back to living the way her father had: she used cash for every purchase. "We don't use our credit cards anymore," she said. "What we have is what we have. We have to rely on the money that we're bringing in."

Many other households were doing the same, in what amounted to a remaking of the terms that had long ruled American finance, and it was reshaping the economy. It was grinding businesses into the ground, sowing fear from China to Guatemala, where factory jobs were dependent on the free-spending ways of Americans. It was making it harder for people like Greg Bailey to get jobs.

In the summer of 2008, the government sent out $100 billion worth of checks to American households in an effort to spur spending. But so many families were so saturated with debts that many used the money just to pay off outstanding bills—Willie Gonzalez among them.

Four years had passed since Gonzalez bought his house in Miami. For the first two years, things had looked fine. Gonzalez's handyman business expanded amid the construction and renovation boom. He brought home as much as $4,000 a month. Then, in the spring of 2005, he secured a job at a liquor distributor. This was a clear step up, a way out of the physically demanding life of pounding fence posts and pouring concrete, and it liberated Gonzalez from the month-to-month worries of working for himself: the job came with a 401(k) retirement plan, health insurance, a guaranteed salary of $2,500 month, plus commissions. "It gave me some security," Gonzalez said. "I was thinking about the future."

Confident and personable, he was well suited for the work. Selling liquor was all about relationships. He got to know the names of his customers' spouses and kids. He asked about their family vacations and birthdays. He celebrated and commiserated over the travails of the Miami Dolphins football team. He liked being the go-to guy, solving problems in a pinch. "If they ran out of something on a busy weekend, if they needed a case of wine or something on short notice, I would bring it right to them," Gonzalez said. "I was the hero."

The money was decent, about $36,000 the first year, and closer to $60,000 the following year. Still, Gonzalez had been spending as if his commissions would keep growing, tapping credit cards to finance what seemed like ordinary expenses—work on his car, dinners out with Ibis, new clothes for the kids. He was making minimum payments while the interest accrued. By March 2006, his balances had swelled beyond $25,000, and he needed a new car. His old one was unreliable, and he had to have solid transportation to make his rounds and bring home his paycheck. So he got a bigger mortgage on his house, paid off the existing loan, and pocketed $84,000, bumping up his monthly payment from $1,800 to $2,300. He bought a Suzuki SUV, with room enough for his family.

Then housing prices started collapsing. As home owners throughout Miami lost their ability to borrow, they stopped going out to eat, which meant Gonzalez's customers were buying a lot less liquor. Some restaurants went out of business. Others shifted from higher-end wines to mass-produced, inexpensive varieties. Gonzalez's commissions fell. In late 2007, his employer eliminated the guaranteed $2,500-a-month salary for all salespeople. In the first half of 2008, he brought home about $3,000 a month. Between his expanded mortgage, his car payments, and the cost of gas and food, he needed $6,000 a month to pay the bills.

"I have a big fear," Gonzalez said, as he laid all this out. "My fear is of losing my house. My income now is not adequate to pay the bills."

Financial planning had entered his thinking for the first time, but it was a perverse kind that involved figuring out which bills he could ignore while hoping for a change in fortunes. "The money's not there," he said. "So now you've got to say, 'Okay, what can we cut?' Now you have to prioritize your bills. Number one is your house. Number two is your car. Credit cards? Cable? I'm behind."

By May 2008, Gonzalez could no longer make his mortgage payment, joining millions of Americans in a state of default.

In July, he started raising Doberman puppies in the backyard, hoping to sell them to raise cash and avert bankruptcy. That month, the government deposited $1,033 into his checking account. He understood that this was an invitation to spend: to buy a new cell phone, jewelry for his wife, or a fence for his yard. With a click of his computer mouse, he sent the whole thing to his mortgage company.

"They think they give you a check to go out and spend some money, but it's not enough," Gonzalez said. "The way the economy is going, people are too scared to spend."

9

Healing Cape Coral

"We're all going to have to tighten the belt."

Reno had given me a gut-level sense that the loss of home equity borrowing would be enough to finally roll back consumer spending. That, by itself, virtually guaranteed a painful economic downturn. But I did not come to appreciate the extent to which the collapse of housing prices could wreck an entire community—and, therefore, many communities in which real estate had been the economic engine—until I visited Cape Coral, Florida.

Cape Coral, a sprawling city alongside the Gulf of Mexico, was one of the hottest real estate markets in the country between 2000 and 2004. The median house price in Cape Coral and its neighboring city of Fort Myers had leaped by 70 percent in those years, and jumped another 45 percent in 2005. But in 2006, prices had nudged down by 2 percent. Over the course of 2007, they dropped nearly 15 percent. Worse, the volume of home sales had plummeted by more than half.

At Cape Coral's City Hall—a glass-fronted building that spoke loudly of the abundant property tax revenues of the 2000s—Mayor Eric Feichthaler had come to the painful conclusion that he would no longer be spending much time at ribbon cuttings. A tax attorney by trade and a Republican by persuasion, Feichthaler called himself a fiscal conservative. He was being forced to put that mantra to the test, slashing away at the municipal budget and figuring out how to make due with less.

The town had grown by nearly half since 2000, its population swelling beyond 150,000. Growth had turned the musty flatlands in the northern reaches of the city into a loose grid of ranch homes painted in the hues of Sunbelt living—lime green, apricot, canary yellow. The mayor had been elected in 2005, in the midst of the boom, on a pledge to help deliver the services and infrastructure needed to accommodate expansion. He was keen to build a new high school to complete the local charter school system. He aimed to widen roads and extend water and sewer lines—which reached only about a third of the city—to limit pollution from leaky septic tanks running off into the gulf. He had hoped to add city parks. But most of those visions were on hold. The real estate furor that had filled city coffers had given way to a devastating bust. The "impact fees" the city charged new developments were drying up fast. In place of christening new facilities, the mayor found himself tending to the detritus of an age of speculative excess.

In the fall of 2007, Cape Coral had laid off fifty building permit inspectors because they weren't needed anymore. The city had handed out some eight hundred new construction permits a month in the midst of the boom. The number for November 2007 was seven. "That's an all-time low," the mayor said.

At a strip of model homes on the west side of town, real estate agents waited for customers to arrive as the sun baked the empty parking lots. The local government had recently inked a contract with a company that would cut the overgrown lawns shrouding hundreds of homes forsaken by speculators, many of them living far from Florida. "Emotionally, it seems blighted," the mayor said.

The yards were an eyesore, a nagging reminder that neighborhoods that were supposed to be filled with retirees enjoying lawn chairs and children playing on swing sets were instead lifeless, sitting dark night after night. The overgrown lawns were also attracting rodents, snakes, and assorted other critters in the semitropical wildness of south Florida.

"People are underwater on their houses and they have just left," Feichthaler said. "That road widening may have to wait. It will be difficult to construct the high school. We know there are needs, but we are going to have to wait a little bit."

Many other parts of the country were staring at similar problems, but southwestern Florida sat at the center of the gathering storm. It was here that housing prices multiplied first and most exuberantly during the boom, and here that the deterioration was unfolding most rapidly. Cape Coral and surrounding Lee County were at the epicenter. As houses were relinquished to red ink and the elements, break-ins were skyrocketing. Those scraggly lawns advertised the emptiness of the homes behind them, attracting vagrants needing a roof, teenagers looking for a place to party, and prostitutes seeking venues for their trade. With more than one-fourth of all homes vacant, residential burglaries had surged by more than one-third in the county. "People that might not normally resort to crime see no other option," said Lee County sheriff Mike Scott. "People have to have money to feed their families."

At the same time, law enforcement was resigned to making due with existing staff, cognizant that the days of getting what it asked for were over. "There's a concern in terms of tax revenue projections and our ability to provide service," Cape Coral police chief Robert Petrovich said. "I don't know that we'll be able to meet the demands of growth. We're all going to have to tighten the belt somehow."

⁓

Florida real estate had long been synonymous with boom and bust, but the cycle of the 2000s housing bubble had packed an unusual intensity. The Internet had made it possible for people ensconced in snowy Minnesota to type "cheap waterfront property" into search engines and quickly encounter no end of ads for properties. Cape Coral had beckoned speculators, retirees, and snowbirds with its thousands of undeveloped lots on a grid of palm-fringed canals, all beyond reach of winter. The city had been gaining familiar big-box retailers and chain restaurants, offering a quintessential slice of American suburbia at far cheaper prices than in more established communities nearby such as Fort Myers and Naples.

But the key element to the boom in Florida was the same as everywhere else: seemingly unlimited quantities of finance. The established dream of waterfront living combined with the easy money disgorged by the banks proved irresistible. This was how a speculator named Joe Carey—one of a crowded influx—wound up in Cape Coral.

Carey had owned rental apartments back in Toledo, Ohio, but Florida seemed like a whole different deal, a veritable money machine. He first visited Cape Coral on vacation with his girlfriend in the winter of 2002. A friend suggested he meet with a real estate agent to check out the local market. Through that agent, Carey discovered he could buy undeveloped quarter-acre lots for as little as $10,000. There were beaches nearby, plus golf courses and boat access to the Caloosahatchee River, whose muddy waters emptied into the Gulf of Mexico. Builders were happy to arrange construction loans and then erect houses in as little as six months. Realtors promised to find buyers before the houses were even finished.

"All you needed was a pulse," Carey said. "The price of dirt was going up. We took that leap of faith and put down $10,000."

Given the lenience of the credit terms, that investment was enough to buy three lots and erect three houses. Carey sold them immediately for about $175,000 each. Then he doubled down, buying new lots, confident that growth was real and would be sustained. In 2003, he became a realtor. The following year, he opened a title company. Then he launched a local office for Keller Williams, the national realty chain. He hired forty realtors.

His timing was impeccable. By 2005, the same lots that had been worth a mere $10,000 when Carey arrived were going for as much as ten times that. Back in Toledo, he had once made as much as $100,000 in a year. In 2005, Carey did $800,000 worth of business. "If you just got up and went to work," he said, "pretty much anybody could become an overnight millionaire."

Cape Coral and the city of Fort Myers, across the river, had blossomed into a metropolitan area of more than half a million. More people were surely on the way, seemingly justifying continued investment. "Jobs were very plentiful," Carey said. "The construction trade was up, stores were opening up, and doctors were coming in. It kind of built its own economy."

The trouble was, the economy was largely comprised of people building and selling Cape Coral.

As national home builders poured in, along with construction workers, roofers, and electricians, a kingdom of real estate materialized, and growth ultimately exceeded demand. The Joe Careys had been buying aggressively on the expectation that enough people would gravitate down from Toledo and Buffalo and other places where January involved a snowblower. The influx would fill the homes coming to life and justify the prices. They had been able to sell and make money in recent years because enough other people believed the story and bought in. In reality, speculators were largely selling to one another, as they were in other hot markets across the country, bidding prices up with the easily obtainable finance. When investors and prospective home buyers figured this out in late 2005, the market reacted with punishing speed. "It was as if someone turned off the faucet," Carey said. "It just came to a screeching halt. When it stopped, people started dumping property."

In October 2007, Carey shut the doors on his realty office. He closed the title company. In December, he went to his old office in a then-quiet strip mall to sell off his remaining furniture. He moved to Georgia to try his luck there.

But the houses left behind from the era of speculation would not be sold off as easily, much like the mortgage-linked securities clogging the balance sheets of major banks. More than nineteen thousand single-family homes and condos were listed on the market in Lee County in December 2007. Fewer than five hundred had sold in the previous month. At that rate, it would take three years for the market to absorb all the homes. "Prices are in a free fall because of this excess inventory," said Gerard Marino, a commercial realtor at RE/MAX Realty Group in Fort Myers.

Entire strip malls had been abandoned, as were the streets in many parts of town. Realty lawn signs lined the curbs, as if election day were approaching and someone named FOR SALE was about to win in a landslide.

Commercial builders were unloading properties at dramatically reduced prices—sometimes even below the cost of construction—adding to the glut. "It's our goal to clear out the inventory," said James P. Dietz, chief financial officer of WCI Communities, a Florida-based home builder. "We have to generate cash to make payroll."

In front of Selling Paradise Realty, an agency set in a strip mall, a sign beckoned customers with a free list of properties facing foreclosure and so-called short sales, meaning the sales price was less than the owner owed the bank. Inside, receptionist Eileen Rodriguez, said the firm could no longer hand out the list. "We can't print it anymore," she explained apologetically. "It's too long."

Two years earlier, in 2005, roughly seventeen hundred houses had been on the market in Cape Coral. By the end of 2007, fifty-five hundred properties were listed for sale, and more than twenty-six hundred of them were short sales, said Bobby Mahan, the firm's broker. "Anybody who bought in 2004 and 2005 owes more money than they paid," he said. "All of it was speculation driven. It was a feeding frenzy. Greed and speculation created the monster."

The glut alone was responsible for pulling home prices down further. And the excess inventory was certain to last a long while, because short sales were extremely difficult to complete. The lender holding the mortgage had to be persuaded to share in the loss and write off some of what was due. As Fran Barbaro in Belmont, Massachusetts, had discovered, simply tracking down the holder of the loan was not easy. Then, the agent had to convince someone sitting far away in a banking center to invest time investigating the particulars of a single piece of Florida property.

"Our real estate market has been devastated by the gross overabundance of inventory," Mahan said. "But you're dealing with a bank in Peoria, Illinois, or Houston, Texas. A short sale is a long and arduous process. Battling the banks is horrendous."

෨

Throughout Cape Coral, foreclosure filings increased fourfold over the course of 2007. Elaine Pellegrino and her daughter, Charlene, had resigned themselves to joining that list. Elaine and her husband had bought their three-bedroom house in northwestern Cape Coral back in 2002 for $97,000, paying no money down. The land was mostly empty then. But as construction crews descended and a thicket of new homes took shape around them, values more than doubled. They refinanced their mortgage and took out cash to buy two businesses—an auto repair shop and a lawn service company—thinking that increased local population would spell extra demand.

"We were thinking we were on the way up," Elaine said. "When we took the money out, there was so much building going on. Cape Coral was the number one booming place in the United States." She pointed across the street, at a nondescript gray box of a home. "That was selling for over $400,000," she said.

But in 2006, her husband suddenly died, leaving Elaine with the two businesses, both failing, plus $207,000 worth of debt against a home that was then worth perhaps $130,000. She was fifty-two years old, disabled, and severely overweight. She did not work, drawing only a monthly Social Security check of about $1,200. Her daughter, a college student, received $325 a month for child support for her two kids. As they stood in their driveway at twilight, their lights the only sign of life on an otherwise darkened street, they had not paid their mortgage in three months.

"What can we do?" her daughter said. "We're probably going to lose the house."

It would not happen immediately. The Pellegrinos were part of a new cohort forged by the real estate bust: they were among those effectively squatting in their own homes. The courts were so stuffed with foreclosures that they could assume they would be able to stay for a while. "We figure we have nine months," Elaine said. "It feels very weird."

Throughout Lee County, the pullback was taking down the broader economy. As people abandoned failed investments, there was less demand for building supply stores and fewer hours for the people who worked at them. Fewer cars on the road meant less business at area repair shops and tire dealers, further straining the local job market. At Rumrunner's, a popular Cape Coral seafood restaurant whose tables looked out on the bobbing lights of a marina, business was down by a third. Furniture dealers were folding. Hardware stores were suffering. At Taco Ardiente in Lehigh Acres, business was down more than three-fourths, complained owner Hugo Lopez. His tables were once full of the Latin American immigrants who filled the ranks of the construction trade. With the work gone, so were the workers.

"It's not just real estate," said Ray Kest, a finance professor at Hodges University in Fort Myers. "It now has permeated everything."

At the end of 2006, Cape Coral's unemployment had been a mere 2.9 percent. By the end of 2008, it was 9.9 percent.

In surrounding Lee County, government agencies, which depended on property taxes for a third of their general funding, were under significant pressure to pare back, as lower property values translated to less revenue. The county public safety department, which operated the ambulance service, was thinking about cutting staff. "That could affect the time required to get an ambulance to the door," said director John Wilson. The county natural resources department had delayed a $2.1 million project aimed at filtering polluted runoff spilling into Lakes Regional Park, a former quarry turned into a waterway dotted by islands and frequented by native waterfowl.

The county department of human services was seeing a substantial increase in applications for a program that helped those in need with their rent and utility bill payments. Half the applicants were saying they had lost jobs or seen their hours reduced.

At Grace United Methodist Church in Cape Coral, Father Jorge Acevedo had grown accustomed to launching aid drives for needy people far away—for health clinics in India and Africa. In 2007, the church was buying Christmas presents for fifty children within the congregation, whose families had lost jobs.

In previous years, Bishop Verot Catholic High School in Fort Myers had raised as much $200,000 by selling goods at a dinner auction. Michael Pfaff, another Toledo transplant turned Cape Coral mortgage broker, had often donated a weekend cruise on his forty-foot catamaran. But Pfaff's business had nearly disappeared, and he had recently sold the boat. The school canceled the annual auction.

"A lot of families just can't spend money the way they used to," said the principal, Father Chris Beretta. To compensate for the lost funds, the school was deferring building maintenance.

Out at the Lee County School District offices in Fort Myers, plans had been shelved to build seven new campuses in coming years. The needed finance was gone. In 2006, at the height of the boom, the district had taken in $56 million in developer impact fees toward building needed classrooms. Its initial projection for 2008 was $25 million. The actual number came in at $5 million, with $3 millon projected for 2009. The new buildings were no longer needed anyway, said school superintendent James W. Browder. Families connected to construction and real estate had moved away, so school enrollments were growing more slowly.

The very scrapping of the new campuses would likely accelerate the local downturn. Each school was to cost as much as $60 million—major projects for the reeling building industry.

❧

Amid this economic disaster, with wealth being destroyed and money in retreat, a former high roller named Kevin Jarrett found himself turning to the state to provide for his family.

In 1995, freshly arrived from Illinois, Jarrett and his wife drove out to Lehigh Acres, then a largely blank patch of land in eastern Lee County, on what had been pasture. A row of model homes boasted linoleum counters and carpeted floors for a mere $1,000 down. Jarrett wrote a check, and he and his wife soon moved into a three-bedroom, two-bathroom house on a corner lot.

He worked at first as a mental health counselor, bringing home about $21,000. By 1998, he was selling real estate for Beazer Homes, a national builder. By 2004, he was working for another builder and bringing in $230,000 a year.

Had Jarrett put some of that money aside, he might have weathered the storm that lay ahead. But he believed in the story he was selling, the transcendent value of Lee County earth. He and his wife bought progressively nicer homes, keeping the older ones to rent, while borrowing against the rising value of one to finance the next. They acquired a taste for $100 dinners. They bought a powerboat and a yellow Corvette convertible. Jarrett printed business cards with a picture of himself behind the wheel, the top down, giving a friendly wave. In the summer of 2006, Jarrett and his wife paid $730,000 for a 2,500-square-foot home in Cape Coral with a pool and picture windows looking out on a canal— Neverland by the sea.

It was a foolish move, a bold bet against everything that was already happening around him. By December 2007, Jarrett had not closed a deal in three months. His income for the year was on pace to come in at $50,000. Yet he needed $17,000 every month just to pay the mortgages on his four properties. Rental income was bringing in only about $3,500 a month. He had not paid two of his mortgages in six months.

Jarrett was supplementing his income by selling MonaVie, a juice marketed for its supposed healing properties that sold for $45 a bottle. Two other troubled realtors had turned him on to it, and now he was inviting people over to his house to try it as a form of sales. Drinking the juice had also essentially become his health plan: Jarrett had recently dropped health insurance for his family, saving about $680 per month. He had applied to join a state-subsidized health plan to cover his nine-year-old daughter.

"I'm in survival mode," he said.

The same would soon be said for much of the country, as Cape Coral's experience spread to Boston and Phoenix and Los Angeles. From the dense suburbs of northern Virginia to communities arrayed across former orchards in Oregon, real estate values were also falling, and local governments were soon cutting services as well, eliminating staff and shelving projects. Families seemingly disconnected from real estate were finding themselves sucked into its orbit, as the economy absorbed the strains of so much paper wealth wiped out so swiftly. The nation, sustained for so long by the idea that the American house was a cash machine, was discovering that homes were really just another source of debt. For many, the bill was past due.

The damage from the rampant speculative excess that unfolded in Cape Coral seeped well beyond its environs. The lending and borrowing that built this local disaster lay at the heart of the financial crisis that was building up, and would soon wash over most of the national economy, upending households and companies far from the red hot real estate markets of Florida, California, Nevada, and Arizona. The breakdown of the financial system had begun in the summer of 2007, when the subprime problems first emerged and lending first got tight. In March 2008, the crisis exacted its first prominent Wall Street victim, as the investment bank Bear Stearns nearly collapsed before the Fed launched the first of a series of unorthodox, government-led financial rescue efforts. The Fed brokered a deal through which JPMorgan Chase purchased Bear Stearns, while putting taxpayers in the position of guaranteeing $29 billion worth of the bank's bad investments.

But the crescendo came six months later, in September, when, in the space of a few momentous days, the government mounted several major rescues. On September 6, with the financial system in near lockdown, the Bush administration effectively nationalized Fannie Mae and Freddie Mac, putting aside its philosophical aversions to such action. Taxpayers were now explicitly responsible for Fannie and Freddie's trillions of dollars'

worth of loans. Later that month, on Sunday, September 14, the government allowed the giant investment bank Lehman Brothers to fail—an
event that would come to be derided by practically every economist as a
terrible mistake, a significant contributor to the fear building in the economy. The same day, the government declined to rescue Merrill Lynch, setting up its distressed sale to Bank of America, adding an ignominious
finish to the story of one of Wall Street's signature trading houses. A mere
two days later, the Fed handed an $85 billion bailout to American Inter-
national Group, the global insurance company whose credit default swaps
had emboldened so many institutions to make recklessly enormous bets
on mortgages—a tab that would soon grow to $170 billion. Had many of
those swaps been allowed to fail at once, said analysts, a broad meltdown
of the financial system might well have followed. "It would have been a
chain reaction," declared Uwe Reinhardt, an economist at Princeton.
"The spillover effects could have been incredible." Late the following
week, federal regulators seized WaMu and swiftly sold it to JPMorgan
Chase.

As seemingly impregnable institutions disappeared into the muck,
their collapses highlighted a sobering truth: the values of the mortgage-
linked securities had always been inscrutable, fluctuating with the value
of mortgages themselves. When housing prices were rising, this had not
been a problem, but amid growing defaults, they threatened to choke
the global economy. Mortgage-linked investments clogged bank balance
sheets. Unlike a share of stock in a company, whose value could be
gleaned by looking at its sales price on a stock exchange, these investments
were created from slicing the pools of mortgages into varying shapes and
sizes. They were worth what someone would pay for them, and in the
fall of 2008, that was close to nothing.

As more loans went bad, this injected even more uncertainty into the
process of calculating their worth. This uncertainty had enormous
implications—not just for financial institutions, but for the broad economy. Because no institution had confidence in the value of its assets,
money sat at a virtual standstill. The world financial system was a tangled
web of interlinking loans, investment guarantees, and insurance policies.
When an investment owned by one bank went bad, so did the investments
to which it was linked as collateral or as insurance. To raise money to
cover their obligations, financial institutions sold whatever they could, and

that lowered the market value of everyone else's investments. Each drop forced banks to pencil in a lower value for the assets left on their own books, and that required more selling to raise cash to maintain their required reserves. The crisis amounted to a global run on the banks. Everyone was at once selling whatever they could to raise capital and hardly anyone was making fresh loans.

The Bush administration finally came to the conclusion that no conventional approach was likely to solve the crisis. Fear and uncertainty had become so deeply entrenched that the problem was systemic. Rather than address trouble on a piecemeal basis, as one institution or another teetered toward collapse, the government had to reckon with the root cause of danger: banks and other financial institutions were stuck with too much garbage on their balance sheets. Until they could get rid if it, most banks would continue to eschew lending. So the administration put together plans for a $700 billion bailout.

"I'm a strong believer in free enterprise, so my natural instinct is to oppose government intervention," President Bush said during a nationally televised speech in late September, beseeching Congress to deliver the bailout funds. "I believe companies that make bad decisions should be allowed to go out of business. Under normal circumstances, I would have followed this course. But these are not normal circumstances. The market is not functioning properly. There has been a widespread loss of confidence, and major sectors of America's financial system are at risk of shutting down."

The Bush White House designated Treasury secretary Henry Paulson as the primary point man for its campaign to gain congressional approval, an ironic casting choice. Paulson had spent most of his career on Wall Street, where he headed Goldman Sachs. He had traveled the globe proselytizing for privatization, deregulation, and smaller government. Yet as one institution after another succumbed to the crisis, there he was on Capitol Hill, warning that government must either take control of broad swaths of the financial system or invite a meltdown. "No one likes to be painting in, you know, an overly dire picture and scaring people," Paulson told the House financial services committee. "But the fact is that if the financial markets are not stabilized, the situation can be very severe."

Paulson did a miserable job administering the bailout, leaving a legacy of distrust around infusing money into financial institutions, stoking a populist backlash that significantly complicates the Obama administration's policies. His vagueness in outlining the plan, his ham-handedness in addressing public outrage, and his basic political insensitivity to the ways of Washington nearly scotched the deal. He arrived on Capitol Hill bearing a crude, three-page proposal for the bailout—$233 billion a page. Even people who had secured mortgages from Washington Mutual at the height of the housing boom presumably had been required to submit more paperwork than that. He called his plan the Troubled Asset Relief Program and said the Treasury would use the money to buy the bad investments on the bank's balance sheets. But he offered scant details about how much the Treasury would pay the banks for these investments, or how it would determine the price. Given the uncertainty of valuing them, this was no minor omission. If the Treasury paid too little, the banks would presumably refuse to sell, and nothing would improve. If the Treasury paid too much, the government would be handing out subsidies to the very Wall Street banks that had helped bring the economy to its knees.

Paulson insisted such concerns were misplaced. The involvement of the government would stabilize the market and boost the prices of mortgage-linked investments, he argued. Once that happened, the Treasury could start selling assets back to Wall Street, and taxpayers would recoup a lot of their money. They might even profit. But this argument played poorly.

"I can put a gun to my neighbor's head and take his college fund for his children and place a bet on a roulette table in Las Vegas, maybe—maybe—I'll triple his money," declared Representative Jeb Hensarling, a Texas Republican. "That is not a risk that my neighbor voluntarily undertook. This is not a risk that the taxpayer wishes to voluntarily undertake."

The public was enraged by the prospect of entrusting such a huge sum to a deeply unpopular administration, and particularly to a man who had earned his money on Wall Street. Paulson was adamant that the bailout not include requirements about how financial institutions could run their businesses or how much they could pay their employees, lest banks be dissuaded from participating. The most objectionable part of the proposal for many was a section that gave the Treasury secretary virtually unlimited power over how he could use the money, with no review permissible by any administrative agency or court. "They sent us a proposal about how to solve the problem that made the secretary of the Treasury the king of the world," said Representative Melvin Watt, a North Carolina Democrat.

Yet, after a few days of theatrics and threats, after a dramatic vote against the bailout in the House followed by negotiations, Congress reluctantly gave Paulson the money—$350 billion immediately, and the promise of a second installment later.

Then, almost as soon as he got the money, Paulson changed his mind about how to use it. Buying toxic assets was suddenly out. Instead, the Treasury opted to inject $250 billion directly into the banks to improve their balance sheets, while aiding banks that issue student loans, auto loans, and credit cards. Another $40 billion went to cover loan guarantees extended to AIG. The rest of the first $350 billion was distributed in smaller pieces to other distressed lenders, such as $6 billion that the Treasury gave to GMAC, the financing arm of General Motors.

Democrats pressed Paulson to use some of the money to aid people in danger of foreclosure, but he rejected those entreaties. "The primary purpose of the bill was to protect our financial system from collapse," Paulson told the House financial services committee in mid-November 2008. "The rescue package was not intended to be an economic stimulus or an economic recovery package." But if Paulson was unwilling to bend his criteria for home owners, he ultimately did so—albeit reluctantly—for American carmakers. In December, General Motors and Chrysler teetered toward bankruptcy, threatening deeper job losses in an industry that directly employed some 240,000 people and 2.3 million more through suppliers. Congress, still bitter about the financial system bailout and distrustful of the people running the auto companies, voted down a proposed rescue package. That prompted the Treasury to reach further into its $700 bailout fund: it agreed to hand over $17.4 billion to automakers to spare them from bankruptcy.

In the fall of 2008, Federal Reserve chairman Bernanke was also forced to face an unfortunate reality: the American economy did not operate in a world walled off from real estate. "The downturn in the housing market has been a key factor underlying both the strained condition of financial markets and the slowdown of the broader economy," he told a congressional panel. The following month, he acknowledged to a roomful of economists in California that the financial system was riddled with failed investments. "The boom in subprime mortgage lending was only a part of a much broader credit boom characterized by an underpricing of risk, excessive leverage, and the creation of complex and opaque financial instruments that proved fragile under stress," Bernanke said. "The unwinding of these developments is the source of the severe financial strain and tight credit that now damp economic growth."

Bernanke's Fed dropped interest rates aggressively through 2008 in a bid to spur economic activity. By the end of the year, rates were effectively zero, meaning that banks could borrow money from other banks for free. The Fed also made use of its power to print money from thin air. Banks are required to reserve a certain percentage of their overall capital at the Fed as an emergency stash. The Fed gave banks credit for holding hundreds of billions of dollars they did not really have to restore their balance sheets and encourage them to lend anew. In this fashion, the Fed created some $1.3 trillion in new money during the latter half of 2008, hoping that this extra liquidity would filter its way to businesses and consumers.

In essence, the Fed was employing an enhanced form of the strategy that Greenspan had used to revive the economy after the Asian financial crisis and the collapse of Long-Term Capital Management in 1998, and again after the technology bust and terrorist attacks in 2001—unleash cheap credit and watch households and businesses put it to use. This time, it didn't work. That is not to say the effort was unnecessary, a question that economists will presumably debate for decades to come. Had the Fed not acted aggressively, the consequences might have been even more painful. Americans might have experienced the second coming of the Great Depression—something that Bernanke, a student of the era, was particularly intent on preventing. But lower interest rates and the dramatic expansion of the Fed's balance sheet did not revive the economy. They did not reverse the loss of jobs, which only accelerated as the months passed, because the financial system was rapidly disintegrating.

Just as Bernanke was flooding the nation with money in an effort to revive the economy, the financial system was taking it away. On Wall Street and in banks across the nation, the people in control of money no longer believed in the sky's-the-limit potential of American real estate. Zero-interest rates or no, the banks were not lending, fearful of diminished business prospects and unclear how many more dollars were going to disappear into the black hole of the financial crisis.

The banker and economic historian Charles R. Morris had essentially forecast this string of events. His book, *The Trillion Dollar Meltdown*, came out in early 2008, before most of the bank collapses. In a particularly trenchant observation, Morris distinguished between previous investment bubbles that had burst in discrete markets, such as technology stocks and real estate, and the unfolding debacle, whose implications were far broader. "Overpriced assets are like poison mushrooms," Morris wrote. "You eat them, you get sick, you learn to avoid them. A credit bubble is different. Credit is the air that financial markets breathe, and when the air is poisoned, there's no place to hide."

By the time Bush left office, the line of applicants for bailout funds was growing long, and the financial system showed no sign of improvement. Fannie and Freddie were counting losses faster than most expected. Citibank was in danger. AIG, whose investment concoctions were once supposed to be a source of comfort in the global economy, was continuing to sow anxiety. Seemingly every state capital and city hall was grappling with a budget shortfall. Connecticut was staring at a $922 million budget deficit. Virginia was confronting a whopping $4 billion shortfall over two years, with lawmakers bandying about words like *draconian* to describe the budget cutting that lay ahead. California was looking at a $42 billion deficit over a year and a half and was about to run out of funds to pay unemployment benefits, while writing more than $30 million worth of checks a day. In New York, Mayor Michael Bloomberg was begging the state legislature not to cut $656 million in aid for his city, warning that he would otherwise have to cut education spending. "We have got down to a level at this point where all the cuts from now on will be in the classroom," Bloomberg said.

The loss of credit tends to be devastating in any economy. The Great Depression has been convincingly blamed on a dramatic contraction of the American banking system, which left little money left to be lent out, thus starving the economy. Similarly, the financial crisis of recent years has proven to be a particularly nettlesome beast.

In Baltimore, a company called Marlin Steel Wire Products, which makes parts for factories that manufacture appliances, was still managing to increase its profits in the summer of 2008. It had just received the two largest orders in its history. The company's president, a likeable and loquacious man named Drew Greenblatt, had designs on expansion. He wanted to buy a robot and hire three more workers. But he needed a $300,000 bank loan to finance the plan. The local branch of Wachovia had been aggressively marketing him loans for years. Yet when Greenblatt called to try to arrange one, he was taken aback by the bank's response.

"The exact words were, 'We're saying no to almost everybody,'" Greenblatt said. "This is why God made banks, for this kind of transaction. This is going to slow down the American economy."

No loan meant one fewer order for the factory in Chicago that made the robot Greenblatt wanted to buy. It meant fewer hours for workers there. It meant less business for the truck driver who would have hauled the robot to Baltimore, and less demand to make trucks. And it meant no help-wanted ads for Marlin Steel Wire Products in Baltimore, where the local unemployment rate reached 8.5 percent at the end of the year.

"I'm stunned," Greenblatt said. "We're at such an exciting inflection point, and this is what a bank is supposed to do. There's sand in the gears."

By the spring of 2009, fear itself had morphed from a symptom of trouble to a leading cause. Poor expectations about the future were becoming self-fulfilling prophesies: even companies that were able to borrow and expand declined to invest in such a troubling economic climate, making pessimistic forecasts a reality.

For nearly forty years, Michael Powell had invested steadily in his demonstrated knack at selling books, employing a unique business model: he sold used and new books side by side at his store in Portland, Oregon. He had added to his business bit by bit, expanding into the largest bookstore in North America—a spacious, no-frills monument to reading that occupies a full square block of his often-drizzly city in the Pacific Northwest.

But in March 2009, Powell scrapped plans for his latest expansion, a $5 million project that would have replaced his original entrance with a two- or three-story building. An architect had already prepared the plans. His bankers had already signaled that credit was no problem, given his track record. Even amid a terrible downturn, his sales were down only about 5 percent over the past year, a testament to his store's fierce local acclaim. But the project no longer looked prudent, Powell said, not with stock markets extinguishing savings, home prices plunging, and jobs disappearing. "It's going to take a period of time to recover," he said. "Whether it's two years or ten years I don't know, but I don't think it's going to be quick. People are nervous."

That gnawing sense of uncertainty was pinning many investors and would-be consumers to the sidelines, making economists concerned about deflation—sustained falling prices—as goods piled up unsold and demand weakened. Deflation was a crucial problem during the depression, and it lay at the heart of Japan's so-called lost decade during the 1990s, when a collapse in real estate prices left banks in tatters. Even as Japan's central bank dropped interest rates to zero in a bid to spur growth, it had little effect because companies and households were too fearful to borrow. And even with interest rates near zero in the United States by 2009, business was winding down, as growth gave way to fear.

"I think we're in deflation right now," said Joe Cortright, an economist at a Portland-based consulting group, Impresa, Inc., speaking in March 2009. "You could fix all the problems in the financial system and we'd still spiral down because of the problem of expectations."

As the financial crisis wound on, banks confronted accusations that they were unhelpfully clinging to their money, depriving the economy of fuel. But Powell's change of plans and the lowered horizons of other Portland-area businesses attested to a complicating reality: even banks that were eager to lend were seeing their best customers demur.

"The banking system has liquidity; that's not the problem," said Raymond P. Davis, president and chief executive officer of Umpqua Bank, a regional lender with operations in Oregon, Washington, and northern California. "The problem is the demand. The problem is trying to get qualified people to borrow. We're as much a victim in all this as anybody."

Portland, a metropolitan area of 2.2 million people, was an ideal window onto the dynamic of fear and lowered expectations assailing the American economy. In good times, Portland tends to grow vigorously, elevated by successful companies such as the computer chip-maker Intel—which employs fifteen thousand people in the area—and the athletic clothing giant Nike. In recent years, Portland has attracted investment and talent with its strict curbs on urban sprawl, abundant parks, thriving culinary scene, and life in proximity to the Pacific coast and the snow-capped volcanic peaks of the Cascades.

But by 2009, Portland had devolved into a symbol of much that was wrong with the American economy. Housing prices were plummeting and foreclosures were skyrocketing. The unemployment rate for the Portland metro area surged from 4.8 percent at the end of 2007 to 8.1 percent at the end of 2008, according to the Labor Department. Intel had recently announced plans to close a local factory that employed nine hundred people, shifting perhaps three hundred of these workers to other positions.

With a major deepwater port on the Columbia River, Portland had benefited from the historic growth of global trade, generating jobs for stevedores, truckers, and warehouse workers. But as a global recession rolled back trade, Portland's docks were a snapshot of diminishing fortunes. Some thirty thousand automobiles filled parking lots at the port, the stranded cargo of withering trade. They had been shipped in from Japan and South Korea, yet sat unclaimed by dealerships as car sales plunged. Slabs of steel sat piled on the docks. Sales had slipped sharply as the falling price of natural gas has slowed the need for steel to construct pipelines in Canada. Volumes of so-called bulk minerals—including potash, a fertilizer railed in from Canada and then shipped to China—had fallen off by more than 12 percent over the past year. Docks once jammed with shipping containers showed visible gaps between the stacks, reflecting diminishing demand for Asian-made furniture and clothing.

The port's executive director, Bill Wyatt, described the decline in starkly deflationary terms: "Why buy today if you think the cost is going to drop more?"

As trade slowed, so did business for Greenbrier, an Oregon-based manufacturer of rail cars. General Electric was seeking to renegotiate a huge order, an eight-year deal worth more than $1 billion. Greenbrier relied upon a $100 million line of bank credit to buy raw materials and pay workers while it waited to collect from its customers. But with the potential loss of business from GE, the company worried that its banker, Bank of America—still struggling to recover from its disastrous bets on mortgages—would view its credit line as a risk and demand significantly higher interest rates. "If you had to go and renegotiate the terms of debt today, they'd rip your face off," said William A. Furman, Greenbrier's president and chief executive officer.

So Furman laid off three hundred workers in the Portland area, seeking to hold on and fend off the next wave of crisis, while spreading trouble further across the area.

"I'm not really spending anything because I don't know what's going to happen," said Alrenzo Ferguson, one of the workers who had lost his job.

෴

In April 2008, Dorothy Thomas moved out of the house on "Crack Avenue." She and her friend Yvonne agreed to leave in exchange for $1,500 from the bank that was foreclosing. They had been staying on as squatters after the foreclosure proceedings began, but were persuaded to surrender the place through the bank's Cash for Keys program. Thomas abandoned most of her furniture, while throwing a few cherished things—photos of her girls, her sheets and towels, some pots and pans— into a storage locker. Then she checked into a homeless shelter.

The shelter was located on a quiet, residential street in Livermore, a town about thirty miles east of Oakland. It was for battered women and substance abusers. Thomas was neither of those. She was merely poor. So she was pretending to be a drug addict in order to stay. She was even attending required counseling sessions, making up stories of craving and pain. "I just emulate the people around me," Thomas said, unable to contain her laughter. "I listen to their stories and I borrow from them."

The shelter was very strict. People were frequently tossed out for arguing, requiring one's best behavior at all times. Thomas had to sign in and out and state her precise purpose for leaving.

But she did not let this new station become a long-term state of desperation. She used it as an opportunity to reconstruct her life. In November, Thomas finally a got a job at a call center for a local chain of orthopedics clinics. She answered the phone and scheduled appointments. It paid $16 an hour—considerably less than she used to make but a whole lot more than nothing. It included full medical and dental benefits plus a retirement account. "It's lifted a huge burden off me," she said. She was so pleased with this development that she had brought a copy of the offer letter to show me when we met a few weeks later.

Her new employer had four offices—one in Livermore and the other three in surrounding towns. She was able to reach three of them using various forms of public transportation. When she told her managers that she could not manage to get to the fourth, they accepted it and inquired no further. And they didn't conduct a credit check. "They don't know that I'm homeless," Thomas said. "They don't know that I'm car-less."

Just as she had for most of her adult life, Thomas was again laboring to keep up appearances in an atmosphere that tested her limited resources. Through a program called Wardrobe for Opportunity, she had been given a leather bag and a couple of business suits.

One night, her coworkers invited her to join them at TGI Friday's for happy hour. But the shelter imposed a 6 P.M. curfew, so she had to decline. "I had to say, 'Oh well, I've got too much to do,'" she said. "And I would have liked to have gone. Apple martini, please!" But she had managed to join her coworkers one afternoon for lunch at a nearby Philly cheese steak place. "It felt so good just to be out eating lunch like a real, normal person," she said.

She wore a crisp white blouse. Her face radiated a calm that had not been there before, with some powder applied to her cheeks. You could once again glimpse the woman who had sold makeup at a department store counter.

"Everything is so much better now," she said.

Her life was far from fixed, and yet she exuded a palpable sense of purpose and self-assurance. She had one foot solidly back in the world of appointments, filing cabinets, and having a reason to wake up in the morning. A long, depressing stretch of hopelessness had given way to the outlines of a future.

She also had a driver's license, which was equally exciting to her, a validation of her place in the world. She thrust it at me as further evidence that she had reclaimed her true identity. The case manager at the shelter had driven her down to a special homeless court, where the judge had wiped out her past record of unpaid fines.

"Now I'm a licensed driver," she said. "I've got a permanent job. I've come a long way. I've got a roof over my head. I feel so good because I feel so normal."

She was saving $800 per paycheck, every two weeks. She had already saved up $1,600. She has no bank account yet, so she cashed the checks at the company credit union and then stashed the money in a safe at the shelter. Her plan was to save up $10,000, get a car, rent another house, and recover the life she had once known.

She had just seen a courtroom television show about a divorce case, in which the wife was deemed entitled to continue living in "the manner in which she was accustomed." That phrase had stuck in Thomas's mind. "Why can't I just get back to my own normal customary lifestyle?" That was feeling possible again.

"We have a saying," Thomas said. "'God may not come when you want him, but he's always on time.'"

Two months later, she had saved up enough to buy a car. She put $3,000 down for a 1999 white Toyota Rav 4, financing another $2,500, which gave her a manageable monthly payment of $168. The car made it much easier to get to work. When she hit the time limit on the shelter in Livermore, she simply drove off to San Leandro and found an available bed at a shelter there. Her plan seemed right on course.

But in late January 2009, with the economy continuing to deteriorate, her employer laid her off. Thomas was again unemployed and reeling.

"That first week, I really slipped under, into a deep, deep depression," she said. "I did feel suicidal. I just felt so knocked off the block. To lose that job was just devastating." She was sobbing. "I'm back at square one," she said.

But then an intense resolve returned to her voice. She was still in a shelter, which meant that she did not have to tap most of her savings. She still had her car, which meant she could apply for many more jobs than she had been able to before. She was pursuing one job at Stanford University Medical Center that paid $22 an hour. She had learned through the training classes in Oakland how to tailor a cover letter, how to write a résumé. Indeed, she had multiple résumés stored up on a little flash drive she kept in her purse.

"I'm a new person now," she said. "I do have marketable job skills this time."

She rattled off all the things she was doing to look for work, keeping herself busy. The very experience of having worked for a few months had restored confidence that had been broken down during those terrible months on "Crack Avenue."

"Things are still going to work out," she said. "I've gained a little ground, and I refuse to give it up."

In Florida, Willie Gonzalez was starting over, too. In September 2008, he had gotten a new job as a distributor for a wine company that promised him a minimum of $40,000 a year, plus commissions. But it wasn't nearly enough to cover his bills, and he had filed for bankruptcy.

At first, his lawyer told him he could probably save the house. But by December, the bank was pursuing foreclosure and Gonzalez's lawyers suggested that he relinquish it and find an affordable rental. He found a 2,500-square-foot house on a full acre of land, giving him room to breed his Dobermans. It was a manageable $2,000 a month. His sister moved in with him and Ibis and their kids. She had been a real estate agent and had earned as much as $5,000 a month during the boom. But amid the bust, she had been cleaning houses for a living, and she could no longer afford her $850 monthly rent.

As spending continued to dry up in Miami, work was becoming an increasingly uncertain proposition. In the middle of January 2009, Gonzalez's employer revoked the minimum guaranteed salary and forced all the distributors to sign letters saying that if they failed to sell $500,000 worth of product within the year, they could be fired. Gonzalez's take-home pay was down to about $2,100 a month. Ibis was bringing home about $1,500 from her accounting job at an appliance store.

"The way I feel now, I'm okay," Gonzalez said in February. He was relieved to be out from under a mortgage that he could not handle. He was pleased to be on a big chunk of land with his family. Yet the future seemed as uncertain as ever. Signing the letter preauthorizing his own firing had felt humiliating. He had made mistakes in his life, the same as most people. He had borrowed more than he could pay back, and he had suffered the consequences. But he was a worker, he kept saying, someone who earned his way.

"I'm not a lazy guy," Gonzalez said. "And I feel threatened where I'm working."

By March, his liquor commissions were still sliding, and he was borrowing money from his daughter to pay the bills. "I regret that I ever quit painting houses," he said. "I'm depressed, and my car needs brakes, and I can't afford to replace them."

᰷

Since the housing bubble burst in 2007, Americans have grown accustomed to living in close proximity to financial disaster. Their economic reality is fraught with deep insecurity. Millions live in perpetual vulnerability to one piece of unfortunate news, one bad break powerful enough to cost them their houses, their life savings, their confidence, their personal dignity. Before I started hanging around job centers, I imagined the homeless as a largely faceless mass of people somehow disconnected from the rest of the economy. They were people not like the rest of us, people whose lives had fallen outside the bounds of even ordinary failure, reaching a state of irredeemable hopelessness. In truth, many such people were devastatingly ordinary; people who had simply exhausted the means of keeping run-of-the-mill reckonings at bay.

In May 2008, Greg Bailey had left the homeless shelter after five weeks there, and his fortunes had improved dramatically. He was among twenty people hired by the Alameda County Registrar of Voters as temporary workers to help prepare for the 2008 elections. They tested voting machines, other needed equipment, and even the ballpoint pens that would be used for provisional ballots. They were paid $18.50 an hour, a veritable jackpot considering the jobs he had been contemplating.

Six months later, the election was over, and so was his job. When he and his coworkers said their good-byes, he said, "It was really emotional. People were hugging and crying. My boss made this speech thanking us all and telling us he was never going to forget us. I was like, 'Man, you're about to make me tear up!'"

But the experience had elevated him. There was a new spring to his step that had not been there before. He wore a snazzy blue athletic suit with white stripes. The bags under eyes were gone. He had saved $4,500 while he had worked on the election job, enough to put down a deposit on an apartment as soon as he secured some stable employment.

For the time being, Bailey was staying in a week-to-week hotel downtown, right around the corner from the job center, but he felt confident that he was on the doorstep of his own apartment. "I'm ready," he said. "I got the money. All I need is the full-time job."

Two months later, as the country posted another month of more than 600,000 layoffs, he sounded freshly beaten down. "There ain't nothing out there," he said. "Nothing."

He had tried to move back with his son's mother, with whom he had a long-running and difficult relationship—a word he avoided. "Well, it's a long something," Bailey said. They were soon fighting again, and he had moved in with a friend.

He had gone online and learned that he qualified for unemployment. He was receiving $229 a week—at least for as long as the state could afford to cut the check. There was talk of a special state election in the spring, and he was hopeful he might get called back to the Alameda County job. He had gone down to the office where laborers tried to pick up temp work for the day, but that had become hopeless, he said. In the spring of 2008, if he showed up at four in the morning—an hour before the place opened—he was almost always one of the first three people there. But when he showed up at the same time in January 2009, there were already twenty-five people in line ahead of him. And they were all waiting for nothing.

"You don't even get called," he said.

Opportunities had become so lean that many people who were trying hard to provide for themselves were coming up empty and rolling backward, bouncing between the real possibility of middle-class success and the equally real possibility of abject poverty. Yet this disturbing reality contained its own solution: all that many Americans needed to recover from their personal financial crises was a good, decent-paying job. Plentiful jobs could improve a great deal of the American economy's trouble.

Some people will always be stuck in poverty. Some will be gripped by substance abuse. Some will fail because of their own foolishness, poor judgment, bad luck, or some combination thereof. But after spending five minutes in any unemployment office, it's obvious that most people want to work. People want to depend on themselves, not the government or charity. If good jobs are there, people will occupy them. People want to feel normal, as Dorothy Thomas put it. They want their own place, as Greg Bailey said again and again—and he did not mean merely having his own physical address. He craved a solid place in society, not a high perch, but a reliable one, a concept that is inextricably linked to having a job. Much of the economy's breakdown—from growing indebtedness to accelerating foreclosures to increasing homelessness—was significantly enhanced by a dearth of good jobs. Too many people had been deprived of an opportunity to occupy their days earning a paycheck that could adequately provide for a decent life.

"The consequences of high neighborhood joblessness are more devastating than those of high neighborhood poverty," writes sociologist

William Julius Wilson in the introduction to *When Work Disappears*. "A neighborhood in which people are poor but employed is different from a neighborhood in which people are poor and jobless. Many of today's problems in the inner-city ghetto neighborhoods—crime, family dissolution, welfare, low levels of social organization, and so on—are fundamentally a consequence of the disappearance of work."

Much the same can be said of middle-class trials. The oversaturation of consumer debt was a function of many forces in the economy, not least the relentlessly marketed idea that shortcuts to wealth were waiting for anyone willing to buy the right stock or refinance a home. But it was also the result of decades in which American paychecks were outstripped by the rising costs of health care and higher education, in which millions of ordinary people have felt the acute need to use credit to pay for everyday life.

The growing reliance upon foreign creditors—not least, China—to finance American spending helped drive household and public debt to stratospheric levels. The only way to reverse this dynamic is for Americans to save rather than speculate. And the only way that can happen is if Americans can harvest earnings to work off our debts, which means we have to work for a living.

There is no panacea for Cape Coral, Portland, or any other part of the American economy. But generating millions of good jobs—jobs that pay enough to finance houses, cars, medical bills, and college—might restore some reality to the Horatio Alger tales that remain a core piece of the American identity. Ensuring that hard work is rewarded will allow people such as Willie Gonzalez and Fran Barbaro, digging out from the excesses of their borrowing and spending, a chance to recover and build a new life. It would supply Greg Bailey and Dorothy Thomas with a way to become the self-sufficient, productive members of society they have always strived to be.

10

Shovel Ready

"These are not bridges to nowhere."

When Barack Obama became the forty-fourth president of the United States on January 20, 2009, he inherited a nation consumed with growing economic anxiety. Three million jobs had disappeared over the previous year, and many analysts were predicting the unemployment rate would soon reach double digits. Obama immediately staked his presidency on an effort to halt the free fall in employment and generate millions of new jobs.

"We remain the most prosperous, powerful nation on earth," Obama declared in his inaugural address. "Our workers are no less productive than when this crisis began. Our minds are no less inventive, our goods and services no less needed than they were last week or last month or last year. Our capacity remains undiminished. But our time of standing pat, of protecting narrow interests and putting off unpleasant decisions—that time has surely passed. Starting today, we must pick ourselves up, dust ourselves off, and begin again the work of remaking America."

To many, Obama appeared to be paraphrasing John Maynard Keynes, the economist whose ideas formed the intellectual basis of Franklin Delano Roosevelt's New Deal, which was instigated in an effort to restore the country's economic vitality in a time of even greater distress. "The resources of nature and men's devices are just as fertile and productive as they were," Keynes wrote in 1930, as the nation descended into the Great Depression. "The rate of our progress towards solving the material problems of life is not less rapid. We are as capable as before of affording for everyone a high standard of life."

The similarity between Obama's and Keynes's words hardly seemed a coincidence. Obama was signaling that his presidency represented a fundamental shift in American philosophy: he would harness government and public spending toward reviving the economy. Alan Greenspan and Milton Friedman, who had steered the nation's economy in thrall to the markets, were out of the picture. The failed experiment in "faith-based regulation" had been relegated to history, along with the notion that government could trust the markets to spread the spoils of economic growth and protect the interests of working Americans. The renewal of the economy would unfold on the ground, with shovels firmly in hand. After two-plus decades in which government had been mostly tossed around as a pejorative, Obama sought to resurrect government as a crucial actor in the economy, not just as a regulator in the public interest but as an enabler of jobs and a guarantor of basic welfare. "The question we ask today is not whether our government is too big or too small, but whether it works," Obama said. "Whether it helps families find jobs at a decent wage, care they can afford, a retirement that is dignified."

A few days before Obama's inaugural address, the unemployment office in Columbia, South Carolina, was jam-packed. In the lobby, dozens of people sat in molded plastic chairs under the pale glow of fluorescent lights, waiting to apply for unemployment checks or job training. People entered the double doors and checked in at the front desk, their queries offering a running commentary of plans gone awry.

"This is the issue," began a woman who needed to extend her check, which was about to run out.

"I never got the call," said a man who suddenly was receiving no check.

"The store has closed," said a young man who needed a form from his previous employer.

"I just need this paper signed, showing that I've been here," said a woman.

Many of the people waiting were guardedly optimistic, a sentiment that was particularly strong among African Americans, who were particularly cognizant of the reality that a black man was days away from becoming president. The unemployment office sat less than a mile from South Carolina's state capitol, where the Confederate flag still flew in a courtyard memorial. "You look around this room, and nobody ever thought they would see this in their lifetime," said Aaron Bellinger, a twenty-five-year-old African American who had been unemployed since the summer, when he lost his job at a call center for Verizon. "For me personally, just having him in office, I'm always going to have hope."

But for Bellinger and many other people there, hope operated alongside awareness that it could take many years to improve the economy. Some were skeptical that the bold talk emanating from the new administration would translate into meaningful change. They were reserving judgment until rhetoric translated into the one thing they needed most—a solid paycheck.

"I haven't seen the change," said Joe Lewis, a fifty-two-year-old African American who had been out of work for four months, since he lost his job as a maintenance worker at a chain of convenience stores that had fallen on hard times. He had come to the unemployment office to arrange an extension of his $180-a-week check, which was going to expire. Lewis had applied for jobs at warehouses, a concrete plant, and a moving company. He had received no offers. He had heard how Obama was planning to unleash hundreds of billions of taxpayer dollars toward construction projects in a stimulus spending bill to create precisely the sorts of jobs he was looking for. But to Lewis, this was just the sound of another politician talking.

"Until he does something, he's just like all the rest of them to me," he said. "He ain't done nothing for me. Everybody's making promises. I got to see what he do."

༄

It was hard to begrudge such sentiments. At the start of 2009, the country was already a full year into a terrible, if belatedly identified, recession, a downturn whose bite had been intensified incalculably by the historic financial crisis in mortgage and derivative investments. In his first weeks in office, President Obama pursued two crucial goals: gaining the passage of a $787 billion, two-year emergency spending plan to pump money through the economy and crafting a new program to restore the flow of money through the financial system.

The so-called stimulus spending plan was Obama's most immediate priority, an effort to unleash spending through the channels that would deliver the most immediate economic benefits, thus preserving jobs that might otherwise be lost. High on the list was aid to the states, all grappling with the loss of tax revenues, to enable them to continue with planned boom-time construction projects—so-called shovel-ready projects. Obama sought additional funds for food stamps and unemployment to allow such programs to be expanded. He asked for money to retrofit federal businesses to make them more energy efficient, a fillip to renewable energy industries. And he sought money to improve schools, to both create construction jobs in the immediate term and improve education for years after. Obama asserted that his plan would create 3 to 4 million jobs in the first two years of his term.

As Obama crafted the plan, he cast it as more than an effort to revive national fortunes in the short term. It was supposed to lay the groundwork for economic growth for years to come. The infrastructure projects to be financed, such as building roads and bridges, had to be selected strategically, to support industries that would generate jobs. He aimed to provide tax incentives to companies that produced energy through renewable sources such as wind and solar. This would not only create jobs in these new industries, he argued, but also diminish the country's imports of oil, allowing Americans to stop sending so many dollars to oil-producing states, such as Saudi Arabia and Venezuela, and put that money to use at home. "This is not just a short-term program to boost employment," President Obama said in his first weekly radio address to the nation. "It's one that will invest in our most important priorities like energy and education, health care and a new infrastructure that are necessary to keep us strong and competitive in the twenty-first century."

But turning that rhetoric into genuinely beneficial policies seemed to require a veritable transformation of the political system, which traditionally runs on compromise, negotiation, and the balancing of interests. These features tend to moderate action, pulling the system away from extremes—often a helpful feature. But as Obama took office, many economists proclaimed that the biggest danger confronting the country was the possibility of too little action, too little government spending. If the government shrank from the magnitude of the troubles, if Washington got bogged down in arguments over the huge costs of spending plans and bank bailouts, nothing short of disaster might result.

When it comes to divvying up capital, American democracy favors power and influence. By and large, powerful lawmakers with seniority in Washington bring home extra dollars to their states and congressional districts. Presidents tend to reward states that deliver votes at election time. In Congress, votes to finance pet projects are exchanged for votes on other pieces of legislation. Horse-trading and the prerogatives of rank generally determine where the money goes.

The moment that Obama began talking up an $800 billion spending plan, he created an atmosphere not unlike that of a children's birthday party as a piñata gets hung from the ceiling. Indeed, even before the new president took office, cities and states around the country sent delegations to Washington to meet with his transition team to make pitches for their prize construction projects. Lobbyists descended: Furniture and carpet dealers sought tax credits for consumers who bought their wares. Hotels asked for tax credits in exchange for hiring laid-off workers. Libraries petitioned for funds. So did aggrieved catfish farmers.

Interest groups and their lobbyists are part and parcel of American democracy. Simply rounding up the votes for the stimulus spending bill required that the Obama team engage these players, courting crucial interests and including the mayors, the governors, and members of Congress as it drafted its plans. Yet this very exercise presented the danger that what was supposed to be a targeted effort to spend money to create jobs over the long term would devolve into another Washington feeding frenzy, with choice cuts of pork handed out to those best positioned to capture it.

"There are members of our caucus who are trying to create a Christmas tree out of this," said Representative Baron P. Hill, an Indiana Democrat who cochaired a coalition of fiscally conservative House Democrats.

༄

In Columbia, South Carolina, Mayor Bob Coble had heard the sound of money emanating from Washington and was mobilizing to capture some for his city.

Like most American communities, Columbia had the two things that were required to make it a viable recipient for some of the stimulus money: it had a lot of work to be done, and it had a lot of people out of work. Though the Carolinas often prompt thoughts of textile mills and tobacco fields, Columbia's metropolitan area—home to 700,000 people—comprises a fairly diverse and modern economy. As South Carolina's capital, the city holds many state government jobs. The University of South Carolina is a major employer. So are hospitals, banks, and insurance companies. The Fort Jackson army base employs 9,200 people. United Parcel Service has a regional distribution hub at the airport. Michelin operates a tire factory in next-door Lexington County, and the Computer Science Corporation develops software in offices north of the city.

Columbia is a perfect example of how the excesses of the financial system had spread broadly, to places that did not share in the bonanza of the technology and housing bubbles. Little real estate speculation unfolded there. Neither the solid brick Georgian homes downtown nor the sprawling ranch houses on the suburban fringes had risen or fallen much in value over the previous decade. Wall Street seemed far removed from the palmetto-dotted streets of the university and the domed capital building downtown. Yet as the toll continued to mount from financial recklessness in Manhattan—as banks continued to cut credit to households and businesses—the consequences were rippling out to Columbia. By late 2008, a state panel was predicting that South Carolina's unemployment rate would reach 14 percent within six months. With property and sales taxes down, the state's budget board had recently announced fresh cuts of $380 million in spending—about 7 percent—with most of that money coming from public schools and health care.

Soft-spoken and inquisitive, Mayor Coble was a lawyer by trade. He had been Columbia's mayor for eighteen years, but the year ahead of him was shaping up as the most pivotal in his tenure. As the incoming Obama administration crafted its plans for the stimulus bill, it was putting a lot of emphasis on large-scale construction projects. Coble had assembled a list of $140 million worth of projects that he said were "shovel-ready"—with the engineering work already completed and the land use rights acquired. All he needed was the money, he said, and then people could be swiftly put to work.

First on his list was the refashioning of North Main Street, a bedraggled corridor of hard-luck retailers lacking sidewalks in many places, with power lines arcing down to the pavement from light posts. The first phase was under way for $19 million, adding brick-paved sidewalks and burying power lines. The mayor was seeking another $54 million to finish the effort. He had a ready template for this project—Main Street, which had been in a similar state of disrepair little more than a decade earlier, before the sidewalks were built out and the power lines buried. Gervais Street was another model. It ran through the trendy Vista neighborhood, where a collection of old brick warehouses and a rail station had been given over to upscale eateries and bars.

Coble was also focused on advancing Innovista, a research campus crafted by the university that centered on potentially high-growth areas such as hydrogen fuel cells. South Carolina had been a key site for the development of the hydrogen bomb in the 1950s. Now, that historical know-how was being put to use for more peaceful purposes, in the effort to produce clean-burning sources of energy. The idea behind Innovista was to cluster university labs with those of private businesses wanting to tap the local expertise. Residential condos would run down the undeveloped banks of the Congaree River, a lure for recruiting top researchers.

Coble presented these construction projects as far more than opportunities to hire people to lay bricks and pour concrete. By redeveloping North Main Street, conditions would be created for new businesses— retailers, restaurants, banks—to take root there, as soon as the economy rebounded, generating a second wave of jobs. The Innovista project would harness Columbia's core intellectual strength to position the city to attract private investment for years to come. "This will be a once-in-a-generation opportunity to transform a city with projects that have been on the books but are hard to fund," the mayor said. "These are not bridges to nowhere."

But turning his list into jobs would not happen easily, if at all—a clear foretaste of the complications and jockeying for spoils that awaited the nation. The state's governor, Mark Sanford, a Republican, firmly opposed the White House's stimulus plan, arguing that it merely exacerbated long-term debt while squandering public money on dubious projects. He was threatening to reject whatever money flowed South Carolina's way, out of pure principle. "Historically, simply throwing government money at a struggling economy hasn't worked," Sanford wrote in an op-ed piece in Columbia's daily newspaper, the *State*. "We would do well to remember this is not Monopoly money. Every single dollar we spend today has to be paid for, by someone, at some point."

Even if the money did make its way to South Carolina, not that much would necessarily reach Columbia. Some of the funds would go directly to the city through grants, but much would be distributed through state agencies such as the Department of Transportation, which had its own list of priority projects.

Nor was there any promise that the mayor's list of projects could deliver jobs over the long haul, after the construction work was done. The Main Street revitalization had returned the shine to Columbia's downtown, but it had not attracted many retailers in the years since. Shopping was generally confined to malls and big-box retailers out on the suburban fringes. The old Macy's downtown was now a museum with a plaza full of sculpture. If Main Street could not easily be transformed into a successful commercial area, North Main Street had even less hope. Main Street runs right up to the capitol dome, where state workers earn decent salaries. It is lined with glass-encased office buildings topped by private dining clubs where business people tuck into crab cakes and prime rib. North Main runs through a largely low-income, high-crime neighborhood, making it even less likely to attract investment. "That's not the place to be putting capital," said David Lockwood, senior vice president at the commercial real estate firm Colliers Keenan. "Nobody is going to invest up there."

In short, in Columbia—as for communities across the country—the imperatives of political fairness and economic benefit appeared to pull in opposite directions. Politically, it was close to impossible for Mayor Coble to sell the idea that the city should focus its limited capital downtown while neglecting lower-income and largely African American neighborhoods to the north. According to the political calculus that dominates budget decisions, the logic was simple: Main Street had gotten new sidewalks and now North Main Street was due a turn. But in economic terms, the surest way to generate the greatest number of jobs over the long haul was to put the stimulus money where people could be induced to spend it and where companies were most likely to hire workers: downtown and near the university. In pure economic terms, Coble's wisest course seemed to be to focus any available dollars on the Innovista project.

If Innovista panned out as planned, it seemed to promise a greater re-turn on investment than the other projects on the mayor's list. The campus would be staffed with high-paid researchers, who would—the city hoped—be persuaded to live in the new riverfront condos. These white-collar work-ers could then distribute their money throughout the community—in the restaurants and bars in the Vista and in the boutiques downtown. The city would pull in property and sales tax revenues and spend the funds on im-proving public schools, attacking crime, expanding social services, and lay-ing the groundwork for other communities to attract businesses and jobs. If all of that happened, it might one day create a Columbia where it made economic sense to fix up the sidewalks of North Main Street, because the city could be confident that people would happily stroll there and spend money.

But that scenario was a political nonstarter. It required an awful lot of goodwill within the local political system. It demanded more trust than people around North Main Street were feeling for government. They could certainly be forgiven for feeling skeptical that such divi-dends would ever trickle down their way while adopting a much more pragmatic mind-set: the new president is scattering money through the country, so give us our share.

༄

When the new administration asked Congress to embrace an $800 bil-lion stimulus plan in late January 2009, it seemed at first that the bill might be passed quickly, amid a new spirit of bipartisanship. "Anyone who belittles cooperation resigns him or herself to a state of permanent legislative gridlock," said Senate minority leader Mitch McConnell, the Kentucky Republican who had engaged in partisan bickering for years. "That is simply no longer acceptable to the American people."

But long-standing ideological tensions soon surfaced, not only around the most effective use of the money—tax cuts versus government spending—but also on arguments about whether the nation could afford to take on more debt. Years of spending and borrowing without limit had put the American economy in this dangerous place. How could more of the same be the way back to safety? "We cannot borrow and spend our way back to prosperity," said Representative John A. Boehner, the Ohio Republican and the House minority leader. "The trillion-dollar spending plan authored by congressional Democrats is chock-full of government programs and projects, most of which won't provide immediate relief to our ailing economy."

Democrats retorted that the debts were in large part the result of profligate financial management under the Bush administration, which waged an expensive war in Iraq without budgeting for it while handing out roughly $2 trillion worth of tax cuts. Spending more public money was a problem, they acknowledged, but the biggest danger was failing to do enough. "We need to compare the cost of this package against the cost of doing nothing," Representative David Obey, a Wisconsin Democrat, said during debate on the House floor. "The cost of doing nothing would be catastrophic."

The fight over tax cuts and government spending was mostly political theater. Economic studies had shown that tax cuts were a generally poor way to stimulate the economy, providing nowhere near the boost delivered by spending. Expanding unemployment insurance and food stamps were particularly effective ways to spark economic growth, because recipients of aid dollars usually spend them immediately. Those two measures along with spending on construction can yield more than $1.50 in increased economic activity for every dollar spent, according to research by Mark Zandi, the chief economist for Moody's Economy.com who also served as an adviser to John McCain's 2008 presidential campaign. Cutting corporate and capital gains taxes—a favorite target of Republicans— garners less than forty cents on the dollar. *True but*

Still, Obama sought conciliation in advance, catering to Republican predilections by devoting roughly one-third of his package to tax cuts in a bid for resounding bipartisan consensus. But in late January, the House passed a stimulus bill on strict party lines; not a single Republican voted for it. As the stimulus plan moved to the Senate, Republicans stripped out spending measures and replaced them with tax cuts while rolling back the overall price tag of the program. The White House then negotiated with three moderate Republicans whose votes were needed to gain the sixty votes necessary to bring the bill to a floor vote. That compromise intensified charges that the plan had been hijacked by political considerations. The former Reagan administration economist Martin Feldstein wrote that it "delivers too little extra employment and income." Jeffrey D. Sachs, an economist at Columbia, called it "an astounding mishmash of tax cuts, public investments, transfer payments and special treats for insiders."

The bill ultimately passed in mid-February, unleashing $787 billion into the economy. Some $282 billion was assigned to tax cuts, split evenly between those for businesses and for individuals. About $50 billion was devoted to roads, bridges, and transportation projects. The plan included $54 billion in aid for states, with most of the money going to local school districts to pay teacher salaries or upgrade buildings. The rest went for unemployment benefits, food stamps, and other aid programs such as Medicaid.

"It's a good plan, but I don't think it's good enough," said Zandi, whose models the White House used to construct the bill.

McConnell, who had only weeks earlier declared obstructionism passé, branded the bill a dangerous turn away from free enterprise. "Where are we going to leave the country in two years if we take all of these steps?" he said. "We will have made a dramatic move in the direction of, indeed, turning America into Western Europe."

Washington has grown accustomed to muddy compromises that can be spun into clear-cut victories by both parties, as their leaders appear on Sunday television talk shows to argue over who won the week. But the economic crisis confronting the country is not well addressed by this traditional mode of politics: the process is a sideshow, and only the results count. Either the government will marshal the resources to stave off a potential economic catastrophe or it won't. The merits of the spending plan adopted can only be assessed once the money reaches its final destinations—the classrooms and state office buildings that are to be upgraded, and the construction workers who are supposed to be employed. Where that money ultimately goes is just the first phase of the process, an initial effort to limit the damage of the recession. Even after the stimulus money is distributed, a more important issue will remain: how best to create jobs that can sustain Americans over the coming decades. Is Innovista or North Main Street the future? Can one thrive without the other?

⁓

Of course, the stimulus bill was merely the initial push from President Obama. Equally important was its effort to fix the financial system. Until the banks were returned to functional health, and again lending money, economic activity was certain to remain sluggish, if not decline. Jobs would continue to disappear from the economy, and more people would show up alongside Greg Bailey at the Oakland job center or Joe Lewis at the Columbia unemployment office, waiting to find something real to replace their hopes.

On this front, the Obama administration by nearly all accounts stumbled badly out of the gate, raising fears that it lacked the political courage to tackle the real problem: the reality that the banking system was effectively insolvent and required perhaps trillions of dollars in fresh taxpayer funds.

By February 2009, economists of every political stripe, even conservative Republicans who saw bailouts as anathema, were all coming to an unpalatable conclusion. The government was going to have to seriously consider nationalizing the banks—seize them and run them until they were functional, at which point they could be sold back into private hands. In a society that prided itself on embracing free enterprise, this was a grave indignity. Yet, given the alarming dysfunction in the financial system and the trillions of dollars' worth of investments that were simply evaporating, even Alan Greenspan had arrived at this view. "It may be necessary to temporarily nationalize some banks in order to facilitate a swift and orderly restructuring," Greenspan said. "I understand that once in a hundred years this is what you do."

But the administration offered a tepid plan for yet another bailout that seemed little more than a continuation of the failed policies of 2008, which had stirred deep public distrust. Obama's Treasury secretary, Timothy Geithner, brought baggage of his own. Geithner was confirmed in his new post only after issuing a mea culpa for failing to pay his taxes. Perhaps more problematic was his résumé: his previous job was chairman of the New York Federal Reserve, where he worked closely with Henry Paulson to craft many of the Bush administration's emergency bailouts. For a public craving a clean break with the past, Geithner amounted to more of a bridge.

As Geithner crafted a new plan to rescue the financial system, the politics of winning congressional approval only got pricklier. The initial bailout was looking at best ineffectual. Congress was frustrated that it could not get a reliable accounting of what had happened to the money. At his confirmation hearing, Geithner got a clear sense of the unhappiness.

"Instead of using the first payment of $350 billion to purchase troubled assets, as the name Troubled Asset Relief Program suggests, the money has been erratically and arbitrarily distributed in a monstrous act of government intervention," complained Republican senator Charles Grassley of Iowa.

Anger about the bailout intensified in late January 2009, when the New York State comptroller disclosed that Wall Street paid out more than $18 billion worth of bonuses in 2008—the sixth-largest haul in history. On talk radio, on television, and in opinion columns, critics furiously denounced the greed that ruled Wall Street and the foolishness of the Bush administration for handing over public money to hucksters. The bonuses represented "financial treason so injurious to the nation that it makes a beggar out of language," said the MSNBC anchor Keith Olbermann. President Obama exuded outrage. "That is the height of irresponsibility," he told reporters. "It's shameful."

Obama followed that condemnation by announcing new rules that would apply to the next phase of bailout funds: a $500,000 cap on annual executive pay for any company receiving the money.

Geithner immediately began building big expectations for a broad new bailout program that could finally eradicate the troubles plaguing the financial system, saying it "will require much more dramatic action on a very substantial scale." He specifically raised the possibility that the Obama administration would pursue the course that Paulson had initially proposed and then quickly shunned—buying bad assets from banks. Each day, details of Geithner's likely plan were leaked to the press, with talk of a government-private partnership that would raise as much as $1.5 trillion to finally buy up and dispose of the bad loans choking bank balance sheets.

But behind the scenes, Geithner was successfully fighting to make the plan look more like Paulson's initial effort than anything new. Amid debate within the administration, Geithner persuaded Obama to forgo stricter limits on executive pay, making sure the $500,000 cap applied only to the most senior executives, according to a report in the New York Times. Geithner also watered down proposed restrictions on how banks would be allowed to use their bailout funds.

When Geithner laid out his new plan publicly in early February, he was pilloried.

In a televised speech from the Treasury's ornate Cash Room, he explained that the second half of the agreed-upon bailout money would be used for fresh injections into banks, but he gave no sense of which ones and how much. He announced that the Fed would print more money—perhaps as much as $1 trillion—and lend it to banks that committed to making student loans and car loans to ease the flow of credit. But he left the details for later. He said the administration would spend $50 billion to help households in danger of losing their homes to foreclosure, but those details, too, awaited another day. On Wall Street, the stock markets immediately cratered. Investors and politicians alike derided Geithner's plan using many of the same pejoratives hurled previously at Paulson's—vague, too few details, incomplete. "There's not a hell of a lot here to get a sense of," complained Senator Robert Menendez, a New Jersey Democrat, as Geithner went to Capitol Hill to present his plan.

Meanwhile, as the perception took hold that the new administration had nothing to offer toward fixing the banks, the reality of the financial system was only worsening. Just as Geithner managed to sow greater confusion, Nouriel Roubini—the New York University economist once dismissed as a Chicken Little, now increasingly looking like a seer—released a report with a sobering detail: before the reckoning was done, financial institutions would write off $3.6 trillion. "The U.S. banking system is effectively insolvent," Roubini asserted.

Obama and Geithner were operating in a poisonous atmosphere with no easy options. They confronted an enormous well of hostility toward the very concept of a Wall Street bailout, one intensified by the news of the bonuses. But without another injection of capital, the financial system was certain to remain crippled and the economy would continue to suffer. Any prospect of generating jobs over the long haul would be immediately undone by the influx of people at unemployment offices.

Public anger only grew in March when word emerged that AIG, the company that had sold billions of dollars worth of credit default swaps, was using taxpayer bailout money to pay $165 million in bonuses to people in the very unit that had generated all the trouble. Obama administration officials took to the airwaves to vent outrage on Sunday morning talk shows amid the rising populist backlash. "There are a lot of terrible things that have happened in the last eighteen months, but what's happened at AIG is the most outrageous," said Lawrence Summers, President

Obama's chief economic adviser, speaking on ABC's *This Week with George Stephanopoulos*. "What that company did, the way it was not regulated, the way no one was watching, what's proved necessary—is outrageous." The fact that Summers had, a decade earlier, played a key role in enabling AIG and other financial institutions to sell derivatives free of regulation was an irony that somehow drew little notice.

Geithner's reputation came in for a fresh beating, as he asserted there was nothing the Treasury could do to prevent the bonuses, though the government by then owned 80 percent of AIG. So unpopular was this assertion that the following day President Obama flatly contradicted it, ordering Geithner to look for a way to invalidate the bonuses. Yet even this seemed more theatrical flourish than substance: AIG needed government money just to survive, and the financial system needed a functioning AIG to prevent trouble from spreading like a pandemic. Whatever money AIG had to hand back to the Treasury was taxpayer money, and if it needed more to survive later on, that was coming from the public, too.

∽

In early 2009, Fran Barbaro was still unemployed, happy to be back living in Belmont Hill, and paying the bills with her unemployment check, child support, and the odd freelance technology project.

She had become an informal adviser to other people negotiating with the banks over the terms of the mortgages they had not previously needed to understand. She was telling people whom to write to and what sorts of modifications to seek. She was continuing to apply for whatever technology jobs were listed online, but the offerings were getting slimmer and slimmer by the week. She was thinking about pursuing a job in the health care industry, the only part of the economy that experts said was still growing. Mostly, she was just hanging on, worrying that she was living through a new depression.

"The world seems to be at a standstill," she said.

The continued fall in housing prices was weighing heavily on the job market. As foreclosures accelerated, more empty houses landed on the market, exacerbating price drops. This made more loans go bad, prompting banks to lend even less, and making prospects that much worse for people sitting at job centers, staring dolefully at meager job listings.

In mid-February, the Obama administration announced a plan to try to stem foreclosures. In a speech in Phoenix, the president said the government would spend $75 billion to compensate banks that agreed to modify the terms of mortgages for home owners who could not make their payments. The plan supplied a fresh $200 billion to Fannie Mae and Freddie Mac to allow them to refinance more mortgages, thus allowing home owners stuck with high rates of interest to seek easier terms. Obama asserted the plan would spare up to 9 million home owners from onerous loan terms and foreclosure.

The plan was targeted to make money most readily available to people who were in danger, particularly those who had fallen behind on their loans. But it offered much less aid for a larger group who presented a more complex problem that might tally up to several hundred billion dollars—those who were making their payments but might simply choose to walk away from their homes because the properties were worth less than they owed the bank. The administration was betting on the sanctity of home ownership, assuming that—whatever the value of their homes— most people would keep making their payments if they could. That calculation may well prove correct. Indeed, recent economic research supports that assumption. But it was no sure thing. Walking away from a home— that is, simply halting the payments and letting the bank foreclose— would certainly damage credit ratings, but it would also save a lot of families a good deal of money, because they could rent similar homes for less than they were now paying toward their mortgages. If that bet proves wrong, a lot of extra foreclosures will result, bringing housing prices down further in the hardest-hit markets—Phoenix, Las Vegas, southern California, and South Florida. And that would make it harder for people to get jobs.

The sentiments of people in hard hit areas suggest that many may indeed walk away. Time and again, in different parts of the country, I have asked people if they own their own homes and received an intially puzzling response: "Well, we're buying it." At first, I took this to mean that they were about to close on the purchase of a home. But, no, what people meant was that they had been making mortgage payments for several years, yet did not feel like true owners. The Ownership Society was supposed to boost a sense of personal responsibility. Home owners would be more inclined to pick up trash and keep an eye out for crime than renters, the theory went. But so many people had been able to become legal owners while putting down so little money that they did not feel a sense of possession. By making finance so lenient, the Ownership Society had managed to cheapen the very concept of ownership.

The moral obligation to pay the bank back increasingly seems like a relic of another era, when the banker was likely to be someone in the neighborhood. Today, when a home owner walks away, they are stiffing an abstract notion of a bank, not a personal relation; an institution they are likely to contact through a call center in India or the Philippines, attached to an insolvent lending operation such as Washington Mutual. Thus, the decision to walk away has for many families become a purely financial calculation shorn of moral consideration: what are the consequences of damaging one's credit versus the benefits of getting out from under a bad mortgage?

All of this raises the distinct possibility that even people who can afford their mortgages will stop paying. The market will then absorb an even larger glut of foreclosed properties, and eventually the Obama administration will need to return with a significantly larger rescue package. There are no easy options. Had it been simple work to reverse the downward spiral of joblessness, foreclosure, and financial crisis, someone would have done it already. Even with Keynes's admonitions for government spending back at the forefront of American debate, the old political comfort zones held reign, limiting the size and scope of the bailouts Obama could reasonably propose. If the stimulus money is distributed willy-nilly, with political considerations trumping strategic coherence, that will merely add to the financial deficit without boosting new industries that can be a source of good jobs. If banks continue to cut back on lending, fewer and fewer private companies will supplement government spending—forcing the government to step up with more or watch the economy slide deeper into the ditch. If the administration cannot promulgate a credible plan to restore order to the financial system, confidence will continue to erode and more pessimistic forecasts will become self-fulfilling prophesies.

Even if these early efforts are successful, if they restore order to the financial system and save millions of jobs—no small accomplishment— they cannot fundamentally fix what ails the American economy. The problems are too entrenched and deep-seated. A whole new kind of economy is required, one that replaces debt with savings and home equity loans with paychecks. One that generates growth not by conjuring up more make-believe finance but by producing goods and services of intrinsic value, and then selling them at home and around the world. An economy that can generate good jobs for decades to come, the sorts of jobs that will allow Americans to afford the features of middle-class life that they once took largely for granted—a home, a decent education, health care, and a comfortable retirement.

In the remaining pages of this book, I will focus directly on how the United States can produce good paychecks in large numbers through growth in two promising industries—biotechnology and renewable energy.

11

Seed Capital

"It's a product you feel good about."

W hat will it take for the United States to exploit its still considerable strengths and rebuild the economy?

How can we transcend the wreckage of the era of easy money and replace it with a more stable economy centered on hard-earned paychecks?
Gone are the days of crafting an enticing new story that unleashes a fresh
wave of investment. Future economic prospects rest on crafting useful
products and services of enduring value.

For reasons now obvious, new regulations are required for the financial
system to ensure that banks, insurance companies, and other institutions
set aside sufficient funds to cover investments that go awry. The spiraling
cost of health care must be contained and brought down, freeing households to spend on other things and lifting a burden from companies that
sow a sense of greater security throughout American society. Education
must be expanded and improved to spread the benefits of economic growth
to more people, for the simple reason that better-paying jobs increasingly
require more sophisticated skills. All of these areas must be addressed to
bring about a healthy economic refashioning. But prospects for genuine renewal ultimately rest upon creating high-quality jobs. A culture of credit
must be replaced by a culture of work, necessitating abundant new jobs
that pay good wages in sustainable industries.

The seeds of renewal will be most effectively planted through the skillful partnership of government incentives, private enterprise, and the research expertise of major universities. Both biotech and renewable energy are success stories that offer models worth studying and emulating going forward. They are potentially enormous sources of jobs in their own right, exemplars of American innovation and technological prowess. More important, their very existence and growth owes largely to government policy that has effectively catalyzed private entrepreneurship and investment, while exploiting university know-how.

Renewable energy has spread rapidly as states adopted laws directing local utilities to buy more electricity from companies that produce it from the wind, sun, and other "clean energy" sources. Biotech has grown as government has crafted tax credits to encourage companies to take risks that would otherwise seem excessive, making use of new technologies and developing new products.

The point is not that biotech will—or must—necessarily become a leading source of jobs, or that Greg Bailey, who invested in job training in the industry, or Fran Barbaro, with her years of experience in high-tech companies, will forge their futures in biotech plants. Rather, the question confronting policy makers is how best to generate a long-term cycle of job creation and rising fortunes—and these are industries that have shown considerable potential for growth in the decades ahead.

During the tech and housing bubbles, growth in one part of the economy rippled out widely. When Eric Bochner was netting his millions at Ariba, the investment wave that produced his wealth also translated into more demand for office chairs made in factories in the Midwest. It filled Greg Bailey and Willie Gonzalez's trucks with products that needed moving. The virtuous cycle of the technology bubble was ultimately propelled by too much borrowed money chasing after a fantasy. The next virtuous cycle must be built upon solid businesses operating in markets that are regulated to prevent excesses, and nurtured by government policies that encourage research and development. That process holds great potential to create enduring jobs that will pay enough to raise living standards and enable ordinary people to spend and save.

Given that government is now spending huge sums of taxpayer money to revive the economy, it should not shirk its decisive role in parceling out these funds strategically, influencing which industries will emerge. This would not be an altogether new role for the government. Back in the FDR administration, the government directed its massive infrastructure campaign toward generating construction jobs—a prominent part of the New Deal that is well known. But more important, as explored by my *New York Times* colleague Louis Uchitelle, the government also elevated some projects from a mere source of short-term construction jobs into the building blocks for new industries. The New Deal financed a necklace of new dams across American rivers. The dams significantly increased the U.S. supply of electricity, a boon to manufacturers. But this extra electricity supply did not become a productive component of the economy until the Roosevelt administration began subsidizing the installment plans under which households purchased new electrical appliances. Before then, such products were too expensive for most families and residential electricity was little used. Once the government began the subsidies, households started buying briskly. Only then did Americans buy appliances in large enough numbers to increase jobs at the factories that made washing machines and other home appliances. It took two ingredients—electricity and finance—for this piece of the New Deal to work, and it took the government to jump-start both of them.

Similar thinking is likely to be required today. To derive maximum economic benefit from each dollar devoted to stimulus spending, the Obama administration will need to offer incentives to companies to create promising products while also seeking to nurture markets that consume those products. Success will depend on whether taxpayers pay for trillions of dollars' worth of one-time-only jobs programs or rather lay down the foundations for a healthy post-crisis economy.

～

Regina Whitaker could be the face of the new American economy.

A decade ago, she was another low-wage, low-skill worker toiling inside one of North Carolina's flagging textile operations, one of the state's many traditional industries under assault from cheap imports pouring in from Asia and Latin America. Today, she has a vastly more rewarding career as a lab technician at a biotechnology company, earning her living in an industry that grew rapidly in North Carolina over the past decade.

That growth is no accident. Biotech has taken root and thrived in North Carolina because the state carefully nurtured it, systematically harnessing its local advantages to attract private capital and generate high-paying jobs—particularly for people without college degrees. North Carolina employed a method that many other states are beginning to replicate in biotech and in other emerging industries, one that the nation as a whole could put to use as it seeks to turn its considerable brainpower and business acumen into profits and jobs over the long term: the state teamed world-class research universities with private capital, while creating incentives for commercial ventures to set up shop.

North Carolina's biotech initiative was directed at solving precisely the problem that now confronts the national economy: it needed high-quality jobs. Over the last three decades, the state directed a steady stream of dollars at its premier research institutions—particularly the public University of North Carolina as well as the private universities Duke and Wake Forest—to encourage them to focus on producing advances in the field. Like Columbia, South Carolina's Innovista initiative, it erected offices, laboratories, and condos near campuses to attract companies willing to locate there and tap the local expertise—but the state did it on a much grander, more coordinated scale. Not least, in 2004, North Carolina launched a training program called BioNetwork, boosting course offerings at community colleges around the state to supply workers with the skills needed to gain lower-level jobs in biotechnology operations.

Whitaker was one of thousands of students who came through the BioNetwork program. In 1997, fresh out of high school, she went to work at a yarn factory in the town of Yadkinville, in North Carolina's Piedmont country. Her mother had worked there for thirty years. So had her cousins, aunts, and uncles. Whitaker figured she would probably spend her lifetime there, too. She worked the night shift, from midnight until eight in the morning, mostly as a quality assurance technician. Amid the ceaseless din of whirring machinery, she made sure the threads of polyester spinning around mechanized bobbins were properly fused into yarn. The product had to meet the requirements of the companies buying it—textile mills that made upholstery for car seats; hosiery mills; a lingerie factory that generated product for Victoria's Secret. She earned about $13 an hour, plus health insurance.

As the years passed, Whitaker imagined other ways to earn a living, while worrying that she might soon be forced to pursue one. Her employer, Unifi Inc., was increasingly setting its sights elsewhere, establishing mills in

China and Brazil. It was cutting production in Yadkinville, going from three working shifts a day to two and administering layoffs and pay cuts. In 2000, the company slashed Whitaker's pay by $1 an hour. She feared this was only the beginning. "I was afraid I wouldn't have a job there in ten years," she said. "I couldn't see spending my life there with the way the market was going. Everything's going overseas."

In the summer of 2001, she quit her job at the yarn plant and enrolled at nearby Forsyth Technical Community College. Serious-minded and intense, she began studying to be a medical assistant, becoming the first person in her family to enroll in a college program. She waited tables part-time and worked at a local pharmacy to bring in cash. Her husband brought home wages from a Dell computer factory. A federal grant paid for much of her tuition and other costs of schooling.

Almost immediately, Whitaker saw a brochure for new classes at the college that sounded especially promising. As part of the BioNetwork program, Forsyth was launching courses in applied science focused on biotechnology. The courses were designed as a passageway to careers in the industry, conferring associate degrees in biotech and related areas. Students gained the lowest certification after 128 hours of course work, which qualified them for entry-level jobs at biomanufacturing facilities that paid between $25,000 and $35,000 a year. Two-year associate degrees in chemical processing technology or the use of biomedical equipment would qualify graduates for jobs in laboratories as analysts, at starting salaries of $35,000 a year.

These workers are the foot soldiers of biotechnology, which involves manipulating the genetic material of cells so they can be used to manufacture pharmaceuticals, fuels, and other chemicals. While biotech may conjure images of people with doctorates pondering cosmic thoughts as they drive toward glass-fronted offices in luxury cars, most of the industry is centered on the nitty-gritty work of manufacturing commercial products, following standard formulas. More than half of North Carolina's biotech workers are engaged in production, and three-fourths of these employees have only a high school diploma. This makes the industry a potentially huge source of fresh paychecks in a state that has been losing lower-skilled, higher-paying jobs in the struggling areas of textiles and tobacco.

"Those guys know that you have to follow standard operating procedures, and that there's quality control involved," said Norman Smit, the director of recruitment for the BioNetwork program in 2007. He concentrated on finding students among the castoffs from textile and furniture-making plants. "They understand manufacturing," he said. "We've grafted onto that the science, the technology and the understanding of how the Food and Drug Administration works. All of the skills are closely tied to the workplace."

Back at the yarn plant, Whitaker had spent some time in the lab, testing the strength of the product using chemical solutions and rudimentary equipment. She had liked the responsibility as well as the peace and quiet. She took satisfaction in putting science to practical use. With this experience in mind, she enrolled in the first biotech classes at Forsyth, joining a group of ten students that included two other former textile workers, a man who had worked in banking, a recent high school graduate, and a man who had lost his job at US Airways. When they graduated in July 2004, all were quickly hired into jobs in biotech. Whitaker took a job at Targacept, a biotech start-up in Winston-Salem.

Targacept's very existence spoke to the transition under way in North Carolina. It was a spin-off from R. J. Reynolds Tobacco. Back when cigarettes made North Carolina rich, the tobacco giant aimed its laboratories at finding ways to manipulate nicotine to cause smokers to crave its products. Targacept was taking that same body of research and putting it to use in the service of medicine. It was studying how nicotine receptors in the brain could be used in developing drugs to attack Alzheimer's disease and schizophrenia. The fledgling company was housed in a new health sciences building erected by Wake Forest University that clustered together university research and private investment. (In another sign of the refashioning under way, some of the old surrounding tobacco fields had been replaced with grapes, as wineries took root.)

Whitaker now spent her days in a lab, assisting with tests by setting up chemical reactions and operating instruments. The drudgery of watching bobbins turn had been replaced by something more interesting. "What I love about my job is it's not the same thing every day," she said.

She got a promotion in 2005, then another in late 2008, bringing her salary to 50 percent more than she was making at the yarn plant. She and her husband purchased a new car, a Nissan Altima. As the recession tightened its grip in early 2009, they were worried about his job at Dell, amid rumors that the local factory might close, but they were far more confident in the endurance of her wages than they would have been had she still been in textiles.

"Before, it was paycheck to paycheck," she said. "It's not that bad now."

༈

Only a couple of decades ago, North Carolina seemed synonymous with decline. Once teeming with prodigious agricultural wealth, the state suffered as tobacco morphed from a valuable cash crop into a public health scourge. Textiles became synonymous with the downside of globalization as work shifted to Latin America and Asia, leaving behind shuttered mills, forsaken workers, and recriminations over the benefits of free trade.

These realities are far from played out. In the rugged Appalachian country in the western reaches of the state, furniture factories remain under relentless assault as lower-cost goods land in the United States from factories in Asia. In Mitchell County alone, some sixteen hundred jobs disappeared between 2000 and 2007—this, in an area of roughly eight thousand total jobs.

Henredon Furniture Industries was a typical casualty. The company made hand-carved wooden bedroom furniture of the highest quality—"the Cadillac of the industry," employees boasted. In the town of Spruce Pine, the company employed more than one thousand people. Many lacked high school diplomas, and a few were illiterate. But they took home $14 an hour, plus health and pension benefits—enough to support families. Yet by the middle of the 1990s, this equation was under assault, and layoffs began. Henredon's four-poster beds sold retail for about $5,000 each. Similar models began showing up from China and the Philippines for less than $2,000. By November 2004, when Henredon finally gave up, eliminating the last 350 jobs in Spruce Pine, the Asian-made beds could be had for less than $1,000.

Philip Wilson had worked at Henredon for twenty-six years, the last fourteen as a master carver. The end of that job meant finding a new one in what stood as the only fast-growing industry in the area: the state prison system. In the spring of 2007, he was waking before dawn and driving into the hills outside town for his 5:30 A.M. shift as a prison guard at a medium-security institution. ("You learn to be on your toes," he said. "You learn to know when somebody's behind you.") Afternoons, he was putting in hours at a used appliance store, installing refrigerators and washing machines to supplement his pay. Still, his income was down nearly one-fifth from what it was back when he was still creating furniture. "You learn to eat before you go to the grocery store," Wilson said. "You don't want to buy too much food."

Spruce Pine was withering. Its brick storefronts were emptying out downtown. Plate glass windows of restaurants were blinded by brown paper and masking tape. "The kids are moving out," said Brenda Smith, a youth pastor at a local teen center. "They can't find anywhere to work. There's Walmart, and that's about it."

Spruce Pine's experience is consistent with what is happening to most communities with large numbers of lower-skilled people. Rural counties in the western part of the state had unemployment rates above 10 percent in 2004, when the national unemployment rate was less than half that level. Overall, North Carolina lost more than a third of its manufacturing jobs—more than 300,000 positions—between the mid-1990s and 2008.

Yet, as a whole, the story of North Carolina as a victim of globalization is outdated. In the 1980s, the state created the North Carolina Biotechnology Center to help develop the industry. It furnishes grants to universities to advance research and dispenses seed capital to promising start-up companies. It recruits established private companies to the state, and supports them by tailoring research and the training of prospective workers to their needs. By 2008, North Carolina's biotech industry employed some fifty-five thousand people scattered across 450 companies, with average salaries of more than $63,000 a year. That was nearly triple the number of workers from a decade earlier.

Outside Durham, a major biotech company, Biogen Idec, operates one of the larger biomanufacturing facilities in the country. Here, it makes its blockbuster multiple sclerosis drug, Avonex, which netted revenues of more than $2.2 billion in 2008.

Inside the plant, the atmosphere is not unlike that of a large brewery—albeit one overseen by people in white lab coats. A spider's web of tubing and pipes carries chemicals to their required places. Huge stainless steel vats rise to high ceilings, holding living cells that are growing in a liquid solution as they produce proteins of therapeutic value. The key to the process is precision: the slightest mistake—improperly raising or lowering the temperature of the solution, or allowing contaminants to seep in—can swiftly ruin a batch of drugs. Deviating from the rules of production courts action from the Food and Drug Administration. However, mastering the regimen is generally not difficult for people who have experience in other types of manufacturing, say the plant's managers.

"We need people who have great attention to detail," said Biogen's vice president for manufacturing, John Cox. "You open the wrong valve, you just sent the product down the drain. It requires discipline." He pointed at a huge vat full of raw materials going into a cancer drug soon approaching tests on human patients. That single batch cost about $3 million to produce. "You don't want to make a mistake with that," he said.

Randy Johnson, forty-six, was perfectly comfortable working amid the pressure. He had successfully completed more than one career transition, and often involuntarily. He had worked in the industries that dominated North Carolina as he was growing up—textiles and tobacco—and had suffered layoffs in both as their fortunes declined. In 2000, he took a leap into something new that seemed to have greater staying power, training to become a computer programmer. He got a job at a major computer company where he earned more than $50,000 a year. He was part of a team that managed Medicaid accounts for the state. But in 2004, the company shipped that work to a much cheaper operation in India, laying off local programmers. A father of two and a home owner, Johnson was suddenly out of work again. Through a friend, he heard about the BioNetwork program. He learned he could enroll without paying tuition because his job was deemed to have been eliminated by trade. So he started classes at a community college, twice a week for three hours a day. After three months, he had his certification. After attending a job fair at the Biotech Center, he landed a job at Biogen. The company was ramping up to begin manufacturing a new drug, and it hired him to be a production supervisor, giving him what he described as "a substantial bump up" from his previous salary.

"It's a very easy transition," he said. "At a supervisory level, so much of what you do is just people related."

But in one key regard, Biogen felt like a new experience. It seemed far more solid than anything he had done before. And he took satisfaction in the product. Instead of helping make cigarettes, he was producing pharmaceuticals. "It's a product you feel very good about," Johnson says. "You feel good about what you do."

Biogen was one of dozens of biotech companies concentrated in the Research Triangle Park just outside of Raleigh-Durham, where modern campuses adorned with modern art and fountains house the research talent culled from nearby universities and increasingly around the globe. But the industry has been expanding further afield, spreading the promise of decent employment even to small towns.

In Pittsboro, a community of twenty-two hundred people some thirty miles west of Raleigh, a low-slung brick building near the center of town was once home to the Kayser-Roth hosiery mill. Until the 1950s, four hundred workers tended to clattering looms that made ladies' stockings. The mill is now a distant memory, but the brick building remains, occupied today by Biolex Therapeutics, a promising biotech start-up. Biolex has developed a process that induces a local plant called duckweed—bane to local ponds—to offer up desired proteins as part of the process of making drugs that treat hepatitis. About ninety people worked there in early 2009, watching over plastic trays of duckweed set up under light tables as they pressed toward the next drug trial. Nearly one-third were production workers. Even the lowest-paid lab technician was taking home far more than the seamstresses ever did back in the era of stockings.

∽

Not everyone who seeks to will make the transition.

The training courses are effectively a requirement for a job, and they can be quite challenging. Regina Whitaker acknowledged that she was fortunate to be in her mid-twenties when she made the decision to quit the yarn plant. "For somebody who has been out of school for ten or fifteen years, it's going to be difficult, but not impossible," she said.

In California, Greg Bailey had trained for a career in biotech but had not secured a job. There were just too many applicants for the available spots, underscoring the need for state-run training programs to take care to match the numbers of people they graduate with the demand for workers.

But so long as some people can take advantage of the biotech opportunity, the states' dollars seem well spent. Biotech operations in North Carolina now pay out roughly $4.5 billion in annual wages. In the

Winston-Salem area, Whitaker distributes what she earns at Targacept throughout other sectors of the economy—to the Nissan dealership that sold her a car, and to the factory in Tennessee that built it; to the restaurants where she can now afford to eat; to the shops that sell clothes and toys for her three-year-old son. The state's biotech companies buy more than $10 billion a year in goods and services from other North Carolina businesses, indirectly supporting another 125,000 jobs. They send $1.4 billion a year toward state and local tax coffers. And this money is not the product of a financial scheme: it stems from a targeted investment in an area that exploits local expertise to devise products of genuine social value, no make-believe required.

Unlike the manufacturing jobs they are replacing, the biotech positions seem largely impervious to the forces that have sent many American paychecks overseas. Fabric is easily sewn in China or Guatemala, where a pair of working hands can be employed at a fraction of the going rate in North Carolina. If quality slips a bit as a result of transferring production far away, increased volume can more than compensate. The risk of having production techniques stolen or emulated by local entrepreneurs in a country with weak patent protections is relatively minor in textiles: they already know how to make yarn in China and Guatemala, and there's not a lot of mystery to it. But in biotech, all of these considerations are substantial. Making bioengineered pharmaceuticals entails less labor and more sophisticated, expensive machinery, best entrusted to higher-skilled hands. A botched process can be lethal, subjecting the company to lawsuits, government action, and bad publicity. The risk of having patents breached or techniques stolen is infinitely greater because the value of a biotech company resides in its intellectual property, which is typically the culmination of years and many millions of dollars in research.

No job is truly safe in a global economy. Risk and reward are both heightened when factories in the Carolinas are pitted against those in Malaysia. Architects in Shanghai now use broadband Internet links to design Manhattan office buildings, taking business away from American operations. Software engineers in Bangalore write code that runs on computers in Seattle. And yet Whitaker's job at the lab in Winston-Salem seems substantially less vulnerable than her previous position at the yarn plant.

For all of these reasons, North Carolina is hardly alone in using its research expertise to focus on biotech. Similar partnerships between private industry, government, and research universities now thrive in San Diego, Boston, San Francisco, Seattle, northern New Jersey, Philadelphia, Los Angeles, and the greater Baltimore-Washington area. Areas that hold promise include Chicago, Detroit, Houston, and St. Louis. Given that some of these areas—particularly Detroit—have lost millions of high-paying manufacturing jobs, the blossoming of biotech could be a particularly meaningful development.

For two decades, practitioners of financial engineering carried the day. They turned Wall Street into a highly profitable casino, while they managed to rake off most of the real dollars for themselves. Spooked and disillusioned by the shenanigans of recent years, the markets now crave products and services that are of tangible value and investments that can be measured using basic arithmetic.

As a society, Americans must get back to living on income that is solid, not synthesized. In place of limitless dependence on foreigners as a source of credit, the United States must find a way to start the transition toward living on its resources. All of this means that the U.S. economy needs a new source of power. Credit default swaps, Cape Coral houses, and loans from China must be replaced as the engine of American economic growth by something sustainable and useful—perhaps bioengineered drugs, or some innovation yet to be dreamed up.

John Maynard Keynes's observation about the endurance of the nation's "resources of nature and men's devices" is as true today as it was in 1930. Rebuilding the American economy will involve several years of difficult transition. It may even involve some "lost" years of Japan-style stagnation before robust growth resumes. But rebuilding is an attainable goal. Despite its obvious structural problems and the economic vulnerability of millions of households, the United States possesses formidable strengths: a highly skilled, adaptable, and enormously productive workforce; enviable business prowess in engineering, research, marketing, and distribution; and world-class universities eager to facilitate turning their research into viable businesses. Though American financial innovation went feral in recent decades and must now be tamed, the basic analytical skill set remains intact, and with the proper incentives and regulatory framework it can once again function in the public interest. American agriculture remains a beacon for the rest of the world in terms of productivity and improvement. In entertainment and other media, the United States may be unmatched in creativity and popularity.

We have sidetracked ourselves through our destructive reach for free money. While we were off pursuing fantastic visions of wealth, we lost touch with the resourcefulness that has long been a hallmark of the nation. These virtues must now be harnessed toward building a new kind of economy. Not a New Economy, 1990s style, but a "retro" variety—albeit, one built upon modern technology and modes of business—in which profit is earned for delivering goods and services of enduring value, providing ample paychecks to American families whose own spending creates jobs and business opportunities for others.

What cannot be emphasized enough is that this blossoming is unlikely to happen if left to the markets alone. Biotech is a classic example of an enterprise that can produce high-wage jobs well into the future, yet is also so risky that its very existence depends on an initial unleashing of public investment. In any given year, the National Institutes of Health, a key federal research agency, may fund as many as twenty-five thousand projects. Researchers and private companies engaged in biotechnology projects may gain some fifty-five hundred patents per year, with perhaps four hundred biotech drugs in some stage of development. Yet by 2002, when the Brookings Institution published a study looking at the development of so-called biotech clusters, only about one hundred biotech drugs had gotten all the way through mandated testing to reach the market. The top ten drugs had accounted for almost all of the sales.

Ultimately, the market should be relied upon to sort the winners from the losers, determining which enterprises attract capital. But given the long odds of success, the government must take the lead in establishing the seed investments that bring biotech ventures into existence, while using its role in financing health care through Medicare and Medicaid to help guarantee demand for the most promising drugs. Just as the Roosevelt administration expanded the electrical grid to produce jobs for workers in appliance factories, the Obama administration now has a chance to use scientific research grants and health care reform to expand employment opportunities for biotech workers.

In the past decade, North Carolina has directed $857 million toward new research and facilities, $135 million toward training workers, $115 million for the biotech center, and more than $100 million in incentives to attract companies. This targeted surge of public money has generated enough momentum to attract a substantial stream of private money. Between 2001 and the middle of 2008, $1.1 billion in venture capital flowed to biosciences companies in North Carolina. The state identified its core strength, and then aggressively used public largesse to catalyze opportunities for private industry.

The benefits of that partnership are still emerging, and the challenges remain enormous, with the state unemployment rate running well above the national average and layoffs continuing. Significant debate within North Carolina focuses on how best to spread the benefits of the higher-wage jobs being produced mostly in the center of the state to the largely rural areas that have continued to suffer as traditional manufacturing work disappears. North Carolina remains divided by great income inequality, and it still suffers a clear dearth of opportunities for less educated people. None of this will be reversed by a single industry or a single government strategy.

Yet, without the public-private partnership, the technical acumen that ultimately attracted venture capital to North Carolina might never have come into being—or, at least, not as quickly. Regina Whitaker might still be at the yarn plant, fretting about a tenuous future—or worse, unemployed.

12

The Renewable Economy

"It's the field of dreams right here."

Newton, Iowa, is the sort of place that seems to take comfort in being ordinary, a small town tucked in the middle of a state in the middle of the country. Its streets run past little houses on tidy squares of lawn and out to endless expanses of corn. Its downtown seems like a movie set for a generic slice of the Midwest circa 1955, with its domed courthouse opposite a bank—the First Newton National Bank. At the Midtown Café, silver-haired men in plaid shirts occupy stools at the counter, flipping through the local paper as they drink their morning coffee. At the Capitol Theater, a hand-lettered sign beckons with MATINEES ON SATURDAYS AND SUNDAYS.

Yet Newton is quite remarkable in another key regard worth contemplating as the nation tries to generate new jobs and navigate its way out of its deep economic crisis. As much as any community in the United States, it has managed to mount an impressive recovery from the devastation of losing its longtime primary employer—Maytag, whose washing machine factory dominated life here for generations before it shut down in October 2007.

Maytag's departure eliminated eighteen hundred jobs from a town of sixteen thousand people. Ten months later, Newton had already gained back nearly seven hundred jobs—by embracing renewable energy. In place of making washing machines, Newton is now aggressively engaged in making the parts of the machinery needed to generate electricity from the wind. With concerns growing about climate change and the American reliance on foreign energy, wind power has huge potential for long-term growth. As in North Carolina, the town has pulled off its renewal by forging a partnership among government, private enterprise, and the local community college system.

In short, Newton is already well on its way to accomplishing what the United States as a whole must do. It has transitioned from a pursuit that could no longer sustain it to something else that seems like it might. It carefully focused on putting its people to work by taking advantage of the community's strengths — not least, the fact that the town sits on the edge of the Great Plains, an expanse of land that experts call "the Saudi Arabia of wind." Turning these unrelenting winds into electricity requires a lot of gear: wind turbines to house the crankshaft; blades to catch the wind; towers to prop hunks of steel and fiberglass high above the land. That gear has to be made somewhere. To which the people of Newton posed a useful question: why not here?

Much of the gear used to turn wind into electricity is so large and so heavy — turbines as big as rail cars, towers that stretch two hundred feet skyward, and blades as long as aircraft wings — that they are most economically built close to where they are needed. In a sense, the forces that have brought jobs to Newton amount to globalization, working in reverse.

"These parts are far too big to be hauling around," said Crugar Tuttle, general manager of one of the new factories in Newton, a plant constructed by a company called TPI Composites, which makes fiberglass blades. "You're going to spend more money hauling them around than you do making them. These are American jobs that are hard to export."

By the end of 2008, the TPI plant was employing three hundred people, many of them former Maytag workers. It planned to hire two hundred more in 2009. Across the road, at the old Maytag factory, another company, Texas-based Trinity Structural Towers, was building the concrete cylinders that hold wind turbines above the ground. It was expected to hire as many as 140 people by the end of 2010.

The apparent safety of these jobs was a comforting prospect for Arie Versendaal, who had worked at Maytag's plant in Newton for two decades when it shut down. His wife had worked there, too. So had his uncle, his grandfather, and most of his friends and neighbors. "I thought I'd be there 'til the end," he said. "It wasn't the end I'd wanted."

Less than a year after Maytag shut down, Versendaal was already started on his new career at TPI. "Life's not over," he said. "I didn't sit around and cry. I went out and got a job."

Crucially, there was a job to go out and get—and not by lucky happenstance. The renewable energy industry had been buoyed by the three dozen states that directed their utilities to buy from clean energy sources instead of coal, oil, and gas in order to curb carbon emissions, which cause global warming. The growth of Iowa factories making gear to harvest electricity from the wind is the product of a concerted effort by local officials and the state to attract investment.

Until recently, most of the gear required for wind power—the turbines, the towers, and the blades—has been made in factories in other countries, such as Germany, Spain, and Denmark, where governments have aggressively promoted the advance of the wind industry. Yet many of the largest wind farms now being constructed have gone up on the Great Plains. Iowa is capitalizing on its proximity to the wind by courting manufacturing companies that are eager to establish factories closer to their customers. Iowa also beckons companies with its thousands of people like Versendaal—skilled at making things, yet unemployed and eager for their next paycheck.

The state's logic has been affirmed. Between 2000 and 2003, Iowa saw twenty-five thousand manufacturing jobs vanish. But over the following five years—a period that saw the nation as a whole lose some 3 million manufacturing jobs—Iowa managed to hold the line, actually gaining six thousand such jobs.

No one believes that renewable energy can fully replace what has been lost on the American factory floor. Versendaal now makes about $13 an hour, far less than the $20 an hour he made at Maytag. But he is engaged in something new, an area of innovation and growth, giving him the sense that the possibilities for advancement are abundant. Unlike so many industries in which expansion has been powered mostly by easy money over the past decade, the factory where Versendaal works is engaged in making something of tangible value.

"I feel like I'm doing something beneficial for mankind and the

United States," he said. "Gas is so high; oil is so high. We've got to get used to depending on ourselves instead of something else, and wind is free. The wind is blowing out there for anybody to use."

෴

Few places needed help as much as Newton—a company town abandoned by its company in a turn of events few had seen coming. Even as the rest of the industrial Midwest succumbed to decline, Newton somehow felt insulated. It was the birthplace of Maytag, and that transcended the bottom line of business.

Maytag made its first washing machine in 1907 before expanding into one of the most recognizable household appliance brands on earth. The company had survived the Great Depression without losing a dime. During World War II, it had put its factories to use making parts for military aircraft. After the war it resumed production at an accelerated clip to serve the expanding American middle class, adding a second plant on the edges of town. Over the generations, as Maytag grew into a global enterprise—buying up companies in Europe and Australia, and adding factories in Mexico and China—it had kept its headquarters in Iowa.

In every conceivable way, Maytag lay at the heart of Newton. Its original factory sat downtown, just a couple of blocks from the town square. The company built a city park, a public swimming center, and a library. When the state community college system sought to set up a local campus in Newton, Maytag handed over an old factory that had been used to make the treads on tanks during the Korean War. Above all, Maytag paid out substantial wages for those willing to endure the grueling work of turning coils of metal into washing machines—$20 an hour and more, enough to finance houses, cars, vacations, weddings, and funerals. The company provided ample health insurance. It paid generous pensions to those who worked there for three decades.

"We had the good life," said Rick Avery, a former president of the local United Auto Workers chapter, which represented Maytag plant workers, and who worked at the company himself for thirty-one years. "Maytag paid better than a lot of the college jobs. It was kind of hard to go anywhere else to beat the benefits. Maytag wasn't afraid to pay the wages and benefits if you were willing to work."

As similar factory towns across the United States saw jobs transferred to factories in Latin America and Asia, and to nonunion plants in the United States, Newton convinced itself that it was immune. The local workforce was proud of its speed and efficiency. Maytag made machines of the highest quality. The company had been in town so long that life was unimaginable without it.

"Newton was an island," said Ted Johnson, who was president of the local chapter of the United Auto Workers when the plant finally closed. "We saw autos go through hard times, other industries, but we still had meat on our barbecues."

The end came, as it so often does, through a corporate merger. In 2005, Whirlpool, the largest appliance manufacturer in the United States, struck an agreement to purchase Maytag, fighting off another suitor, the Chinese company Haier. By the following year, the Newton factory was doomed. Whirlpool let it be known that it would shift production to lower-cost plants. On the last day, as the factory's final shift shut down, people hung out in the parking lot for hours, as if uncertain what they were supposed to do next. They hugged one another and felt numb. "It was like somebody died," said Mary Durbala, who had worked at the factory for twenty years. "You were just in total shock. And then you went home and you cried."

Workers unloaded their memorabilia at Pappy's Antique Mall: matchbooks, buttons, award plaques, and coffee mugs, all of it adorned with the company logo. "If it said Maytag on it, we bought it," said Susie Jones, the store manager. "At first, I thought the stuff had value. Then, it was out of the kindness of my heart. And now I don't have any heart left. It don't sell. People are mad at them. They ripped out our soul."

State and county economic development officials quickly sought a new source of jobs. They brought in a consultant with experience in communities that had lost major employers. At a hastily convened town hall meeting, he urged them to settle on a new identity or risk succumbing to downward mobility.

"It was a call to arms," recalled Kimberly M. Didier, executive director of the Newton Development Corporation, a nonprofit that courts investment for the town. "He basically said if we didn't do something ourselves, nobody was going to lose any sleep over it. We had to decide what we wanted to be."

In early 2007, the state's Department of Economic Development added the shuttered Maytag factory to a list of empty facilities it showed to companies thinking of setting up in Iowa. It was the largest standing structure in the state.

Iowa was already focused on attracting investment in wind power—a campaign that had brought an American turbine-maker, Clipper, to the Cedar Rapids area, and a Danish tower manufacturer to the small town of Keokuk. The state's pitch was all about geography: within a six-hundred-mile radius of Iowa, some $5.7 billion worth of turbines was projected to be installed each year between 2008 and 2014, mostly in North Dakota, South Dakota, Minnesota, and Iowa itself. The state was prepared to train sufficient numbers of workers in the required skills, having launched a program in wind energy and turbine technology at Iowa Lakes Community College. When that program began in 2004, it had about sixteen students. By 2007, the enrollment had swelled to one hundred, and the demand for graduates was intense.

"It's hard to stay in the program, because all these companies are constantly trying to offer you jobs," said Carter Frank, who graduated in the first class.

Now, the wind was blowing Newton's way.

In June 2007, the city government and surrounding Jasper County dispatched a team of economic development officials to the American Wind Energy Association trade show in Los Angeles. They ensconced themselves at the state of Iowa's booth and gave their pitch to dozens of curious companies. One of the companies that stopped by was TPI Composites. Weeks later, its chief operating officer was in Newton to have a look.

Based in Arizona, TPI was about to get a contract to supply General Electric with the blades for its turbines. Making blades involves layering strips of fiberglass into molds, requiring a long unbroken work space. The Maytag plant was too short. So Didier and her crew showed TPI an undeveloped piece of land on the edges of town.

In what seemed an unlikely competition, TPI was comparing Newton to a site in Mexico for its next factory. Mexico had the obvious wage advantage. But Newton had location. General Electric would deploy its turbines across the Great Plains. The local officials laid out maps. Newton was just off Interstate 80, and it had rail links, making it easy to bring in raw materials and ship out finished products. Former Maytag employees were waiting to take up jobs. The new branch of the Des Moines Area Community College—the campus set up in the former Maytag factory—was ready to train them in the particulars of making turbine blades.

That pitch carried the day. In exchange for $6 million in state and local tax sweeteners, TPI picked Newton.

"You go where your customer wants you to be," said Crugar Tuttle, who was brought in to head the construction of the plant. He had worked for a host of established companies in a thirty-five-year-long career in manufacturing—Johnson & Johnson, Motorola, General Electric. Now, he would build something from scratch.

As a condition of the tax breaks, TPI promised to hire five hundred people by 2010. "Getting five hundred jobs in one swoop is like winning the lottery," said Newton's mayor, Chaz Allen. "We don't have to just roll over and die. We can grow this place."

By late 2007, TPI was breaking ground, turning a pancake-flat expanse into a new factory. Three feet of snow and minus-thirty-degree temperatures slowed construction. The summer brought floods, turning the site into a sprawling mud pit. A tornado snipped away a thirty-two-foot-high utility door like a child's toy. But by August 2008, the factory was up and running.

"It's the field of dreams right here," said Tuttle. He wore a blue plaid button-down shirt over khakis. He joked with people on the factory floor in his easygoing southern drawl as he made the rounds. But his intensity was evident as he checked the particulars of their work.

"The demand for blades exceeds the supply for the next three to four years," he said. "Everybody in the wind industry is in a massive hurry to build out capacity."

Moments later, he and two dozen workers gazed up excitedly as an overhead crane lifted the first-ever blade from its mold and carried it toward an empty patch of concrete at the factory's back end. One man hummed the theme from *Jaws* as the blade slipped past. Larry Crady, a round-faced man with a goatee—a former Maytagger—looked up at the blade and grinned.

"I like this job more than I did Maytag," he said. "I feel like I'm doing something to improve our country, rather than just building a washing machine."

Asked how long he spent at the washing machine factory, Crady responded precisely: "Twenty-three point six years"—which was to say, 6.4 years short of drawing the pension whose famously generous terms compelled so many to spend their lives inside an airless hangar, getting squirted by oil and burned by welding torches. "That's what everyone in Newton was waiting on," he said. "You could get that thirty and out and then retire. It was everyone's dream." His wife was there, too. She fell three years short.

By the end, Crady was earning $23 an hour. Combined with his wife's wages, they were bringing home about $1,050 per week, after taxes. They bought a four-bedroom house in town, with plenty of room for their two kids. Now, his wife was working at a local telephone directory company. Together, they were bringing home less than $900 a week.

"We had to change our lifestyle," he said. Their boating trips to nearby Red Rock Lake were less frequent. They eliminated cable television and shopped at discount supermarkets. His son's soccer team was skipping out-of-town tournaments. Still, Crady felt fortunate to have found work in Newton. Most of the other available jobs were in Des Moines, a thirty-mile drive away, and they paid about the same as TPI.

"You're not going to find twenty-one- and twenty-two-dollar-an-hour jobs anymore," he said. "This is what everyone's making. You just accept it."

Terri Rock was overseeing TPI's human resources office. Cheerful and upbeat, she occupied the same position at Maytag's corporate headquarters. In her last years there, her job was mostly spent ending other people's jobs. "There was a lot of heartache," Rock said. "This is a small town, and you'd have to let people go and then see them at the grocery store with their families. It was a real tough job at the end."

Now, she was launching fresh careers, hiring as many as twenty people a week, and enjoying the creative spirit of a start-up. "We're not stuck with the mentality of 'this is how we've done it for the last thirty-five years,'" she said.

The first crews she hired required company training to learn the precise craft of making turbine blades. In another bit of reverse globalization, TPI dispatched them to China to train at a factory it operates there. Then they came home and put their skills to use in Newton.

The tidy downtown was showing fresh signs of life by the summer of 2008, the pain of Maytag's demise already fading. At Courtyard Floral, the end of Maytag spelled a steep drop in sales, particularly around holidays like Valentine's Day and Mother's Day, when it used to run several van-loads of flowers a week to the washing machine plant. But when TPI sent its workers to China for training, the company ordered bouquets for the spouses left at home. Since then, new orders were filtering in as spending power returned.

Across the street at NetWork Realty, broker Dennis Combs said the housing market was starting to stabilize as jobs were replaced. "We've gone from Maytag, which wasn't upgrading their antiquated plant, to something that's cutting-edge technology," he said. "Something that every politician is screaming this country has to have."

At Uncle Nancy's Coffeehouse & Eatery, on the other side of the square, talk of unemployment checks and foreclosures was now tempered by conversation about job leads and looming investment.

"We're seeing hope," said the mayor.

The effort to attract jobs in wind power was ongoing. Didier, the head of the Newton Development Corporation, was trying to attract turbine manufacturers and providers of raw materials and parts. "This is in its infancy," she said. "Automobiles, washer-dryers, and other appliances have become commodities in their retirement phase. We're in the beginning of this. How our economy functions is changing. We built this whole thing around oil, and now we've got to replace that."

⁓

Newton is a particularly successful exponent of the embrace of renewable energy, but hundreds of communities are employing similar strategies. Across industrial America, from the faded steel towns of western Pennsylvania to communities in Michigan reeling from the loss of auto industry jobs, many factory towns are starting to retool to make the equipment needed to produce energy from renewable sources, jockeying for a slice of a potentially enormous market.

Ever since the end of the Civil War, Toledo, Ohio, had been a major center of glass production, exploiting the nearby abundance of sand and natural gas. But its glass factories have been assailed in recent times—first, by the shift from bottles toward aluminum cans, and more recently by the decline of the American auto industry. Fewer cars made in Detroit spelled less demand for windshields made in Toledo. The city lost nearly one-third of its manufacturing jobs between 2000 and 2008, according to the Labor Department. From its lifeless downtown to the industrial suburbs, many of the city's factories sit boarded up and abandoned.

But by 2008, a new enterprise was absorbing many Toledo factories: making solar panels, a business that could eventually replace significant numbers of lost jobs. "The green we're interested in is cash," said Norman W. Johnston, a former chemical industry executive who started a solar cell factory called Solar Fields in Toledo in 2003. "This is the thing we can do to get from the Rust Belt to the Renewables Belt."

The same skills that go into making other glass products can easily be applied to make solar cells. "It's such an adjunct to the glass industry," Johnston said. "It's basically a glass sandwich."

At the center of the trend is Pilkington, one of the largest glassmakers in the world, with operations in twenty-eight different countries and thirty-six thousand employees around the globe. Pilkington bought a glassmaker that had been operating a factory in Toledo since the 1890s. In the 1970s, amid the oil shocks, Pilkington launched a solar division to make photovoltaic cells, but then aborted the initiative in the early 1980s, concentrating on its core business: selling glass products to the automakers. Later that decade, it unleashed a new solar venture, this time with better technology. That proved to be a fortuitous decision. In 2007 and 2008, as auto sales plunged by 30 percent, the solar business grew by 40 percent.

"Solar was one of those things where every year it was, 'Next year it's really going to happen,'" said Pilkington's vice president for sales and marketing Stephen E. Weidner, speaking in the summer of 2008. "Next year has finally come."

The University of Toledo, a local research university, was increasingly focused on fueling the city's commercial push into solar energy. In the late 1990s, the university had only two faculty members with an interest in solar power. By 2008, there were fifteen, advising fifty graduate students. The university was licensing technologies spawned in its labs and encouraging faculty members to launch their own businesses, while helping them gain start-up capital from the state.

"The job of the lab is not finished until the technology is in production," said the university president, Lloyd A. Jacobs. "We're not about figuring out how many angels can dance on the head of a pin."

A university incubator was helping companies get off the ground, offering low-rent laboratory space, offices, and guidance securing finance. One of the earliest companies sprung from the incubator, Xunlight, secured $7 million in finance from a Swiss venture capital firm and a Washington-based private equity firm, using that money to buy a vacant factory, where it set up an assembly line in 2007 to test how to make thin and especially flexible solar cells on strips of stainless steel. The following year, Xunlight gained a fresh $22 million in investment to expand production. By early 2009, the company had eighty-eight employees and planned to double its workforce over the following year. Roughly one-third of those people were engineers with salaries between $60,000 and $90,000 a year. Assembly workers earned between $30,000 and $50,000.

"It's a second opportunity," said assembly supervisor Matt McGilvery, one of the early hires.

Sly and prone to wisecracks, McGilvery is precisely the sort of talented and industrious person who has been left behind by the million as American manufacturing jobs have withered in recent years. Now in his mid-fifties, he spent a decade at a factory that made steel coils that sit on the backs of tractor trailers, earning $23 an hour, before that business hit on hard times and he was laid off. With computers proliferating across the factory floor, he worried that he had become a fossil.

"I'm hateful, really, of that damn computer," he said. "I come from a time when you drew the plan by hand, you had to watch and cut and pay attention. Now, everything's computer-controlled. You're nothing but a robot. You just put the part in and you push a button. After years of that, I thought, 'Nobody's going to want me.'"

But Xunlight was engaged in the manufacture of a product that had only recently come into existence. That meant it had to design and fabricate the machinery it required by itself—a custom job. No computer could be entrusted with this task. Suddenly, McGilvery's seemingly anachronistic technique was back in demand.

His paycheck was a lot smaller than it used to be. But the trajectory looked good. "The hope is that two years from now everything is smoking," he said, "and that envelope will slide across the table."

His confidence had returned, along with his sense of job security. "The money that people are dumping into this tells me it's a huge market," he said.

&

Money had indeed been pouring into green businesses at a clip reminiscent of past investment booms. In 2007, alternative energy businesses raised $14.8 billion through initial public offerings on stock markets, considerably more than the $11.6 billion captured by tech stock offerings in 1998, at the height of that boom. Some $5 billion in venture capital poured into clean energy businesses in North America in 2007, and nearly $6 billion in 2008.

Among leaders in industrial communities, the hope is that the arrival of turbine plants and solar cell factories will catalyze demand for raw materials and components, putting people to work in steel foundries and generating fresh orders at machine shops. It could create work for the construction crews needed to build new plants, the truckers who haul goods, and the mechanics who service the trucks. It could increase demand for a broad range of services, from accounting and legal to real estate and landscaping, as the industry boosts overall economic activity. The extra wages would filter through communities, from restaurants and retailers to hardware stores and dry cleaners.

"It's the renewal of the manufacturing base," said Tuttle, TPI's general manager in Newton. "It will feed into a whole local industry of people making stuff. Manufacturing has been in decline for decades. This is our greatest chance to turn it around."

A multitude of environmental and foreign policy considerations argues for the transition from coal and oil toward renewable forms of energy. There is the need to curb greenhouse gas emissions in the face of mounting worries about climate change. There is the imperative to lessen American dependence on foreign oil, with the geopolitical messiness and trade deficits that such dependence entails.

Yet the courtship of investment by state and local governments has less to do with these lofty aims and everything to do with creating paychecks. In a report released in 2008, the Energy Department concluded that the United States could make wind energy the source of one-fifth of its electricity by 2030, up from about 2 percent. That would require nearly $500 billion in new construction, while adding some 550,000 jobs. Many of these new jobs would be concentrated around the Great Lakes, the region hardest hit by the cuts in manufacturing jobs—4 million nationwide—over the last decade. Add in solar energy along with generating power from crops, and the continued embrace of renewable energy would create as many as 5 million jobs by 2030, asserts Daniel M. Kammen, director of the Renewable and Appropriate Energy Laboratory at the University of California–Berkeley. Most of these jobs could be filled by people with a high school diploma but less than a four-year college degree—precisely the sorts of workers who have seen opportunities evaporating in recent decades.

Such job projection numbers, perhaps tinged with wishful thinking, are at the center of an extraordinary political moment. On the campaign trail in the fall of 2008, Barack Obama promised to direct tens of billions of dollars toward spurring so-called green-collar jobs. He pledged to make renewable forms of energy the source of at least one-tenth of the nation's electrical supply by 2012, and at least one-fourth by 2025.

But significant obstacles sit in the way of the expansion of renewable energy. The wind of the Great Plains is a long way from the major U.S. cities where electricity is needed most. For wind turbines in South Dakota to power industry near Chicago, the government and power companies will need to sponsor an expensive build-out of the existing transmission system. Thousands of miles of modern power lines must be extended. Many utilities are resistant to buying wind and solar energy because they deliver power only when the wind is blowing or the sun is shining. Technologies that allow wind and solar energy to be stored for later use, such as large batteries, are a primary area of ongoing research, but such solutions are far from complete.

Wind and solar cannot compete on cost with existing coal-fired electrical generating plants—at least not without a system that forces the coal plants to pay for the pollution they emit. Wind and solar can increasingly compete with new coal-fired plants, but only so long as they receive subsidies from the federal government, compensating for the subsidies that have long been lavished on traditional carbon-based sources of energy. Currently, the government subsidizes renewable energy by allowing those companies that use it to produce electricity to collect tax credits. These credits have been a crucial inducement. During 2008, with the credits in place, a fresh $17 billion in investment flowed to American wind farms, and the United States began to edge out Germany as the largest generator of wind power in the world, with enough capacity to power 7 million homes. This expansion added thirteen thousand manufacturing jobs.

When Congress allowed such tax credits to expire in 2000, 2002, and 2004, the installation of wind turbines fell off dramatically. "You're going to see development come to a halt if the production tax credit is not extended," said Ruth E. Leistensnider, an attorney with the law firm Nixon Peabody in Albany, New York, who helps major developers gain required land use permits to construct wind farms. The stimulus spending bill adopted by Congress in February 2009 extended the tax credits for three years, easing some uncertainty about the prospects of companies devoted to wind energy.

Still, the financial crisis slowed the pace of development, making investment harder to secure. During the first nine months of 2008, renewable energy and power conservation ventures received $3 billion in investment capital, up from $1.9 billion during the same period in 2007, but larger projects were having an increasingly tough time getting funding.

Before the slowdown, as many as eighteen large banks and financial institutions were eager to finance the installation of wind turbines and solar cells, availing themselves of federal tax incentives. Such finance is crucial, particularly for wind farms, which tend to rely on bank loans for as much as half of the costs of acquiring land and installing the gear. But with banks in virtual hibernation, the number of willing lenders had slipped to four by the beginning of 2009, according to Keith Martin, a tax and project finance specialist with the law firm Chadbourne & Parke.

The finance squeeze prompted layoffs in some factories making wind and solar gear, much to the consternation of local officials. "I thought if there was any industry that was bulletproof, it was that industry," the mayor of West Fargo, North Dakota, Rich Mattern, told the *New York Times* in February. In his town, DMI Industries of Fargo operated a plant making towers for wind turbines. Despite the fact that the Dakotas offer some of the better locations for wind farms on earth, DMI had recently announced plans to lay off one-fifth of its workforce because of flagging sales.

᪗

Longer term, however, renewable energy has gathered what many analysts say is unstoppable momentum. In Texas, the oil baron T. Boone Pickens is pressing ahead—albeit more slowly than originally conceived—with his much-touted plans to develop what would be the largest wind farm in the world. Not least, state laws requiring utilities to buy renewable energy give the market a government mandate. Meanwhile, the Obama administration has signaled that it is likely to embrace some form of new regulatory system that will force coal-fired electricity plants to pay for the pollution they emit. That would make wind, solar, and other renewable fuels competitive in terms of the cost of producing electricity. And that would likely spur more private investment into those areas.

As much as anything, the growing potential of renewable energy as a source of paychecks reflects the changing dynamic between business, labor, and environmentalists. For decades, environmental groups and industry have battled ceaselessly, with their interests generally cast as mutually exclusive. Pollution controls sought by those concerned about blue skies, public health, or endangered species seemed to come at the expense of the corporate bottom line.

But as the market for renewable energy has taken shape, major companies have come to see profits. General Electric is now a major supplier of wind turbines. BP has unleashed a corporate strategy to change its image from an oil company into an energy company that produces whatever makes the most sense. "We're investing billions in renewable energy today, for a better tomorrow," proclaimed a full-page newspaper ad run by JPMorgan Chase in January 2009, complete with an illustration of wind turbines, as the bank tried to reassure investors it has a plan to move past the financial crisis. Meanwhile, environmentalists have come to tout job creation as one of the benefits of pressing ahead with a cleaner-burning energy regime, combining traditional concerns about global warming with a targeted appeal to the national bottom line.

In the early 1990s, Chris Rose, an environmental attorney in Alaska, spent much of his time mobilizing activists to try to stop projects. He and his community challenged the merits of power lines to nowhere. They sought to make more of the state off-limits to the exploration of oil and gas conglomerates. They tangled with unions eager for the jobs that would accrue from such undertakings. These days, Rose runs a nonprofit group that lobbies for the advancement of renewable energy. "Now, I'm *for* big projects," he says. He is working to promote a wind farm just outside Anchorage. He is advocating for a geothermal project that could cost several billion dollars. All the forces seem to be aligning—profit, job creation, and environmental protection.

Back in 2001, the American Wind Energy Association, a trade group, drew about a thousand attendees and twenty-five exhibitors to Washington, D.C., for its annual show. At its show in June 2008, more than twelve thousand people and 770 exhibitors jammed a convention center in Houston. On the showroom floor, booths offered myriad services for companies building out wind farms, from construction companies to firms that negotiate with farmers for land-use agreements. One business offered climbing harnesses that allow technicians to mount the towers to service turbines. Another specialized in surveying local wind conditions. At a booth run by the Spanish turbine-maker, Acciona, visitors padded up carpeted steps to a sleek hulk shaped like an airplane cockpit—the company's newest model. Once installed, it sat some three hundred feet above the ground, this single turbine capable of powering as many as two thousand homes.

"Five years ago, we were all walking around in Birkenstocks," said John M. Brown, then the managing director of a Colorado-based turbine manufacturer, Entegrity Wind Systems, Inc. "Now it's all suits. You go to a seminar, and it's getting taught by lawyers and bankers."

At Entegrity's booth, a steady procession of emissaries from multiple states arrived to tout the benefits of setting up the next factory within their borders. Texas, Florida, Louisiana, Alabama, Colorado, Michigan, Ohio, Idaho, and Nebraska had all stopped in. "Everyone wants us to build a plant in their state," said the company's director of sales, Mark Boumansour. "They call us all the time."

In a rented ballroom at a hotel across the street, Iowa's governor, Chet Culver—his cheeks boyishly pink, his head topped with a shock of hair the color of corn silk—presided over a reception for companies already in his state, or perhaps on the way. "We are blessed with certainly some of the best wind in the world," the governor said, as one hundred or so people looked on, many wearing name tags identifying them as executives of multinational companies. "We're putting the pieces together. We certainly invite you to give our state a try."

⌇

The promises of wind and solar are considerable, and yet the distress of American factory workers is so great—and particularly in the Midwest—that many are certain to be left behind.

Even as the TPI plant swiftly expanded in Newton, Ted Johnson, the former Maytag union president, sat in the old UAW hall, where a litany of former workers passed through each day, swapping leads about potential jobs and commiserating over the difficulties of starting over. Though the new wind power jobs were a considerable addition to the local economy, hundreds of former Maytag workers remained without work, Johnson among them.

Joblessness was a state of affairs he had never known before. At forty-five, he had slipped from relative comfort of his adult years into the sort of poverty he had last known as a child. "I grew up in southern Iowa with nothing," Johnson said. His father was a self-employed welder. His mother worked at an overall factory. "Nobody had anything. If somebody got a new car, everybody heard about it. If somebody got air-conditioning, that was a big deal."

After high school, Johnson worked at a small machine shop for about $6 an hour. Then Maytag hired him, doubling his wages. As the years passed and his wages grew, he gained comforts he had not known as a boy—his own house with a garage and a deck, a new truck, regular health care.

But when Maytag shut down, his $1,100-a-week paycheck was replaced by a $360-a-week unemployment check. He and his wife divorced, turning a two-income household into a no-income household. He sold off his truck, with its $550-a-month payment. He sold his dining room table and chairs, and his refrigerator, all in the hopes of being able to keep making his $900 monthly mortgage payment. It was not enough. In late 2007, he surrendered his house to foreclosure. He and his teenage daughter moved into a rental with a friend.

All the while, Johnson found his next job beyond reach. He had put in dozens of applications, from sales jobs at Lowe's and Home Depot to TPI. He had yet to secure an interview. He thought of the protests he had led against Maytag's management over the years, the pictures of him in the local paper demanding that the company honor its commitments. "I guess I'm blackballed because of what I did with the union," he said.

Johnson's unemployment benefits ran out in May 2008. He no longer had health insurance. He broke a tooth where the filling had been, but he couldn't afford to get it fixed. When he ran out of medication for high blood pressure, he went two months without it, before a local clinic took pity on him and gave him some samples. When his daughter complained of constant headaches, he paid $1,500 out of pocket for an MRI. The doctor found a cyst on her brain.

How was she doing now? Johnson froze at the question. He was a grown man with gray hair combed into a widow's peak, a black Harley-Davidson T-shirt tight across his barrel chest. He had long earned a living with his hands and paid his own way. He was unaccustomed to being the object of charitable concern. He tried to compose himself, but he burst into tears.

"I'm sorry," he said.

Johnson had recently signed up for a state insurance program for the poor so his daughter could see a neurologist. He had signed up for food stamps.

"Do you know how much it sucked to apply for assistance from the state?" he said. "There's a lot of things you get from working. No, I never had it growing up. But once you got it for twenty-one years, you kind of like to see it through. You feel so irresponsible. You feel kind of stupid."

He was willing to take almost any job. A position at TPI or some other factory would be terrific, even at much reduced pay. Still, he worried about larger issues, about the future of a way of life that had sustained people like him for decades. "Thirteen dollars an hour, is it enough to live on?" he asked. "Probably. But is it enough to support a community, a car dealership, to attract doctors to the hospital and sustain them? No, it isn't enough. We're living in a $22-an-hour economy. You cannot drive the standard of living down and expect to support the economy."

Johnson's formulation prompts basic questions: As finance surges into wind and solar energy, how far can these industries go? How much value can the American economy derive from a potentially global transition toward a new energy regime?

In the visions of the state officials courting investment, this is only the beginning, the first phase of something potentially enormous that will eventually spill far beyond the factory floor.

"I'm into renewable energy because I'm into economic development," said Ohio's lieutenant governor, Lee Fisher, who directs his state's efforts to attract investors. "One of the best ways to capture the loss of manufacturing jobs is to take our core competency in manufacturing and match it with the needs of the renewable energy industry. We're trying to move people from $7-an-hour jobs to careers."

Despite its recent gains, the United States sits well behind Europe in terms of manufacturing wind power gear and solar panels, in what amounts to the squandering of a historical legacy. Wind power took off as a modern enterprise in California in the 1970s, as the oil shocks of the era lent urgency to a search for alternative supplies of energy. By the mid-1980s, California was home to some 90 percent of the world's installed wind power capacity. But as the oil shocks passed and prices dropped, federal subsidies for wind disappeared, and so did momentum for the wind industry. Meanwhile, Europe began aggressively promoting wind power, seizing the initiative both in installing turbines and in improving the technology. As the United States now reenters the very industry it once dominated, it is being forced to rely upon the innovation of foreign companies, sending most of the revenues to Europe.

Solar is a similar story. All the way back in 1908, a researcher at the Carnegie Steel Company used copper coils to fashion a box that could store energy from the sun. In 1954, Bell Labs pioneered the first solar cell that could generate enough electricity to power ordinary equipment. Later that decade, the architect Frank Bridges designed the world's first solar-heated commercial office building, using the sun's rays to heat water. Through the 1960s and '70s, American researchers and companies refined uses of photovoltaic cells that turned the sun's energy into electricity, with the oil shocks again lending urgency to the effort. But as cheap oil returned and the initiative cooled in the United States, Europe and Japan captured the lead in design, manufacture, and deployment of the technology.

The best outcome for American industry is that the continued emergence of renewable energy is accompanied by a concerted research effort that positions domestic companies to capture the high-value business of designing systems and then selling them to the world. Along the way, the industry could amass enough scale to trigger the much-touted resurgence of manufacturing, restoring jobs and making use of skills that are already fading.

"You have to reinvest in industrial capacity," said Randy Udall, an energy consultant in Carbondale, Colorado. "You've got to get serious about this. This is not child's play. You use wind to revitalize the Rust Belt. You make steel again. You bring it home. We ought to be planting wind turbines as if they were trees."

In the town of West Branch, just east of Iowa City, the Spanish company Acciona opened a new factory in 2007 to make the turbine it had debuted at the Houston trade show. The future of its operation there amounts to a test of the promise of wind power—whether it is really a big enough force to revive struggling pieces of American manufacturing.

Acciona is best known as a developer of wind farms, acquiring land use rights and then installing turbines made by someone else. Much like TPI, it needed a source of turbines near the Great Plains, and it decided to build its own. It settled on an empty factory in West Branch that had formerly been used to make hydraulic pumps. When that factory closed in 2004, it wiped out 130 jobs in a town of little more than two thousand people.

As a condition for state tax incentives, Acciona agreed to hire at least 109 people at $16 an hour. By the beginning of 2009, it had already hired 170 people—many of them workers from the former hydraulic pump factory.

"It's a thing of the future," said one worker, Steve Jennings. "It looked like an open door to me." Plain-spoken and amiable, Jennings, fifty, had worked for a dozen years at a local machine shop when it went bankrupt in 1992. After a few odd jobs, he landed at the hydraulic pump factory, where he made $14 an hour. When that plant shut down seven years later in a consolidation, he took a position at a heating and air-conditioning company for $9 an hour, without benefits. "I wanted to work," he said. "I didn't want to go on unemployment."

When he heard that a wind turbine plant was coming in, five miles from his house, he was among the first to apply. He soon became a team leader, making nearly $20 an hour—more than he had ever brought home before.

"It seemed like manufacturing was going away," Jennings says. "Everything was going overseas. But I think this is here to stay."

Acciona poured $23 million into expanding the facility. It built its first turbine in West Branch in December 2007, made two hundred in 2008, and planned to double production in 2009.

But by March 2009, as the credit crunch slowed the development of wind farms, Acciona slowed production and laid off fifty-five people at the West Branch plant—Jennings among them. The layoffs highlighted the tenuous nature of all efforts aimed at economic renewal absent the restoration of the financial system.

Longer term, Acciona's mode of production raises a fundamental question about the extent to which the emerging industry of renewable energy can deliver additional paychecks: the company does not fabricate its products in Iowa. Rather, it assembles its turbines out of finished parts that lie stacked across the concrete floor of the factory—the hub, like a hollow steel ball, with holes for the bolts that attach to the blades; the frames, like shipping containers, which serve as the chassis; the shaft, a hefty cone of steel. All of these parts were being shipped in from Europe, racking up sales for companies on the other side of the Atlantic.

"There's not that many companies left in the U.S. that can do this," explained the plant's general manager, Adrian E. LaTrace.

Acciona was seeking American suppliers. LaTrace figured his company's demand would be part of a wave that would compel increased steelmaking in the United States, along with the work of making parts.

The basics of making a wind turbine tap into skills that have long been in place. For the American economy, the merits of this enterprise ultimately hinge on whether he is right—whether the influx of new factories will indeed revive the manufacturing base, bringing back the sorts of jobs whose disappearance has been so wrenching.

"Michigan, Ohio, that's the Rust Belt," LaTrace said. "We could be purchasing these components from those states. We've got the attention of the folks in the auto industry. This thing has critical mass."

13

Insourcing the Future

"No free lunch for the United States"

Whatever the engines of the new American economy prove to be — whether renewable energy comes to employ millions of people, or biotech expands, or some other industry emerges — growth will ultimately require investment. The government can supply it in the immediate term to generate demand for goods and services, thereby creating some jobs, but this is not a long-term solution for the troubles of the U.S. economy. Eventually, after hundreds of billions of public dollars are unleashed, private investment will need to take over, creating and maintaining the businesses that can generate good paychecks.

Where will this money come from?

Some will come from American investors. But in a global economy in which the fastest growth is likely to accrue elsewhere — particularly as the United States grapples with restoring order to its financial system — much will eventually wash in from abroad. This is something that Americans must embrace as part of the fix. After the global recession lifts, foreigners will again buy American companies, and American workers will increasingly draw their paychecks from companies headquartered in Frankfurt, Mexico City, Shanghai, and Tokyo.

In years past, this reality caused enormous friction in U.S. politics, yet it is something with which Americans must make their peace if they are to accrue the capital needed to finance businesses and generate growth. There is simply no alternative. We need the money, and selling companies to foreigners is a better way of raising it than continuing to lean on the foreign central banks, whose aggressive purchases of American debt have enabled Americans to spend beyond their incomes for many years. Indeed, the idea of keeping American companies in purely American hands has as much reality to it as never growing up.

Despite the headline-catching deals that have ultimately been scotched—such as the effort by Dubai Ports World, a company from the United Arab Emirates, to buy several American ports in 2006—growing volumes of foreign investment and direct foreign control of previously domestic firms is already an established facet of American commercial life. Between 1998 and the fall of 2008, foreign companies paid more than $2 trillion for major stakes in U.S. firms or to set up new operations in the United States. With little notice, a Saudi Arabian conglomerate bought a plastic maker in Massachusetts. A French company set up a new factory in Adrian, Michigan, adding 189 automotive jobs to an area synonymous with auto industry layoffs. A British company bought a cough syrup manufacturer in New Jersey. Since 2004, the German industrial conglomerate Siemens has invested more than $17 billion in American companies, acquiring factories that make water treatment equipment, medical devices, and laboratory testing gear, in addition to a company that develops business management software.

Many factors explain this surge. In the mid-2000s, the dollar's relatively weak value against major currencies such as the euro and the Japanese yen made American companies a bargain for foreign purchasers. While global confidence in the U.S. financial system has been severely shaken, the United States remains the world's largest market for nearly everything, and buying an American company typically continues to be the swiftest way for a foreign firm to capture a piece. In the last couple of years, with credit tight, American companies have been particularly keen for investment of any sort—a reality with potential staying power.

The tensions tripped by higher-profile, controversial deals reflect a U.S.-centric view of the world that has not served the national interest. For many Americans, globalization has become just another word for Americanization. Capital, technology, and culture are supposed to flow from the United States, spreading suburban-style living, big-box retail stores, fast food, and Hollywood entertainment to every corner of the earth. So when the money travels in the opposite direction, it presents a challenge to American self-image.

In the 1980s, as an ascendant Japan expanded into foreign markets and snapped up trophy properties such as Rockefeller Center, jingoistic warnings circulated as if the nation were under attack. "Where Will Japan Strike Next?" asked an ominous 1989 *Fortune* magazine cover. The following year, Sony struck a deal to buy the Hollywood icon Columbia Pictures. "I wonder if it's bad for America," the music and film producer David Geffen told the *Washington Post*. The same story quoted an economist warning that Sony might use Columbia to beam Japanese "propaganda" into the United States. Even supposedly straight news analysis was permeated with a sense of foreboding. "Should You Work for the Japanese?" asked a 1990 *Fortune* magazine headline over a story that analyzed the pros and cons of such a career move while brazenly trading in crude stereotypes. "Be ready to deal with a certain level of vagueness," warned a graphic. "Expect to spend a lot of energy just figuring out what's going on."

In 2005, when the Chinese state-owned energy company, CNOOC Limited tried to buy the American concern Unocal, Congress scuttled the deal by branding it a threat to national security, though Unocal then controlled less than one-quarter of a percent of the global oil supply. "The object of China's actions is inexorably to supplant the United States as the world's premier economic power and, if necessary, to defeat us militarily," warned Frank J. Gaffney Jr., a former Reagan administration Pentagon official, speaking during a congressional hearing at which he urged Congress to bar the deal. The following year came the outcry that scuttled the Dubai Ports deal.

More recent fears have centered on so-called sovereign wealth funds—huge state-financed investment pools stocked with the proceeds of Saudi Arabia's oil sales, China's burgeoning exports, and the excess savings of other nations from Singapore to Kuwait. Such funds invested some $21.5 billion in American companies in 2007 alone. The influx sparked worries that foreign governments would skew markets by investing to improve the fortunes of their national companies or in pursuit of political goals. "This is a phenomenon that could be called the growth of state capitalism as opposed to market capitalism," said Jeffrey E. Garten, a trade expert at the Yale School of Management. "The United States has not ever been on the receiving end of this before."

Such concerns are legitimate, given that the money is directly controlled by governments, and the numbers are large enough to move markets. But these worries have combined with alarmist and xenophobic fears to spawn knee-jerk loathing of all foreign money. As major U.S. banks stumbled under the weight of their bad mortgage investments in early 2008, prompting some to practically beg for fresh investment from Chinese and Middle Eastern firms, some pundits portrayed this as an ominous loss of national prestige. "Do we want the communists to own the banks, or the terrorists?" asked Jim Cramer, the hyperventilating market analyst in a television appearance on the financial news channel CNBC. "I'll take any of it, I guess, because we're so desperate."

Yet what was most striking, as another surge of foreign capital opportunistically picked up slices of the American banking industry, was how little protest it ultimately engendered. Senator Charles E. Schumer, the pugnacious New York Democrat, had played a leading role in killing the port takeover by the Dubai company. He had long led the charge against China on trade issues, accusing Beijing of manipulating currency markets while threatening to impose punitive trade tariffs. But as Wall Street descended into grave peril, Schumer was suddenly not bothered by the prospect of Chinese and Middle Eastern firms capturing stakes in American financial institutions.

"It would be good if these companies didn't need all this capital and better if the capital was available in the United States," he said. "But given the situation that these institutions find themselves in and the fact that there's a pretty strong credit squeeze, there's only two choices: Have foreign companies invest in these firms or have massive layoffs."

⁓

Of course, as we have already seen, Americans have been living on a different flavor of foreign largesse for many years, predominantly through the purchase of Treasury bonds by China's central bank and other foreign institutions. Oddly, this reality has proven far less controversial than foreigners buying stakes in American companies, though it presents far more destabilizing possibilities. Government bonds can be sold on a whim, with the mere click of a computer mouse, sending the value of the dollar plummeting at any time. Companies, on the other hand, are less easily unloaded, making their purchase a more stable force in the American economy.

For a host of reasons, the United States must seriously endeavor to wean itself from dependence on foreign purchases of American debt. The greater the foreign ownership of Treasury bills, the larger the consequences that could arise from a panic about the value of the dollar. Should, say, the Saudi government, fearing the wrath of al-Qaeda, decide to stop bankrolling the U.S. Treasury, it could quickly sell large quantities of Treasury bills. That would press the value of the dollar down and force U.S. interest rates higher, putting the brakes on the economy. Should China ever become worried that the Saudis were on the verge of such a panic, it might opt to sell some of its own dollar holdings ahead of the expected plunge in the currency, bringing about the same dangerous outcome. Both of these scenarios remain highly unlikely, given that neither China nor Saudi Arabia would rationally pursue a policy that runs the risk of diminishing the value of their own enormous holdings of dollars. But the minute one becomes convinced that the other is about to push the button on selling dollar holdings, preemptive selling immediately becomes a potentially rational course.

Furthermore, China cannot forever continue to deposit increasingly enormous amounts of its national savings into the U.S. Treasury. And the more American debt China owns, the more vulnerable the American economy is to an abrupt pullback if and when Beijing loses it appetite for the dollar. "Chimerica" has endured as long as it has because it has satisfied the immediate needs of both countries. But its endurance ties American fortunes to China's willingness to keep handing over money. In some sense, the partnership was disbanded as the global recession tightened the volume of global trade. As the United States lost spending power in the wake of the housing bust, China has lost export sales. By December 2008, China's exports were declining for the first time in seven years. As China's exports continued to evaporate through the early months of 2009, that gave China fewer dollars, raising the likelihood that Beijing would eventually moderate its purchases of U.S. Treasury bonds. Meanwhile, after years of effectively investing its national savings in Florida beachfront property, China has been showing greater interest in putting that money to work at home. In November 2008, as the global recession deepened, China announced plans for its own $586 billion stimulus spending program aimed at generating domestic demand for Chinese goods to compensate for the loss of demand around the world.

The financial crisis also appears to have caused the Chinese government to reassess the merits of buying so much American debt. After using the United States as a safe-deposit box for its national savings for a decade, China's leaders are clearly shaken by the turmoil on Wall Street. In May 2008, the chairman of China's banking regulatory commission, Liu Mingkang, excoriated his American counterparts for delivering the subprime mortgage crisis and the resulting worldwide financial crisis, an event he said was "counteracting the course of global civilization." These words hardly suggested that Americans could take for granted China's continued debt purchases. "Does moneymaking or doing business justify the regulators in ignoring their duty for prudential supervision and their job of preventing misbehavior?" Liu asked.

In January 2009, the sense of an unfolding reassessment intensified as premier Wen Jiabao, speaking at the World Economic Forum in Davos, Switzerland, pinned the blame for the global downturn on an "excessive expansion of financial institutions in blind pursuit of profit," regulatory failure, and an "unsustainable model of development, characterized by prolonged low savings and high consumption." Wen did not name the United States, but no other nation fit that description. In March, Premier Wen made his thinking more explicit. "We have lent a huge amount of money to the U.S," he said at a press conference in Beijing. "Of course we are concerned about the safety of our assets. To be honest, I am definitely a little worried." Later that month, China's central bank governor released a paper calling for the International Monetary Fund to create a new global currency to replace dependence on the dollar.

Americans' low savings and high consumption have, of course, been financed by Chinese high savings and low consumption. Banking on the continuation of that arrangement would be foolish. It must end eventually, as all things do. All of which argues that Americans must embrace direct foreign investment into domestic companies as a way of raising needed investment. Treasury bills are fungible assets that can be dumped at any time, unlike factories and warehouses and research centers. When foreigners own American companies, they are genuinely invested in the United States in a way that cannot be said of those who merely control billions of dollars' worth of electronic blips. For that reason, many economists argue that attracting foreign investment is the most palatable way to square American debts, the most stabilizing option on the menu.

"To the extent that the United States continues to have low levels of savings, well, the rest of the world, they are not going to give us that excess for free," said Matthew J. Slaughter, an economist at Dartmouth College. "We have to sell them something. There's no metaphorical free lunch for the United States."

Americans have been getting good value for the slices of companies they have been surrendering to foreign hands: expanded access to global markets, advanced technologies, and jobs—typically good jobs. Some have called these jobs the product of "insourcing," offsetting some of the losses from outsourcing, in which work is shipped overseas. Between 1998 and 2006, the number of Americans working for foreign companies with operations in the United States swelled from 4.7 million to 5.3 million. By 2006, these affiliates of foreign companies reinvested more than $65 billion of what they earned in the United States, according to Matthew Slaughter. They paid out more than $335 billion in wages and salaries, or average annual compensation of more than $66,000—that is, nearly a third higher than the average private-sector job in the United States.

Even as the American auto industry sought tens of billions of dollars of public money to stave off bankruptcy in late 2008 and into 2009, some expansion was under way, courtesy of foreign investment. While General Motors, Ford, and Chrysler delivered the grisly news of plant closures, Volkswagen, the German automaker, announced plans to invest $1 billion in a new factory in Chattanooga, Tennessee, where it expected to begin producing some 250,000 cars a year in 2012.

This was the sort of story that explained why many state governors— particularly those in the Rust Belt—were courting foreign money relentlessly. "We don't want to just be victims of the global economy," said Michigan governor Jennifer M. Granholm, a Canadian-born Democrat who has traveled frequently to Japan and Europe in search of investment since taking office in 2003. "Pursuing international investment is one strategy to get jobs."

Holland, Michigan, was already reaping the benefits of making its peace with working for foreigners. In 2004, a factory on the fringes of town that made wastewater treatment equipment was suffering declining fortunes and shedding workers—another tale of woe in a state that has lost more than 300,000 manufacturing jobs over the last decade. Then Siemens, the German industrial conglomerate, paid $954 million for the factory's parent company, US Filter. Suddenly the plant's fortunes were reversed.

For Siemens, the deal was all about increasing sales to American utilities, while also securing fresh technology it could use to tap into markets from China to Algeria. "There's just not enough clean water in the world, and everybody has to be conscious of how to use and reuse it," said George Nolen, president and chief executive of Siemens Corporation, the U.S. subsidiary of Siemens AG, which is based in Munich. "A lot of the innovation remains in the United States." For Holland, a town of thirty-four thousand people on the eastern lip of Lake Michigan, the deal signaled the arrival of a deep-pocketed industrial titan—a rare bit of good news against a backdrop of deterioration.

Holland is home to some of the largest office furniture makers in the world, among them Herman Miller, which makes the mesh-covered Aeron chair, now a ubiquitous prop in the white-collar American workplace. In the late 1990s, as the technology boom filled office parks from Silicon Valley to Boston, Holland's factories cashed in by making the chairs. But as that bubble burst, Holland's furniture plants laid off thousands. In the years since, auto parts factories in the town shed jobs, adding to a local crisis of employment. Holland hit bottom in 2003, when a Life Savers factory shut down to escape the high cost of sugar in the United States—a protected industry—shifting production over the border to Canada.

But Holland is a salvage-minded place, exhibiting the craft and opportunism required for the United States to find its way to a new economy. When the Baker Furniture company shut down, a developer turned its old brick factory into loft-space apartments and offices, with original wood floors and exposed brick walls lending an air of urban chic. A French auto interior designer set up shop upstairs. When Pfizer, the pharmaceutical giant, announced plans to shut its Holland factory, local officials quickly persuaded the company to hand over a laboratory to Michigan State University. The university intends to use the lab as an incubator for renewable energy businesses, making space available at subsidized rates for promising start-up companies. Downtown, the CityFlats Hotel opened in early 2008, a monument to natural light, sleek design, and energy efficiency, with "green" certification to prove it. Furnished with recycled glass tiles, cork floors, and other renewable materials, the hotel was the brainchild of Charles Reid, president of Charter House Innovations, whose local factory makes furniture out of recycled materials. "We're a design company that happens to manufacture," Reid explained over dinner at his penthouse restaurant, where pendant lights of unusual shapes cast a sophisticated glow. "I'm trying to keep our guys working."

His factory workforce had tripled to one hundred in recent years, as the company gained sales by designing furniture for fast-food restaurants. The CityFlats was to be a showcase for the next potential area of growth: Reid planned to license his brand to other hoteliers, selling them the furnishings and generating more jobs for his factory.

Into this creative atmosphere landed Siemens, sparking a mixture of hope and concern. The Holland factory had already had one experience with foreign owners, and it was miserable. The previous owner was Vivendi, the French water company that briefly reinvented itself as a media conglomerate in a strategy that made sense only to the investment bankers who brokered the deals. As the water company launched Internet businesses and bought Hollywood film and music studios, it yielded a confused jumble of ill-fitting parts that was soon dismantled.

For the managers in Holland, being part of Vivendi posed a fundamental problem: the French company was in the business of managing wastewater plants. It ordered the Holland factory not to supply its competitors with equipment, thus depressing potential sales.

"Our international business collapsed," complained David J. Spyker, who had been the plant manager. He grew to loath meetings with his French overseers. "You were called over to get instructions, and all the orders had been made behind the scenes before you arrived. If I never have to make another trip to Paris, it's too soon."

Now, with Siemens in charge, Spyker would be making trips to Munich, among other places. He was elevated to a senior vice president in a

Siemens wastewater division, with responsibility for thirteen factories scattered around the globe.

Spyker worried about the German reputation for bureaucracy, but the pluses of joining the Siemens empire seemed abundant. The company had a presence in 190 countries. He could tap this network to boost sales, particularly in fast-growing countries such as China, where government ministries influence purchasing decisions for multiple state-owned companies, and where relationships often carry the day. "Now, we weren't just dealing with a purchasing agent who might deign to see us," Spyker said. "Now, we're dealing at the ministry level."

Two years after Siemens bought the Holland factory, it delivered capital for an expansion. In exchange for more than $1.4 million in state and local tax credits, the German company promised to hire 80 people in Holland. By early 2008, it had vastly exceeded the target. The workforce had multiplied from 105 to 237, with most jobs paying $45,000 a year. The factory had added a night shift. It was shipping its gear around the world, supplying the Olympic village in Beijing ahead of the 2008 summer games. Revenues had tripled, the company reported.

"I don't feel German, I'm still an American, but I have the ability to leverage off a German company," said Spyker. "It's certainly given us the growth we were looking for. Globalization has been good for Holland."

On the factory floor, listlessness and worries about the future had been replaced by a sense of purpose.

"Before, people didn't see where the next paycheck was coming from," said Jeff Whipple, a manufacturing supervisor who has worked at the plant since 1995. "Morale has definitely improved. People see the benefit of having a strong parent behind them. We went from scraping by on a forty-hour week to where forty-eight hours is a normal week."

છ

Elsewhere in Michigan, still the home of the Big Three automakers, talk of foreign ownership as salvation was hard to swallow. Up the road in the town of Muskegon, a German company, MAHLE Engine Components, purchased an auto parts factory from the bankrupt American firm Dana Corporation in 2007. Workers there had hoped being part of a well-financed multinational company would shelter them from the storm ravaging the auto industry. But three months later, MAHLE announced plans to shutter the factory, eliminating more than one hundred local jobs, while shifting most of the production to Mexico.

"When you're owned by somebody that has operations around the world, with trade the way it is, that's a recipe for disaster," said Jeff Beegle, president of the United Auto Workers Local 637, the union that represented 120 of the workers. "These global corporations have a lot to gain by leaving and going to lower-cost countries."

In Greenville, sixty miles northeast of Holland, the community was still reeling from its own disastrous experience with a foreign company, the Swedish conglomerate Electrolux Group. For decades, the dominant source of paychecks in town had been a mammoth refrigerator factory on the banks of the Flat River—the largest such plant in North America. In a community of eight thousand people, the Electrolux factory was the workplace for twenty-seven hundred. Much like Maytag in Newton, Iowa, its wages provided the trappings of middle-class life for much of the community. But in 2006, Electrolux shut down the factory and transferred production to Mexico. The old plant was soon demolished, leaving a bald patch of gravel along the river. Two years after they lost their jobs, many former Electrolux workers remained without work, their unemployment benefits expiring. Restaurants, hardware stores, and auto dealers were suffering plummeting sales amid a general loss of spending power, prompting them to lay off their own workers.

"Everybody talks about Electrolux around here the way the rest of the country talks about Katrina," said Becky Gebhart, manager of Montcalm Area Health Center, a nonprofit medical clinic that opened in Greenville in November 2007 to serve people with little or no health insurance—many of them people who lost jobs at the refrigerator plant. "We've been running at full capacity since the day we opened the door."

On Main Street, Huck Huckleberry, the stocky proprietor of a restaurant that bears his name, had shrunk his staff from thirty-two to twelve since Electrolux left, while cutting health benefits—his own included. "It's heartbreaking," he said, as AC/DC's *Highway to Hell* blared through his mostly empty dining room at lunchtime. "When people here were making a living, they bought houses, cars, paid for shoes. On weekends, mom and dad would get groceries, then come in and have a steak and a beer, and life is good. They quit coming."

Several businesses had shut down on the block—a sports bar, an office supply store. The real estate agency next door was barely hanging on. The barbershop had let one barber go. Two tattoo parlors had opened up. "You're not going to run your local economy on tattoo places," Huckelberry said.

For Governor Granholm, the decision by Electrolux to abandon Greenville was especially disappointing. She had publicly vowed that she would persuade the company to stay, marshaling a package of more than $120 million in state and local tax credits. The city had offered to build Electrolux a new plant. The local union, a branch of the UAW, agreed to relinquish $33 million a year in wages.

"They said, 'There is nothing you can do to compensate for the fact that we are able to pay $1.57 an hour in Mexico,'" Granholm recalled. "That's when I started to say, 'NAFTA and CAFTA have given us the shafta,'" she added, using the acronyms for the North American and Central American free trade agreements. "You cannot tell me this has been good." Yet Granholm was resolute that more foreign investment was probably the quickest way to bring new business to her state. "I've got to get jobs for our people," she said.

Greenville's city manager, George Bosanic, impatiently dismissed the notion that his community was a victim. A solar panel factory had recently opened up in a new industrial park. Skilled labor would always be in demand for one pursuit or another, he figured, and Greenville had plenty on hand. The future was promising enough, he said, provided the community sought out fresh investment to bring jobs. And he felt no compunction to discriminate. One foreign company had abruptly leveled the local economy with a decision made in a boardroom in Sweden, but if another was willing to come, Bosanic would lay out the welcome mat.

"We know this is a global economy, and companies are going to come and go," Bosanic said. "It's a matter of taking advantage of what opportunities there are."

Conclusion

In J. M. Barrie's tale, Peter Pan never returns from Neverland. He brings the Darling children back to London along with the Lost Boys, who are adopted and sent off to school. But Pan keeps the make-believe going, while occasionally dropping in on Wendy to invite her to return.

Americans do not have that luxury. We have gotten tired of make-believe suppers. We have simply lost belief in the stories that once propelled our economy. Indeed, we have lost belief in the very concept of stories as a means of making money change hands. Investors have been tricked one time too many. They will not play along again—at least not anytime soon.

From here, the American economy succeeds or fails on the strength of its ability to sustain itself. We can no longer depend on the largesse of foreign creditors that have bought our debt and urged us to buy their countries' goods, resulting in enormous trade deficits. Rather than binging on finance borrowed against a supposedly fantastic future, we must figure out how to generate enough income to live on—as individual households and as a society. Perhaps the source of future jobs is biotech or renewable energy; perhaps it will be some other industry developed through the careful, sensible use of resources. In any event, a new era is upon us.

Of immediate concern is preventing the economy from spiraling down into the sort of hole that captured Japan during the 1990s, as retrenchment begot retrenchment until a whole decade passed in fear and stagnation. We will find out soon whether the stimulus spending package unleashed at the beginning of Obama's tenure spares us this fate, creating enough demand for goods and services and enough new jobs to prevent a broader disaster. We will see whether the Obama administration succeeds in restoring confidence to the financial system, a prerequisite for a return to economic growth, and whether the growing threat of foreclosure can be arrested.

But the greater test will be with us for many years, as the government and business together seek to develop areas of the economy that can create long-term sustenance for millions of people—not through slick marketing and financial engineering but through the less glamorous work of fulfilling genuine societal needs, by harnessing American prowess to create American products and services that are of genuine value and offer lasting benefits, and by getting back to honest work for honest pay. In the simplest terms, the American economy must find a way to replace credit cards and home equity loans with paychecks and savings accounts.

This must be a collective enterprise. It must be spurred by government, using public money in the form of tax incentives and research dollars to encourage particularly productive industries. It must be supervised by government to prevent the excesses that tend to result when we hand our fates over to unregulated markets, as we have learned the hard way. Fairy dust is no longer the primary raw material on Wall Street, and good riddance. We have lost our belief in Alan Greenspan's Neverland of a free market utopia. Americans must relinquish the idea that the market, left to its own devices, will maximize prosperity for all and ensure sustainable economic progress. Left to its own devices, the market synthesizes credit default swaps worth more than human creation and sells option ARM mortgages to people who think they are wonderful until they turn deadly solemn. Recuperating from the consequences of our flight may take many years. Like the Lost Boys, the American economy has come to crave a little parental supervision, appreciating the merits of regulation.

The market must be returned to its proper station. It is still the central organizing principle of American economic policy, as it should be. The market remains the most efficient way to allocate capital, a powerful force for economic progress. Whatever industries emerge as the most promising sources of jobs, private enterprise—not government spending—must be the engine of economic growth; private companies, not Uncle Sam, will sign most of the paychecks. But the market is a tool, not an all-encompassing system. It needs supervision to ensure that it functions in our collective interest. The seminal economist Adam Smith gave us the metaphor of the invisible hand to describe the functioning of the market. When everyone pursues their own self-interest, the invisible hand moves capital to where it can best be used. Today, however, as financial institutions disintegrate, millions of families surrender their homes to foreclosure, and the job market grows punishingly bleak, the invisible hand is being dusted for fingerprints. Government supervision is back, and it must offer a guiding hand, nudging the markets to function according to the national interest.

President Obama's ascension to the White House delivered a clear signal of the nation's new relationship with the market. From his first day in office, he promised to resurrect government as a powerful tool in rebuilding the economy, generating jobs, and reregulating the financial system. Yet he also took pains to underscore that American fortunes will remain tied to free enterprise. "Its power to generate wealth and expand freedom is unmatched," Obama said in his inaugural address. "But this crisis has reminded us that without a watchful eye, the market can spin out of control, and that a nation cannot prosper long when it favors only the prosperous. The success of our economy has always depended not just on the size of our gross domestic product, but on the reach of our prosperity; on our ability to extend opportunity to every willing heart, not out of charity, but because it is the surest route to our common good."

Blaming free enterprise for the economic disaster that has befallen the United States would be like blaming automobiles for fatal car accidents, as opposed to blaming reckless drivers, people who neglect to wear seat belts, and authorities who fail to enforce traffic laws. The form of capitalism that has been operative in the United States since the 1980s represents a departure from the virtues of the free enterprise system, a distortion of an older, more trustworthy way of economic life in which the government was a partner, a perversion molded by the people in control of money to make more of it flow their way. But the merits of the free enterprise system remain unchallenged, awaiting updated rules and incentives that can guide it and shape it and make it work for the benefit of more people.

Millions of people have seen their lives upended as the American economy has crash-landed from its extended sojourn in Neverland. The United States need not have experienced the terrible pain of this recession and the global financial crisis it has triggered. The economy was governed by the deregulators for a dangerously long time. Those who recognized it along the way sounded their warnings, only to be dismissed. There was simply too much money getting made by keeping the make-believe going. That allowed the consequences of the inevitable crash to build up to devastating proportions.

The intensity of the recession that followed was a direct result of a massive abdication of regulatory authority, one that enabled Wall Street and Madison Avenue to get rich by selling the dream of immediate wealth—the sort of wealth that could only have been sustained in a fantasy land. The pain resulting from that terrible miscalculation has landed hardest on those who did not even share in the spoils of better days. Greg Bailey missed out. His feet never left the ground. And yet he has been dragged down just the same by the collapse of make-believe, paying the costs of the reckoning now under way.

It is also true that this moment presents an extraordinary opportunity, a chance to start over, crafting the proper rules for the financial system, augmenting the social safety net, expanding the availability and affordability of health care, while focusing on areas of core economic strength. Amid the crisis, politics has aligned such that the powers that be feel an imperative to spend trillions of dollars toward the construction of a more sustainable economy. If that money is scattered carelessly, divvied up as pork, that will be a terrible squandering. If it is harnessed strategically, it could create useful facilities, industries, and ways of life that will be with us for a long time, from improved schools and research centers to new medical technologies and forms of energy.

We have indeed left Neverland, and the economy has become quite a mess in our absence. All the more reason to dust ourselves off as quickly as we can and start fixing up the country where we really live, replacing make-believe with the hard work of constructing a new economy that is both solid and sustainable.

Notes

Introduction: Dust Ourselves Off

5 "This economy is flexible": Edmund L. Andrews and Robert Pear, "Bush Confident on Economy, Vetoes Domestic Spending Bill," *New York Times*, November 14, 2007, p. A20.

7 "You can listen to these economists": Peter S. Goodman, "More Arrows Seen Pointing Toward a Recession," *New York Times*, August 1, 2008, p. A1.

7 "All my cousins already know": Ibid.

9 By 2008, consumer credit exceeded $2.6 trillion: Federal Reserve Board data, household liabilities, consumer credit, via Haver Analytics, last updated December 11, 2008.

10 By October 2008, those same weekly earnings: Bureau of Labor Statistics, Average Weekly Earnings, 1982 Dollars, Total Private, Series ID: CES0500000031.

10 "For middle- and low-wage workers": Telephone interview with Jared Bernstein, February 22, 2009.

11 But compensation for the American rank and file: Analysis of federal data provided on request by Jared Bernstein, senior economist, Economic Policy Institute, Washington, D.C.

11 In recent decades, only the elite: Claudia Goldin and Lawrence F. Katz, *The Race Between Education and Technology* (Cambridge, Mass.: Belknap Press of Harvard University Press, 2008), pp. 45–46.

11 The highlights include the declining power of unions: See, for example, Robert Z. Lawrence, *Blue-Collar Blues: Is Trade to Blame for Rising US Income Inequality* (Washington, D.C.: Peter G. Peterson Institute for International Economics, 2008), and Goldin and Katz, *Race Between Education and Technology.*

11 The researchers found a fourfold increase: Teresa A. Sullivan, Elizabeth Warren, and Jay Lawrence Westbrook, *The Fragile Middle Class: Americans in Debt* (New Haven, Conn.: Yale University Press, 2000), pp. 2–3.

12 This trend was worst for those at the lower end: Jacob S. Hacker and Elisabeth Jacobs, "The Rising Instability of American Family Incomes, 1969–2004: Evidence from the Panel Study of Income Dynamics," Economic Policy Institute Briefing Paper Number 213. In April 2007 the Congressional Budget Office released a report that analyzed Social Security data, "Trends in Earnings Variability Over the Past 20 Years," available online at http://www .cbo.gov/ftpdocs/80xx/doc8007/04-17-EarningsVariability.pdf. That study appeared to challenge the basic findings of the Hacker and Jacobs study, noting that volatility in individual incomes had changed little through the 1980s and 1990s. But in a response to that study, Hacker argued that the CBO report looked only at individual incomes and not at family incomes. Given that many families are now comprised of two incomes, this is an important distinction, he argued, and a contention that seems convincing. If the failure rate of jet engines had remained constant over two decades, while the percentage of planes that went from one engine to two increased significantly, one would reasonably worry about a deterioration of air safety. The Hacker response to the CBO report may be seen online at http://economistsview .typepad.com/economistsview/2007/04/does_the_cbo_re.html.

12 Most families tie their purchases: Peter Gosselin, *High Wire: The Precarious Financial Lives of American Families* (New York: Basic Books, 2008), p. 12.

12 But a second income typically does not get: Elizabeth Warren and Amelia Warren Tyagi, *The Two-Income Trap* (New York: Basic Books, 2003).

13 For households headed by workers in their mid-forties: Jacob S. Hacker, *The Great Risk Shift: The New Economic Insecurity and the Decline of the American Dream* (New York: Oxford University Press, 2006), p. 126.

13 Between 1983 and 1998: Ibid., p. 122.

13 "There is indeed much to be said for the ownership society": Robert J. Shiller, *Irrational Exuberance*, 2nd ed. (New York: Doubleday, 2005), p. xvii.

13 "Saving for the future seemed almost irrelevant": Ibid., pp. 35–36.

14 In the course of the year, the stock market had wiped out: Vikas Bajaj, "Markets Limp into 2009 After a Bruising Year," *New York Times*, January 1, 2009, p. A1.

14 Some 50 million Americans whose retirement savings: Eleanor Laise, "Big Slide in 401(k)s Spurs Calls for Change," *Wall Street Journal*, January 8, 2009, p. A1.

15 "Our entire economy is in danger": President George W. Bush, speech to the nation, September 24, 2008, transcript online at http://www.nytimes.com/2008/09/24/business/economy/24text-bush.html?pagewanted=1&_r=2.

15 "The open question is whether": Interview with Kenneth S. Rogoff, July 16, 2008; see Peter S. Goodman, "On Every Front, Anxious Questions and Uncomfortable Answers," *New York Times*, July 19, 2008, p. A10.

15 For a mere $99.95: Cyrus Sanati, "Mini-Madoff Turns Heads at Toy Fair," *New York Times* DealBook, February 17, 2009, http://dealbook.blogs.nytimes .com/2009/02/17/mini-madoff-turns-heads-at-toy-fair/?scp=1&sq=Mini-Mad off%20Turns%20Heads%20at%20Toy%20Fair&st=cse.

16 "I don't want to go to school": J. M. Barrie, *Peter Pan* (New York: Henry Holt, 2003), p. 146.

18 "What do they want from us, anyway?": Michael Kinsley, "Let's Have Another Cup of Coffee," *New York Times*, November 14, 2008, p. A33.

1. The Credit Diet

24 "Beware of thinking all your own": Benjamin Franklin, "Advice to a Young Tradesman," Sparks Edition, Volume 2, p. 87, as cited in Max Weber, *The Protestant Ethic and the Spirit of Capitalism*, 3rd ed., originally published in German (Los Angeles: Roxbury Publishing Co., 2002), p. 15.

31 The economy was shedding hundreds of thousands of jobs: Bureau of Labor Statistics, Unemployment Rate, Black or African American, Seasonally Adjusted, Series ID: LNS14000006.

32 "financial decadence": David Brooks, "The Great Seduction," *New York Times*, June 10, 2008, p. A23.

33 "We're talking about health": Kim Severson, "Good News About Rising Food Prices," *New York Times*, April 2, 2008, p. F1.

34 "The middle-class employer became conscious": Max Weber, *The Protestant Ethic and the Spirit of Capitalism*, 3rd ed., originally published in German (Los Angeles: Roxbury Publishing Co., 2002), p. 120 (italics original).

34 "work constitutes a particular defense": Ibid., p. 105.

34 The grateful recipient of this heroism: Horatio Alger Jr., *Ragged Dick* (New York: Street and Smith Corp., 1868; reprint 1926).

35 "In the long run, we are all dead": John Maynard Keynes, *A Tract on Monetary Reform* (London: MacMillan, 1923), p. 80, as cited in Charles Robert McCann Jr., ed., *The Elgar Dictionary of Economic Quotations* (Northhampton, Mass.: Edward Elgar Publishing, 2003), p. 88.

35 "government mismanagement": Transcript of Milton Friedman in an interview with Richard Heffner on television program *The Open Mind*, December 7, 1975, available online at http://www.theopenmind.tv/tom/searcharchive_episode_transcript.asp?id=494.

36 The result was fat profits: Anthony S. Campagna, *The Economy in the Reagan Years* (Westport, Conn.: Greenwood Press, 1994), pp. 168–75.

38 Before the books were closed: Niall Ferguson, *The Ascent of Money: A Financial History of the World* (New York: Penguin Press, 2008), pp. 253–59.

39 Between 1980 and 2007, the value of mortgage-backed securities: Ibid., pp. 259–60.

40 The banks together came up with $3.6 billion: Alan Greenspan, *The Age of Turbulence: Adventures in a New World* (New York: Penguin Press, 2007), pp. 193–94; Ferguson, *Ascent of Money*, pp. 320–29.

40 "will surely lead to the breakdown": George Soros, *The Crisis of Global Capitalism* (New York: Public Affairs, 1998), p. 176.

41 "Risks in financial markets": Peter S. Goodman, "Taking Hard New Look at a Greenspan Legacy," *New York Times*, October 8, 2008, p. A1.

41 By facing the harsh reality and acting in their self-interest": Greenspan, *Age of Turbulence*, p. 195.

41 "not judgment but panic": Ibid.

2. Profits of Neverland

44 By day's end, they had nearly quadrupled: "Price of Ariba Stock Almost Quadruples on Its First Trading Day," *Wall Street Journal*, June 24, 1999, p. B9.

45 "The era of green-field opportunities": Clinton Wilder, "Online Procurement Vendor's IPO Sizzles," *Information Week*, June 28, 1999, p. 144.

45 "By anyone's measuring stick": Mel Duvall, "Betting on the Next Big Payoff," *Interactive Week from ZDWire*, April 26, 1999.

46 "Something really big is going on": Bob Austrian, "New Business E-conomy Report," cited in "Business-to-Business E-Commerce Is Enabling the $50 Trillion New E-Conomy, Says Banc of America Securities B2B Strategist Analyst," PR Newswire, February 7, 2000.

46 "Through the Ariba B2B Commerce platform": Ariba press release, August 16, 2000, "ABN Amro Furthers Alliance with Ariba by Integrating Comprehensive Financial Services Engine into Ariba B2B Commerce Platform, available online at http://files.shareholder.com/downloads/ABN/0x0x146458/a3f7bca1-26a6-4850-806c-b4a6ba48343b/2000-08-16-en.pdf.

51 "Their old business model went away": Interview with Mark Sunshine in New York, August 12, 2008.

52 At the end of the day, the company's twenty-four-year-old vice president: Laurence Zuckerman, "With Internet Cachet, Not Profit, a New Stock Is Wall St.'s Darling," *New York Times*, August 10, 1995, p. A1.

52 "Tech stardom started, as usual": Randall E. Stross, "How Yahoo! Won The Search Wars," *Fortune*, March 2, 1998, p. 148.

52 By then, stocks trading on the Nasdaq: Nasdaq composite market capitalization, via Haver Analytics.

53 Far from a dispassionate judge of value: John Maynard Keynes, *The General Theory of Employment, Interest and Money* (New York: Harcourt, Brace, Jovanovich, 1964), p. 156.

53 "A conventional valuation which is established": Ibid., p. 154, as cited in Eugene N. White, "Bubbles and Busts: The 1990s in the Mirror of the 1920s," in Paul W. Rhode and Gianni Toniolo, ed., *The Global Economy in the 1990s* (Cambridge: Cambridge University Press, 2006), p. 198.

53 "Prices change in substantial measure": Shiller in 1991, as quoted in White, "Bubbles and Busts," p. 198.

53 "It's insanity": Andrew Bary, "Market Mania: Share Prices Are Rising Even as Earning's Growth Slows," *Barron's*, May 27, 1996, p. 15.

53 "irrational exuberance": Alan Greenspan, Remarks at American Enterprise Dinner in Washington, D.C., December 5, 1996, Transcript by Federal Document Clearing House.

53 "The waves of the business cycle": Steven Weber, "The End of the Business Cycle?" *Foreign Affairs* 76(4), 1997, pp. 65–82, as cited in Shiller, *Irrational Exuberance*, p. 119.

54 "Stock prices could double": James K. Glassman and Kevin A. Hassett, *Dow 36,000: The New Strategy for Profiting from the Coming Rise in the Stock Market* (New York: Three Rivers Press, 1999), p. 4.

54 "No area of inquiry is more ripe": Ibid., p. 14.

54 "The message I have is reassuring": Landon Thomas Jr., "Glassman Is Half-Full: The Julia Child of Investing Is Driving the True Believers Mad," *New York Observer*, October 15, 2000.

55 "Let's light this candle": See this ad on YouTube at http://www.youtube.com/watch?v=WOKDK0g1Gno&feature=related.

55 "I'm a stockbroker, son": See this ad on YouTube at www.youtube.com/watch?v=uK0ziaFHMFM&feature=related.

56 "If you're out of this sector": Lisa Reilly Cullen, "The Triple Digit Club," *Money*, December 1999, p. 170.

58 Even the spread of legalized gambling: Shiller, *Irrational Exuberance*, pp. 31–55.

59 "We can be the one company": Mark Leibovich, *The New Imperialists:*

How Five Restless Kids Grew Up to Virtually Rule Your World (Paramus, N.J.: Prentice Hall Press, 2002), p. 116.

60 "As business leaders melded themselves": Thomas Frank, *One Market Under God: Extreme Capitalism, Market Populism, and the End of Economic Democracy* (New York: Doubleday, 2000), p. 36.

62 "Oh, well, the reason we're doing software": Leibovich, *New Imperialists,* p. 16.

62 Then and only then could Webvan: Greg Ip, "On a High Wire: The Bull Market in Stocks Has Defied Skeptics, But We Are Now Where No Bull Has Gone Before," *Wall Street Journal,* p. C1.

3. The Debts of the New Economy

66 Between 1997 and 2001, local and long-distance telephone companies: Estimate from RHK, a San Francisco research firm; cited in Peter S. Goodman, "Telecom Sector May Find Past Is Its Future," *Washington Post,* Monday, July 8, 2002, p. A1.

67 During the same period, the price of leasing a transmission line: Interview with Eli Noam, professor of finance at Columbia University Business School, July 2002.

67 By the end of 2001, the eight largest telecom companies: Estimate from Scott Cleland, the Precursor Group, July 2002.

67 "Demand was poised to go up 30: Telephone interview with Leo Hindery, July 2002.

67 Instead, Ebbers reprimanded them for using too much coffee: Peter S. Goodman and Renae Merle, "End of Its Merger Run Led to WorldCom's Fall," *Washington Post,* June 30, 2002.

69 "As long as the music is playing": Scott Patterson, "Ahead of the Tape," *Wall Street Journal,*" July 26, 2007, p. C1.

69 In April 2002, WorldCom's board forced Ebbers: Christopher Stern, "WorldCom's CEO Resigns as Firm's Stock Slumps," *Washington Post,* May 1, 2002, p. A1.

69 "You look at Andy Grove's speeches": Telephone interview with John Sidgmore, June 2002.

70 Between 1989 and 1999, the total outstanding debt: Kevin Phillips, *Bad Money: Reckless Finance, Failed Politics, and the Global Crisis of American Capitalism* (New York: Viking, 2008), p. 45.

70 Between 1992 and 2001, telecommunications roughly doubled: Joseph E. Stiglitz, *The Roaring Nineties: A New History of the World's Most Prosperous Decade* (New York: W. W. Norton, 2003), pp. 91–92.

71 By the end of the 1990s, the national unemployment rate: Bureau of Labor Statistics, Labor Force Statistics from the Current Population Survey,

Unemployment Rate, 16 Years and Over, Seasonally Adjusted, Series ID: LNS14000000.

74 In 2000, as President Bill Clinton presided over the last: The mock documentary, "The Final Days," can be seen online at http://www.youtube .com/watch?v=7n2fl9r9n9A.

75 "It is time for America once again to try living": Richard J. Herrnstein and Charles Murray, *The Bell Curve: Intelligence and Class Structure in American Life* (New York: Free Press, 1994), pp. 551–52.

76 "lack of thrift or proper money management": James R. Kluegel and Eliot R. Smith, *Beliefs About Inequality: Americans' Views of What Is and What Ought to Be* (New York: Walter de Gruyter, 1986), p. 37, as cited in William Julius Wilson, *When Work Disappears: The World of the New Urban Poor* (New York: Vintage Books, 1997), pp. 159–60.

77 When the Republicans delivered a third bill: For this history, see John F. Harris, *The Survivor: Bill Clinton in the White House* (New York: Random House, 2005), pp. 230–39.

77 "makes a mockery of his pledge": Jerry Gray, "Amid Praise, a Peppering of Criticism and Dismay," *New York Times*, August 1, 1996, p. A23.

78 "predictably bad public policy": Telephone interview with Peter Edelman, March 21, 2008.

78 It was preferable to sign the measure": Hillary Rodham Clinton, *Living History* (New York: Simon & Schuster, 2003), p. 369.

78 "A long time ago, I concluded": Transcript of Bill Clinton's news conference on welfare at the White House, July 31, 1996, via U.S. Newswire.

78 "as an opportunity to bring everyone": Ibid.

78 By August 2000, the welfare rolls had declined: Melissa Healy, "Welfare Rolls Fall to Half of '96 Numbers," *Los Angeles Times*, August 23, 2000, p. A12.

78 As unemployment fell from 6.8 percent to 4 percent: "Changes in the Economic Resources of Low-Income Households with Children," Congressional Budget Office, May 2007. Available online at http://www.cbo.gov/ftpdocs/ 81xx/doc8113/05-16-Low-Income.pdf.

78 The percentage of single mothers: "Single Mothers Retain Nearly All Their Employment and Wage Gains in the Current Economic Slowdown," Urban Institute, Single Parents' Earning Monitor, January 2003. Available online at http://www.urban.org/UploadedPDF/410605_SPEM _3.pdf.

79 Between 2000 and 2005, income for poor families: Analysis of federal data by Jared Bernstein, senior economist, Economic Policy Institute, Washington, D.C.

79 During the same period, family income for households: Rebecca Blank

and Brian Kovak, "The Growing Problem of Disconnected Single Mothers," National Poverty Center Working Paper Series, #07-28, Table 1, p. 44.

79 By 2007, the number of children in poverty: Census Bureau data, Historical Poverty Tables, Table 3, Poverty Status of People by Age, Race and Hispanic Origin: 1959 to 2007, available online at http://www.census.gov/hhes/www/poverty/histpov/hstpov3.xls.

79 Though he recognized the bubble: Alan Greenspan, *The Age of Turbulence: Adventures in a New World* (New York: Penguin Press, 2007), p. 171.

79 "People would stop me on the street": Ibid., p. 198.

79 "A stock market boom, of course": Ibid., p. 174.

80 The pullback destroyed $8.5 trillion: Stiglitz, *Roaring Nineties*, pp. 5–6.

80 In a historical context, the technology bubble: Ibid., p. 9.

80 "Financial and non-financial bubbles": Interview with Alan S. Blinder, July 17, 2008.

80 Between 2000 and 2002, the total value of retirement accounts: Stiglitz, *Roaring Nineties*, p. 7.

4. Full Faith

84 In 1987, American imports exceeded: Richard Duncan, *The Dollar Crisis: Causes, Consequences, Cures* (Singapore: John Wiley & Sons [Asia], 2003), p. 178.

84 The financial system lending out all this money: Federal flow of funds data, as cited in Kevin Phillips, *Bad Money: Reckless Finance, Failed Politics, and the Global Crisis of American Capitalism* (New York: Viking, 2008), p. 43.

86 By early 2009, China was reporting: Brad Setser and Arpanda Pandey, "China's $1.7 Trillion Bet: China's External Portfolio and Dollar Reserves," Council on Foreign Relations, Center for Geoeconomic Studies, Working Paper, January 2009, p. 1.

87 Setser said that some 65 percent: Ibid.

87 "Chimerica": Niall Ferguson, *The Ascent of Money: A Financial History of the World* (New York: Penguin Press, 2008), p. 335.

89 "Get ready for the biggest coming-out party": Bill Powell, "China's Great Step Forward," *Fortune*, September 17, 2001, p. 128.

89 "It's all made in China": Bill Powell, "It's All Made in China Now," *Fortune*, March 4, 2002, p. 121.

89 "No country plays the world economic game": Ted C. Fishman, *China Inc.: How the Rise of the Next Superpower Challenges America and the World* (New York: Scribner, 2005), p. 1.

90 "the China price": Ibid., p. 177.

90 "absolutely center stage": Clay Chandler, "Inside the New China," *Fortune*, October 4, 2004, p. 84.

91 Over the next three years, exports expanded: Chinese Customs data, via Haver Analytics (China: Merchandise Exports, free on board), last updated January 21, 2009.

91 Exports specifically to the United States: China Customs data, via Haver Analytics (China: Cumulative Exports to the U.S.), last updated January 12, 2009.

93 In Zhejiang Jintiande's showroom: Peter S. Goodman, "China's Silk Noose Tightens; Italy's Textile Industry Feels Squeeze from Low-Cost Competitor," *Washington Post*, December 18, 2003, p. E1.

94 In parts of Jiangxi—a major source of laborers: Interview with Zhou Daming, sociologist at Sun Yat-Sen University, Guangzhou, China, January 2006.

94 "He calls me 'older sister' ": Interview with Wang Chunguang, sociologist at the Chinese Academy of Social Sciences, Beijing, China, January 2006.

98 Revulsion with corruption: Dali L. Yang, *Remaking the Chinese Leviathan: Market Transition and the Politics of Governance in China* (Stanford, Calif.: Stanford University Press, 2004), p. 220.

98 Three million people attended: "China Contemplates Change," The *Economist* Intelligence Unit, October 12, 2005.

98 Paramilitary troops were often required: Joseph Kahn, "China's 'Haves' Stir the 'Have Nots' to Violence," *New York Times*, December 31, 2004, p. A1.

99 We're ordinary people": Interview with Wang Jijing in Fawang, Shandong province, China, March 17, 2004. See also Peter S. Goodman, "Chinese Farmers Pay Price in Drive to Build Golf Centers," *Washington Post*, April 13, 2004, p. E1.

100 By the year the golf course arrived: According to an account in the Chinese newspaper *Southern Weekend (Nanfang Zhoumou)*.

100 "Of course the price was not very high": Interview with a Qihe County land bureau official in Dezhou, China, March 18, 2004.

100 the men were all arrested: Interview with Wang's wife, Fawang, China, March 17, 2004.

102 "extra careful": Peter S. Goodman, "In China, Building Worries; As Housing Keeps Going Up, Some Fear the Bubble Will Burst," *Washington Post*, March 5, 2003, p. E1.

102 Overall, the country's banks had about one-tenth: Report in *China Securities Times*, as cited in Goodman, "In China, Building Worries."

103 "Financial reform is the most difficult": Interview with Chinese premier Wen Jiabao, with *Washington Post* editors and China-based correspondents, Beijing, China, November 21, 2003.

104 "I know very well how uneven": Ibid.

105 Major projects, including many of the skyscrapers: See, for example, Yan Sun, *Corruption and Market in Contemporary China* (Ithaca, N.Y.: Cornell University Press, 2004).

106 "Certain key positions have become corruption disaster areas": Duan Hongqing and Wang Heyan, "China's Converging Fight Against Corruption," *Caijing*, July 23, 2007, cover story.

106 "Ordinary people in China often say": Cited in Peter S. Goodman, "China's Leaders Back Private Property," *Washington Post*, December 23, 2003, p. A1.

5. Home Rich

111 By the first half of 2005, in the midst of the boom: Merrill Lynch estimate, cited in Charles R. Morris, *The Trillion Dollar Meltdown: Easy Money, High Rollers, and the Great Credit Crash* (New York: Public Affairs, 2008), p. 66.

112 In such fashion, total U.S. mortgage debt: Federal Reserve Board data, via Haver Analytics; mortgage debt outstanding, quarterly, last updated January 9, 2009.

112 Over the same period, housing prices: S&P/Case-Shiller Home Price Index, U.S. National, S&P, Fiserv and MacroMarkets LLC, via Haver Analytics.

113 "Stock market shares are too volatile": Robert J. Shiller, *Irrational Exuberance*, 2nd ed. (New York: Doubleday, 2005), pp. 79–80.

113 "The market isn't acting rationally": Shawn Tully, "Is the Housing Boom Over?," *Fortune*, September 20, 2004, p. 90.

113 By the end of 2005, that ratio was up: Mark Zandi, *Financial Shock: A 360° Look at the Subprime Mortgage Implosion, and How to Avoid the Next Financial Crisis* (Upper Saddle River, N.J.: Pearson Education, 2009), pp. 163–64.

113 By the peak of the boom in 2005: Floyd Norris, "Housing Market's Upside: Affordability," *New York Times*, March 7, 2009, p. B3.

114 "The bad outcome could be": Shiller, *Irrational Exuberance*, pp. xv–xvi.

114 a year in which local housing prices jumped by one-fifth: S&P/Case-Shiller Home Price Index, Los Angeles, S&P, Fiserv and MacroMarkets LLC, via Haver Analytics.

114 "It could mean we've seen the end of the boom-bust cycle": Susanne Trimbath, "Real Estate; No More Boom Bust Blues," *Los Angeles Times*, July 20, 2003, p. M3.

114 "We have driven a stake through the heart": Daniel Vasquez, "Real Estate Experts Bust Bubble Fears," *San Jose Mercury News*, May 8, 2003, p. 1C.

115 "Any analogy to stock market pricing": Remarks by Chairman Alan Greenspan, at the annual convention of the Independent Community Bankers of America, Orlando, Florida, March 4, 2003. Transcript available online at http://www.federalreserve.gov/boarddocs/speeches/2003/20030304/default.htm.

115 And the academic literature had already shown: Kevin Phillips, *Bad Money: Reckless Finance, Failed Politics and the Global Crisis of American Capitalism* (New York: Viking, 2008), p. 12.

115 In 1997, President Clinton persuaded Congress: Vikas Bajaj and David Leonhardt, "Tax Break May Have Helped Cause Housing Bubble," *New York Times*, December 18, 2008, p. A1.

116 Clinton's secretary of housing and urban development: David Streitfeld and Gretchen Morgenson, "Building Flawed American Dreams," *New York Times*, October 18, 2008, p. A1.

116 "Don't apologize when you make a loan": Greg Ip, James R. Hagerty, and Jonathan Karp, "Housing Bust Fuels Blame Game," *Wall Street Journal*, March 19, 2008, p. A1.

116 In 2002, Bush explicitly challenged lenders: Ibid.

116 "Part of economic security is owning": Jo Becker, Sheryl Gay Stoltenberg, and Stephen Labaton, "White House Philosophy Stoked Mortgage Bonfire," *New York Times*, December 21, 2008, p. A1.

116 The White House and members of Congress . . . pressured the government-sponsored mortgage companies: Ibid.

116 Fannie was already working toward a goal: Charles Duhigg, "Pressured to Take More Risk, Fannie Reached Tipping Point," *New York Times*, October 4, 2008, p. A1.

117 "We didn't really know what we were buying": Ibid.

117 "to target borrowers who would have trouble": E-mail from David A. Andrukonis to chief executive Dick Syron, September 7, 2004; released by Rep. Henry Waxman at the House Committee on Oversight and Government Reform, December 9, 2008, available online at http://oversight.house.gov/story.asp?ID=2252.

117 "When money is free": George Soros, *The New Paradigm for Financial Markets: The Credit Crisis of 2008 and What It Means* (New York: Public Affairs, 2008), p. xv.

117 More than a third of those loans were for more than the purchase price: Morris, *Trillion Dollar Meltdown*, p. 69.

118 Between 2000 and 2006, the percentage of subprime borrowers: Data from First American CoreLogic, as cited in ibid.

118 "The game was certainly different": E-mail from Nan Lanros, July 23, 2008.

119 As a result, Countrywide and other mortgage companies: Gretchen Morgenson, "Debt Watchdogs: Tamed of Caught Napping?," *New York Times*, December 6, 2008, p. A1.

119 It touted them to retirees on fixed incomes: According to an internal company training manual, and confirmed in interviews with former Washington Mutual sales agents in Irvine, San Diego, and Chicago, November 2008; see Peter S. Goodman and Gretchen Morgenson, "Saying Yes, WaMu Built an Empire on Shaky Loans," *New York Times*, December 27, 2008, p. A1.

120 "I saw it as a death trap": Telephone interview with Barbara Fronek-Cooper, November 12, 2008.

122 "In our world, it was tolerated": Interview with Sherri Zaback, San Diego, California, November 19, 2008.

122 "I'd lie if I said every piece of documentation": Interview with John David Parsons at the Richard J. Donovan Correctional Facility, California, December 13, 2008.

122 In Downey, a heavily Latino community southeast of Los Angeles: Interview with former Washington Mutual salesman, Los Angeles metropolitan area, November 20, 2008.

124 Their seals of approval gave investors assurance: See, for example, Morgenson, "Debt Watchdogs."

124 Between 2005 and 2008, Fannie alone purchased: Duhigg, "Pressured to Take More Risk."

125 "The risks inherent in mortgage lending": Zandi, *Financial Shock*, p. 3.

125 By the fall of 2008, one-tenth of all home owners: Data from the Mortgage Bankers Association, as cited in E. Scott Reckard, "Mortgages; 1 in 10 Loans Past Due," *Los Angeles Times*, December 6, 2008, p. C1.

125 Among those with option ARM loans, nearly one-fourth: Analysis by Mahesh Swaminathan, mortgage strategist at Credit Suisse, as cited in Dina ElBoghdady and Sarah Cohen, "The Growing Foreclosure Crisis," *Washington Post*, January 17, 2009, p. A1.

125 Among those who had fallen into delinquency: Ibid.

125 Between 2000 and 2007, the number of Latino households: Census data, cited in Susan Schmidt and Maurice Tamman, "Housing Push for Hispanics Spawns Wave of Foreclosures," *Wall Street Journal*, January 5, 2009, p. A1.

125 But by late 2008, as foreclosures mounted: Census data, home ownership rate, Hispanic, quarterly, via Haver Analytics, last updated October 28, 2008.

126 From the middle of 2006 through the middle of 2007, Countrywide's chief executive: Morgenson, "Debt Watchdogs."

126 a member of the Horatio Alger Association's Hall of Fame: Paul Muolo and Mathew Padilla, *Chain of Blame: How Wall Street Caused the Mortgage and Credit Crisis* (Hoboken, N.J.: John Wiley & Sons, 2008), p. 2.

126 Between 2001 and 2007, Washington Mutual's chief executive: Data provided by the Corporate Library, a research firm, as cited in Goodman and Morgenson, "Saying Yes, WaMu Built an Empire on Shaky Loans."

6. Locked Out

129 They were convinced by supposedly sophisticated computer models: See, for example, Joe Nocera, "Risk Management," *New York Times Magazine*, January 2, 2009, p. MM 24.

129 By the end of 2007, the notional value of credit default swaps: International Swaps and Derivatives Association, 2007 Market Survey.

130 "Proposals to bring even minimalist regulation": Telephone interview with Alan S. Blinder, October 1, 2008.

130 "financial weapons of mass destruction": Warren Buffett, Letter to shareholders of Berkshire Hathaway, Inc., February 21, 2003, p. 15.

131 "significant gaps and weaknesses": "Financial Derivatives: Actions Needed to Protect the Financial System," General Accounting Office Report to Congress, May 18, 1994, p. 8. Report Number GAO/GGD-94-133. Available online at http://archive.gao.gov/t2pbat3/151647.pdf.

131 The report noted that the worldwide volume: Ibid., p. 3.

131 "The sudden failure or abrupt withdrawal": Testimony of Charles A. Bowsher, Comptroller General of the United States, to the House of Representatives, Committee on Energy and Commerce, Subcommittee on Telecommunications and Finance, May 19, 1994, p. 2. GAO Report Number GAO/T-GGD-94-150. Available online at http://archive.gao.gov/t2pbat3/151679.pdf.

131 "currently unregulated": Ibid., p. 4.

131 He was joined by Arthur Levitt: Transcript of Hearing of the Telecommunications and Finance Subcommittee of the House Energy and Commerce Committee, May 25, 1994, via Federal News Service.

132 "Were we to endeavor to do that": Ibid.

132 "It's like dealing with a professor": Telephone interview with Arthur Levitt, October 1, 2008.

132 "The market was completely opaque": "A Conversation with Brooksley Born," *Washington Lawyer*, October 2003. Available online at http://www.dcbar.org/for_lawyers/resources/legends_in_the_law/born.cfm.

132 "Greenspan told Brooksley": Interview with Michael Greenberger, New York City, September 15, 2008.

133 "He said, 'You're going to cause the greatest financial crisis'": Telephone interview with Lawrence Summers, October 7, 2008.

133 "There is a very fundamental trade-off": Transcript of Senate Agriculture Committee Hearing, February 10, 2000.

134 "provide regulatory relief": President Clinton's Statement on Signing the Consolidated Appropriations Act FY 2001, December 21, 2000. Weekly Compilation of Presidential Documents, 3167–3174, volume 36, issue 52. ISSN: 0511-4187.

134 By 2003, the balance had grown lopsided: Bureau of Economic Analysis, as cited in Kevin Phillips, *Bad Money: Reckless Finance, Failed Politics and the Global Crisis of American Capitalism* (New York: Viking, 2008).

134 Over the same basic time frame, jobs in finance grew: Bureau of Labor Statistics, Current Employment Statistics Survey (National), Financial Activities, All Employees, Seasonally Adjusted, Series ID: CES5500000001.

134 By comparison, more than 14 million manufacturing jobs: Bureau of Labor Statistics, Current Employment Statistics Survey (National), Manufacturing, All Employees, Seasonally Adjusted, Series ID: CES3000000001.

134 "The nation's financial system is at the heart": Transcript of Hearing of the Senate Banking, Housing and Urban Affairs Committee, June 17, 1998.

134 The following year, Rubin took a senior executive job at Citibank: Eric Dash and Louise Story, "Rubin Leaving Citigroup; Smith Barney for Sale," *New York Times*, January 10, 2009, p. B1.

135 "The consequence of such action": Prepared Testimony of George M. James, managing director, Morgan Stanley Dean Witter & Co., House Banking and Financial Services Committee, July 17, 1998.

135 "The American OTC derivatives market": Transcript of Hearing of Senate Agriculture, Nutrition and Forestry Committee, Panel One, July 30, 1998.

135 "There was no political reality": Telephone interview with Robert Rubin, September 2008.

135 Freed of regulatory oversight, the notional value of credit default swaps: Data from the International Swaps and Derivatives Association.

135 By 2008, the notional value of all financial derivatives: Charles R. Morris, *The Trillion Dollar Meltdown: Easy Money, High Rollers, and the Great Credit Crash* (New York: Public Affairs, 2008), p. xii.

135 "the market for products that derive from real things": John Lanchester, "Melting into Air," *New Yorker*, November 10, 2008, p. 83.

136 "If there's one person to blame": Telephone interview with Frank Partnoy, October 7, 2008.

136 "It is remarkable how much trust we have": Transcript of Alan Greenspan's remarks delivered at the Sandra Day O'Connor Project Conference at Georgetown Law School, Washington, D.C., October 2, 2008. Available online at http://www.law.georgetown.edu/news/documents/Greenspan.pdf.

137 "Those of us who have looked to the self-interest": Edmund L. Andrews, "Greenspan Concedes Flaws in Deregulatory Approach," New York Times, October 23, 2008, p. B1.

138 Housing prices were plummeting: S&P/Case-Shiller Home Price Index, Composite 20, S&P, Fiserv, and MacroMarkets LLC, via Haver Analytics, last updated January 27, 2009.

139 Before the end of 2008, Nouriel Roubini: Erica Martin and Rhonda Schaffler, "Roubini Sees Worst Recession in 40 Years, Stocks Drop," Bloomberg, October 14, 2008.

139 And by February 2009, Mark Zandi: Peter S. Goodman, "Sharper Downturn Clouds Obama Spending Plan," New York Times, February 27, 2009, p. A1.

7. Lost Work

142 It would climb from a relatively modest: Bureau of Labor Statistics, Labor Force Statistics from the Current Population Survey, Unemployment Rate, Seasonally Adjusted, 16 Years and Older, Series ID: LNS14000000.

145 By January 2009, more than 2.6 million Americans: Bureau of Labor Statistics, Current Population Survey, Number Unemployed for 27 Weeks and Over, Series ID: LNS13008636.

147 "The jobs are there": Interview with John Garamendi, Oakland, California, February 13, 2008.

151 "if inner city blacks are experiencing the greatest problems": William Julius Wilson, When Work Disappears: The World of the New Urban Poor (New York: Vintage Books, 1997), p. xx.

151 Indeed, by early 2009, the unemployment rate among white college graduates: Bureau of Labor Statistics, Current Population Survey, Unemployment Rate, 20 Years and Older, Bachelor's Degree and Higher, White, Seasonally Adjusted, Series ID: LNS14000027.

151 Among Asian college graduates, the unemployment rate: Bureau of Labor Statistics, Current Population Survey, Unemployment Rate, 25 Years and Older, Bachelor's Degree and Higher, Asian, Not Seasonally Adjusted, Series ID: LNU04032300.

151 More than half a million retail jobs: Bureau of Labor Statistics, Current Employment Statistics Survey, Retail Trade, All Employees, Seasonally Adjusted, Series ID: CES4200000001.

151 Some twenty-three thousand accounting and bookkeeping jobs: Bureau of Labor Statistics, Current Employment Statistics Survey, Professional and Business Services, Accounting and Bookkeeping (NAICS Code: 5412), All Employees, Seasonally Adjusted, Series ID: CES6054120001.

151 By January 2009, there were fifteen thousand fewer legal services jobs: Bureau of Labor Statistics, Current Employment Statistics Survey, Professional and Business Services, Legal Services (NAICS Code: 5411), All Employees, Seasonally Adjusted, Series ID: CES6054110001.

155 By January 2009, some 7.8 million Americans were working part-time: Bureau of Labor Statistics, Current Population Survey, Employment Level—Part-Time for Economic Reasons, All Industries, All Education Levels, All Origins, All Marital Statuses, Seasonally Adjusted, Series ID LNS12032194.

156 The so-called underemployment rate: Bureau of Labor Statistics, Current Population Survey, Total Unemployed, Plus All Marginally Attached Workers Plus Total Employed Part-time for Economic Reasons, as a Percent of All Civilian Labor Force Plus All Marginally Attached Workers, Seasonally Adjusted, Series ID: LNS13327709.

156 During the first half of 2008, more than one-fourth of college graduates: Andrew Sum and Ishkar Khatiwada, "Beyond Official Unemployment: Measuring the Size and Incidence of Labor Underutilization Problems Among U.S. Workers in 2008," Center for Labor Market Studies, Northeastern University, August 2008.

157 "When you go into a recession": Peter S. Goodman, "Toughest Summer Job This Year Is Finding One," *New York Times*, May 25, 2008, p. A1.

157 "have lost jobs in this economic downturn": Ibid.

157 Nationally, the welfare rolls: Jason DeParle, "Welfare Aid Isn't Growing as Economy Drops Off," *New York Times*, February 1, 2009.

158 Michigan, where unemployment was: Ibid.

158 "There is ample reason to be concerned": Ibid.

158 "When we started this, Democratic and Republican": Ibid.

159 By 2002, the percentage had dropped: Pamela Loprest and Sheila Zedlewski, "The Changing Role of Welfare in the Lives of Low-Income Familes with Children," Urban Institute, Occasional Paper Number 73, August 2006, p. 23. Available online at http://www.urban.org/UploadedPDF/311357_occa73.pdf.

159 More than 35 percent of welfare recipients: Ibid., p. 18.

159 By January 2009, less than one-third of African American adults: Bureau of Labor Statistics, Current Population Survey, Employment-Population Ratio, Less Than a High School Diploma, 25 Years and Over, Black or African American, Not Seasonally Adjusted, Series ID: LNU02327671.

159 Among adult Latinos lacking a high school diploma: Bureau of Labor

Statistics, Current Population Survey, Employment-Population Ratio, Less Than a High School Diploma, 25 Years and Over, Hispanic or Latino, Not Seasonally Adjusted, Series ID: LNU02327663.

160 "The labor market for low-income women": Interview with Randy Albelda at the meeting of the American Economic Association, New Orleans, Louisiana, January 5, 2008.

161 That was triple the pace in Japan: Robert I. Lerman, "Are Skills the Problem?," published in Timothy J. Bartik and Susan N. Houseman, ed., *A Future of Good Jobs?* (Kalamazoo, Mich.: W. E. Upjohn Institute for Employment Research, 2008), p. 18.

161 Indeed, by 2006, nearly one-fifth of adults: Paul Osterman, "Improving Job Quality," published in Bartik and Houseman, ed., *A Future of Good Jobs?*, p. 204.

161 Among people working in low-wage jobs from 1995 to 2001: Brett Theodos and Robert Bednarzik, "Earnings Mobility and Low-Wage Workers in the United States," *Monthly Labor Review* 129(7) (2006), pp. 34–47; as cited in Osterman, "Improving Job Quality," in Bartik and Houseman, ed., *A Future of Good Jobs?*, p. 205.

161 For the first time since the government began keeping records: Census Bureau data, as cited in David Leonhardt, "For Many, a Boom That Wasn't," *New York Times*, April 9, 2008, p. C1.

161 Those with doctorates: Robert Z. Lawrence, *Blue Collar Blues: Is Trade to Blame for Rising US Income Inequality* (Washington, D.C.: Peter G. Peterson Institute for International Economics, 2008), p. 1.

161 At the same time, corporate profits: Ibid.

161 Over the next eight years, the economy added: Bureau of Labor Statistics, Current Employment Statistics Survey (national).

162 In the most recent expansion, payrolls had increased: Analysis of Census and Bureau of Labor Statistics data conducted by Lakshman Achuthan, managing director, Economic Cycle Research Institute, as cited in Floyd Norris, "Shallow Recessions, Shallow Recoveries," *New York Times*, August 30, 2008, p. C3.

162 Yet after the recessions in 1990 and in 2001: Analysis of Bureau of Labor Statistics data by Andrew Stettner and Sylvia A. Allegretto, "The Rising Stakes of Job Loss," research paper released jointly by the Economic Policy Institute and the National Employment Law Project joint briefing paper.

162 As late as 2003, with the economy again expanding: Bureau of Labor Statistics data, Business Employment Dynamics, Gross Job Gains, Total Private, Seasonally Adjusted, Series ID: BDS0000000000000000110001LQ5.

162 Among those who found full-time jobs: Lawrence Mishel, Jared Bernstein,

and Heidi Shierholz, *The State of Working America 2008/2009* (Ithaca, N.Y.: Cornell University Press, 2009), p. 260; Henry S. Farber, "What Do We Know About Job Loss in the United States," Federal Reserve Bank of Chicago, Economic Perspectives 2Q (2005), pp. 13–27.

162 By February 2009, fewer than 63 percent: Bureau of Labor Statistics, Labor Force Statistics from the Current Population Survey, Employment-Population Ratio, 20 Years and Over, Seasonally Adjusted, Series ID: LNS 12300024.

163 All suffered falling rates of employment: Bureau of Labor Statistics, Labor Force Statistics from the Current Population Survey, Employment-Population Ratio, Bachelor's Degree and Higher, 25 Years and Over, White, Not Seasonally Adjusted, Series ID: LNU02327670.

163 By early 2009, only 55 percent: Bureau of Labor Statistics, Labor Force Statistics from the Current Population Survey, Employment-Population Ratio, 16 Years and Over, Black or African American Men, Seasonally Adjusted, Series ID: LNS 12300007.

163 One study found that, since the 1980s: Timothy J. Bartik and Susan N. Houseman, ed., *A Future of Good Jobs?* (Kalamazoo, Mich.: W. E. Upjohn Institute for Employment Research, 2008), p. 5.

163 Latinos suffered: Bureau of Labor Statistics, Labor Force Statistics from the Current Population Survey, Employment-Population Ratio, 16 Years and Over, Hispanic or Latino, Seasonally Adjusted, Series ID: LNS 12300009.

163 And during the last decade, it never dropped below: Bureau of Labor Statistics, Current Population Survey, Average Weeks Unemployed, Seasonally Adjusted, Series ID: LNS13008275.

164 A widely cited 1992 study: George J. Borjas, Richard Freeman, and Lawrence F. Katz, "On the Labor Market Effects of Immigration and Trade," in Borjas, Freeman, and Katz, eds., *Immigration and the Work Force: Economic Consequences for the United States and Source Areas* (Chicago: University of Chicago Press), pp. 213–44.

164 The expansion of the high school ranks: Claudia Goldin and Lawrence F. Katz, *The Race Between Education and Technology* (Cambridge, Mass.: Belknap Press of Harvard University Press, 2008), p. 165.

165 "For the first time on record": David Leonhardt, "The Big Fix," *New York Times Magazine*, February 1, 2009, p. 48.

165 "Companies today would rather not go": Phone interview with Dean Baker, January 2008.

166 Service industries, by contrast: Lawrence Mishel, Jared Bernstein, and Sylvia Allegretto, *The State of Working America 2004–05* (Ithaca, N.Y.: Cornell University Press, 2005), as cited in Jacob S. Hacker, *The Great*

Risk Shift: The New Economic Insecurity and the Decline of the American Dream (New York: Oxford University Press, 2006), p. 81.

166 This boosted stock values: Bartik and Houseman, ed., *A Future of Good Jobs?*, p. 6.

8. Waking Up to the New Thrift

171 "Fundamental factors": Chairman Ben S. Bernanke, "The Housing Market and Subprime Lending," a speech to the 2007 International Monetary Conference in Cape Town, South Africa, June 5, 2007. Transcript available online at http://www.federalreserve.gov/newsevents/speech/bernanke20070605a .htm.

172 "These subprime losses are wildly out": Ben Stein, "Chicken Little's Brethren, on the Trading Floor," *New York Times*, August 12, 2007, p. BU6.

172 "Direct evidence of such spillovers": Ben S. Bernanke, "The Recent Financial Turmoil and Its Economic and Policy Consequences," speech to the Economic Club of New York, New York City, October 15, 2007. Transcript available online at http://www.federalreserve.gov/newsevents/speech/ bernanke20071015a.htm.

173 "Bernanke did not see the magnitude": Suzy Jagger, "Ben Bernanke Under Fire Ahead of Fed Rate Meeting," *Times* (London), January 29, 2008, as cited in Ethan S. Harris, *Ben Bernanke's Fed: The Federal Reserve After Greenspan* (Boston: Harvard Business Press, 2008), p. 182.

173 "Bernanke was caught asleep": Dean Baker, "Does Bernanke Have to Go?," *Perspective*, Center for Economic and Policy Research, February 18, 2008, cited in Harris, *Ben Bernanke's Fed*, p. 182.

174 "Credit issues are there": Jonathan Stempel, "New Century, Subprime Lenders Rebound a Bit (update 2)," Reuters News, March 6, 2007.

174 "The fundamentals of the economy": Glenn Somerville, "Bush Says U.S. Economy Strong despite stock swings (update3)," Reuters News, August 8, 2007.

174 "Our economy obviously is going through a tough time": Remarks by President George W. Bush to the Economic Club of New York, New York Hilton, March 14, 2008.

174 "Should the government bail out": News conference with President George W. Bush, July 15, 2008. Transcript from CQ Transcriptions, LLC.

175 As speculators jumped in: Data from First American LoanPerformance; cited in Peter S. Goodman, "Homeowners Feel the Pinch of Lost Equity," *New York Times*, November 8, 2007, p. A1.

175 That year, Washoe County handed out: Bureau of the Census, New Private Housing Units, Washoe County, Nevada, via Haver Analytics.

180 "Get down to Disney World": President George W. Bush, speaking at

O'Hare International Airport, Chicago, September 27, 2001, Federal News Service, as cited in "Excerpts from Bush Speech on Travel," *New York Times*, September 28, 2001, p. B6.

180 "Rather go to bed supperless": Benjamin Franklin, *Autobiography of Benjamin Franklin* (New York: Macmillan, 1921), p. 184.

180 "People have changed their view of debt": John Kenneth Galbraith, *The Affluent Society* (Boston: Houghton Mifflin, 1958), pp. 200–201, 206, as cited in Lendol Calder, *Financing the American Dream: A Cultural History of Consumer Credit* (Princeton, N.J.: Princeton University Press, 1999), p. 25.

180 "Today Middletown lives by a credit economy": Robert S. Lynd and Helen Merrell Lynd, *Middletown: A Study in Modern American Culture* (New York: Harcourt, Brace, and Company, 1929), p. 45.

181 "The contractor is extensively financed": Ibid.

181 "If one misses two months' rent": Ibid., p. 105.

181 Untrained in such matters": Ibid.

181 By 1926, two out of every three cars: Martha L. Olney, *Buy Now, Pay Later: Advertising, Credit and Consumer Durables in the 1920s* (Chapel Hill: University of North Carolina Press, 1991), p. 96, as cited in Calder, *Financing the American Dream*, p. 19.

181 For the burgeoning middle class": Joseph Nocera, *A Piece of the Action: How the Middle Class Joined the Money Class* (New York: Simon & Schuster, 1994), p. 21.

181 In 1958, Bank of America unleashed: Ibid., pp. 15–33.

182 Over the three decades that followed, the national consumer debt load: Ibid., pp. 9–10.

182 "the myth of lost economic virtue": Calder, *Financing the American Dream*, p. 28.

183 "People have come to view credit": Phone interview with Michelle Jones, as cited in Peter S. Goodman, "Economy Fitful, Americans Start to Pay as They Go," *New York Times*, February 5, 2008, p. A1.

183 But not until the early 1980s did it enjoy wide usage: Louise Story, "Home Equity Frenzy Was a Bank Ad Come True," *New York Times*, August 15, 2008, p. A1.

183 "There's got to be at least $25,000": Ibid.

183 "You don't have to sell your home": Ibid.

183 Between 1990 and the end of 2007, the outstanding balance of home equity loans: Federal Reserve Board data, Mortgage Debt, 1-4 Family Homes, Home Equity Loans, quarterly, via Haver Analytics.

183 By the middle of 2008, Americans were on the hook for $2.56 trillion: Federal Reserve Board data, as cited in Gretchen Morgenson, "Given a Shovel, Digging Deeper into Debt," *New York Times*, July 20, 2008, p. A1.

183 By 2008, Americans were surrendering 14.5 percent: Ibid.

184 These people—which is to say roughly one-third of all households: Data derived from an analysis of Federal Reserve data by Moody's Economy .com.

184 Many of those put out of work had since taken jobs: See, for example, Louis Uchitelle, *The Disposable American: Layoffs and Their Consequences* (New York: Random House, 2006).

184 The share of Americans who worked at least twenty hours: Lawrence Mishel, Jared Bernstein, and Sylvia Allegretto, *The State of Working America 2004/2005* (Ithaca, N.Y.: Cornell University Press, 2005), as cited in Jacob S. Hacker, *The Great Risk Shift: The New Economic Insecurity and the Decline of the American Dream* (New York: Oxford University Press, 2006), p. 37.

184 When Americans got sick: Ibid., pp. 136–64.

184 But as companies rolled back benefits: Ibid.

184 Many took on bigger mortgages: See, for example, Robert H. Frank, *Falling Behind: How Rising Inequality Harms the Middle Class* (Berkeley and Los Angeles: University of California Press, 2007), p. 80.

184 The cost of a college education soared: Tamara Draut, "The Growing College Gap," published in James Lardner and David A. Smith eds., *Inequality Matters: The Growing Economic Divide in America and Its Poisonous Consequences* (New York: New Press, 2005), pp. 92–93.

184 Three decades ago, federal Pell grants: Ibid., p. 93.

185 Among graduates from private colleges, the share of those in hock: Hacker, *Great Risk Shift*, p. 75.

185 But under even the most conservative estimate—with five cents of every dollar spent: Mark Zandi, *Financial Shock: A 360° Look at the Subprime Mortgage Implosion, and How to Avoid the Next Financial Crisis* (Upper Saddle River, N.J.: Pearson Education, 2009), p. 74.

186 Between 2004 and 2006, Americans pulled roughly $840 billion: Updated estimates provided by economist James Kennedy, presented in Alan Greenspan and James Kennedy, "Estimates of Home Mortgage Originations, Repayments, and Debt on One-to-Four-Family Residences," Federal Reserve Board FEDS working paper no. 2005-41.

186 Nationwide, home equity withdrawals: Data provided by Moody's Economy.com, based on an analysis of Federal Reserve data supplemented by an examination of Equifax credit reports.

186 Home equity withdrawals had fallen to 8 percent: Ibid.

186 By the first half of 2008, home equity withdrawals nationally fell off: Updated estimates provided by Greenspan and Kennedy, "Estimates of Home Mortgage Originations."

186 Between July and September, consumer spending dropped: Peter S. Good-man, "Economy Shrinks with Consumers Leading the Way," *New York Times*, October 30, 2008, p. A1.

186 "We live in a small town": Phone interview with Elena Gamble, as cited in Goodman, "Economy Fitful."

9. Healing Cape Coral

190 The median house price in Cape Coral: Florida Association of Realtors data, cited in Peter S. Goodman, "This Is the Sound of a Bubble Bursting," *New York Times*, December 23, 2007, p. C1.

190 Worse, the volume of home sales: Florida Association of Realtors data.

191 "That's an all-time low": The account from Cape Coral and surrounding Lee County throughout this chapter is based on interviews conducted in December 2007; some of these interviews were a basis for a story. See Goodman, "This Is the Sound of a Bubble Bursting." *New York Times*, December 23, 2007, Sunday Business section.

195 Throughout Cape Coral, foreclosure filings: Data provided by RealtyTrac, Inc.

196 By the end of 2008, it was 9.7 percent: Bureau of Labor Statistics, Local Area Unemployment Statistics, Cape Coral City, Florida, Not Seasonally Adjusted, Series ID: LAUCT12014006.

197 Half the applicants were saying: Interview with program manager Kim Hustad, December 2007.

197 The actual number came in at $5 million: Christina Cepero, "Lee County Schools Get Slight Budget Bump," *News-Press*, September 8, 2008, p. B1.

199 The Fed brokered a deal: Andrew Ross Sorkin, "JP Morgan Pays $2 a Share for Bear Stearns," *New York Times*, March 17, 2008, p. A1; Landon Thomas Jr. and Eric Dash, "Seeking Fast Deal, JP Morgan Quintuples Bear Stearns Bid," *New York Times*, March 25, 2008, p. C1.

199 Taxpayers were now explicitly responsible: Zacahary A. Goldfarb, David Cho, and Binyamin Appelbaum, "Treasury to Rescue Fannie and Freddie," *Washington Post*, September 7, 2008, p. A1.

200 The same day, the government declined to rescue Merrill Lynch: Andrew Ross Sorkin, "Bids to Halt Crisis Reshape Landscape of Wall Street," *New York Times*, September 15, 2008, p. A1.

200 A mere two days later, the Fed handed an $85 billion: Jim Puzzanghera, "Bailout Funds Going Quickly; AIG's Rescue Tab Grows to $150 Billion," *Los Angeles Times*, November 11, 2008, p. A1.

200 "It would have been a chain reaction": L. Andrews, Michael J. de la Merced, and Mary Williams Walsh, "Fed's $85 Billion Loan Rescues Insurer," *New York Times*, September 16, 2008, p. A1.

200 Late the following week, federal regulators seized WaMu: Eric Dash and Andrew Ross Sorkin, "In Largest Bank Failure, U.S. Seizes then Sells," *New York Times*, September 26, 2008, p. A1.

201 "I'm a strong believer in free enterprise": President George W. Bush, Speech to the nation, September 24, 2008, transcript online at http://www.nytimes.com/2008/09/24/business/economy/24text-bush.html?pagewanted =1&_r=2.

201 "No one likes to be painting in": Ibid.

202 "I can put a gun to my neighbor's head": Transcript of a hearing before the House Financial Services Committee, September 24, 2008.

203 Another $40 billion went to cover loan guarantees: Jim Puzzanghera, "Bailout Funds Going Quickly," *Los Angeles Times*, November 11, 2008, p. A1.

203 The rest of the first $350 billion was distributed: Binyamin Appelbaum, "Treasury's Bailout Promises Runneth Over," *Washington Post*, December 31, 2008, p. D3.

203 In December, General Motors and Chrysler: Louis Uchitelle, "If Detroit Falls, Foreign Makers Could Be Buffer," *New York Times*, November 17, 2008, p. A1.

203 That prompted the Treasury to reach further: John D. McKinnon and John D. Stoll, "U.S. Throws Lifeline to Detroit," *Wall Street Journal*, December 20, 2008, p. A1.

203 "The downturn in the housing market": Transcript of a hearing before the House Financial Services Committee, September 24, 2008, panel II.

204 "The boom in subprime mortgage lending": Ben S. Bernanke, "The Future of Mortgage Finance in the United States," speech given to the UC-Berkeley/UCLA Symposium, "The Mortgage Meltdown, the Economy, and Public Policy," Berkeley, California, October 31, 2008. Transcript online at http://www.federalreserve.gov/newsevents/speech/bernanke20081031a.htm.

204 In this fashion, the Fed created some $1.3 trillion: Peter S. Goodman, "Printing Money and Its Price," *New York Times*, December 27, 2008, p. WK1.

205 "Overpriced assets are like poison mushrooms": Charles R. Morris, *The Trillion Dollar Meltdown: Easy Money, High Rollers, and the Great Credit Crash* (New York: Public Affairs, 2008), p. xii.

205 Seemingly every state capital: Gregory B. Hladky, "In Fiscal Balance, a Sisyphus-Like Labor," *New York Times*, January 25, 2009, p. CT2.

205 Virginia was confronting a whopping $4 billion shortfall: Anita Kumar, "Lawmakers Say Kaine Failed to Cut Enough," *Washington Post*, January 21, 2009, p. B1.

205 California was looking at a $42 billion deficit: Stu Woo, "Schwarzenegger Urges Action on Budget," *Wall Street Journal*, January 16, 2009, p. A4.

205 about to run out of funds to pay unemployment benefits: Marc Lifsher, "State Labors to Meet Jobless Demand," *Los Angeles Times*, January 19, 2009, p. C1.

205 "We have got down to a level": David W. Chen, "Mayor Pleads for Sustenance, Not Cuts, from the State," *New York Times*, January 23, 2009, p. A21.

205 The Great Depression has been convincingly blamed: Niall Ferguson, *The Ascent of Money: A Financial History of the World* (New York: Penguin Press, 2008), p. 9.

206 "The exact words were": Peter S. Goodman, "Worried Banks Sharply Reduce Business Loans," *New York Times*, July 28, 2008, p. A1.

206 And it meant no help-wanted ads: Bureau of Labor Statistics, Local Area Unemployment Statistics, Baltimore, Maryland, Not Seasonally Adjusted, Series ID: LAUPA24005006G.

207 "It's going to take a period of time": Interview with Michael Powell, Portland, Oregon, March 10, 2009.

207 "I think we're in deflation": Interview with Joe Cortright, Portland, Oregon, March 10, 2009.

207 "The banking system has liquidity": Interview with Raymond P. Davis, Portland, Oregon, March 11, 2009.

208 "Why buy today": Interview with Bill Wyatt, Portland, Oregon, March 13, 2009.

208 "If you had to go and renegotiate": Interview with William A. Furman, Portland, Oregon, March 11, 2009.

209 "I'm not really spending": Interview with Alrenzo Ferguson, Portland, Oregon, March 12, 2009.

214 "The consequences of high neighborhood joblessness": William Julius Wilson, *When Work Disappears: The World of the New Urban Poor* (New York: Vintage Books, 1997), p. xiii.

10. Shovel Ready

216 "We remain the most prosperous": Transcript of President Barack Obama, inaugural address, January 20, 2009. Available online at http://www.nytimes.com/2009/01/20/us/politics/20text-obama.html?_r=1&pagewanted=all.

216 "The resources of nature and men's devices": John Maynard Keynes, "The Great Slump of 1930," *Nation & Athenæum*, December 20 and December 27, 1930 (first ed.), London. Available online at http://www.gutenberg.ca/ebooks/keynes-slump/keynes-slump-00-h.html.

217 "The question we ask": Transcript of President Barack Obama, inaugural address, January 20, 2009.

219 This is not just a short-term program": Peter Baker, "Obama, in Effort to

Build Support, Lays Out Details of $825 Billion Stimulus Plan," *New York Times*, January 25, 2009, p. A20.

220 Lobbyists descended: Martin Vaughan, "Lobbyists Give Wish Lists for Stimulus Tax Breaks," Dow Jones News Service, December 23, 2008.

220 Hotels asked for tax credits: Ibid.

220 So did aggrieved catfish farmers: James Oliphant and Richard Simon, "Obama Plan Stimulating Lobbyists," *Chicago Tribune*, December 14, 2008.

220 "There are members of our caucus": Paul Kane and Michael D. Shear, "'Green Jobs' Compete for Stimulus Aid," *Washington Post*, December 24, 2008, p. A1.

222 "This will be a once-in-a-generation opportunity": Interview with Mayor Bob Coble, December 10, 2008.

222 "Historically, simply throwing government money": Mark Sanford, "Sanford: Stimulus Would Hurt, Not Help," *The State*, February 15, 2009.

223 "That's not the place": Interview with David Lockwood, December 12, 2008.

224 "Anyone who belittles cooperation": Jackie Calmes and David Herszenhorn, "Obama Pressing for a Quick Jolt to the Economy," *New York Times*, January 24, 2009, p. A1.

224 "We cannot borrow and spend": Peter Baker, "Obama, in Effort to Build Support, Lays Out Details of $825 Billion Stimulus Plan," *New York Times*, January 25, 2009, p. A20.

225 "We need to compare the cost": Jonathan Weisman, "House Passes Stimulus Package," *Wall Street Journal*, January 29, 2009, p. A1.

225 Those two measures along with spending: Mark Zandi, "The Economic Impact of the American Recovery and Reinvestment Act," January 21, 2009, p. 9, available online at http://www.economy.com/mark-zandi/documents/Economic_Stimulus_House_Plan_012109.pdf.

225 Still, Obama sought conciliation in advance: Paul Kane and Michael D. Shear, "Obama Seeks GOP Backing for Stimulus," *Washington Post*, January 24, 2009, p. A4.

225 "delivers too little": "Take Charge; The Stimulus Bill Requires President Obama's Intervention," *Washington Post*, February 1, 2009, p. B6.

225 "an astounding mishmash": Ibid.

226 About $50 billion was devoted to roads: Shailagh Murray and Paul Kane, "Congress Reaches Stimulus Accord," *Washington Post*, February 12, 2009, p. A12; Greg Hitt and Jonathan Weisman, "Congress Strikes $789 Billion Stimulus Deal," *Wall Street Journal*, February 12, 2009, p. A1.

226 The plan included $54 billion in aid for states: Hitt and Weisman, "Congress Strikes $789 Billion Stimulus Deal."

226 "It's a good plan": Ibid.

226 "Where are we going": James R. Carroll, "Area Senators at Odds on Stimulus Measure," *Louisville Courier-Journal*, February 11, 2009, p. A4.

227 "It may be necessary:" Krishna Guha and Edward Luce, "Greenspan Backs Bank Nationalization," *Financial Times*, February 18, 2009.

228 "Instead of using the first payment": Deborah Solomon, "Geithner Apologizes, Calls for Dramatic Action," *Wall Street Journal*, January 22, 2009, p. A3.

228 Anger about the bailout intensified: Ben White, "What Red Ink? Wall Street Paid Hefty Bonuses," *New York Times*, January 29, 2009, p. A1.

228 "financial treason": *Countdown with Keith Olbermann*, MSNBC, transcript, January 29, 2008.

228 "That is the height of irresponsibility": *Nightly Business Report*, PBS transcript, January 29, 2008.

228 a $500,000 cap: Stephen Labaton and Vikas Bajaj, "Executive Pay Limits Seek to Alter Corporate Culture," *New York Times*, February 5, 2009, p. A1.

228 "will require much more dramatic action": Ibid.

228 Each day, details of Geithner's likely plan: David Cho and Lori Montgomery, "New Bailout May Top $1.5 Trillion," *Washington Post*, February 10, 2009, p. A1.

228 Geithner also watered down: Stepen Labaton and Edmund L. Andrews, "Geithner Said to Have Prevailed on the Bailout," *New York Times*, February 10, 2009, p. A1.

229 "There's not a hell": Michael R. Crittenden, "The Bailout Plan: Treasury Secretary Gets a Chilly Reception," *Wall Street Journal*, February 11, 2009, p. A2.

229 before the reckoning was done, financial institutions: Nouriel Roubini, "It's Time to Nationalize Insolvent Banking Systems," Nouriel Roubini's Global EconoMonitor, February 10, 2009, http://www.rgemonitor.com (subscription required).

229 Public anger only grew in March: David Cho and Brady Dennis, "Bailout King AIG Still to Pay Millions in Bonuses," *Washington Post*, March 15, 2009, p. A1.

229 "There are a lot of terrible things": Edmund L. Andrews and Peter Baker, "Bonus Money at Troubled AIG Draws Heavy Criticism," *New York Times*, March 16, 2009, p. A1.

230 So unpopular was this assertion: Edmund L. Andrews and Jackie Calmcs, "Obama in Effort to Undo Bonuses Granted by AIG," *New York Times*, March 17, 2009, p. A1.

231 Indeed, recent economic research: Christopher L. Foote, Paul S. Willen, and Kristopher Gerardi, "Negative Equity and Foreclosure: Theory and

Evidence," Federal Reserve Bank of Boston, Public Policy Discussion Papers, Federal Reserve Bank of Boston, June 5, 2008, Paper Number 08-03, available online at http://www.bos.frb.org/economic/ppdp/2008/ppdp0803.pdf.

231 Walking away from a home: David Leonhardt, "Bailout Likely to Focus on Most Afflicted Homeowners," *New York Times*, February 17, 2009, p. A1.

11. Seed Capital

236 Only then did Americans buy: Louis Uchitelle, "Maybe It Can't: A Trap in Obama's Spending Plan," *New York Times*, December 21, 2008, p. WK4.

238 This makes the industry a potentially huge source: "Profile of the Bioman-ufacturing Workforce," North Carolina Biotechnology Center, 2003.

238 "Those guys know that you have to follow": Interview with Norman Smit, recruitment director, North Carolina BioNetwork program, March 28, 2007; see Peter S. Goodman, "In N.C., A Second Industrial Revolution," *Washington Post*, September 3, 2007, p. A1.

240 In Mitchell County alone, some sixteen hundred jobs: Interview with San-dra F. Buchanan, branch manager, North Carolina Employment Security Commission, Spruce Pine, North Carolina, April 18, 2007.

241 Overall, North Carolina lost more than a third: Bureau of Labor Statistics data, State and Area Employment, Hours and Earnings, North Carolina, Statewide, Manufacturing, Series ID: SMS3700000300000001.

241 By 2008, North Carolina's biotech industry employed: Data from the North Carolina Biotechnology Center.

244 The state's biotech companies buy: "Evidence and Opportunity: Biotech-nology Impacts in North Carolina," a report prepared for the North Carolina Biotechnology Center by Battelle Technology Partnership Prac-tice, November 2008, p. ES-13. Available online at http://www.ncbiotech .org/biotechnology_in_nc/battelle/battelleReport.pdf.

245 Areas that hold promise include: Joseph Cortright and Heike Mayer, "Signs of Life: The Growth of Biotechnology Centers in the U.S.," Brook-ings Institution Center on Urban and Metropolitan Policy, 2002, p. 11.

246 The top ten drugs: Ibid., p. 9.

246 In the past decade, North Carolina has directed: "North Carolina's Biotechnology Investment Tops Billion Dollar Mark," press release from North Carolina Biotechnology Center, November 20, 2008. Available on-line at http://www.ncbiotech.org/news_and_events/industry_news/battelle _billion_nov08.html.

247 Between 2001 and the middle of 2008, $1.1 billion in venture capital: "Ev-idence and Opportunity: Biotechnology Impacts in North Carolina," a re-port prepared for the North Carolina Biotechnology Center by Battelle Technology Partnership Practice, November 2008, p. 29.

247 North Carolina remains divided: See, for example, "State of the North Carolina Workforce: An Assessment of the State's Labor Force Demand and Supply, 2007–2017," published by the North Carolina Commission on Workforce Development, January 2007.

12. The Renewable Economy

250 Iowa managed to hold the line: Bureau of Labor Statistics data, State and Area Employment, Hours and Earnings, Iowa, Statewide, Manufacturing, All Employees, Series ID: SMS19000003000000001.

251 Over the generations, as Maytag grew: Maytag history drawn from the Web site of the Maytag Collector's Club at http://www.maytagclub.com/main .htm, and from the corporate Web site timeline at http://www.maytag.com/ content.jsp?name=146.

257 "The job of the lab": Interview with Lloyd A. Jacobs, Toledo, Ohio, September 4, 2008.

259 In 2007, alternative energy businesses raised $14.8 billion: Data from Dealogic, as cited in Karen Richardson, "A Quarter Much Like the Last One," *Wall Street Journal*, June 26, 2008, p. C1.

259 Some $5 billion in venture capital: Ibid.

259 In a report released in 2008, the Energy Department concluded: U.S. Department of Energy report, "20% Wind Energy by 2030: Increasing Wind Energy's Contribution to U.S. Electricity Supply," July 2008, Appendix C, "Wind Related Jobs and Economic Development," pp. 204–5. Available online at http://www.20percentwind.org/20percent_wind_energy_report _revOct08.pdf. The report's appendix refers to the creation of 3 million job years, which is roughly equivalent to 550,000 actual positions, according to the study's authors.

259 Many of these new jobs would be concentrated around the Great Lakes: Ibid., p. 207.

260 Add in solar energy along with generating power: Telephone interview with Daniel Kammen, August 26, 2008.

260 Most of these jobs could be filled: Van Jones, *The Green Collar Economy: How One Solution Can Fix Our Two Biggest Problems* (New York: HarperOne, 2008), p. 12.

260 He pledged to make renewable forms of energy: Barack Obama and Joe Biden, "New Energy for America," a campaign issue brief, available online at http://www.barackobama.com/pdf/factsheet_energy_speech_080308.pdf.

260 Thousands of miles of modern power lines: U.S. Department of Energy, "20% Wind Energy by 2030."

261 This expansion added thirteen thousand manufacturing jobs: "American Wind Energy Association (AWEA) Notes Top Wind Industry Accomplish-

ments of 2008," a press release from the AWEA, available online at http://www.awea.org/newsroom/releases/Year_End_Wrap_Up_22Dec08.html.

261 When Congress allowed such tax credits: Data from the American Wind Energy Association.

261 "You're going to see development": Interview with Ruth E. Leistensnider, Houston, Texas, June 3, 2008.

261 The stimulus spending bill adopted by Congress: Dave DeWitte, "Stimulus Aids Wind Industry in Iowa, Nation," *Cedar Rapids Gazette*, McClatchy-Tribune Regional News, February 14, 2009, available online at http://www.gazetteonline.com.

261 During the first nine months of 2008, renewable energy: Claire Cain Miller, "In Silicon Valley, Venture Capitalists Turn Cautious and Focus on the Short Term," *New York Times*, January 5, 2009, p. B4.

261 But with banks in virtual hibernation: Ibid.

261 Despite the fact that the Dakotas offer: Kate Galbraith, "Dark Days for Green Energy," *New York Times*, February 4, 2009, p. B1.

262 Meanwhile, the Obama administration has signaled: John M. Broder, "In Obama's Team, Two Camps on Climate," *New York Times*, January 2, 2009.

262 "We're investing billions": "The Way Forward," an ad for JPMorgan Chase and Co., in *New York Times*, January 6, 2009, p. A26.

265 "I'm into renewable energy": Interview with Lee Fisher, Houston, Texas, June 2, 2008.

266 Through the 1960s and '70s, American researchers: Research drawn from U.S. Department of Energy, "The History of Solar," Energy Efficiency and Renewable Energy, available online at http://www1.eere.energy.gov/solar/pdfs/solar_timeline.pdf.

13. Insourcing the Future

270 Between 1998 and the fall of 2008, foreign companies paid: Foreign Direct Investment in the U.S.: Balance of Payments and Direct Investment Position Data; quarterly, not seasonally adjusted. Available online at http://bea.gov/international/di1fdibal.htm.

271 "Where Japan Will Strike": Gene Bylinsky, "Where Japan Will Strike Next," *Fortune*, September 25, 1989, p. 42.

271 "I wonder if it's bad": Paul Farhi and Stuart Auerbach, "Reports of Bid by Sony Raise Questions," *Washington Post*, September 27, 1989, p. B1.

271 "Be ready to deal": Susan Moffat, "Should You Work for the Japanese?," *Fortune*, December 3, 1990, p. 107.

271 "The object of China's actions": Joel Havemann and Elizabeth Douglass, "Lawmakers Seek to Stop CNOOC Bid," *Los Angeles Times*, July 14, 2005, p. C1.

271 More recent fears have centered on so-called sovereign wealth funds: Data from Thomson financial, as cited in Peter S. Goodman and Louise Story, "Overseas Investors Buy Aggressively in U.S.," *New York Times*, January 20, 2008, p. A1.

271 "This is a phenomenon": Goodman and Story, "Overseas Investors Buy Aggressively in U.S."

272 "Do we want the communists": Ibid.

272 "It would be good": Ibid.

273 By December 2008, China's exports were declining: Andrew Batson and Gordon Fairclough, "Slowdown in China Gets Worse, Increasing Global Woes," *Wall Street Journal*, December 11, 2008, p. A1.

274 In November 2008 . . . China announced plans: David Barboza, "China Unveils Sweeping Plan for Economy," *New York Times*, November 10, 2008, p. A1.

274 "counteracting the course of global civilization": Edward Wong, "Booming China Faults U.S. Policy on the Economy," *New York Times*, June 17, 2008, p. A1.

274 "We have lent a huge amount": Michael Wines, "China's Leader Says He Is 'Worried' Over U.S. Treasuries," *New York Times*, March 14, 2009, p. A1.

274 Later that month, China's central bank: David Barboza, "China Urges New Money Reserve to Replace Dollar," *New York Times*, March 23, 2009, p. A5.

275 Between 1998 and 2006, the number of Americans working: Thomas Anderson, "U.S. Affiliates of Foreign Companies: Operations in 2006," Survey of Current Business, August 2008, p. 186, Table 1. Available online at http://bea.gov/scb/pdf/2008/08%20August/0808_affiliate.pdf.

275 They paid out more than $335 billion in wages: Mathew J. Slaughter, "Insourcing Mergers and Acquisitions," December 2007, a study underwritten by the Organization for International Investment, a Washington lobbying firm financed by foreign companies.

275 While General Motors, Ford, and Chrysler delivered: Kate Linebaugh, "Europeans Raise Pressure on Detroit," *Wall Street Journal*, January 5, 2009, p. B1.

275 "We don't want to just be victims": Interview with Governor Jennifer M. Granholm, Greenville, Michigan, March 6, 2008.

276 In 2004, a factory on the fringes of town: Bureau of Labor Statistics, State and Area Employment, Michigan, Statewide, Manufacturing, Series ID: SMS26000000300000001.

276 "There's just not enough clean water": Telephone interview with George Nolen, February 29, 2008.

279 "When you're owned by somebody": Telephone interview with Jeff Beegle, March 5, 2008.

280 "They said, 'There is nothing you can do' ": Granholm interview, March 6, 2008.

Conclusion

283 "Its power to generate wealth: Transcript of President Barack Obama's inaugural address, January 20, 2009, available online at http://www.cnn.com/2009/POLITICS/01/20/obama.politics.

Acknowledgments

First and foremost, I thank the dozens of people who willingly opened up their lives to public scrutiny, speaking to me for many hours over many months on faith that their struggles and aspirations would further the cause of economic renewal—in particular, Dorothy Thomas, Greg Bailey, Willie Gonzalez, Fran Barbaro, Eric Bochner, Marshall Whittey, and Michael Pfaff.

This project began as a newspaper story centered on a forward-looking question posed by Larry Ingrassia, who oversees the business section of the *New York Times*, where I've been lucky enough to work since 2007: what happens to American society as we are finally forced to live within our means? I'm tremendously grateful to Larry for his sharp thinking, and for allowing me to pursue this question at length early in my *Times* career, generously providing me a book leave just as the economic and financial crisis put considerable strain on his staff.

I'm grateful to *Times* editors Bill Keller, Jill Abramson, John Geddes, Rick Berke, and Glenn Kramon for their support of the project, and for continuing to champion ambitious journalism at a time when so many other institutions are in retreat.

Tim O'Brien, the *Times*'s Sunday business editor, has been a remarkable journalistic resource, a fountain of good ideas, and a valued friend.

Several of these chapters began as stories written for him. I'm fortunate to work for Winnie O'Kelly, a first-rate editor whose keen eye, enthusiasm, and intelligence always make things interesting. Tom Redburn taught me a great deal about economic coverage. Thanks to Adam Bryant, David Joachim, Allison Mitchell, Jeff Sommer, Liz Alderman, David Gillen, Jose Lopez, Seth Feaster, and Mark Getzfred for consistently elevating the paper's business and economic coverage, while making the *Times* a rewarding place to work.

I've also been fortunate to write frequently for the Week in Review section, an ideal opportunity to explore the economic terrain, thanks to Sam Tanenhaus, Dave Smith, Marc Charney, and Tom Kuntz.

Thanks to my *Times* colleagues, whose criticisms and insights have challenged my thinking, helped me formulate ideas, led me to valuable sources of information, and provided diversionary companionship, among them David Leonhardt, Gretchen Morgenson, Floyd Norris, Vikas Bajaj, Michael Grynbaum, Michael Powell, Charles Duhigg, Michael Barbaro, Jad Mouawad, Barry Meier, Andrew Martin, Steve Lohr, Joe Nocera, William Neumann, Catherine Rampell, Jack Healy, Michael Schmidt, Kim Severson, Steve Greenhouse, Diana Henriques, and Louise Story. Ken Belson has been a great friend and colleague for two decades.

Parts of this book draw on reporting I conducted during a decade at the *Washington Post*, an institution with which I remain enormously proud to be associated. Don Graham, Len Downie, Steve Coll, and Robert Kaiser oversaw a culture of creativity and sky's-the-limit ambition. Jill Drew gave me a coveted chance to cover technology in the midst of the boom years and then sent me to my dream job in Shanghai, while allowing me to roam from Sudan to Indonesia. Larry Roberts never took his eye off the big story. Foreign editors Phil Bennett and David Hoffman sharpened my thinking about China and the global economy. Thanks to Fred Barbash, Carlos Lozada, Dan Beyers, Mary Hadar, Bill Hamilton, Steve Levingston, and Howard Schneider for keen editing. Nell Henderson, Steve Pearlstein, and Paul Blustein patiently initiated me into the ways of economic thinking.

While at the *Post*, I flagrantly stole as many tricks as possible from a hugely talented group of writers, among them Mark Leibovich, Paul Farhi, John Schwartz, Scott Wilson, Chris Stern, Lena Sun, Gabriel

Escobar, Peter Slevin, Vernon Loeb, Bart Gellman, Dafna Linzer, and Steve Mufson.

During my years in Asia, I was grateful to draw on the journalistic thinking and companionship of many friends and colleagues, among them Hannah Beech, Brook Larmer, John Pomfret, Phil Pan, Sarah Schafer, Gady Epstein, Ed Gargan, Odilon Couzin, Yuen Chan, Christopher Choa, Nina Train Choa, Mark Magnier, Richard MacGregor, Kath Cummins, Jen Lin-Liu, Evan Osnos, Michael Lev, Akiko Kashiwagi, Eva Woo, Ed Cody, Barbara Demick, Arthur Kroeber, Joe Kahn, David Barboza, Jim Areddy, Chris Torrens, Jason Cai, Tony Faiola, Doug Struck, Maureen Fan, Alec Sirken, and Paul French.

During my years covering technology, I was fortunate to draw on the wise counsel of experienced people willing to help teach me about their world, not least Blair Levin, Scott Cleland, Mike Mills, Leo Hindery, Jonathan Askin, and a few others best not named publicly.

At the Oakland Private Industry Council, Gay Plair Cobb introduced me to many people struggling to find jobs whose life experiences form the backbone of the book. My old friend Chris Rose initiated me to the world of renewable energy.

Over the years, dozens of economists have patiently answered elementary questions and schooled me in the particulars of their discipline and offered up voluminous reams of data. I'm particularly grateful to Mark Zandi, Brad Setser, Ken Rogoff, Mark Weisbrot, Dean Baker, Nouriel Roubini, Allen Sinai, Alan Blinder, and Jonathan Anderson. At the Labor Department, Steve Hipple graciously walked me through many government databases.

David Segal, a wise friend, colleague, and confidante for more than a decade, read early versions of the manuscript and applied his considerable intellect toward improving it. Justin Gillis—one of the sharpest minds in the news business—kindly read drafts of chapters and offered valuable suggestions, as did the excellent and generous Jared Bernstein. Thanks much to others who read portions of early drafts and shared their insights—Robert Barbera, Larry Flowers, Brad Burns, and Lou Uchitelle.

I thank my agent, Jim Rutman, for his faith, advocacy, and grace under pressure. My editor at Times Books, Robin Dennis, masterfully helped forge the pieces into a book. Paul Golob helped shape the initial concept and enthusiastically took on the project.

Thanks to Alex Ward for gracefully and enthusiastically helping keep the newsroom and the publisher on the same page.

I am enormously grateful to my children, Leah and Eli, who patiently waited through many a session at the keyboard and whose precocious and incisive questions aided my mission to demystify this thing called economics. Thanks to my parents, Arnold and Elise Goodman, for generously helping me find time to write the book and supporting the effort. Thanks to Joshua Shulman and M. P. Dunleavey for their enduring friendship. Ed Segel at Reed College and Peter Zinoman at the University of California, Berkeley, have been substantial intellectual mentors. My cousins Mark Merin and Cathleen Williams have never failed to challenge my thinking in three decades of running debate over various dinner tables.

Most of all, I thank Deanna Fei, my ultimate editor and critic, my inspiration and refuge, my partner and my love, and the smartest, most beautiful person I know. I can't imagine life without her and I don't want to try.

Index

Macao, 106
Madoff, Bernard, 14, 15
Mahan, Bobby, 195
MAHLE Engine Components, 278–79
Malaysia, 40, 86
manufacturing, 134, 165–67, 236, 237
    foreign investment in U.S. companies
        and, 269–80
    jobs, 134, 165–67, 241, 244, 250–51,
        256, 258, 259, 261
    post–World War II, 165
    see also specific industries
Mao Zedong, 89, 97, 101
"Market Mania" (article), 53
Markey, Ed, 130–31
Marlin Steel Wire Products, 205–6
mass transit, 31
Maytag, 248–53, 254, 256, 264, 279
McCain, John, 225
McConnell, Mitch, 224, 226
McGilvery, Matt, 258
McKelvey, Ed, 162
McLean, Bethany, 61
media, 50, 246
    on mortgage crisis, 172
    on 1990s tech boom, 60–61
    *see also specific publications and
        programs*
median wage, 10, 161
Medicaid, 226, 242, 246
Medicare, 246
Menendez, Robert, 229
mergers, corporate, 36, 61, 69
Merhaut, Lisa, 187
Merrill Lynch, 14, 52, 200
Merton, Robert, 39
Metz, Michael, 53
Mexico, 73, 251, 253, 279
Miami, 6, 71, 109, 110, 187–88, 212
Michigan, 155, 158, 275–80
Microsoft, 175
middle class, 2, 19
Middletown (Lynd and Lynd), 180–81
Moody's, 124, 125, 225
Morgan Stanley, 135

Morris, Charles R., 205
mortgage-linked investments, 39, 69,
    124–26, 127
    2007–2009 crisis, 127–40, 200, 202,
        218, 229–30
mortgages, 9, 38–39, 83, 107, 184
    adjustable rate, 25, 118–24, 125,
        137–39, 282
    fixed-rate, 119, 177
    mid-2000s easy money policy, 83–84,
        108–26
    refinancing, 110, 119–20, 127, 138,
        153, 195, 231
    S&L debacle and, 38
    second, 11, 83, 183
    subprime, 117–24, 125, 137–39,
        171–76, 199, 204
    2008–2009 crisis, 14, 16, 18, 127–40,
        171–89, 190–215, 218, 231–33, 272
    variable-rate, 24
    Wall Street and, 124–26
Motorola, 90
Mozilo, Angelo R., 126
Murray, Charles, 75–76
mutual funds, 58

NAFTA, 280
Nasdaq, 24, 52
    2000 collapse, 61, 80
National Bureau of Economic Research,
    7–8
National Institutes of Health, 246
Netscape, 52
Nevada, 6, 19, 186
    housing market, 174–79, 199, 231
New Deal, 35, 216, 236
New Economy, 53–56, 64–82, 90, 112,
    114, 160, 246
    debt, 64–82, 112
New Thrift, 177–89
Newton, Iowa, 248–56
New York, 205
New Yorker, 135
New York Times, 5, 18, 33, 117, 157, 165,
    172, 228, 236

Nike, 207
9/11 terrorist attacks, 83, 179–80
Nixon, Richard, 84
  economic policies of, 84–85
Nocera, Joseph, 181
Nortel, 68
North Carolina, 19, 154, 236
  biotech industry, 236–47
North Carolina Biotechnology Center, 241
North Dakota, 261
Norway, 118

Oakland, California, 4–5, 6, 26–32,
    80–81, 141–45, 186
Obama, Barack, 17–18, 88, 216, 283
  economic policies, 18, 202, 216–33,
    246, 282, 283
  effort to fix banking system, 226–32
  inaugural address, 216–17, 283
  renewable energy policy, 260, 262
  stimulus plan, 18, 88, 216–26
Obey, David, 225
Ohio, 19, 193, 256–57, 265
oil, 89, 219, 250, 259, 262, 271
  crisis, 8
Oklahoma, 186
Olbermann, Keith, 228
Omega Apparel, 97
One Market Under God (Frank), 59–60
Oppenheimer & Company, 53
option ARMs, 137–38, 139
Oracle, 62
Oregon, 9, 206–9
Osterman, Paul, 161
over-the-counter (OTC) derivatives, 131,
    135
Ownership Society, 12–13, 116–17,
    231–32

Palo Alto, California, 43
Parsons, John David, 122
part-time employment, 155–56
Paulson, Hank, 173–74, 201, 227
  bailout plan, 201–4, 228
"payday loans," 11

Pellegrino, Elaine, 195–96
Pell grants, 184–85
pensions, 12–13, 58, 184
People's Bank of China, 87, 103, 107
Peter Pan (Barrie), 16–17, 281
Pets.com, 45, 50
Pfizer, 276–77
pharmaceuticals, 238, 239, 241, 244, 246
Philadelphia, 245
philanthropy, 34, 197
Philippines, 164, 240
Phoenix, 186, 199, 231
Pickens, T. Boone, 261–62
Piece of the Action, A (Nocera), 181
Pilkington, 257
plumbers, 111
police, 192
politics, 220, 269–70
  banking crisis and, 227
  2009 stimulus plan and, 220–26, 232
pollution, 250, 259, 262
Ponzi scheme, of Madoff, 14, 15
pork bellies, 47
Portland, Oregon, 9, 206–9
ports, 9, 208
  Dubai Ports World deal, 270, 271, 272
pound, British, 86
poverty, 7, 75–79, 214
  Clinton-era welfare reform and, 75–79
  of 2007–2009, 79
Powell, Michael, 206–7
Powell's Books, 206–7
Prince, Charles, 69
Private Industry Council, 146, 148
privatization, 12, 201
productivity, 10–11
property values, 138
Protestant work ethic, 33–34, 54
public opinion, 202
  on TARP bailout, 202–3, 229

Qualcomm, 59

Race Between Education and Technology,
    The (Goldin and Katz), 164, 165

About the Author

PETER S. GOODMAN is the national economics correspondent for *The New York Times* and a contributor to the paper's groundbreaking fall 2008 series, "The Reckoning." Previously, he covered the Internet bubble and bust as *The Washington Post*'s telecommunications reporter, and served as the *Post*'s China-based Asian economics correspondent. He lives in New York City.